MAIN STREET AND BEYOND

THE WORLD

OF THE

WALL STREET

JOURNAL

Edited by Charles Preston

With an Introduction by Vermont Royster,
Editor, The Wall Street Journal

SIMON AND SCHUSTER

NEW YORK, 1959

CONTENTS

CORNER OF BROAD AND WALL

THE WORLD AROUND US

THE FRUITS OF FREEDOM

THE FACE OF THE PAST

THE FACE OF THE LAND

THE FACE OF POLITICS

THE FACE OF THE FUTURE

ACKNOWLEDGMENTS

To edit a collection of writing from seventy years of *The Wall Street Journal* implies on the part of the compiler a presumptuousness which is matched only by his obligations to scores of the newspaper's contributors.

The span of my obligations ranges from 1889 to the present and includes writers and editors who have long since written their last "30"—veterans still going strong and neophyte reporters excitedly filing their first stories. Though it is impossible to name them individually, I thank them all and beg their forgiveness for overlooking some of their favored stories.

For permission to perform unfettered research through the *Journal* files and meander through microfilmed issues covering decades of news events, I express my gratitude to Bernard Kilgore, president of Dow Jones and Co., Inc. For invaluable help in organization and for his continued inspiration throughout this task, I am grateful to Editor Vermont Royster.

A full measure of thanks must also be extended to the writers and editors I badgered during their working hours: William F. Kerby, Buren H. McCormack, Robert Bottorff and Warren Phillips are just a few.

The library staff of *The Wall Street Journal,* particularly Florence Wagner and Philip Wisner, also Emil Berger, must be singled out for their patience in the face of my persevering queries.

Outside of the *Journal* staff, I accord a special nod of gratitude to Herbert L. Alexander and William Clifford for their support and encouragement during the inception and execution of this project.

CHARLES PRESTON

INTRODUCTION

By Vermont Royster

Charles H. Dow, the man who started it all, was a Connecticut
farm boy who spent a decade as a journeyman reporter on the Main
Streets of New England before a job on the long since departed
New York Mail brought him to report the ups and downs of Wall
Street. Two years in the city were enough to convince him that the
kind of reporting he learned covering the City Halls of Springfield,
Massachusetts, and Providence, Rhode Island, should be applied to
the boardrooms and antechambers of business. In 1880, when he
was thirty-one years old, he persuaded two of his friends to this
then somewhat revolutionary idea and founded Dow Jones and
Company as a financial news service for private clients. This proved
so successful that he soon decided to put out a whole newspaper
which would specialize in business news. And so, on the afternoon
of July 8, 1889, the first issue of *The Wall Street Journal*, a small
four-page pamphlet, was cranked out of an old Campbell flatbed
press and distributed to a few hundred readers within a carrier-
boy's walk of the corner of Broad and Wall.

Many of the changes seventy years have wrought in the world of
business and in the newspaper he founded to inform people about
it would surprise Charles Dow. Like most of his contemporaries, he
had faith that this country would grow, ever westward and ever
bigger, but he could hardly have foreseen the extent of the changes
this would bring in the business of the nation. He would be pleasantly surprised, of course, to find that his little newspaper, born on
that flatbed press in a ramshackle building next to the Stock Exchange, has changed and grown with the country until today it is
the only real national newspaper. He would be fascinated with the
technological progress that permits it to be published simultaneously in five different places (New York, Chicago, Washington, San
Francisco and Dallas) and delivered each morning to cities and
hamlets scattered all across the country, so that the little old lady
in Dubuque can be as informed as the banker on Broad Street.

These changes in technology and the changes made by his successors on his newspaper have combined to give *The Wall Street Journal* more than six hundred thousand subscribers, of whom more than half a million are far removed from Wall Street, and to make it the seventh largest newspaper in the country.

This book, which Charles Preston has culled from the rich variety of *The Wall Street Journal,* would amaze Dow. Some of the subject matter—the articles on how executives live or how a stock trader operates—would, of course, seem familiar to him, even though he might be puzzled at the extensive treatment they received in a daily newspaper. But I wonder what he would think of the article re-printed here, "Confident Teen-agers," which is in essence a socio-logical study, or the kind of foreign reporting represented by "Mr. Okada's Rise," which seeks to give added depth to a Japanese business story by telling it in terms of a Japanese auto worker. In Dow's day news was thought of as a fleeting thing, and he would be astonished to see how many of the modern *Wall Street Journal*'s articles still make interesting reading long afterward.

No doubt about it: today's *Wall Street Journal* is vastly different from Dow's. And not merely in size, or in the resources it can now bring to bear to cover a fast-moving story or to probe a situation which may take weeks to uncover. Its very approach to journalism has undergone a revolution. It has vastly broadened the concept of what constitutes "business" news, or, rather, what constitutes news important to its readers. Indeed, there is hardly any subject of public interest, from medicine to education, that his paper now considers outside its realm. Equally revolutionary is its treatment of these subjects. On the one hand the major events of the day are packaged tightly for quick reading by the hurried man; yet along with this brevity important subjects are covered at length and depth for those who may wish to know more about the subject than simply that "something happened yesterday."

Yet for all this difference, to which many people have contributed, there is a great deal about his paper today that I think Charles Dow would understand. Dow himself always believed, and wrote, that business was something more than balance sheets and ticker tape and that information about it was not the private province of brokers and tycoons. In writing even about high finance Dow used homely analogy and the language of everyday life, although in his day *The Wall Street Journal* did not reach a wide audience. Neither as a writer nor as a person did he ever lose touch with Main Street.

Consider, for example, his use of familiar imagery in this editorial comment about the public in the stock market, as pertinent in 1959 as it was in 1929 or 1889: "Nobody who plants corn digs up the kernels in a day or two to see if the corn has sprouted, but in stocks most people want to open an account at noon and get their profit before night."

Or this readily grasped description of the way the stock market moves: "In the game called the tug-of-war a score of men, an equal number being at each end of the rope, pull against each other to see which party is stronger. In the game called stock-market speculation, the speculators are at liberty to take sides, and the side which they join invariably wins because in stock-exchange parlance 'everybody is stronger than anybody.' When everybody takes hold on the bull side, the market goes up very easily, but, as it goes up, one after the other lets go until the advance halts. Meantime, those who have let go sometimes go around and take hold on the other side."

A man who can write so simply would hardly be surprised that his newspaper has won so many readers today by describing for them in clear language what is going on in business. Nor would Dow be too surprised, I think, to discover that this book includes many articles that have nothing to do with business at all but just deal with subjects that interest people—that it includes good writing on such matters as books, theater, sports, art and music—although he might wonder at the variety of it.

For Charles Dow grasped early two simple principles of journalism. First, that business, like any other human activity, is people; therefore to understand it or explain it you have to look at what people are doing, thinking and feeling about matters seemingly remote from "business." And second, that readers who are interested in these matters are also interested in a wide range of others. That very first issue, in 1889, contained brief items of financial news and a table of security prices, but it also carried a Page One story reporting that the 75-round heavyweight bout between Jake Kilrain and John L. Sullivan, being fought with bare knuckles, was still continuing in Richburg, Mississippi, with Sullivan having the upper hand and expected to win.

Plainly, Charles Dow was primarily a reporter who happened to turn his hand to business news. If, afterward, he was thought of as a stock-market expert it was because he brought to a study of the stock exchange and its movements the observational powers of a good newspaperman.

Once he wrote: "The [stock] market is always to be considered as having three movements, all going on at the same time. The first is the narrow movement from day to day. The second is the short swing running from two weeks to a month or more. The third is the main movement covering at least four years in its duration." Refined and elaborated upon by others, this statement is the basis for what is now known as the "Dow Theory." Dow himself never heard of it. He may have made an original contribution to stock-market theory, but he was just offering the cogent observation of a working journalist to explain what was happening.

And, finally, there is one other thing about the subsequent history of *The Wall Street Journal* that I think would not have surprised Charles Dow. He would have expected it, like the business community it served, to grow not in an unruffled stream but in bumpy stages. This volume itself is a memory book of some of the bumps the nation took, from the panic of '93 to the modern perils of global war. And it was inevitable that a newspaper which lived through these years should share the bumps and be changed by them.

To those who work on it, a newspaper is a living, growing thing; its readers too, as every editor learns, come to have a curiosity and an interest about its growth, about the past life, the personality and the habits of this neighbor who drops into the home or office every day. In the case of *The Wall Street Journal* the path from 1889 to 1959 was a tortuous one.

When Charles Dow died in 1902 the newspaper passed to another New England newspaperman, Clarence W. Barron. Edward T. Jones, one of the original partners, had already withdrawn, and the other major stockholder, Charles Bergstrasser, was willing to sell his interest. Barron, then forty-seven years old and already publisher of a financial paper in Boston, bought Dow's paper in time to take it into the fabulous era that ended in 1929.

Clarence Barron was himself a fabulous man. Starting as a reporter on the Boston *Daily News,* he had switched to the *Transcript* and there had been assigned to cover financial news. When that paper started a special financial page, one of the first of its kind in the country, it attracted so much attention that the page's editor, like Dow in New York, decided to strike out for himself. In 1887 Barron, then thirty-two, founded the Boston News Bureau, first as a financial service and then as a financial newspaper. In 1897 he started the *Philadelphia Financial Journal,* and thus was in a position, by buying Dow Jones and Company, to establish himself in the three financial centers of that time.

The purchase of the New York paper made Barron one of the biggest publishers of the day. He lived up to the adjective in size and personality. Of only medium height, Barron was wide in girth, weighing more than three hundred pounds, and gargantuan in his appetite for food and zest for living. Driven by a boundless energy, he was on the go constantly, wearing out his male secretaries on an average of every two years because he started dictating in the morning before he got up and was still dictating after he had gone to bed. He would dictate in staccato sentences while in the bathtub, while dummy at bridge, at meals, sunning himself, in the barber's chair, and even in the men's room. He was a study in perpetual motion, and his associates rarely knew from one day to the next whether he would be in Boston, New York or London.

Many of these dictated memos went to the editors of his various publications, some of whom received as many as a hundred notes a day from him. I suspect their patience was sorely tried, but the result of this driving by an electric personality was a different tempo on *The Wall Street Journal*. Barron named William Peter Hamilton, an English journalist and brilliant writer who had trained under Dow, as its editor, and after World War I he took on a young man from Indiana, Kenneth C. Hogate, who soon became the paper's managing editor. Under the direction of these two, driven by the Barron whirlwind, the paper boomed along with the country.

When Barron took over, the circulation of *The Wall Street Journal* was about 7,000; there are no accurate records before 1911. By 1920 it had more than doubled, reaching 18,750. By this time the paper was already connected to the other financial centers through a telegraph tie-in with the Barron publications there. It was thus ready to capitalize on that era of history known as the Twenties, when nearly everybody, from St. Louis to San Francisco, had his eye on Wall Street. In that roaring decade the circulation of *The Wall Street Journal* climbed to 50,000. And in terms of prestige and influence it was even larger than its circulation.

In most ways the paper had changed little from the days of Dow. It was still concerned chiefly with the stock markets and the financial news of corporations owned by the public; if anything, it concentrated more on this field. Earnings reports, annual meetings, dividends, sales and profit (or loss) figures: these were the grist of the news. The paper itself would be put together from the compact items that had appeared earlier on the tickers of the Dow Jones News Service which, as the news developed, had fed them quickly into brokerage offices. But it was during this period that two moves were made which were to have a profound effect on the subsequent history of the paper.

A morning edition (the afternoon edition was later dropped) was started with the twofold idea that much could be done to improve the quality by allowing a little extra time for editing and for organizing the news and that the paper could find a wider readership if there was a little more time to get it to the subscribers. The second move, which was originated by Hogate after Barron's death in 1928, was similar and it rested on an awareness that business was a nation-wide interest. Established already in Boston, Philadelphia and New York, the company decided to reach all the way across the country. The result was the Pacific Coast Edition of *The Wall Street Journal,* separately edited (as were all of Barron's papers) but drawing on the same basic news supply.

There was only one catch in this idea. Events proved Hogate a bit ahead of the time, for the first edition of the Pacific Coast paper rolled off the presses in San Francisco on October 21, 1929.

The depression was as much a traumatic experience for the newspaper of Dow and Barron as it was for the country. Its circulation went on a toboggan slide, and from its peak of 50,000 it shrank relentlessly until by the low point of the depression the two editions, New York and San Francisco, had between them only 28,000 subscribers. In depression America there seemed to be no place, or at least no economic place, for a newspaper specializing in business. Wall Street was in disfavor, the business community itself was being battered by the bright young men of the New Deal, and few people had any money anyway. Even the recovery period of the mid-Thirties brought circulation up to only 30,000. The future was not very bright, to put it mildly.

This book is, among other things, evidence of what that shock did to *The Wall Street Journal.* The results are already familiar to the paper's readers, who now embrace not merely men of finance but farmers, lawyers, doctors, college professors, small businessmen, housewives, other newspaper editors, labor leaders and indeed almost anyone who is interested in what goes on in the world around them. You will see some of the results yourself as you browse through this volume.

But a newspaper does not suddenly grow so spectacularly in the span of two decades (incidentally, its Wall Street readers today number hardly more than in Barron's day) without a revolution. The story of that revolution is not without meaning for other journalists, for sociologists of America, for economists and for politicians. It is also the story of an exciting adventure.

Like most revolutions, this one was begun by a few men of ideas who may not have fully grasped what they were starting.

As far back as the mid-Twenties Kenneth Hogate, who was to become president of the company soon after Barron's death, had felt a need for a somewhat broader news coverage, and one of his moves was to strengthen the Washington bureau. Hogate, like Dow, was a newspaperman who happened to land in the business-news field; prior to joining *The Wall Street Journal* he had worked on his father's country paper in Danville, Indiana, and had been on the news staff of the Cleveland *News* and the Detroit *News*. So for a new Washington bureau chief he turned to an experienced general newspaperman on the United Press, William H. Grimes, another Midwesterner who had also worked in Cleveland. He also began to hire a number of young reporters, judging them not by their knowledge of business and finance but by their promise as newspapermen. Among these was Bernard Kilgore, a fellow Hoosier just out of DePauw University.

Hogate also conceived the idea that *The Wall Street Journal* could perform a useful service for its readers by printing each day a summary of the general news from all over the world, if it were skillfully done so that depth and brevity could be packaged together. This was the origin of the "What's News" feature on today's front page and another step toward a broader newspaper. Grimes, by then managing editor, launched this new feature in 1934, and, as luck would have it, the first such column was written by Kilgore, then a 25-year-old special writer. An extra impetus to enlarging the vistas came from an unexpected source; the advent of the New Deal suddenly made government and political news not merely an important but an essential part of "business" news. First under Grimes, and later under Kilgore, the Washington bureau was built up until it was, as it is now, one of the largest of any newspaper.

Meanwhile, a significant change was taking place elsewhere in the paper. Thomas F. Woodlock, a scholarly Irishman, had worked with Dow in the early days of *The Wall Street Journal* and then left for other fields. In 1930 Hogate brought him back as a contributing editor. Woodlock was a man of wide knowledge and interests, of philosophic mind and prolific pen. *The Wall Street Journal*'s editorial columns began to blossom with essays on Plato or John Stuart Mill and with thoughtful examinations of the issues of the day against the background of the principles on which Western thought had developed. He stretched the intellectual dimensions of the editorial page. A man of deep Christian faith, a firm believer in the immutability of certain fundamental principles of thought and action, Woodlock laid the foundation for an editorial policy that would rest on a clear moral and philosophic base.

Quietly and unobtrusively this process of broadening the paper went on all during the Thirties, but its discernible effects were small and its effect on circulation was practically nothing. By 1940 it was clear some drastic measures were needed if *The Wall Street*

Journal was to be anything more than a small stock-market paper of limited circulation and influence. As it turned out, what was needed was a transfusion of new ideas.

That came in 1941. First, Hogate moved Grimes up to editor and made Kilgore—who had been a reporter, news editor and Washington bureau chief—the paper's managing editor. Then, when illness struck down Hogate, Kilgore was named vice-president and general manager at the age of thirty-five, and the revolution got under way in earnest.

With Grimes providing the leavening of experience and Kilgore the daring to "do everything differently" the modern *Wall Street Journal* was created by building a new edifice atop the old foundations. Within the space of a few years the front page was completely revamped by developing a type of news story which, while dealing with current events, was not tied down by yesterday's developments. This permitted the staff to dig into a situation over a period of several days, write about it with care and then give the reader a comprehensive report. The "What's News" column was strengthened in scope and manpower (it now takes sixteen man-hours daily to produce what it takes you six minutes to read) to cover all the "spot" news of the day, with the details, where necessary, carried in separate stories inside the paper. The concept of appropriate news for *The Wall Street Journal* was enlarged past Dow's wildest dreams. The hard core of Dow's paper—accurate and full coverage of corporate affairs and the stock market—was still there, but it was reorganized, more carefully packaged, and no longer allowed to dominate the paper.

Nor was this all the revolution. The Pacific Coast edition, heretofore separately edited, was made a replica of the New York edition on Kilgore's conviction that readers everywhere really wanted and needed the same news and that all would profit by having it edited by one good team of editors. The "regional" concept, which accepted the idea that people in different parts of the country somehow differed in interests, was buried. All this rapid change put immense strains on the staff and raised huge technical problems—no one had ever tried before to publish the same paper on the same day in New York and San Francisco.

There was, perforce, a good deal of experimenting and quite a bit of improvisation. There was the problem, for one, of trying to develop stories that would interest readers in Des Moines and Sacramento, that would explain complicated economic and political matters in terms understood by the nonexpert reader without alienating the expert with oversimplification. Inevitably mistakes were made, ideas tried and abandoned. But the very act of trying to put out a national newspaper itself shaped the product and increased the resources for producing a national newspaper. For example, when the paper wanted to do a story on the effects of wartime price controls on consumer buying it could quickly check on the situation on both sides of the continent. Since this was not just a New York story or a San Francisco story it automatically became a "team" story that had to be written from a national viewpoint. Furthermore, since a "Wall Street" paper naturally met a certain sales resistance on the nation's main streets, it was imperative that extra effort be put into good writing and editing as well as into the reporting. The formula story of old newspaper days simply would not do.

For the most part this challenge was thrown at young men who accepted it with enthusiasm and tackled it with *élan;* from them emerged the men who shape today's *Wall Street Journal.* William F. Kerby succeeded Kilgore as managing editor and Buren H. McCormack succeeded him. In San Francisco Robert Bottorff was wrestling with the sticky problem of making that experimental edition work. The present editor was in Washington learning to translate the complexities of government into understandable language. All were well on the youngish side of forty. Grimes, who was not yet fifty, was by contrast the "Old Man" who sometimes had to keep the enthusiasm from running riot and who in the meantime was slowly turning *The Wall Street Journal's* editorial page into a voice of national influence. Not since the days of Dow had the paper had an editor who could use simple language to drive home a point with such force, but Grimes had a more wide-ranging mind than either Dow or Hamilton and a sharper pen than Woodlock.

It's hardly surprising that there was an electric air in the news shop just off Wall Street. It communicated itself to people like Joseph Ackell, who had to invent better ways of producing a single newspaper from multiple plants, and to Robert Feemster, who had to sell both the readers and the advertisers a product that had never existed before.

The results are perhaps best told in a few statistics. In 1941, the circulation of *The Wall Street Journal* was 32,600. By the end of the war it had once more crossed 50,000. Two years later it was double this figure. In 1951 it passed 200,000. In 1955 it was 365,000. And in 1959, as this is written, it is 620,000. It was to keep pace with this circulation that the other publishing plants were added in Dallas, in Chicago and in Washington.

It would be idle to deny that the men who have seen this happen are not proud of the record. But what happens today behind the scenes of *The Wall Street Journal* is, for me, as fascinating a story as its history.

In the summer of 1956 I sat in the Cow Palace outside of San Francisco where Harold Stassen was trying to discourage the Republicans from renominating Vice-President Nixon. In the late afternoon I went down to the paper's subterranean press booth and wrote a bit of commentary which was put on the leased wire direct to the New York newsroom. An hour later I journeyed to *The Wall Street Journal*'s publishing office in downtown San Francisco, and as I walked in the door a copy boy handed me a printed proof of the article I had just written. In that space of time it had gone by teletype 3,000 miles across the country, been edited for my awkward spelling, had a headline written for it, and returned by wire 3,000 miles across the country to be set in type automatically.

The incident illustrates how both conscious design and the pressure of necessity have made *The Wall Street Journal*'s operation an unusual combination of diversity and centralization. All editions of the paper today are printed by an electronic system developed by Dow Jones research; the copy is punched on a tape, very similar to that used by the familiar teletypewriter, and this tape is then fed into a transcontinental wire. At each of the printing plants the incoming tape is then used to activate a line-casting machine. The result is that each plant gets exactly the same type, including at times the same typographical errors. Technologically this centralization is essential; it also contributes to the quality of the product.

The newspaper today has, including its five main publishing offices, fourteen news bureaus across the country staffed by 194 full-time correspondents, making it the most widespread domestic news-gathering organization maintained by any newspaper. All these bureaus, together with the Dow Jones News Service (Dow's original enterprise in modern dress), are tied together by 86,006 miles of leased telegraphic wires. The paper also maintains eight foreign bureaus. Since the paper is also supplied by the Associated Press and United Press International, the total volume of wordage to be handled is staggering. Without firm control by the editors in New York, the result would be nothing but chaos. They must decide each day under pressure of deadlines what stories are to be used, see that they are edited and assigned their proper place in a newspaper of compact size.

A by-product of this necessity for order in compact size is that one group of editors gets a look at the entire product and can be alert for "holes" in the reporting, bad writing or distortions due to the fact that one reporter may see only a part of the story. For example, when President Eisenhower made his decision to fight over Quemoy, if need be, it was a Washington story, a Far Eastern story, a diplomatic story and a domestic political story. In an older tradition these would have been handled separately, requiring the reader to read many different articles to get the whole import. The *Journal* could take the reports from its eighteen-man Washington bureau, the dispatches from its Far Eastern correspondent and its London bureau, the soundings of public opinion probed by its staff newsmen in a score or more of U.S. towns, and put them all together in one manageable package. A story of this nature may run to 2,000 words or more; but the reader who wants to pass it by can get the main developments from the "What's News" summary, and the reader who wants to know more has it all available to him.

Where time permits this method can be greatly expanded; it is not unusual for a half-dozen reporters to work for several weeks on a single story under an editor who is responsible for the direction and the actual writing. With a different type of story one man may do the whole job from start to finish. The assignment of credit on team operations—the "byline"—goes to the man who contributed the major part, although sometimes it is so much a joint effort that there is no byline at all. As a consequence, many stories included in this volume were the product of more people than the man whose name appears on them. The senior editors rarely get bylines, although they add an extra quality to the result.

Few newspaper stories are literature, but the *Journal*'s system permits it to make an obsession of good writing, or at least craftsmanlike writing. A frequent scene is a group of editors arguing, even in the late afternoon with the deadline approaching, whether a certain sentence "reads" right or whether the information in the twelfth paragraph should be moved up to the third paragraph to make the story easier to follow. No one's copy is immune to this type of critical examination. Since all writers have a touch of the prima donna, sparks sometimes fly, but mutual respect prevents serious conflagrations and the sparks do help preserve a bit of the electric air that marked the early days of the revolution.

Meanwhile, the broadening process has continued. Besides widening the concept of what constitutes business news, the *Journal* has widened its ideas of what will interest readers. Except for daily sports and the routine transgressions of the flesh, which fill a large part of most newspapers, there are today practically no subjects of public interest outside *The Wall Street Journal*'s province; and even sports and sin sometimes make its pages. This widening horizon is especially true of the editorial page, which in addition to questions of political philosophy ranges into the field of literature, art, music, education, science or the theater. As John Brooks recently observed in *Harper's* Magazine, the paper is now catching the attention of "eggheads" who may not have even a nodding acquaintance with Wall Street. Back in 1947 Grimes won the paper its first Pulitzer Prize for his distinguished editorial writing; the present editor won it in 1953; other journalistic awards have accumulated over the past several years.

Yet for all the changes, much remains the same. *The Wall Street Journal* still aims at complete financial coverage and still devotes the major part of its columns to the business of the nation. Oliver J. Gingold, who began as a reporter under Dow, still edits the "Abreast of the Market" column. The original financial service, begun with handwritten bulletins, flourishes as a high-speed news ticker that reaches from coast to coast and originates much financial news for the *Journal's* editors. The paper remains independent in its news judgments and its editorial opinions.

In the latter it is accused by some of being too conservative, by others as having become too liberal, by still others as just being cantankerous. To this Grimes once wrote what is perhaps the best reply: "On our editorial page we make no pretense of walking down the middle of the road. Our comments and interpretations are made from a definite point of view. We believe in the individual, in his wisdom and his decency. We oppose all infringements on individual rights whether they stem from attempts at private monopoly, labor-union monopoly or from an overgrowing government. People will say we are conservative or even reactionary. We are not much interested in labels, but if we were to choose one, we would say we are radical—just as radical as the Christian doctrine." Charles Dow would never quarrel with that.

Out of so much history Mr. Preston could easily have drawn a book twice this size. As it is, every reader of *The Wall Street Journal* is sure to have a complaint because this or that story which he especially remembers is not included in this anthology. I have myself a few favorites that are missing here. But Mr. Preston is a stranger, as it were, to the family; he could look upon the work of seventy years with an unprejudiced eye. To go through so many years of faded newsprint was a Herculean labor, and I marvel at the skill with which he has sifted out the ephemeral, which must of course be the bulk of it, and has chosen those things that still retain a gloss.

Personally I am an easy victim of nostalgia. No one would pretend that the little item on the panic of 1893, drawn from one of Dow's early issues, is as good a story as the reprise by two veterans of '29. Yet the spare account of the event I don't remember has a special appeal because it gives life to history. I am drawn, too, by the stories that recapture President Roosevelt and the New Deal; perhaps it is because I remember them well. But rereading all these stories, I find them in a way more interesting than the ones that appeared in this morning's newspaper; the present is too close for us to see it, or appreciate it fully.

You will discover your own favorites. If you are stock-market-minded, try "Boiler Room Boom" and, if you have a sense of humor, "Nicely Nicely's Broker's Tip." If you are fascinated by life in the executive suites, there's something to be learned from "Throat Cutting"—or maybe from the extensive report on "How to Get Fired." If yours is a strenuous life, show your wife "Golf and Freedom." If it's a relaxed one, don't show her "Shall We Dance?"; instead, take time to reflect on "Eggheads in Action" or to consider "A Definition of Democracy." Or if you think the proper study of mankind is man, go out in the byways for the "Saga of a Salesman" and the young couples "In Their Twenties" to whose door the salesman brings the riches of America. You can see how those riches are spent by people as varied as "Farmer G." and "Multimillionaire F." And you can also learn how, now and then, death comes to a business.

The choices are as varied as life. To be reminded how varied that is, I hope you will turn to "The Quiet Force in Arkansas" and the two articles that take you, years apart, across the heartland of U.S. 40. You may find it pleasant, too, to renew old acquaintances with F.D.R., Harry Truman and Robert Taft. Beyond is the whole wide world, and you can visit Russians in "Mr. Meged Builds a Dream House" or untutored Africans in the poignant piece on the "Barefoot Girl." Wars, cold or hot, are of course a part of the story; so also is the burden of taxes and the treadmill of inflation.

But enough. In the stored memory of seventy years it is all there, and Mr. Preston, rummaging through the old chests, has found at least one souvenir to fit each mood and time. As host, I can only make you welcome, show you about the house, and tell you something of the people who filled the album on the table—Dow, Hamilton, Barron, Hogate, Woodlock, Grimes, Kilgore. I hope you will enjoy the memories, for they reach from Wall Street all the way out to Main Street and beyond.

MAIN STREET

❀

PEOPLE MAKE MONEY

Lesson in Retailing

SPRINGFIELD, Ill.—Looking for a formula for successful retailing?

Then try that used by Myers Bros. department store here—methods that have been tested since 1886 and which are responsible for the store's current annual volume of nearly $5 million, plus a net that is considerably above average for a store of its class.

Myers Bros. sales, expanded some fivefold in little more than a decade, are running 13 per cent ahead of a year ago this year, though department store sales nationally were up only 4 per cent in the first seven months of 1953 compared with last year, according to the Federal Reserve System. But the real worth of the Myers' formula shows up in profit statistics. Myers Bros. is netting 50 per cent more from its operations this year than a year ago, whereas the average department store has found rising costs have nullified the sales gain and profit is just matching a year ago.

At Myers Bros. the inventory is turned over four and a quarter times a year. According to National Retail Dry Goods Association statistics, the average department store in its class turns over inventory only three and a half times a year.

Moreover, the inventory turnover isn't achieved by cut-rate merchandising either. The firm holds to the 40 per cent markup which is more or less standard in the merchandising field.

In the first six months of this year the store's total selling costs on all merchandise sold amounted to 22.4 per cent of gross, plus rent of about 5 per cent. Industry comparisons for the first six months aren't available yet. But average department store selling

1

costs in 1952 amounted to 32.5 per cent of gross, according to the Harvard University School of Business.

The formula for this success story?

Build your store into a community institution by participating in every local activity which comes along. Handle nothing but first-class merchandise which you back 100 per cent by adjusting complaints as they come up. Follow a one-price policy for everybody. Maintain cost controls over each department so you know where you are going. Make shopping easy and emphasize the quality of your goods with wide aisles, spacious merchandising displays, air-conditioned quarters and modern decorating. Instill a family spirit in your employees. Spend 4 per cent of your gross for advertising to put your message across.

The store is located in the basement and first four floors of a ten-story, 80-by-180-foot structure built on the site of the law office occupied by Abraham Lincoln and William H. Herndon from 1843 to 1861.

It is run by two sets of first-cousin Myers brothers: Albert II, James and Stanley, sons of cofounder Albert Myers; and Alan and Louis, sons of cofounder Louis Myers. The original Myers brothers, Albert and Louis, founded the firm in 1886.

"We own the building," says crisp-voiced 44-year-old Stanley Myers, the energetic general manager of the store. Then he adds: "We don't owe anyone anything, either. Except for seasonal borrowings we have no reason for going into debt."

Watch the Myerses in action for an idea of how these results are being attained. Alan Myers, 49-year-old president of the firm, has an office on the first floor just off the shoe salon. It's a tiny six-by-six room scarcely large enough for a desk and a chair. But it's big enough, for Mr. Myers' office really is the entire store. You're apt to find him anywhere, perhaps in the hosiery department examining some new stock, in the gift shop talking to a customer or on the walk inspecting a window display.

"This store of ours grew from a handshake business," says he. Then he adds: "And we're still shaking hands."

"We try to get acquainted with all of our customers. That gives personality to the way we do business," says Stanley Myers.

The list of organizations that various members of the clan belong to includes every community enterprise. If there is a bond drive, a fund-raising campaign, a state fair promotion or anything else going on in town, Myers Bros. Store will be in on it, most likely with one of the Myerses serving as a campaign officer.

"It means a lot of work and little leisure time for us," admits athletic, 36-year-old Albert Myers, manager of advertising and men's clothing. "Our wives all kick because we are on the go so much, but that's the way you get ahead in this business."

In the store the Myerses strive hard to provide a personalized service and to satisfy the customer.

Walk around the store with Alan Myers and a town lady interrupts. She wants assistance in selecting a dress for a funeral. Can Mr. Myers help? Mr. Myers can and does.

Myers Bros. follows an extremely lenient exchange policy, and frequently when merchandise doesn't live up to expectations the store will make good even though the manufacturer won't.

"We stand behind our merchandise one hundred per cent," says Alan Myers.

A check of the records shows that the firm's ratio of exchanges and losses is averaging 6.6 per cent of total gross volume. That's a high figure, but the Myers clan figures it worth while.

In accepting exchanges the store tried a separate return desk, then dropped the idea. Now each exchange is handled at the counter where the original sale was made. This gives the department's buyer a chance to ascertain causes of the complaint and to make any adjustments necessary for avoiding repetition. It also gives the department's salespeople an opportunity for reselling the customer.

On the sales floor, Myers Bros. holds firmly to one price. Once when one of the town's businessmen purchased $102.50 worth of merchandise, he attempted to pay the total with a $100 check.

"Surely you're not going to quibble over $2.50 on a sale of this size, are you?" he asked.

A store official firmly replied that the store's one-price policy was maintained at all times. The customer walked away in a huff without the merchandise.

He returned several hours later, though, to apologize. "I wouldn't cut my price," said he. "Why should you cut yours?"

The firm has an intricate cost accounting system which spotlights exactly how each of the store's 96 departments is faring at all times. Each department is operated as an independent store, being held accountable for a percentage of rent according to the space it occupies, a percentage of the advertising budget based on sales volume, a salary budget also based on sales, and other costs in proportion to its size. Profits on sales also are tabulated for each department. So at the end of the month, management can tell at a glance which departments are making or losing money and why.

Of course, several departments, such as men's work clothes or the Chatfield Shop (women's expensive garments) are operated mainly as a customer service or for prestige. This is considered when departments are evaluated.

Department turnover of merchandise also is carefully tabulated, and the inventory held in a 60-to-90-day range.

Careful buying is viewed as the best safeguard against the overstocking which sometimes forces cut-rate sales in merchandising. Myers Bros. seldom goes in for cleanup sales, preferring to control its inventories through the purchasing department.

It does use advertising promotions extensively, however, usually trying to have a community tie-in with them.

Advertising spending is scheduled through the year with each month's apportionment based on sales expectations for that month. Thus, December, which usually accounts for 15 per cent of the year's total sales, gets 15 per cent of the year's advertising budget. Over-all advertising expenditures amount to 4 per cent of the store's gross revenues.

The store participates actively in all the county fairs in the neighborhood, passing out novelties such as pickle forks, bottle openers, baby show banks, pencils, writing pads and other items aimed at building goodwill.

"We generate a lot of business in the small towns around here that way," says Albert Myers.

Approximately 60 per cent of sales are made on credit, chiefly charge accounts. On 30-to-60-day accounts no interest is charged. On longer accounts interest usually is one half of one per cent a month on the unpaid balance. Terms on soft merchandise usually are limited to six months, though on expensive items, such as fur coats, a year and a half may be allowed for A-1 customers. Hard-goods terms run up to a year.

Currently, the firm is collecting 55 per cent of its debt outstanding each month. Its write-offs of bad debts are running less than one half of one per cent.

To keep better track of its accounts, the firm this month installed a cycle billing system in its credit department.

In handling its personnel, Myers Bros. seeks to create a small-store, family spirit among its 240 full-time employees. The average employee has been with the firm for over six years, with 18 on the payrolls for 25 or more years and one with the firm for 50 years.

Salespeople work on a commission ranging from 4¾ per cent to 8 per cent of gross sales.

RAY VICKER

August 13, 1953

"I always stop in just in case my husband has made a deposit."

A Small-Town Bank

CEDARHURST, N.Y.—Shortly after Mr. and Mrs. Frank Fisher moved to this attractive little Long Island community, they opened an account in the Peninsula National Bank.

A few days later, a distraught Mrs. Fisher walked into the bank. Her husband was at his job at a nearby airport. Their household furnishings had just arrived from New England. She had found herself in the midst of a clutter of unpacked barrels, trunks and boxes. To make matters worse, gas, electricity and telephone service had not yet been connected. Could the bank help?

The bank could and did. A member of the staff quickly located a handyman to take over the unpacking job and also arranged for gas, electric and phone service.

This incident, while perhaps a little out of the ordinary, is an example of the "personal touch" which has enabled Peninsula National to grow and prosper while hundreds of similar banks throughout the nation have been swept out of existence, chiefly through mergers. "We try to be good neighbors," explains Peninsula's President Charles J. Machleid.

The bank mortality rate has been rising steadily in recent years. Last year, 126 banks left the scene, compared with 113 in 1952 and with 89 in as recent a year as 1948. In most cases, the pressure of competition from bigger neighbors is a major factor in decisions to sell out.

Peninsula National's competitive situation would gray the hair of a less aggressive banker than Charles Machleid. Right in its own Nassau County are Franklin National Bank, with assets ten times Peninsula's $22.6 million, and Meadow Brook National Bank, about five times Peninsula's size. Both Franklin National and Meadow Brook have growing systems of branches, some of which are within a few miles of Peninsula. Meadow Brook, in fact, a couple of months ago acquired two branches in Peninsula's "Five Towns" area (Cedarhurst plus neighboring Lawrence, Hewlett, Woodmere and Inwood). In addition, of course, Peninsula must compete with the big banks of New York City, only a few miles away.

A look at the figures, however, shows Peninsula has more than held its own. Without benefit of mergers, its deposits jumped from $12.2 million at the end of 1947 to $19.4 million at December 31, 1953—a gain of 59 per cent. That compares with an average gain of 21 per cent for all banks throughout the nation.

The bank has done equally well profitwise. Net earnings last year were $133,041, up 85 per cent over the previous year. The 1953 profit was equal to 13.2 per cent of the bank's capital funds, compared with an average figure of 7.4 per cent for banks of the same size classification in the New York Federal Reserve District.

Much of the credit for the bank's success must go to its public-relations program. This program is aimed at winning friends—and, of course, new business—for the bank.

Near the door of the bank's office there is a fishbowl filled with coins. Anyone needing coins for a parking meter can make his own change. "We don't know how we come out on it," says Robley F. De Mott, vice-president in charge of public relations. "And we don't care."

Another goodwill-getter in the lobby is a well-stocked umbrella stand. On rainy days, customers can help themselves, although the bank, of course, hopes most of the umbrellas eventually will be returned.

Overcaution on that score almost got the umbrella venture off to a bad start. The first supply was ordered with big initials, "PNB," printed on the umbrella tops. Vice-President De Mott tried one on a rainy day; gibes of friends quickly convinced him the bank should skip the big label.

Three years ago, the bank hired Mrs. Marvin Lobel, long-time Cedarhurst resident, as a new business representative. Tillie Lobel's job is unusual. She drops in on newcomers to the community for a social chat.

Not long ago she visited a housewife who had just moved to the community with her husband and her teen-aged daughter. Mrs. X was very unhappy. Her daughter, a college freshman, had no friends in Cedarhurst. Friendly neighbors had invited Mrs. X to join them in a canasta game, but she preferred mah-jongg and was "just dying for a game."

Mrs. Lobel found these problems easy to solve. She sent her own daughter, also a college freshman, to see the friendless teen-ager, introduce her to other girls in Cedarhurst. She knew a group of women who also liked mah-jongg and arranged for them to get acquainted with Mrs. X.

Mrs. Lobel and many other Peninsula employees belong to a raft of community organizations. Public-Relations Director De Mott is president of the Five Towns Kiwanis Club and is active in the American Legion, the Hewlett-Woodmere Exchange Club, the Family Service Association (a welfare group), the Lawrence-Cedarhurst Merchants Association and the Boy Scouts.

Mr. De Mott works at winning friends for the bank while they're young. With the enthusiastic co-operation of school officials, he lectures on banking to classes in a local high school and to seventh- and eighth-graders at three local schools. Two more grade schools will be added next fall.

The bank sponsors essay contests in the grade schools, with the contestants writing on banking subjects. The winners get cash prizes donated by the bank. For the past five years, the bank also has presented cash awards to the Lawrence High School seniors with the highest averages in business subjects.

Mr. De Mott never mentions Peninsula in his school talks, distributes no advertising material. The bank has no part in judging the essays nor does it make any use of the winning essays. Peninsula takes group pictures of the classes Mr. De Mott addresses; the photos are exhibited in the bank's lobby for a brief period and then presented to the classes.

Mr. De Mott watches closely for word of Five Towners leaving on vacations or opening new businesses. Residents embarking for Europe often have found in their staterooms a bottle of champagne, compliments of Peninsula National. The bank is careful to always send flowers to the opening of a local shop.

President Machleid keeps a close eye on all the bank's operations, occasionally participating actively in negotiation of loans amounting to only a few thousand dollars. Active in banking since 1910, he put in six years as a national bank examiner before coming to Peninsula as cashier in 1931.

The bank up to this year paid a 10 per cent employee bonus each year. This has been replaced by a new employee profit-sharing program. Mr. Machleid meets with Peninsula's 52 employees regularly to discuss bank problems and practices.

"My wife and I have had no children," says Mr. Machleid. "But I think of the bank's employees as my own family."

This attitude has paid off in a remarkably small number of personnel changes. In 1953, according to Jerome W. McDermott, comptroller, the bank had no turnover at all. Annual turnover for banks generally runs as high as 25 per cent.

Founded in 1920 by a group of local citizens, Peninsula has remained community-owned. The bulk of its 316 stockholders lives in the Five Towns area. The typical stockholder has relatively few shares; average holdings are 71 shares. Biggest single stockholder owns less than 7 per cent of the outstanding stock.

By 1950, the bank's business had grown so fast that a second office was opened in neighboring Hewlett. Peninsula officials are careful to call the new building an office, not a branch. "We're not a branch bank," insists Mr. De Mott.

LINDLEY H. CLARK

May 25, 1954

"Say It with Flowers"

BOSTON, Mass.—A onetime newsboy helped coin a famous slogan, "Say It with Flowers," and is now one of New England's best-known florists.

He is Henry Penn, who operates a highly successful shop at 124 Tremont Street here. This small business has grown steadily for more than half a century. Its sales volume has multiplied more than 20 times since Mr. Penn moved to his present location about 30 years ago.

Mr. Penn's capsule formula for a successful florist business: Know your flowers well, how to buy them economically, arrange them attractively, and make them move across the counter to the customer.

The florist stresses the importance of sizing up the mood of the potential buyer and satisfying that mood with the appropriate blossom. For instance, for a man obviously beset by some personal trouble, cheerful red roses would be in order. For a young fellow in a party spirit, either gardenias or orchids would be prescribed. The aim is to give the buyer what he wants before he even knows himself—a neat trick, perhaps, but one that the Penn shop has perfected to keep its cash register ringing regularly.

Born on the north side of Boston in a tenement district, Henry Penn sold newspapers on the streets at the age of ten. One day a pushcart vendor peddling white pond lilies asked newsboys to sell his product at five cents a bunch. The boys were to collect a cent and a half for each bunch sold. These were the first flowers young Penn had seen outside the Boston Public Gardens. From then on they became the prime interest in his life—both vocation and avocation.

Before long, at the age of 12, he had his own flower cart, and newsboys were selling the flowers he bought from florists at the end of each day. His next move was to a shop on Chapman Place behind the famous Parker House, then to a larger place on Bromfield Street and, finally, to his present Tremont Street location.

Mr. Penn, a past president of the Society of American Florists, believes early and continuous advertising has had much to do with the growth of his business. He first used ads almost 50 years ago when public sales promotion was thought "undignified" and even somewhat unethical for florists. He places ads in all five Boston papers daily and Sunday plus an unobtrusive "Flowers by Wire" on the obituary notice page.

In addition, he sends free boutonnieres to members of the Advertising and Rotary clubs at their weekly luncheon meetings. Prominent in local civic affairs, he is president of the Beacon Street Temple and has served in countless philanthropic organizations and community welfare projects. Mr. Penn numbers his personal friends in the hundreds, many of them steadfast customers, and is never too busy for a chat with a worry-burdened customer in his private office.

The importance of building a solid reputation in this manner by word-of-mouth goodwill, he asserts, cannot be overemphasized for a small businessman. Proof of the commercial payoff of a respected and widely known community "name": Over 70 per cent of his sales are by phone, the flowers bought sight unseen.

Mr. Penn buys his flowers from nurseries and greenhouses within a 100-mile radius of Boston and from wholesale flower marts on the city's south side. Prices fluctuate directly with supply and demand.

Unseasonable weather cuts supply and sends prices up. Holiday demand—Christmas, Easter, Mother's Day, Valentine's Day—also effects a jump of about a third in price. Customers are apt to complain when a dozen red roses sells for $6 to $8 during the Yuletide season when $4 to $6 is the normal asking price. It's the bidding for additional stock against a constant greenhouse supply that's responsible.

The main staples in the Penn business are roses for the average bouquet, gardenias for the average corsage and orchids for the "carriage trade." Incidentally, a large per cent of his Vanda orchids are flown in from Honolulu; an enterprising Harvard student is paying his tuition by handling the shipments.

Two keys to small-business success, suggests this flower merchant, are an ability to innovate sales-appealing devices on your own and the readiness to adopt other new trade wrinkles as fast as they appear. One Penn creation was the heart-shaped box of violets for Valentine's Day. It caught on and was picked up by retail florists throughout the country. One Valentine's Day he sold 240,000 violets in such boxes, said to be the largest amount ever sold by one shop.

Another Penn creation that has had nationwide acceptance is the "durable" memorial wreath. For years florists had received annual complaints that the standard wreaths of roses and oak leaves placed on the graves of war dead and ex-servicemen on Memorial Day failed to survive more than 24 hours or so. Henry Penn devised a wreath of prepared roses and oak leaves treated with a shellaclike preservative. The Penn wreath now fills most Memorial Day orders.

He is also quick to introduce new species or unusual types to the local scene. Currently he has brought Peruvian cypress and the ming tree to the Boston area. An authority on pollinization and cross-breeding, he has featured many creations at horticultural shows. Only a person well acquainted with the latest greenhouse practices would know that it's now possible to obtain chrysanthemums in June as well as the traditional September. It's done by covering the plants with black cloth early during the summer nights so that they get additional "sleep" and mature quickly out of season.

The physical appearance of his shop is another of Mr. Penn's strong cards. With two large display windows facing the street, he features a floral display in one, a seasonal tie-in (such as bunnies at Easter, a model of a wedding-gowned bride in June) in the other. Within the cool interior of the shop is a profuse abundance of flowers of every description covering almost every foot of floor space. Along each side of the shop run large glass refrigerators containing a wide variety of flowers; the customer is taken right into the "visual iceboxes" to make his choice.

Mr. Penn is also proud of his relationship with the firm's 36 em-

ployees. It's more like that of father and son than of boss and hired
hand; personal problems of all kinds are discussed and, if possible,
solved within the confines of his small photo-crowded office. He has
almost no turnover; the employees' length of service averages 18
years; one has been there 42 years.

One of the big "days" for florists is, of course, Mother's Day.
Henry Penn played a major role in launching that now commercially important institution. Anna Jarvis, of Chicago, had originally
conceived the idea of duplicating the old English observance of
"Amotherin' Day" in this country. Her proposal met with lukewarm
response and on a visit to Boston she discussed her disappointment
with Mr. Penn.

He suggested pushing the idea of a white carnation in a man's
lapel for a dead mother, a red carnation for a still-living parent.
Why carnations? Every year in May New England nurseries and
florists wound up with a surfeit of white carnations raised in an-
ticipation of the Memorial Day demand. Mr. Penn further suggested
the second Sunday in May as the date of the new "day" to spread
out the carnation-buying period and thus ease the annual glut. He
"sold" this idea to ministers in the Boston area, who then "sold"
it to their congregations, and a commercial bonanza was on its way.
Incidentally, Mr. Penn deplores the fact that stores of all kinds are
taking advantage of what was originally intended to be a simple
one-flower tribute.

He was also in on the creation of another big money-making
scheme for florists—"Flowers by Wire," or the Florists Telegraphic
Delivery Association. That organization, which now numbers about
8,000 florists and does a $120 million annual business, grew out of a
florists' convention attended by 57 delegates in Chicago some 30
years ago. Many florists had long exchanged orders with shops in
other cities and many florists had failed to receive payment for
those out-of-town orders. Accordingly, they set up a clearinghouse
in Detroit with which each member posted a cash bond to cover
nonpayment of bills. The F.T.D.A. deducts one per cent of the
membership dues for clearing of bills, one per cent for publicity and
advertising.

RICHARD M. RUTTER

August 30, 1948

Discount Houses—1954

A speakeasy flavor, a contempt for carpeted floors and frills, and secret co-operation from many publicly hostile manufacturers.

These are the main makings of a formula that's feeding the rapid growth of discount houses across the land. These stores manage to slash prices because they pinch pennies on operating costs and ring up mass sales volume at a small profit markup per unit. Surprising as it may sound, many discounters say they get their merchandise directly from some of the very manufacturers and distributors who profess to decry their price cutting, especially on wares whose retail values are supposed to be fixed under state "fair trade" laws.

The lower prices of the discount houses are the key to their volume selling, of course. But most of them use a little psychology as an added customer lure.

A large proportion of them, for example, require special "identification" or "membership" cards of shoppers, and occasionally even "references." In some states, this is partly to enable them to argue that they haven't been violating "fair trade" laws because they haven't been selling to the "general public." More often than not, though, the main reason for admission cards is to create a hush-hush, speakeasy atmosphere that will make the customer feel he is a privileged insider.

Most discount houses mail such cards by the thousands to employees or members of any club, labor union, church organization, factory, school or other body that will take them. In New York's E. J. Korvette Co. stores, anyone walking in from the street need only stop by an open rack at the door and pick up a handful of "confidential identification cards" authorizing himself, his friends and relatives to obtain discounts there. Another discount house near New York's Union Square has a sign in its window proclaiming: "We honor cards from any discount house in the city."

To help keep prices low, the discount houses draw on an armory of cost-cutting weapons. Many of them dispense with deliveries, fancy wrappings, frilly store furnishings and displays.

Says one discounter: "Most U.S. citizens may still prefer to buy in department stores, walk on rugs and get smiled at by salesclerks—but there is a segment of the public that would rather pay less and carry home a toaster in an unwrapped box."

Often operating in relatively small and crowded stores, the discount houses also shave labor costs by aiming at a high sales total per salesman. "One of our salesmen will sell three watches for us in the time he might take to sell two in a regular jewelry shop," says a Chicago discounter.

The maintenance of credit departments is another expense eliminated by most discount houses; they sell for cash, though some steer customers to finance companies to work out "budget payment plans" on large purchases.

Only a minority service appliances or other wares or accept returned goods; most save on this also, though generally they sell things such as appliances with a warranty that promises defective articles will be replaced if the customer brings them directly to the manufacturer or distributor.

Advertising is another cost that discount operators keep down to a sliver in their budgets. "We don't advertise in the newspapers or on the radio, but we usually send out some sort of circular showing retail list prices and our prices," says Gill H. De Witt, a Houston discount house executive.

His circulars go principally to employee clubs of large companies. "And everyone from the smallest peon to the highest executive buys with us," he boasts. "In fact, we have more trouble from company wheels trying to save a buck on a yard of carpet than we do with the little fellows."

Masters, a big Manhattan discount house, is another one that does direct-mail advertising. Typical bargains touted in one of its recent flyers: Three-quarter-horsepower, 1953-model Philco room air conditioners, "list price $379.95, your price $224.95," and 21-inch "famous make" table model television sets, "list price $199.95, your price $129.50." The same circular even advertises copies of the Bible, "your price 99 cents."

Perhaps the majority of discount houses, however, rely almost solely on mailing out "membership cards" and on word-of-mouth advertising to cultivate customers. Here, in general, is how they work it:

A discount house will approach executives of a factory, labor union, church group, fraternal organization, credit union, farm cooperative, military reservation or some other body with a large number of members or employees. The discounter will say he has goods available at special cut-rate prices and will seek to persuade the executive it would be good employee relations to allow "discount cards" to be distributed to members or employees of his organization.

The cards might be distributed to workers at a factory, for example, accompanied by a letter like this: "Your company has been successful in negotiating arrangements with the ABC Discount House permitting all employees to purchase appliances, giftware and other items at discounts ranging up to 50 per cent. Enclosed is a buying card which will serve to identify you as an employee of your company entitled to this discount."

A Chicago discounter figures that with his group approach he can reach as many as a thousand potential customers in one campaign. Yet the cost is very small. He thinks at least one in every ten first contacted will come in. They, in turn, talk about buys when on the job, so others come in later.

The Wm. E. Phillips Co., a Los Angeles discount house, is one which mails "admission cards" to big business firms in its area. The 200,000-odd card holders look over catalogs at their places of employment, then go to Phillips' downtown store to make their cut-price purchases.

McDonnell Aircraft Co., one of the largest employers in the St. Louis area, now has cards and catalogs from about ten discount houses on a large service rack in the employees' cafeteria, where workers can pick them up.

Though the discounters generally do little advertising themselves, they sell mostly nationally advertised brand-name products to obtain the shopper's confidence and to cash in on the manufacturer's national advertising.

Many merchants have long wondered where the discount houses get the wares they sell, since most manufacturers of branded products rail against the practice of undercutting their "suggested retail prices" or "fair trade" prices.

A few producers, notably Sunbeam and General Electric in the appliance field, have backed up their protests with lawsuits and injunctions against stores caught ignoring "fair trade" prices on their products. But Los Angeles' Wm. E. Phillips Co. is one of many discount houses that claim they get the bulk of their goods direct from manufacturers. "The manufacturer says he's opposed to discount operations out of one side of his mouth and sells to the discount houses anyway," says William Semsrott, an official of Associated Retailers of St. Louis, a trade organization of "regular" retailers.

"All this talk about manufacturers not wanting to sell us is hooey," says a Detroit discount house operator. "All they're interested in is moving the stuff. They tell the big stores they won't trade with us, then their salesmen rush over to us and take our orders." A Better Business Bureau official in Los Angeles says: "Some manufacturers are concerned with the discount house problem, but a heck of a lot aren't."

Often sales are made not directly by manufacturers but by whole-sale distributors, only a small proportion of whom face any real risk of retaliation by the manufacturer for selling to discount houses.

A salesman for one of the biggest New York distributors of appliances and other housewares confides: "We're supposed to 'fair-trade,' too, but we're in a position to give five per cent off and we do. We're interested in selling merchandise and the discount houses buy big, so we sell to them."

A G.E. official admits his company's products show up in discount houses "because in most cases we have no control over what parties our distributors sell to."

In some less common cases, discount house men say they buy directly from other retailers. The retailer may be overstocked and willing to unload at distress prices. Or he may get a better wholesale price himself if he buys in big volume, say 50 or 100 carloads, taking half the shipment for his own use and diverting the other half to some discount house, usually in another city. Or else a retailer who normally orders 50 watches, for example, may decide it's worth his while to buy 500 and contract to sell the extra 450 to a discount house at a slight profit.

March 9, 1954

Welcoming Services

WILMETTE, Ill.—Carrie Baker Buck, a chatty, 76-year-old grand-mother, hurries up the walk toward the new-looking six-room home and the young housewife at the door.

"Hello there, Mrs. Miossi," says Mrs. Buck. "What a nice house you have here. I hope moving wasn't too tiring. Welcome to Wilmette."

For 31 years Mrs. Buck has been greeting newcomers to this attractive Chicago suburb in much the manner that she welcomed Blanche Miossi last week; over the years, she has extended her activities to other communities. Mrs. Buck, in fact, is a professional welcomer, the president of a growing company that expects to gross a record $50,000 this year, four times the total of a decade ago.

The current prosperity of welcoming services such as the one Mrs. Buck runs here stems in part at least from today's tighter business competition, though the boom in new families, of course, has helped, too. In the scramble for new customers, a lot of firms are discovering that welcoming services provide a fast—and cheap—means of sales promotion. Through a myriad of welcoming organizations scattered across the country, merchants are busily attempting to woo community newcomers with hefty cash discounts and outright gifts. Welcoming services, most of them private firms, are paid varying fees by merchants to deliver the "greetings."

Some newcomers, to be sure, resent this admittedly commercial application of what was once just the neighborly thing to do. But most housewives, apparently, are so overwhelmed by the shower of free merchandise that all else is quickly forgotten. One new resident of Evanston, Illinois, for instance, happily reckoned she received about $95 worth of gifts and discounts through a local welcoming service.

A lot of welcoming groups, consequently, are enjoying record business at a time the general economy is only beginning to pull out of the recession. Their success can best be gauged by the boom being experienced by the biggest of the welcoming services, New York's Welcome Wagon, Inc. In its 30th and best year, this private company, which handles more than 50 per cent of the country's welcoming business, claims to have a record 60,000 "sponsor" firms at present spread through more than 2,000 communities in the 48 states. In 1957, by comparison, Welcome Wagon serviced 20 per cent fewer firms in about 10 per cent less communities. The company, which draws its name from the covered wagons sent out from frontier towns to welcome newcomers, currently employs about 5,000 "hostesses," most of them housewives or widows, about 10 per cent more than a year ago.

Welcome Wagon (whose hostesses welcomed the Eisenhowers to the White House) has greeters operating in Hawaii and all the provinces of Canada, and plans are being made to service merchants in Puerto Rico, Alaska, Mexico, Venezuela and West Germany.

Many smaller welcoming services, most of them operating in suburban towns near big metropolitan areas, also find business is expanding. Mrs. Buck's company, Welcomers of Wilmette, claims at present to have about 400 sponsors in the Chicago area, more than ever and twice the total of five years ago. Talks with some of these sponsors indicate why Mrs. Buck's company—and others like it—are doing well.

"It's the best form of advertising we've got," says Ted Hansen, part owner of a Chicago fish shop chain now enjoying its best year. "The welcoming service gets people in for us," he explains. "We can carry the ball from there." Mr. Hansen's company uses Welcomers to circulate cards that can be traded by new residents for a pound of fried shrimp or some chicken.

Liquor dealers find the service is helping their sales. "This is the biggest year we've had," exclaims Vincent Ratcliffe, a partner in 12-year-old Ratcliffe's Ranger Wine Shop of Chicago. Sales through June were 5 per cent higher than in 1957, he reports, and profits also are up. Through Welcomers, the firm sends around cards worth a case of pop.

ALFRED L. MALABRE

August 20, 1958

One-Man Concerns

In Camden, New Jersey, Mrs. N., a 59-year-old widow, pores day and night over production charts, engineering drawings and financial accounts, determined to keep alive an enterprise founded on the basis of a product her late husband invented some 40 years ago.

The company she heads employs 75 people. Its sales last year exceeded $1 million. Profits have been sufficient to permit Mrs. N. to draw a $20,000 annual salary.

"It's nothing elaborate, but at least I'm in business for myself."

Despite the firm's success, however, its continued existence is in jeopardy. Accustomed to doing everything herself, Mrs. N. has never trained an understudy; her only child, a daughter—24 years old and unmarried—has so far shown little inclination to carry on the business. "There isn't a person there who could take over if the widow were to pass on or be forced into sudden retirement," says a close associate.

Mrs. N. is not unlike lots of other proprietors of business enterprises. Many owner-managers allow their firms to drift into this same predicament, unaware of or unwilling to face the problem of their own succession. However, an increasing number of top executives these days are tackling the problem—and they're getting a powerful assist, for various reasons, from educators, bankers and bureaucrats.

Mitchel Stern, 53-year-old bachelor president and chief stockholder of a company that forges fire escapes and other metal products in a plant not far from Mrs. N.'s premises, is one executive who's determined to keep his company alive. Mr. Stern started out in business for himself as a broker of structural steel shapes in 1932, when the steel company that was employing him at $75 a week let him go in favor of an engineering-school graduate willing to take $10. The firm he heads today, Camden Iron Works, keeps 50 people busy producing close to $1 million of wares annually.

Mr. Stern has no close relatives to provide for; one nephew, in fact, is a competitor of his. Still, he has enough pride in his organization to want to see it survive him—and he has a strong sense of loyalty toward the men who work for him. Right now, he's footing bills for extracurricular education designed to prepare his key executives for broader management responsibilities. He's also setting up a stock plan to vest them with ownership in the company along with their advancement.

Sentimental, perhaps, but foresight of this kind pays off in the present as well. Herbert Barchoff, 41-year-old president of New York's Eastern Rolling Mills, Inc., a company that helps its executives broaden their educational backgrounds, puts it this way: "The problem of bringing up second-line management goes farther than providing for one's own succession—it goes to the very roots of corporate growth." Capable lower-level executives, he figures, permit the business to operate in a more orderly fashion and take greater advantage of its opportunities.

To help its men ready themselves for more responsible positions, Eastern will underwrite practically any self-improvement course that promising employees care to undertake. Last month, for example, Eastern's young comptroller, Nathan Angstreich, completed night studies for a master's degree in finance at a New York university. The company had picked up the tab on his tuition all the way. Next month, Eastern's vice-president, Jack Rothschild, will be studying cost reduction for a week at Cornell, courtesy of the company. "Our sales in the past couple of years have doubled, to over $4 million a year," says Mr. Barchoff, "but I'm even prouder of our advances in management."

A concern without a backstop for its one-man management some- times can survive—if it's lucky. Erie Bottling Corp. of Erie, Pennsyl- vania, was left about as headless as a company could be when its 43-year-old president, Grafton Perkins, died of a heart attack last November. Mr. Perkins had been carrying Erie's executive load him- self. The company's three surviving stockholders, none of whom was active in the business, took a chance: They named Erie's best truck driver—pop salesman as general manager and hoped for the best.

Walter Kontje, the new general manager, had little formal edu- cation. Almost all of his adult life had been spent as a pop peddler. He'd never had anyone to boss; now he had a going organization of 25 men to run. But it didn't take him long to catch on. In nine months on his new job, he's been so successful in boosting sales and production—while at the same time actually cutting down on the labor force and reducing costs—that Erie's owners recently awarded him a handsome pay boost and are now cutting him in on the profits. "He really grew into that job," says one of Erie's elated owners.

Few firms escape unscathed, however, when the curtain falls on a one-man show. Far more typical than the good fortune of Erie's owners, for example, was the experience of the New York adver- tising firm of Cecil & Presbrey, Inc. Cecil & Presbrey's door didn't close immediately when its board chairman, James M. Cecil, passed on. First there was a withering away of the company's principal accounts. Then came the end.

A man can be a great builder of businesses and yet be a total flop at providing for his own succession. A typical example, perhaps, was Royce Martin, chairman and president of Electric Auto-Lite Co. of Toledo until he died of a heart attack just over two years ago. Since Mr. Martin had taken over as president in 1933, the company's sales had gone from $14 million to nearly $300 million a year. But Mr. Martin, a friendly man who'd once put in seven years as a financial agent for the Mexican revolutionary Pancho Villa, wasn't given to delegating responsibility to others; a month before he died he was active in planning the company's television shows.

Mr. Martin named more than 23 vice-presidents in his time but gave them little opportunity to make their own decisions. When he died, it fell to a senior partner in the company's law firm to suggest a successor. A man eventually was chosen: James P. Falvey, then vice-president in charge of industrial relations. But much valuable time had been lost. Had Mr. Falvey been given authority earlier, he might also have sped the firm's diversification, tightened its dealings with labor and cleared out overage executives faster—measures generally credited with having pulled the company out of a profits tailspin that began in 1954.

Henry Blackstone, 40-year-old chairman and president of Servo Corp. of America, believes stockholders have a right to expect "independence from one-man management." The company, which he formed 10 years ago to act as a consultant in engineering and research, now employs 300, mostly in the manufacture of electronic control systems, in a plant just outside New York City.

Mr. Blackstone's formula for promoting such independence has three ingredients. First, he reports, Servo goes to "considerably greater expense than is justified by the job opening itself" to determine the executive potential of an individual before taking him on. Second, it rotates its executives in varying jobs. For example, Robert Baxter, now production manager, also has served Servo as director of purchasing and as chief accountant, while David Key, who started with the company four years ago as a helper in its machine shop, has served also in production control and engineering and is now getting a taste of selling.

Finally, Mr. Blackstone has organized his key personnel into three committees of four to seven men in each of three departments—sales, engineering and business. These committees meet once a week for three hours or longer to discuss "all problems in their own fields." Says Mr. Blackstone: "These conferences serve our day-to-day needs by keeping everyone in step and our longer-range aims by exposing young executives with relatively little experience to the broader management of the company." Like Eastern Rolling Mills and Camden Iron Works, Servo also underwrites the cost of outside education for executives—on the basis of 50 per cent when they sign up and the other 50 per cent upon successful completion of their studies.

MITCHELL GORDON

July 20, 1956

The Food Giant

A. & P. is more than you may think.

It is the clerk at the checkout counter, true; he and his colleagues between dawn and dusk today will ring up more than double the sales of any other food chains. But A. & P. is also a salmon fisherman tossing in a small boat north of Alaska's Aleutian Islands. It is the engineer of an indoor railroad in Westchester County, New York. It is a field worker, sleeping in a shanty and going out by day to harvest carrots and celery in California's fabulously fertile Salinas Valley. It is the silver-tongued promoter, traveling from town to town and convincing local folk they should set up new real-estate ventures. It is a lady in white turban and smock, making macaroni in a Brooklyn factory. It is a weather-beaten fellow in the coffee-growing backlands of Brazil.

The Great Atlantic & Pacific Tea Company has, in its 99 years of evolution, indeed grown great. Long ago it became vastly more than a tea company, of course; walk into the A. & P. at Newport, Vermont, and you can even buy nowadays an Orlon sweater, a bathroom scale, a bow tie, a folding card table, a towel, a pencil sharpener, a pop-up toaster or a drip-dry slip. Still, in one respect the company's title remains, even to this day, a little overboastful.

In the West there are 11 states in which A. & P. sells nothing at all; the empire includes Arkansas only by grace of a token three stores, Minnesota with two, Oklahoma and Nebraska with one apiece. Founded in New York City, the company's stores have never really taken hold outside the eastern half of the nation. But this, of course, is not exactly an accident, nor entirely a defeat. Since the chain's principle of operation is to achieve low costs and low prices through enormous volume of sales, A. & P. has deliberately put its stores in the counties where some 75 per cent of American families live.

Says an official of a rival chain: "One A. & P. urban store in New York has more people within walking distance than some of our rural stores out West have within driving distance." The city in which A. & P. is most dominant, however, appears to be not New York but Milwaukee, where a survey by the Milwaukee *Journal* indicates 43.9 per cent of the families buy most of their groceries from the chain, up from 39.8 per cent three years ago.

There are 4,046 of the A. & P. stores in the U.S., plus 151 in

Canada. Mere numbers mean little; the chain actually hit its numerical peak of 15,422 shops back in 1930. But today's bigger stores handle far more traffic—sales have spurted $2.2 billion above the $2.5 billion total of just a decade ago. Where do all those groceries come from?

To a surprisingly large extent they come from A. & P. itself. It is, for instance, either first or second among the world's kneaders and beaters of bread and cake dough, with bakeries in 36 cities. A vegetable oil refinery at Terre Haute, Indiana, turns out salad dressings and mayonnaise. Milk is evaporated, powdered and packaged in Wisconsin. One Brooklyn plant is busy cooking candy while another is making a variety of wares from peanut butter to extracts. Fish sticks are cooked in Boston. A. & P. makes dog food, slices bacon, packs preserves and ketchup, cures cheese, prints butter, stirs up baking powder and even washes its own laundry.

In the sunny town of Salinas, California, which lies like a quartered tomato in the center of a bed of green farmland, are two sprawling sheds where A. & P. "prepackages" in transparent bags vegetables which it has bought in the field and harvested itself. "They have the bankroll and we don't," comments a man who competes in buying, "so they can afford to get the better patches." By eliminating the packer's profit on celery and carrots, shippers estimate, A. & P. could save 15 cents a crate—and the crates roll out by the carload.

An airlift this year flew around 350 fishermen, cannery workers and maintenance men from Seattle nearly 2,000 miles northward to Alaska's Bristol Bay, for a salmon operation conducted jointly with two other companies. Nearly 5,000 tons of supplies, "everything from a screwdriver to a lead pencil," came by boat. With its other canneries on the Alaska Panhandle and on Puget Sound, A. & P. put up over $4 million of salmon, wholesale value f.o.b. Seattle, for its stores in 1957, and probably boosted that 20 per cent this year.

Equally far-flung, and much more important, is the system which puts Eight O'Clock, Red Circle and Bokar coffee on A. & P. shelves. It starts in Brazil and Colombia, where a battalion of buyers roams the interior, sampling and making selections. In Santos and other cities the company washes, separates and blends its beans, then ships them north to 13 U.S. coffee plants for further blending and roasting. Over a quarter-billion pounds, it is estimated, will have been handled this year; A. & P. apparently is outranked in coffee roasting only by General Foods.

What foodstuff it does not process itself, A. & P. must buy ready-made from others, of course. In so doing it often places emphasis not on nationally advertised brands but on items bearing its own private labels—produced by the same manufacturers, in many instances, but priced cheaper. These labels have made Ann Page and Jane Parker among the most noted nonexistent ladies in America.

It's an educated guess of top canners, for example, that more than half of the chain's tinned fruit is sold under its private labels (Iona and others). A meat packer figures that A. & P.'s private (Super Right) cuts now take 95 per cent of the chain's meat sales. Rival chains, too, have plunged heavily into private brands, but A. & P. has at times led the stampede. "When it put a private-brand vegetable oil (Dexola) on the market three years ago, every other major chain followed with its own private label," comments a manufacturing executive. "They believe if A. & P. does it, it must be the smart thing to do."

One top executive of the chain insists, "We don't push our own brands." An examination of advertising in cities across the land reveals scant mention of anything but A. & P.'s private labels, however. An excursion into a typical store, in Madison, New Jersey, indicates clear preference granted to private-label products manufactured or purchased by A. & P. In the jams-and-jellies section, to cite one, the Ann Page label occupies four shelves while the bottom shelf is devoted to a few jars of national brands: Crosse & Blackwell, Kraft, Louis Sherry, Welch, White House, Keiller, Chivers, Big Top. But as a competing chain's president notes, A. & P. rarely makes the mistake of having an important national brand product completely unavailable—"If a woman is determined to have Heinz ketchup, she'll be given no excuse for doing her shopping elsewhere."

To such a housewife, the A. & P. is embodied in its store manager, a man of great power who can okay the cashing of her checks, yet a friendly fellow who takes time out to explain that he doesn't issue trading stamps the way his competitors do because he's intent on giving her low prices. If you talk heart to heart with this manager he will reveal most of this is an illusion, purposefully created; an A. & P. store manager is in fact a key carrier, an errand runner, a housekeeper and a bookkeeper, but a man granted hardly any executive discretion.

His price change list comes to him every Monday, for insertion in a loose-leaf price book, and he dare not diverge from that book except to mark down perishables at the end of the week. In smaller cities he delivers his ads in person to the newspaper, but in the form of mats which are handed to him from above. He supervises store personnel, making sure they are neatly dressed, not loafing or leaning on the scales, but can hire no one—even a part-time stocker—without investigation and approval by his superiors.

If he figures he can sell more by piling up displays in the aisles, he is likely to be countermanded by an order to keep the aisles clear for grocery cart traffic. He orders merchandise, basing his volume on inventories and past sales performance, but has little choice of what he will or will not stock. He is instructed to emphasize customer relations, so he is friendly and tries to keep his clerks in a friendly mood. When a customer complains a cake was stale, he gives back her 29 cents without questioning her word. He cashes a check cheerfully, but knows if it turns out bad he will be given a rough time; he is forbidden to accept personal checks for over $100 and can cash no out-of-town checks at all.

If decisions are not made in the store, where are they made?

All basic policies are set in New York City, on Lexington Avenue off 43rd Street, inside the Graybar Building, on the twenty-second floor: international headquarters of A. & P. The visitor will be not so much dazzled as sobered; as he steps out of the elevator the mood is set by polished tables, an American flag, high-backed leather chairs, and some oil paintings showing A. & P. men doing laudable things, such as inspecting oranges in the grove before buying.

Here is where President Ralph Burger and hosts of associates set their ambitious sales goals and their unambitious price markup policies, debate how fast to push the building of new stores and the introduction of nonfoods into old ones, ponder the adequacy of their $4.4 million reserve for self-insurance, worry over their rent bills (running at $43.4 million annually, up $7.7 million in just two years, and still rising), reconfirm the policy of incurring no debt, chat and sometimes quarrel with high executives of companies from which they buy, and, currently, plan the dissolution of a number of subsidiaries, whose activities will be transferred directly to the company.

"Meetings—lots of meetings," observes one of the chief participants wearily. "Still, there's something new, don't you know, every day."

Apart from policy making, a large proportion of A. & P.'s operational activity also is "nationalized," but by no means entirely in New York. For instance, the national nerve center for all buying of fresh produce is Chicago, where experts constantly receive via phone and teletype price and quality reports from field buyers in Florida, Texas and other producing areas, decide which are the best buys, and flash back instructions to the field.

All seafood buying—even of fish which flipped fins in the Pacific Ocean—is synchronized from Boston. Baltimore buys the frozen orange juice. Egg-and-poultry purchasing centers in New York; national meat buying is all run from Chicago.

All in all, centralization is an outstanding characteristic that sets

A. & P. aside from its major chain competitors, in the opinion of one major supplier whose views are echoed by others. Says he: "Everybody is responsible to the Graybar Building; they seem much more conscious of central control." Much of this control is exercised by combing masses of figures that pour into headquarters. Chief statistician of the corporation is John Reilly, in his thirty-sixth year with A. & P.; backing him up is bespectacled John Ehrgott, who has spent 41 years in service.

Nevertheless, A. & P. since 1925 has enjoyed a measure of decentralization in its retailing operation. It is now split into seven divisions, each equipped with its own president and other officers though none is incorporated.

The Eastern Division comprises New York City and immediate vicinity and—rather weirdly—Los Angeles and Seattle. The Central Division is headquartered in Pittsburgh and includes such cities as Cleveland, Buffalo and Altoona. The Southern Division, covering the most territory, is centered at Jacksonville, Florida, but stretches from Charlotte, North Carolina, to New Orleans and Dallas. The Atlantic Division is based on Philadelphia, including such towns as Richmond and Scranton. Boston is headquarters of the New England Division, which sweeps north and westward to include Canada. The Central Western Division, based on Detroit, takes in Indianapolis, Toledo and other cities. And the Middle Western Division has its officers in a large red-brick warehouse in a drab industrial section of Chicago; it includes such cities as Milwaukee, St. Louis and Kansas City.

The provincial chieftains are unquestionably possessed of considerable power in their own domains. The manufacturer of any nationally advertised food item, for instance, must sell his product to each one individually (but if it is a new item, he must clear it first with the Graybar Building). It can be contended, however, that the more important task of the regional leaders is to play a grass-roots role in the shaping of centralized national policy. Ten members of the A. & P. board of directors are presidents or chairmen of these fiefdoms; it is reported that all the little presidents fly in once a month to confer with big President Burger.

Each division is broken down further into "units." Each unit is headed by a divisional vice-president and centers around a warehouse which feeds goods to its food shops. It is the unit which actually sets prices, under policy filtering down from above; it prepares the ads; it approves hirings (except for store managers and assistant managers, who must be approved at division headquarters); it is staffed by roaming supervisors, each of whom bosses about 10 stores.

The principal architect of the A. & P. empire, the late John Hartford, used to tell his associates that "the really ideal store would be one in which we'd have no employees." Self-service was a move in that direction, but as things have turned out A. & P. has masses of employees—145,000 of them, of whom many work part-time.

Employee loyalty and morale are high, by the account of most outsiders having contact with the chain. Money does not seem to be the chief method of achieving this, though wages are generally equal to those of competitors and, especially in nonunion areas, occasionally higher. No incentive payments or bonuses for exceptional performance are granted.

One stimulant is strict adherence to promotion from within the organization, which gives every young store clerk, though he may lack much formal education, the feeling that he can climb from the bottom to the top, as those now at the top have done. How much can you make up there? Well, the salaries of divisional presidents range from the $54,645 drawn by Francis Bucher, 57, of Central Western to the $92,645 pulled down by Robert M. Smith, 66, of Southern. A couple of divisional chairmen, 79-year-old William M. Byrnes of Eastern and 82-year-old Oliver C. Adams of Atlantic and Southern, receive $105,221 apiece.

Apart from encouraging the drive of ambition, there's evidence that A. & P. discovered before *McCall's* magazine did just how useful "togetherness" can be. Outside working hours A. & P. employees are likely to be found dancing together, picnicking together, golfing together. One lowly ex-employee recalls considerable "influence" for every able-bodied employee to get out on Sunday to play softball.

Besides employing people, A. & P. is the catalyst of thousands of small business ventures. One example is trucking; the chain does not tote its own goods but contracts with others to do so. Every small trucker must file reports to the Interstate Commerce Commission; if he doesn't want to be bothered, A. & P. will make these out for him and call him in merely to sign.

The company's real-estate promoters, operating out of New York City, stir up plenty of activity by others. Here is an actual but somewhat disguised case:

First, the A. & P. men studied a town in upstate New York, determining that it has a year-round population of around 4,000 and draws from an area of 12,000 souls, both figures swelling considerably during summer vacation time. This, they decided, would support a much larger store than they had in the town, which was being obscured by a newer and larger Grand Union shop.

Next they found a suitable four-and-a-half-acre tract of land, owned by a fellow we shall call Hamilton Jones, and sat down and negotiated its sale for about $45,000. But A. & P. didn't buy the land; its men had scouted up a group of prospective buyers. After that, they interested another group in leasing the land for 75 years at better than $5,000 annually, guaranteed, plus an escalator sum depending upon financial success of the venture.

Of course, A. & P. needed a store on the land. So the second group, having incorporated as High Hills Shopping Center, Inc., was offered drawings of the structure desired. It was introduced to a likely contractor to put up the building. And A. & P. signed a 10-year lease, at about $35,000 annual rental, with two five-year options to renew at higher rentals, for more than 14,000 square feet of space. That left another 11,000 or so square feet available for other tenants, and A. & P. insisted upon no veto over these. Since A. & P. stores are known to draw traffic, most of this space already has been leased.

Many competitors have felt that A. & P. has been slow in abandoning its older and smaller stores. Indeed, there has been resistance within the high command; some ranking company executives feel the chain has been "going overboard" in creating as many super-supermarkets as it has. At least one regional chief is determined not to close any small stores where doing so would throw business to local rivals; he cites instances where he is keeping some old stores that are not particularly profitable and letting his profitable big new stores "carry them."

Nevertheless, President Burger has pledged the company "to continue its modernization program in order to protect its business, insofar as available funds permit," and new stores are rising. A. & P. will open in Pasadena, California, next February, for instance, a 26,000-square-foot market, its biggest yet in southern California.

Every bit as important as stores, in the A. & P. system, is the efficient flow of goods through its warehouses. And these are being modernized, too. Prize example is completion this year of a distribution center on a 50-acre site in Westchester County, north of New York City. A rail siding of the New York Central runs through the 175,000-square-foot warehouse, permitting simultaneous indoor unloading of 13 freight cars. On the opposite side of the building is a ramp with ports to unload and load 43 trailer trucks. Inside, transport is handled by a miniature railroad, with five-foot cars pulled by underfloor conveyor chain. This block-long beehive will, among many other things, candle 2.5 million eggs a week and ripen 5,000 stalks of bananas.

December 15, 1958

Death of a Business

Back in 1925 two young Cleveland businessmen went into the fuel oil business. Their assets consisted of a lot of ambition and $30,000 in cash, three fourths of it borrowed from friends.

Twenty-three years later, after weathering a war and a depression, the partners were doing $50 million worth of business annually. The road ahead, businesswise, looked bright and prosperous.

Yet in August 1948, the two partners sold out to a larger oil company. It was one of those mergers of big and little businesses that Washington seems so concerned about; competition in the nation's oil distribution business was reduced by one small part.

What happened? Was there a "squeeze" by big business? Was little business whipped by too tough competition? Was there a plot to monopolize oil in the Cleveland area?

W. W. Vandeveer, one of the partners, has written his story of what happened to one venture in private enterprise:

While the Federal Government investigates, prosecutes and holds hearings on how big business is growing bigger by gobbling up its smaller competitors, thousands of small businesses are being forced to seek refuge in mergers with other companies because of the Government's own regulations.

Our company—Allied Oil Company, Inc., and its subsidiaries—was merged with the Ashland Oil & Refining Company on August 3, 1948. On that day my partner and I were out of business—a business that we had built from scratch over a period of 23 years. On that day the number of competing oil companies in the United States was reduced by one.

We were not the victims of unfair trade practices. We were not gobbled up by any private monopoly. We were not threatened by any of our competitors—big or little. We sought to merge because of the threats held over our heads by the Government that has been giving lip service to the encouragement of small business and to the preservation of competitive enterprise.

We were ready, willing and able to carry on for many more years of successful business life. We have faced the business hazards of depression years, war years and years of postwar reconstruction. We were not a couple of doddering old men looking for a safe, quiet place to piece out the rest of our days. We knew we could continue to increase our service to our community—and do it profitably—but Uncle Sam's tax laws backed us into a corner, where we had only one of two choices: sell out or face the risk of personal bankruptcy at the time of our respective deaths.

If our story were the story of only one small business, it would hardly be worth the telling. It is, however, the story of thousands of independent, closely held business concerns. The liquidation and merging of these thousands of small businesses is reducing the area of competition and threatening our system of individual enterprise.

It is time to study the problem of mergeritis from the viewpoint of the small business that has been merged. It is time to determine the composite causes that make liquidation or the merger route such a popular road to business suicide. We do not need more road blocks on big business. We need an open road that will give small business the incentive and opportunity to stay independent.

The story of the Allied merger shows how government regulations encourage the sales of small business and reduce competition. Allied Oil was born, like thousands of American enterprises, on a shoestring. Its pattern of growth was that followed by many an American company.

Except for the NRA code days and the years of the Petroleum Administration for War, the business grew outside the shadow of government restrictions. We were free to compete for the fuel business of industrial consumers. In that competition with natural-gas suppliers, coal and oil companies, we had to show industrial plants how Allied Oil could help them reduce their operating and manufacturing costs. We did this by teaching their personnel more efficient fuel practices, by searching the country for lower-cost materials, and by devising new, lower-cost transportation methods.

During these years of growth and diversification, we plowed back practically every cent of the company's earnings into new facilities and in addition borrowed substantial sums from local banks and life insurance companies in order to further increase our service to the community and to tide us over many a tight spot. Our expanding facilities each year served more and more customers with lower-cost fuels and better service and provided more and more persons with employment on the Allied Oil payroll.

With such an apparent record of success, why were we forced to sell out? To begin with, the tax laws encourage small businessmen to take their earnings in capital gains instead of paying taxes on current income. To do this you have to sell out. Amos and Andy were not the first to make this discovery. They were the first to get wide publicity for using the capital-gains route to hold on to a larger share of their earnings.

The second impelling cause of our action grew heavier each passing year. The more earnings plowed back, the more the company grew, the greater its assets and earning value became and estate taxes assumed increased importance. The value of the organization was in its nature as a going concern based on earning power. It wasn't the tons of steel, the ships, the storage terminals and other physical properties, but the annual earning potential of a smoothly functioning unit that determined the value of the company.

Each owner knew that the untimely death of the other would set in motion a series of events that could wipe out the earning power of the company and bankrupt the surviving owner as well as the kin of the deceased. There was no established market value of the shares of the company. They were substantially all held by the two chief owners. How would "value" for inheritance and estate tax purposes be determined? Largely by capitalization of past and potential earnings.

The value so determined could easily exceed the realization that could have been actually procured under market conditions such as we have experienced and, unless government attitudes are changed, seem likely to experience for an indefinite time into the future. Inheritance and estate taxes, determined on such a basis, would have greatly exceeded the estate value (liquid assets) held outside of Allied by either owner. Having never been able to pay out much in the way of earnings, their eggs were all in one basket. To meet such taxes, the heirs of the deceased stockholder would have to find a purchaser for a minority stock interest in the company.

Where and at what price could such a purchaser be found? The survivor might have to go into debt in order to buy such stock to protect himself. There might even have to be either a forced sale of the total properties or a liquidation of assets piecemeal. The effect on Allied Oil employees, customers and loan makers, to say nothing of the two principals and their heirs, might have been disastrous. We could not escape the inevitability of putting our estates in order.

There were several possible courses of action and all were studied carefully and thoroughly. One solution was to issue and sell common stock to the public. Allied properties were appraised by a capable firm of engineers in 1945 and a basis established for proper stock issue. The stock market turned down, however, and new issues could find a market only on the basis of bargain-counter prices. Investors were not rushing to buy new issues of anybody's common stock.

After working on the possibility of selling common stock to the public, we found it necessary to find another solution.

We started a market survey of companies capable of buying Allied's little organization. Several oil companies were interested in making the deal. Our prime objective was to insure a continuation of the Allied organization on a sound and growing basis. That is why the exchange of assets for preferred and common stock of the Ashland Oil & Refining Company was finally accepted.

We were satisfied that Allied would continue to serve the market as it had in the past. We were satisfied that our customers would be taken care of. We were convinced that our employees would be treated with dignity and fairness as becomes their abilities.

All in all, it seemed the best arrangement for everyone who had an interest in Allied. It was the only way out for two individuals who had conceived and built up a business and which in other times or under different circumstances they would have carried on for the rest of their business lives.

That is the story of the Allied Oil merger and its contribution to the concentration of economic power in America.

While Allied Oil was an independent, going concern, we did not ask for government guarantees on prices, income and profits. We would still be in business except for the unrealistic tax laws that forced us to sell our company.

The owners of Allied Oil have been merged out of business. As one of the two owners, neither ex post facto investigations, decrees nor educts by a paternal Government can bring me back to life as a competitive factor in the oil-marketing business.

August 25, 1949

EDITORIAL FEATURE

THEY SPEND IT, TOO

Young Dr. B.

AUGUSTA, Ga.—A couple of months ago Dr. Lawrence B., one of this city's newer physicians, purchased a Cadillac. Thus, at the age of 32, he achieved what General Motors Corp. fondly considers a mark of success and simultaneously elevated his family to the two-car class.

But the young doctor notes regretfully: "This is not quite as good as it sounds."

"A patient owed me $100 and I knew he couldn't pay, but he was a used-car dealer so I bought a used 1950 Cadillac from him," Dr. B. explains. "I put up $400 cash and deducted $100 from the price. Then I borrowed the rest, $800, from the bank."

Dr. B. could easily afford the $1,300 automobile, or even a new one if he wanted it. He figures his income this year will be $25,000. But, while this income will be an impressive 1,000 per cent above what he was making as recently as three years ago, the doctor feels that it, too, is "not quite as good as it sounds."

Responsibilities and expenses have been growing right along with income. In the last five years he has acquired a wife and three children, bought a house and started medical practice. In between, he's gone on a whopper of a buying spree for such diverse items as a washing machine, an electrocardiograph and 666⅔ pine tree seedlings. In the process he has put himself more than $34,000 in debt.

"I'm paying out so much on the house, the car, insurance and interest on the loans, I just can't seem to put anything aside," he says. "I guess my current assets would run around $500 to $700."

Dr. B., whose identity has been mildly disguised, stays too busy with his growing practice to do much worrying about the future these days. This capable-looking young man with his relaxed manner and ready smile is not the fretful type, anyhow. But every once in a while, he concedes, he gets concerned about the snail-slow growth of his savings.

"I figure I've got maybe twenty-five good years ahead of me and then nothing," he says. "Practically everybody these days has some sort of pension, but so far doctors don't even come under Social Security. I don't have any regular savings plan; I'd like to get some investments going, buy some common stock and let it grow. But I can't seem to get my hands on any money that I can just put aside.

"You know," he adds, "if I should have a coronary right now, that would be it. No disability insurance."

Dr. B. believes some of his problems would disappear if more of his patients would pay him what they owe. During the three years he's been in practice, he's turned over $5,000 worth of unpaid bills to a collection agency. "They collected $1,000, but I've kissed off the rest," he says. "At any particular moment, my overdue bills run around $9,000 to $10,000. If I could just get paid I could pay off my debts and maybe invest a little money."

Dr. B. was born in Augusta on July 3, 1923, into a family "with a mess of doctors on both sides." Now he's one of four Dr. B.s practicing in Augusta. He graduated from Holy Cross University in Worcester, Massachusetts, in 1943 and went on to medical school at the University of Georgia. Thanks to the accelerated schedule of the Navy Reserve V-12 program, which he joined, he won his medical sheepskin three years later, in 1946.

Then came a year as an intern at the university hospital. Salary: $15 a month. "It wasn't much," he says, "but the hospital took care of all my expenses. They've gone up since then, interns are in short supply, and I think they pay $150 a month now." The Navy called him up in April 1947, gave him the rank of lieutenant (junior grade) and sent him to Guam. Twenty-four months later he was discharged, but at age 26 he still had three years of medical training ahead of him.

He spent two years as a medical resident at Emory University in Atlanta, gradually taking on more and more responsibility and being trained at the same time. For his third year he did research work at Emory.

While in Atlanta, in September 1951, Dr. B. married a Pennsylvania girl, the daughter of family friends. They set up housekeeping on his salary of $2,400 a year.

Looking back on that first year, he muses, "I don't see how we did it. But we didn't have many expenses. We paid $67 a month for an efficiency apartment. I had a car that was all paid for. I was working and studying all the time so we never went out much."

In July 1952, about the time his first son was born, the young M.D. came to Augusta and rented an office, taking the first big step toward cashing in on his years of training. The move set off some staggering changes in the life of the B. family, sending their income soaring and allowing them to go on a long-deferred buying splurge.

Before Dr. B. could even begin practice he was hit with a major expense—$4,000 for office equipment and furniture, including such items as an examining table for $265, electrocardiograph for $875 and ordinary office furniture. Dr. B. paid for the equipment by borrowing from the bank, the first of several loans he would find necessary during the next three years. He's since repaid $1,000 but the $3,000 balance costs him $75 twice a year, or 5 per cent. In addition he purchased an X-ray machine from the A. S. Aloe Co., for $1,200, now paid off via the installment route.

During the next three years the B. family kept growing. A second son was born in September 1953, and a third in December 1954. And the young doctor's practice prospered. During the first six months he averaged seven patients a day; last year he had 10 a day and now he's getting 15 to 20 daily.

From the $55-a-month bungalow they rented when they came to Augusta, the B.s moved into a $28,500 home purchased last September. They bought a new car, a 1953 Chevrolet for which Dr. B. was able to pay $1,200 in cash from his earnings plus trading in his old car, an Oldsmobile. They bought a Necchi sewing machine for $275, a Hotpoint washing machine for $275, a Hotpoint refrigerator for $300 and a Hotpoint stove for another $300, paying cash for the appliances.

Their whole scale of living took a sharp rise. They hired a cook for $20 a week. They joined a country club for $200 a year in dues and "who knows how much extra when you count the things you sign for." They took trips to the mountains and trips to Florida, spending $300 to $400 for a vacation. Once Dr. B. counted up what he'd spent for clothing in the past year and it came to about $275; he figures his wife spends less, maybe $250 a year. They began buying food without "sparing the money," spending "$5 a day at least," the doctor estimates.

The doctor took on new insurance to supplement a $10,000 Metropolitan Life Insurance Co. policy he took out in 1947. When he signed up for that policy in 1947 it was for endowment, and premiums cost him $145 twice a year. "I went 'way over my head," he recalls. "I was making $15 a month and I could no more carry the premiums than fly." He switched the policy to term life insurance at $100 a year.

He now has about $70,000 worth of life insurance, all term policies. In addition to the usual policies on his house and automobiles, he carries physicians' liability insurance to protect him from possible lawsuits charging him with malpractice. This costs him $100 a year.

"I don't know where we got all the money," he says, looking back. A substantial portion of the cash for this wave of spending came from the doctor's rising income. But some of it was borrowed and some was given to him.

During 1953, his first full year of practice, Dr. B. had gross income of $18,466. "That was a very good year, lots of night calls, and collections were good," he recalls. After paying out his office expenses, he had net income of $10,887.

In 1954, he says, he had more patients than in 1953, but "we felt a very definite slump in this area. People not only postponed their bills, they just didn't pay them." His gross income that year was $17,495; net was $9,917.

This year he figures his income for the first six months was $12,000 and it will hit $25,000 for the year. "That will be more like it," he says. Office expenses will stay about the same as earlier years, he hopes, so he should have net income for the year of around $16,000.

He foresees a peak gross income during his career of around $32,-000 to $33,000 yearly. "If I used all my time, I guess I could make $35,000," he says, "but I want to see something of my family."

Dr. B. charges $5 for an office visit, $6 for a house visit, $7 for a house visit between five and 11 P.M. and $10 if he has to make a call after 11 P.M. "I'm in one of the lowest-paying specialties, internal medicine and heart disease," he notes. "The ones who really make it are the surgeons. I spend an hour with a patient, giving him all kinds of tests, send him a bill for $25 and he gripes. But if a surgeon does a little hernia operation and sends a bill for $150 or more they don't bat an eyelash."

He adds: "People should always ask a doctor how much he's going to charge. Some charges by doctors are just ridiculous; we have some here who really gouge their patients. I guess any community does. A doctor should be able to tell you approximately how much treatment is going to cost, just like selling anything else. The doctor who says, 'Just don't worry about that now' is usually the same one who'll turn right around and gouge his patient."

CHARLES N. STABLER, JR.

August 12, 1955

Farmer G.'s Budget

BLOOMINGTON, Ill.—Americans bothered by budget balancing may take comfort from the case of 44-year-old farmer Wilbur G.

Mr. G., who is classed in his community as a solid, conservative citizen, seldom knows how much he's earning until a year ends. During the past decade, his income has bounced up and down like a man on a pogo stick—all the way from a high of $22,227 in 1950 to a loss of $11,562 in 1952.

How does Mr. G. balance his outgo with his uncertain income? He doesn't even try. Says he: "We buy whatever we need when we need it, even if we haven't got the money saved."

The carefree conservatism of Mr. G. may seem paradoxical. Yet it fits the facts of his financial life as a farmer. Mr. G., whose 160 acres of tall corn and green pasture land are about 20 miles north of this central-Illinois city, netted $11,015, before taxes, in 1954. He borrows heavily to finance both personal needs and his cattle-feeding business. Last year this borrowing hit $72,600. His savings are next to nil. "When my bank account gets below $1,000, I just borrow some more money," he explains lightly.

In other respects, Mr. G. is indeed a conservative man. He almost always manages to clear his debts within a year, when he markets his fattened steers, hogs and lambs, and so his banker does not hesitate to okay the next yearly borrowing spree. Mr. G. spends freely on new farm machinery and on increasing his herds. But, though his farm home is well equipped with appliances, he spends relatively little on clothing, furniture, food and entertainment. Mr. G. spends nothing on tobacco or liquor. "The strongest thing I drink is iced tea," says he.

"I bought two suits a few years ago and they'll fill my needs for some time yet," he says. His wife, Evelyn, makes three fourths of the clothes worn by herself and their two daughters and orders most of the rest from a Sears catalog. "A new coat marked down one half wouldn't tempt me unless I needed it," she says. "I bought one last year and won't need another until about 1957."

All the family's living-room furniture except a TV set, and all the furniture in their three bedrooms, was theirs before they moved to their present farm home in 1945. "We'll buy new furniture someday but we have no plans to get any in the immediate future," says Mrs. G.

And because the family grows its own meat, milk, eggs and much of its fruit and vegetable needs, spending for food is relatively low. "I do my grocery shopping once every two weeks at a supermarket twenty miles from the farm, and I spend only about $15 each time—maybe a little more in winter," Mrs. G. declares.

Many a storekeeper or salesman, were he to sit in on this conversation, might consider the G. family ripe for some long-delayed consumer goods spending. But Farmer G. plunks his earnings and borrowings alike into one bank account and makes no systematic effort to separate business and personal withdrawals. When he gets his hands on a packet of cash, he usually already has it earmarked in his mind for a new piece of farming equipment rather than a new sofa or suit or a high-priced car; needless to say, nearby farm implement dealers don't object one bit.

"I've now got my eye on a power manure spreader that will save me work," he confides. "I may get a new forage chopper to replace my 1952 machine, too. And I'd like to have a new grain-seeding drill but haven't decided yet that I need it $600 worth.

"I sometimes buy on the pay-later plan, but I only pay interest to the bank," he adds. He shies away from financing charges, gets his borrowed capital at 5 per cent, payable at maturity.

While Mr. G.'s income is subject to sharp fluctuations, he still does much better than the "average" farmer. During the past 10 years he's averaged over $11,000 a year, before taxes. A study by the Federal Agricultural Marketing Service, undertaken for the year 1953, showed average farm net income was only $1,707.

While farm income generally has been declining, Mr. G. has buoyed up his fortunes by high-volume operations, heavy reliance on machinery and efficient farming. These measures have largely offset occasional downswings in cattle prices.

Six-foot, 195-pound Mr. G. isn't worried about the future. "I figure industry has kept on going up so agriculture is due to go up, too," he explains.

Besides, Farmer G. knows—and his banker knows—that standing behind him is a farm whose value has grown nearly fivefold since he bought it in 1945, due to property improvements, equipment additions and increased land values. When he moved onto the farm in 1945, his net worth was $17,000; today, his banker puts it conservatively at $78,000.

He feeds about 150 steers, 400 hogs and several hundred lambs, using a rented 240 acres in addition to his own 160. To feed his animals, he grows corn, oats and hay; last year he also bought 75,500 pounds of protein supplement.

"When I married Evelyn back in 1935 and brought her home to the 160-acre farm I was renting then about eight miles from here, in the next county, we had an oilstove and a bed and that's about all," Wilbur G. recalls.

In the years that followed, Evelyn shouldered part of the work load as Wilbur rented an additional 160 acres. He was a small-scale dairyman then, and she helped milk the cows and worked with him in the fields. After John was born in 1939, followed by Mary in 1942 and Nadine in 1943, Evelyn took the children to the fields with her to save spending hard-earned cash for hired help.

"My household appliances consisted of a secondhand gasoline-powered washing machine and a kerosene-burning refrigerator," Mrs. G. recalls. "We didn't have electricity. I did my ironing with flatirons heated on the kitchen stove."

In 1944, after one rented farm had been sold and the landlord's son took possession of the second, Wilbur and Evelyn decided to buy a farm of their own. They borrowed $10,000 from a relative and $24,000 from a bank—since repaid—to buy what was regarded then as one of the poorest farms in the county.

"A fellow told me when I moved here that the rabbits even starved to death on this run-down place," Mr. G. says, his lean, sunburned face widening in a grin. "A neighbor predicted I'd be broke in two years."

But Mr. G. didn't follow the local custom of using the land to try to grow crops for sale, as his predecessors had. Instead, he decided to use his eroded farm to fatten cattle for market.

When he moved onto his new farm on March 1, 1945, he brought with him from his former farm property which, after deduction of debts, had a net value of $9,000. This included 28 dairy cows which he later sold to buy feeder cattle, 16 brood sows, 38 feeding hogs, two horses, 577 lambs, 150 laying hens, machinery and equipment worth $4,415, and quantities of corn, oats, hay and protein supplement for feed.

Another $8,000 in savings brought his net worth at that time to $17,000. Instead of applying this $8,000 toward the purchase price of the farm, which would have eliminated the need to borrow it all, he used his savings to buy gasoline, seed, fertilizer and other first-year operating necessities.

Last year's $91,562 gross, after deduction of operating expenses, came to $19,089. An inventory reduction of $8,074, resulting mostly from selling more livestock than he bought, brought Mr. G.'s net to $11,015.

What Mr. G. earns, he earns without government help—in this day of active Federal farm planning—and he's proud of it. "I could have taken a loan on five-thousand bushels of my corn last year under the price support program and made an easy ten cents a bushel by delivering it to the Government, because I could have bought corn for feed for a dime less a bushel on the open market than the Government would have paid me," he says. Then he adds: "But I have a farming system I want to see work without depending on the Government. I like to make my own decisions."

Mr. G. figures he has netted a total of $110,480 since he bought his farm in 1945. Most of it was spent, aside from general living expenses, on fully paying off the $24,000 bank mortgage and $10,000 private debt that financed the farm, enlarging his herds, building up his arsenal of farming equipment and his farm structures, and improving his home, both structurally and by equipping it with labor-saving appliances.

Before examining how he plows back profits into his farming operation, take a look at how Farmer G. has been able to make life more pleasant for his family at their farmhouse, a white-painted building which stands on a knoll 100 yards off a county road and which has withstood sun and snow for 30 years. He figures he has put more than $3,000 into the house, counting appliances, in the past 10 years—but has made that amount go far by careful, conservative spending.

"Shortly after I bought the farm, which already had electricity, I put in a pressure water system, a bathroom complete with water softener and electric water heater, laid out a sewage disposal system and installed a modern sink in the kitchen," recalls Mr. G. "These improvements cost me $765, which I borrowed. I did all the work myself.

"In 1946," he continues, "I glassed in the front porch, at a cost of $350, and installed an electric range, which set me back $150. We got a General Electric refrigerator in 1947 for $200, and an International Harvester food freezer in 1948 for $365. I got $100 off list price on the freezer because it was a discontinued model. In September of 1953 we got a second freezer, a $400 Sears job."

The second home freezer is symbolic of the careful investments the G. family has made in comfortable and economical rural living since they bought their farm. As a farmer who raises some of the tenderest beef a packing house ever bought, Wilbur G. became disgusted when he purchased a hindquarter of beef described by the local butcher as "the choicest meat we can get out of Chicago."

"It was so tough we could hardly eat it," he recalls.

Since they bought their 1948 International Harvester freezer, the G. family had kept the two or three hogs they butchered each year. But there wasn't room in the freezer for a whole side of beef too. The Sears home freezer provided the added space for packing away 500 pounds of beef at a time, and the G.s enjoy their meals a great deal more now.

At Christmas in 1953, three months after the second freezer was bought, Santa Claus delivered Evelyn an ABC automatic washer and a Westinghouse electric dryer. They cost "about $400," Mr. G. says.

"Those are the two things I'd hate most to do without now," Mrs. G. says of the washer and dryer.

Latest appliance purchased was a Philco console 21-inch television set, bought in 1954 for $385. "I paid $165 under list for that," Wilbur G. boasts.

Evelyn G. also has acquired an electric iron, a milk pasteurizer and a number of other electrical gadgets in recent years. These purchases, plus remodeling the kitchen at a cost that's "hard to figure," are what run the grand total spent for the house to more than $3,000 in the 10 years.

Added to this is a Nash bought in 1952 to replace the Pontiac Wilbur G. drove for 10 years. The 1952 model was traded in for a glistening red-and-black Nash Ambassador in May 1954.

These purchases were not paid for out of savings from previous earnings but were almost all bought on credit—with the lump sums Mr. G. borrows from his bank several times a year against future cattle receipts to finance, for the most part, his farm operating expenses. These loans are all funneled into the family's personal checking account. Household expenses, too, are paid for out of these bank advances.

Mrs. G. says she has tried keeping accounts of these household expenses but gave it up each time after a couple of weeks. "When you have to stay within a budget household accounts may be okay, but when you're going to spend it anyway there's not much point in keeping them," says her husband.

Despite this seemingly easygoing attitude toward spending, the buying habits of Mrs. G. appear on closer examination to be just as conservative and thrifty as her husband's way of hunting for discounted appliance bargains.

"If I see something downtown that's on sale I may buy it if we need it," says Mrs. G. "I don't mind buying ahead if it's something I know we need. But I never lose my self-control."

Besides holding back on buying of clothes and furniture, Mrs. G. gets a good many food bargains by buying in bulk, and she makes economical use of her two freezers.

The tight clay soil of their farm won't grow potatoes, and Mrs. G. bought 400 pounds of the tubers last year at $4 a hundred-pound sack. She uses lots of flour for her baking, too, and buys six 25-pound bags a year at $1.85 each. She used 300 pounds of sugar in packaging fruit for the freezer last year, paying $9 for a 100-pound sack.

In her two 17-cubic-foot home freezers Evelyn G. has 25 pounds of pork and 250 pounds of beef left from the 725 pounds packed away at butchering time last January. She also has "I don't know how many" quarts of frozen strawberries, homemade applesauce, home-grown cherries, corn, tomatoes and other fruits and vegetables. Likewise under the lid of one food chest are several fat loaves of foil-wrapped bread baked last week and an assortment of pies, rolls and other pastry ready to be thawed or baked whenever needed.

Mrs. G. figures her food bill last year, excluding home-grown victuals, came to about $500. The outlay for clothing was "not over $300." Medical expenses last year were another $500, mostly for 15-year-old John, who has recurring attacks of rheumatic fever; the family doesn't carry any health insurance. Life insurance premiums took $270 more. ("I only carry $10,000 of life insurance and would be vulnerable to an insurance salesman, but none ever comes around," notes Mr. G.)

Then there was $1,481 for the Federal income tax collector, $69 for household electricity, $75 for coal for the living-room stove (the house still has no central heating), and $75 for gas and oil for pleasure driving. Plus $2,120 for the new Nash and $385 for the TV set. That all totaled $5,775.

Most of the rest was plowed back into the farm—with a mere $176 left over as savings. The plowing back takes the form of retiring that part of his debt used to buy new machinery, for example, instead of to pay operating costs.

"Don't forget you have to make out checks in the morning for the landlord, phone bill, grocer, and payments on the car and television set."

"I think expanding my farm is fundamental," says Wilbur G. "High volume is the first need for a profitable farm. I don't think a small-scale farmer, however efficient, can make a comfortable living."

Such a program takes capital and Wilbur G., of course, borrows a hefty share of it. "I figure if I ever get to where I could use all my own money for capital I won't be operating as big as I should."

BURTON P. SAUER

September 2, 1955

Security-Seeker Mr. H.

JACKSONVILLE, Fla.—"I suppose if I were willing to take a chance I could be making $3,000 or $4,000 a year more, but I can't afford to gamble. We're on a tight budget, and the money has to keep rolling in."

These few words sum up the sit-tight philosophy of Grayson H., a security-conscious white-collar worker who's earning $5,005 a year. Like many Americans, Mr. H. is in debt; he's making regular payments on a home, a range, a washing machine, a refrigerator, a television set and a used car.

But there's nothing reckless about his spending. For example, Mr. H. recently had his eye on a new $2,400 Ford. After a one-third down payment, the monthly installments, spread over 39 months, came to $70. "My wife studied our budget all one evening and finally said we couldn't go over $50 a month," recalls Mr. H. So the H.s settled for a two-year-old Packard. The payments: $37.37 a month for two years.

Mr. H. is 25 years old, slightly above average height, slim and blond. He has two children. In the two years he's lived in Jacksonville his careful budget balancing has won him a high credit rating. Says he: "I've always worked my way and I've always paid everything I owed. I'm proud of that."

Mr. H. works for Prudential Insurance Co. of America. He's one of that financial giant's 47,040 employees.

The personnel department lists him as an assistant underwriter, Ordinary New Business Division, South Central Home Office, Jacksonville. Employed October 1, 1953. Salary: $96.25 weekly; $81.19 after income tax and other deductions. By Prudential's civil-service-type rating system he's at job level 10. (The levels go from one through 13 and then into management.)

"I like working for Pru; it's about as secure as you can get," says Mr. H. seriously. "I figure I'll stay as long as there's opportunity for advancement, but not if I get stymied."

At age 30 Mr. H. wants to be earning $8,000 a year. At 40, near $10,000, "preferably more, but I'm being realistic." By the time he is 50 years old, the young underwriter wants a salary of $12,000 a year and "I hope to be netting $3,000 to $4,000 a year from investments, maybe a store or some rental houses."

"You know," comments an amused Prudential executive, "the funny thing is he's got that figured just about right."

Once in his brief career the young insurance man had a fling at a job which offered him potentially greater earnings but little security. "I disliked it immensely," he says.

He was selling insurance for Acacia Life Insurance Co., with his earnings to a large extent dependent on his sales. "Sometimes you'd be sitting there wondering where the rent money was coming from," he recalls. "I didn't like it one bit."

A sizable portion of his present salary is committed in advance to a series of installment loan payments. The last 18 months, biggest buying period in the nation's history, have also been costly months for this office worker and his 24-year-old wife, Joan.

Largest bill is for the mortgage on their new house; that's $54 a month, including insurance. Monthly payments on appliances come to $34. The television set costs $11.50 a month.

The secondhand Packard is the third car Mr. H. has owned; all have been used. In August 1951, while he was working in Washington for Acacia Life, he bought a 1946 Dodge for $945. In July 1952 he traded in the Dodge for a 1949 Pontiac which cost $1,495.

After his flirtation with the new Ford, Mr. H. bought the 1953 Packard for $1,295, getting $500 trade-in for the Pontiac.

The local bank checked Mr. H.'s credit thoroughly. It found that, since the beginning of 1954, the young man had opened more than a half-dozen credit accounts in Jacksonville and had paid or was paying them all out as agreed. Last week the bank agreed to lend him $800 on the car. According to the bank's installment credit manager, "We consider it a good loan."

In addition to that loan, Mr. H. still owes about $750 on his appliances and some $7,800 on his house.

When the H.s first came to Jacksonville in 1953 they moved into an apartment costing $85 a month. Counting the appliances they bought to go with their new house, they're still paying about the same figure, but the new homeowner notes, "We're getting something for it."

"We spent quite a while looking for a house," he recalls. "We had to find something with either no down payment or a very small one." He's not eligible for a low-down-payment Veterans Administration loan.

The family looked first among Jacksonville's numerous housing developments but they didn't see anything they liked. "Then we saw an ad for a no-down-payment house at the beach," remembers Mr. H. "But when we got to it, there was a line of forty people waiting to get in."

Only slightly discouraged, the H.s kept looking. But they had decided on the beach, a series of communities strung out along the seashore east of Jacksonville.

The house-hunting H.s found a builder in Neptune Beach who promised to put up the place they wanted at a price they could afford. And on last May 19 they moved in, adding their minute portion to the biggest building boom in history.

"We got a nice, well-constructed house for $8,250. It's small but it has three bedrooms," says Mr. H. "Couldn't find anything like that in Washington."

Ironically, when the builder tried to place the F.H.A. mortgage on the property, it failed to meet standards of Prudential, the nation's largest private holder of home mortgages. The lot on which the house stands was too small, explains Mr. H., so the mortgage was taken by another company.

At the time they bought the house, the H.s had $700 in the bank, the most they've ever had. "The house took care of that," says Mr. H. with a grim little smile. They now have $100 in the bank.

Says a Prudential executive about this thin cash position: "It's not too unusual. Practically everyone who works for a large corporation these days has most of the things people used to save for taken care of—pension plans, health insurance and so on. About the only thing you really have to save for is the education of your children."

Another major monthly bill is life insurance. Security-seeking Mr. H., who describes himself as a "firm believer," carries $33,000 on his life. Part of this, $15,000, comes under a Prudential plan which costs him 14 cents a week per thousand. His total insurance bill is $31 a month, which Mr. H. counts partly as savings.

The young man is overinsured, says the Prudential man. He explains that insurance totaling five times annual salary—or $25,000 worth in the case of Mr. H.—is considered adequate by some top insurance industry spokesmen. The national average is about one year's salary.

Other budget items: Food costs about $20 a week. "We really have to watch it and sometimes it goes over," admits Mr. H. His lunches are provided by Prudential.

"We eat meat every night," says Mr. H. "About three times a month we'll have steak and then another three times a month it will be spaghetti and meatballs. Then we eat a lot of chicken, meat loaf and ham."

Operating a car costs him $15 a month in gasoline and oil. Mr. H. alternates with another Prudential employee on the 16-mile drive between his seashore home and the company's big new building here.

Electricity is "pretty high," $18 a month. Water is about $1 a month; garbage collection by a private contractor is $1.50 monthly; telephone $4.90 monthly; daily newspaper $2 monthly; fuel about $30 a year, coming all at once in the winter months.

Recreation costs practically nothing. "We go to a movie about once a month. The rest of the time we have the beach."

The H.s also spend very little on clothing, and doctors' bills don't run more than $2 or $3 a month, Mr. H. figures.

"I guess between the two of us we wouldn't spend over $200 a year on clothes," says Mr. H. "I bought a suit this summer for $28 and also a pair of pants for $6. My wife bought a dress last week for $8.

"I don't have anything like a hobby," declares Mr. H. "I sometimes piddle around the house trying to fix things up. In the evenings we watch TV or go for a little ride."

The family rarely eats out and Mrs. H. gets a permanent wave once a year and "maybe one or two lipsticks a year, that's all."

They are regular churchgoers and each Sunday the family puts $1 in the collection box. "I wish it could be more," says Mr. H.

On the income side, Mr. H. has been helped considerably this year by overtime wages. "We've been very busy, getting about two thousand applications to examine a week, and we've worked long hours. The first six months this year I got $600 in overtime."

This was a temporary situation and the pressure now is easing. Mr. H. is glad. "I liked the extra money," he says, "but it was blood money. I never used to see anything of the kids."

He's looking forward to his regular annual raise next month. On job level 10, this will amount to $4.90 a week. "It will be $3.88 after deductions. We've already figured it out," he says.

"We've had some rough times, but things are going more smoothly now," says Mr. H. "But there's going to be nothing else big bought for some time, I assure you."

Mr. H. can't even guess when he'll be able to buy his first new automobile. As fairly definite future purchases he wants only an electric mixer for his wife, a lawn mower and some garden tools and a rain gutter for the house.

CHARLES N. STABLER, JR.

September 7, 1955

Multimillionaire F.

CHICAGO—When Robert F., a sandy-haired, 66-year-old Midwest industrialist, slices a golf ball into the rough, his companions sometimes ask why he dallies among the weeds looking for it. "It may only be a seventy-five-cent ball to you," he replies lightheartedly, "but I had to earn $3.75 to buy it."

On his trips to the golf course, Mr. F. drives a new air-conditioned Fleetwood Cadillac he purchased this spring. The car was priced at $5,000, but he had to earn $25,000 to pay for it. Similarly, the $1,000 R.C.A. color television set in his living room represents $5,000 gross.

Mr. F. is not being victimized by price-packing dealers. His finances are so unusual because he is among those few toilers who earn over $1 million a year. He can take home only 20 cents of each $1 he earns; the other 80 per cent of his income goes to Uncle Sam.

Some pretty strong opinions about taxes are voiced by Mr. F., especially about the way the present tax structure hinders the accumulation or attraction of capital for development of small or new businesses. But he says he doesn't begrudge his own hefty payments—and there's no reason to doubt that he means it. With his stock holdings and other property worth $85 million at today's market prices, he says he has reached the point of nonchalance about additional money.

"I don't have any desire to be the richest man in the cemetery," says he. "The idea of increasing my money never occurs to me." But his money goes right on piling up just the same—"automatically," as he phrases it.

What is life like in this highest economic bracket? How does a multimillionaire earn his money? How does he spend it? What is his daily routine like, at home and at the office? What does he think about while most other folks are worrying about meeting their bills?

Mr. F.'s income is like that of the auto worker and the home builder, the salesman and the Congressman, in one respect at least. It is going up in this boom year 1955.

He and his easy-smiling, silver-haired wife, Mary, expect to file a

1955 joint return showing a gross of about $1,500,000, a tax of around $1,200,000 and a net of about $300,000. Through the last 10 years their average annual gross has been just a shade over $1 million.

The F.s' income primarily is derived from dividends collected in four installments a year. The biggest checks, around $300,000 each, come every March, June, September and December from the company which Mr. F. now serves as nonsalaried chairman, and which he helped build from a hole-in-the-wall concern into a world-wide operation with a list of products which are household names in every American home. A couple of dozen other smaller checks arrive in the mail through the year to make up the balance.

Bespectacled Mr. F. doesn't look like the average man's conception of a multimillionaire. He looks more like a quiet bookkeeper in the middle-income bracket who didn't start to go ahead until after the kids left home. That impression is emphasized by the fact that he inspires co-operation through friendliness rather than through the power of the dollars in his pocket.

Despite the high taxes, $300,000 in disposable income is no small sum, most people would admit. But even though he lives extremely well, Mr. F. spends considerably under what he earns. This was true even when he was earning only $10 a week when he started out in 1912 with his present company—as a bookkeeper.

He doesn't bother keeping a budget of personal expenditures and lets employees handle spending details. But he estimates that living expenses, clothes, cost of maintaining three homes, a fleet of cars and a staff of nine servants are costing him $1,000 to $1,150 a week of his approximately $6,000-a-week take-home pay.

"I don't believe in spending money just for the sake of spending money," says Mr. F. Then he adds: "If there were something I wanted badly, I'd get it; but there's nothing I know of that I want."

Catch him in his office and he may be wearing a $160 Brooks Bros. dark-blue suit, a $7 white shirt and a blue silk tie. He won't know how much the tie is worth, for his wife buys all of them along with his shorts and socks.

Says he: "My wife buys the ties and then hangs them in a closet. I grab any one I can reach when I need one. She says I usually get the wrong one to go with the suit I'm wearing."

He buys a new $150 or $160 suit once or twice a year, and then perhaps only when his wife tells him a shine is beginning to appear on an old one. "Sometimes she goes downtown, picks out a suit, then calls me to go try it on," says he.

The F.s own a town house, a massive pile of red brick on an avenue that once was Gold Coast row in the metropolitan city where

Mr. F.'s plant is located. They have owned it since World War I, and it would be hard to estimate its value today.

The F.s now prefer to live in another home, their spacious, gabled, Victorian-style 12-room cottage set in five acres in a fashionable section beside a lake not far from the plant. Five years ago the F.s built a third home, a rambling 15-room $300,000 place designed for outdoor living and located near Palm Beach, Florida. Their dream is to spend winters in Florida and summers on the Midwestern lake. In preparation for that step Mr. F. has been delegating company reins to younger men.

Mr. F. admits to two extravagances—his automobiles and his boat. The F.s have three Cadillacs in town—1952 and 1953 sedans and the new 1955 sedan. In Florida, they have a 1954 Lincoln sedan and a 1954 Plymouth station wagon.

Mr. F. prefers to drive the new Fleetwood. Mrs. F. can't drive, so a chauffeur is employed. Besides their chauffeur there are two maids, a cook and a gardener at the lake cottage, with a total payroll of about $12,000 annually plus keep. A caretaking couple for the Florida place costs $5,200 a year.

Like most boatowners, Mr. F. has found that his 50-foot custom-built fishing boat maintained in Florida costs money to have around. He estimates he has put $90,000 into it in the six years he has had it and he pays $7,000 a year to the two-man crew. Occasionally he goes deep-sea fishing off Florida with the boat.

"I fish because I don't know what else to do down there," says he. "I would rather work." The biggest fish he ever caught was a 103-pound white marlin.

Two years ago he bought a $175,000 twin-engined plane on which he traded an earlier model. The plane is less of an extravagance than the boat, though. He rents it to the company when company planes aren't able to handle executive traffic, and recoups some of his operating costs.

Moreover, most of his own flying is for business reasons. Traveling for pleasure isn't his idea of a good time, primarily because of his early years as a traveling salesman with the firm, following his bookkeeping stint.

"For twenty years I spent one third of my time in railroad sleepers," says he.

The plane is outfitted with lounge chairs, a sofa, a small bar, an electric heater for warming food, a refrigerator, a radio telephone, a desk and a library. The desk usually serves as a card table for gin rummy games, Mr. F.'s favorite indoor sport. His limit is one fourth of a cent a point, with a 25-cent side bet.

Once in a while you might see Mr. F. at a race track, especially during the Florida winter racing season. A $10 bet is his limit, and he never loses enough to even slightly dent his pile. A systematic man, he tried developing systems when playing the horses. Ruefully, he says: "None of them worked."

A typical day finds Mr. F. rising at 7:30 A.M., in a double bedroom he shares with his wife. He takes only a few minutes to dress, wash and shave with his Gillette safety razor. After a quick breakfast of oatmeal, bacon and toast, he heads for the garage.

At 8:20 he is behind the wheel of his new blue Cadillac heading toward the plant, as the air conditioner churns a cool breeze across the seats. It is a 25-minute drive to his office through fringe city traffic.

By 8:45 Mr. F. is seated behind the glass-topped desk of his walnut-paneled, 24-by-18-foot office overlooking the plant. A neat stack of papers waits on the desk for him. The paperweight is a one-inch section of coaxial cable, a memento from a utility company, one of several firms Mr. F. serves as a director.

He has devised a simple but effective system for handling the steady stream of visitors to his office. There is a pair of tiny flags on his desk—one green, the other red. Anyone peering through the window in the office door who sees the green flag up is free to enter. The red one means Mr. F. is already occupied and not to be disturbed. The green flag flies most of the time.

His first problem of the day involves a sales contract which is expiring shortly. He studies the situation, then calls a conference of several plant executives. The question of how to protect the company's marketing position is discussed from all angles.

Next comes a conference with production and engineering officials. Discussion centers on where a new plant should be located.

The conference is broken by lunch in the executives' lunchroom of the plant, where company brass rub elbows at long tables in a family-style atmosphere. Mr. F. has a cold ham sandwich and a dish of ice cream, skipping coffee.

"I like coffee but coffee doesn't like me," says he.

After lunch, there comes a long conference with company lawyers concerning litigation involving the concern. The afternoon is nearly over when the lawyers sweep up their papers and troop from the office. Mr. F. cleans up his desk, tucks some work into his briefcase, then heads for home at 5:30 P.M.

A half hour's drive brings him to the stately cottage on the lake. The maid has a gin-and-tonic handy. He relaxes with it on the porch, watching the yawls scooting across the lake in the late-afternoon sunshine.

A second drink puts him in the mood for dinner. Mr. F. handles his drinking like everything else he does, in moderation. Occasionally at a company party he may relax enough to join in a barbershop quartet. But he is too quiet and dignified to be the "life of the party."

Though Mr. F. could afford steak three times a day, he prefers hamburger. Dinner consists of broiled hamburger, without onions, mashed potatoes, corn on the cob and ice cream. Mr. F. eats with a healthy appetite, especially enjoying the corn on the cob. He likes corn so well that he plants four different crops of it in a plot of ground behind the house and has sweet corn from his garden from June to September. He lets the gardener do the work, though.

"I go out once a week and take a look at it," says he.

At 7:30 P.M. he relaxes with a pile of newspapers and magazines and some company reports which he feels must be studied before morning. By 9:30 he is ready for bed, but he admits he has a hard time falling asleep. Currently, his bedside book is *Wine of Youth*, by Robert Wilder.

Saturday Mr. F. puts in a half day at the office, then lugs paper work home with him to study while loafing on the porch. If any company reports aren't finished by Saturday night he may work through Sunday, too.

Two nights a week he and Mrs. F. head for a neighborhood movie or a party. Mr. F. enjoys the movie if it is a light comedy, but he goes somewhat reluctantly to the party.

"It's awfully hard to find reasons to say no to the family," says Mr. F. Mrs. F. is a friendly woman who enjoys meeting people and enjoys partying.

Occasional visits to their only son, now 41, and daughter-in-law across town round out their socializing. The four subteen grandchildren always are a magnet.

On other nights the F.s stay home and watch television. A joint favorite is the Ed Sullivan program. Mr. F. also likes the baseball game on a Saturday or Sunday afternoon and the Friday night fights.

The F.s have two color TV sets, a Columbia in the town house and an R.C.A. at the lake. He bought the Columbia a year ago and the R.C.A. in June, paying $1,000 cash for each.

There is a business reason behind those color sets, though. Mr. F.'s company has an interest in television, so he keeps track of programs and new developments in this field.

Mr. F. makes no pretense about being an art collector or a culture vulture of any kind. His idea of real music is Mary Martin and Ezio Pinza singing "Some Enchanted Evening," or perhaps a medley of *Showboat* tunes.

He has no hobbies, has no weight problem to stimulate any program of exercising, is seldom found in a night club and would rather work than do anything else.

The F.s aren't regular churchgoers. But Mr. F. thinks religion has a place in every man's life. "A man should do what he is convinced is right, and leave it at that," says he.

With taxes as they are, it is obvious that today you don't accumulate $85 million in a savings account. Mr. F. didn't. He began accumulating stock in his company when certificates weren't worth much more than wallpaper. It was after Mr. F. climbed to the presidency of the firm that the company really went to town.

Today each company share is worth $80 to $90 and stock dividends and splits totaling over 45 to one have increased Mr. F.'s holdings over 25 times. Now as he tots up his and his wife's stock—in his company and others—he finds it is worth $85 million at current market values. Their holdings return the $1,500,000 in dividends.

"I don't think that money ever was much of a motive with me," says he. "I work not to increase my wealth, but because I have a desire to build up the company and make better jobs for the people who are working here. When I make the company bigger, the value of my stock in the company automatically goes up. But that's only incidental."

Despite Mr. F.'s unconcern for the dollar, his wrath rises when he discusses the present tax structure.

"When a fellow is in my income bracket, he automatically goes into the oil business," says he. Mr. F. now invests all his surplus income in oil.

Tax laws permit the oil operator to charge losses for dry holes against current income. Even if there is a strike, intangible costs may be written off. In short, for the purpose of encouraging oil exploration, Uncle Sam carries some of the risks if the million-a-year man fails to strike oil, while the man has a better chance of hanging on to any money he might make than has the average investor.

"I feel I'm thoroughly justified in doing anything within legal means to reduce my income taxes, though I have no intention of trying to evade them," says Mr. F. "This is a legal way to escape confiscation of earnings."

Nine years ago Mr. F. sank $50,000 into his first oil well. He hit a producer which is still pumping oil for him. Then, in 1948, he formed three oil-prospecting companies of his own and hired a $15,000-a-year manager to take detail off his shoulders. Today he has over $3 million invested in various oil ventures and has 18 employees in his oil companies.

Mr. F.'s case illustrates that anybody who makes a lot of money may have to establish a company or two just to manage the income which keeps rolling in.

Mr. F. donates about $100,000 a year to various charities. To help him weed out the worthy cases, he established a foundation. However, establishing a foundation automatically made him a target for every professional charity collector in the country. Hardly a day goes by without somebody soliciting a contribution from him.

RAY VICKER

August 30, 1955

Psychologists' Lowdown on "Difficult" Buyers

LOS ANGELES—How do you sell the buyer with a difficult personality?

The "bully" who won't let you past the door, no matter what you do? The "expert" who knows your product better than you do and won't let you get a word in edgewise? The "timid soul" who keeps procrastinating for fear of exerting his own authority or revealing his ignorance.

A nine-year-old management advisory firm here founded and largely staffed by psychology professors from the University of Southern California claims to offer a set of keys to these problems. The organization, Psychology Services, Inc., gave some of this city's leading sales managers a peek at its new merchandising package at a dinner here this week.

The aim of the evening was to sell the assembled sales managers on enrolling their salesmen in a clinic slated to get under way early in the year. Its fees: $125 a head for 24 hours of sessions, or a flat fee of $1,250 for a group of 10 to 20 people.

The firm embarked on its new plan for a fairly mundane reason: It lost its defense contracts—mostly psychological projects for the Air Force—which had accounted for as much as 80 per cent of its $200,000 to $250,000 annual volume. Says Dr. Floyd L. Ruch (pronounced Roo), founder and president of the company, author of *Psychology and Life* and head of the U.S.C. Psychology Department's business and industrial program, "We decided to go more heavily into the business field—and what better area to do it in than by increasing human efficiency and thus raising the profit element in the sales dollar?"

Dr. Ruch and three colleagues, Professor Franklin W. Gilchrist of U.S.C., A. Bruce Rozet, education director for the National Management Association, and Stuart Atkins, former sales chief for the Winfield Arms Corp. and Max Factor & Co., made it clear their techniques weren't designed to cleanse the buyer of his difficult personality. "We're not even going to try to make him a happy man —we're only out to show you how to sell him," Dr. Gilchrist stated.

Boiled down, their technique consists first of all in determining which of half a dozen principal personality categories best describes the particular buyer. "This is done," explained Mr. Atkins, "first by maintaining silence but demonstrating an acceptance of what's being said; then getting the buyer to summarize his complete position. The technique also serves to show the buyer flaws in his own thinking and to provide the seller with gentle leads that will permit him to exert the strategy appropriate to the personality he's dealing with."

Here's how that works out in practice, Mr. Rozet resumed: First of all, you've decided whether he's primarily the "bully" type, who, if you can get in to see him at all, takes pleasure in playing with the salesman as a cat plays with a ball. Or he's the "silent sufferer" whose objections you can't answer simply because he doesn't voice them. Or he's the "fence sitter" who just can't make up his mind, the "know-it-all expert" or the unauthoritative "timid soul."

There's a highly effective way for dealing with each of these types, the psychologists maintained. As one of them put it: "You'll be surprised at how easy it is to topple these people over."

The "bully" type, they suggest, basically is a coward who, if you stand up to him in a pleasant but forceful manner, can be won over by concrete proof you're the person who can help him. The "timid soul," on the other hand, must above all be spoken to in private and presented with the proposition in its simplest form, where all he's required to do is sign it. The "expert" must be treated as such and offered the sales pitch principally as a fund of additional information to his already complete knowledge of the subject.

Sound easy? The U.S.C. psychologists and their colleagues maintain that it isn't. Identifying the type of difficult personality involved, they explain, requires skill because the individual is often a combination of types which frequently remain obscure even to himself. The strategy by which they're won over—and the psychologists wouldn't predict 100 per cent success against every problem buyer— requires some knowledge of the buyer's background and interests.

November 21, 1957

ALL AGES AND SIZES

Confident Teen-agers

NEW YORK—In 1939, the year Hitler's armies marched into Poland, the year the Yankees clubbed Cincinnati in four straight World Series games, were born Judy, Anita, Howard, Mike and Wesley.

A year later, when Nazi bombers fired London night after night and FDR was elected America's only third-term President, were born Shellie, Joyce and Gail.

These war babies are today's teen-agers, variously described as one of the nation's most aggravating social problems and as the most promising generation ever. The teen-agers' parents, now mostly in their mid-40s, were among the groups hard hit by the depression. As for the youngsters, their first memories are of World War II; they've grown up amidst the nation's greatest power and prosperity.

The teens reflect, sometimes unconsciously, the complex forces of their and their parents' decades. But the teens' talk, ideas and activities mainly mirror their own time, something often overlooked by both critics and apologists. Here, lifted wildly from conversational context, are the teen-agers talking:

Judy: "I been to lots of night clubs. On my last date we went to Le Cupidon. The dancing is out of this world. They've got a bongo drum player; I love the drums; you ought to hear him play a piece from *Mr. Wonderful.*"

Gail: "I hoard my money. I love the feel of dollars."

Howard: "I hope to be a dentist fifteen years from now, make maybe $20,000 a year. The security of being a dentist appeals to me. I want four or five kids, and I want money assured."

Wesley: "Sometimes we play poker on Friday nights. You don't spend any more than on a date, and you might make a little."

Joyce: "I hope to be married; I'm going to business school instead of college, and I'd like my husband to be making $200 to $250 a week, and I'd like to live about forty miles out of the city."

Mike: "I'd vote for Stevenson, because I'm a Democrat. I might prefer Lausche or Symington, but Symington isn't well enough

*"Why did they call it 'flaming youth' in your generation,
but in mine it's 'delinquency'?"*

known and Lausche is a Catholic. Al Smith showed a Catholic can't get elected President."

If any single impression comes from these teen-agers, some living in a residential section of New York City, some in a Connecticut commuter suburb, it is their feeling of confidence. They have confidence in themselves, and by and large they're certain the nation's economy will enable them to fulfill the lives to which they now aspire. They quite freely admit that at 16, 17 or 18, plans are in large part dreams. But almost without exception they argue that their opportunities for the future are far better than were their parents' chances when they were teen-agers.

In this and in other ways, these youngsters may or may not be typical of their generation. They come from widely varied economic and cultural backgrounds, but none is from the slums, and none will inherit a job or large fortune. They see their differences in their own terms. Says Gail, blue-eyed daughter of a commercial artist living in the suburbs: "Joyce and I are typical of our high school, but I guess we're not too typical of teen-agers in the city. They're more mature than we are; they go out on school nights and things like that."

In some cases, these teen-agers' parents had to postpone marriage and families or forget about hoped-for careers because of the depression of the 1930s. The teens don't think this will happen to them.

Their explanation: The Government now has a firm grip on the economy (which, the teen-agers indicate, is as it should be) and "won't let" another crash come about.

"I don't think we could have a depression for a long time anyway," says Shellie, an attractive black-haired, dark-eyed daughter of a New York City clothing store operator. "The Government has stepped in so much, and the public is different now. At least I don't worry about it." (Shellie isn't too much given to worrying about anything. "The hell with doing homework tonight," she said one recent evening. "I've got the brains, so why work so hard all the time?")

Shellie's school friend Al, a half-bashful but quietly determined son of a working couple, chimes in to modify Shellie's views. "The Government hasn't taken things over, it's regulated things," he holds. "But I can't see where we'll have another depression. Wages may go down, but then steak may be fifty cents a pound instead of a dollar like now, so you'd be about as well off."

An exception is Gail, who blurts out, "I'm scared to death of it," when informal talk is twisted suddenly to the possibility of an economic crash. Gail is interested in the doldrums of the 1930s as a historic event; she questions her parents about their life then, explaining that her interest was spurred by a high-school history class. (Gail perhaps reflects the high-school rebel. A pretty girl with well-scrubbed freshness, she refuses to "go steady," complains that her dates "don't have much imagination, they just won't be nonconformists," and, unlike other members of her set, argues "there must be more juvenile delinquency than before.")

The teen-agers already make up a potent market force. They have money of their own, and they strongly influence many of their parents' purchases. Teen-age dollars are major underpinnings of such businesses as phonograph records and motion pictures; most department stores and many specialty shops have departments catering especially to teen-age tastes and budgets.

Economically and socially, the teen-agers will be more important in the next few years—because their numbers will be increasing so rapidly. In 1950 there were in the U.S. about 10.6 million youngsters from 15 to 19 years of age. By mid-1955 this number had grown to about 11.2 million. But statisticians figure by 1960 the 15-to-19-year-olds will total more nearly 13.4 million, and more than 19.1 million in 1970.

Nor are the teen-agers strangers to work. Afterschool and summer jobs are easy to find and money from such work doesn't have to go for family support, as often was the case a couple of decades ago.

Wesley never has had an allowance from his parents, but he earns

$1.25 an hour waiting on customers in a suburban bakery-delicatessen. At 17, he's owned two cars—a 1939 Ford which "kind of wore out" and a 1948 Mercury. "I smashed that up last Thanksgiving Day, ran into another car," he reports. Wes, a slim, curly-haired son of an electronics industry executive, also buys some of his own clothing.

Mike gets 50 cents a day for lunch at school, $2.50 a week for working around the house and whatever else he can earn in part-time jobs. He bought a 1937 Plymouth for $35 when he got his driver's license a year ago. The jalopy lasted about a year.

Joyce, who hopes to get a full-time job this summer, has an allowance of $3 a week, plus 40 cents a day for lunch.

Some oldsters might decry the teen-agers' faith in the Government's ability to stall off any serious economic downturn. But the same oldsters likely would applaud some of the teens' cautious attitude toward credit. Sitting in a suburban living room, chatting about past, present and future personal spending, Joyce, Gail, Mike and Wesley agreed that they hope they'll never become heavy users of installment credit.

They further agreed that it would be better to go without a television set for a year than to buy it on installments. "I'd prefer to buy for cash," says Mike. "That way things are your own, and it costs less." Credit, adds Wesley, "is all right for necessities, like a car if a man needs it in his job."

Both Joyce and Gail select their own clothing, but Mother is standing in the background if it's a major purchase such as a coat or expensive dress. Neither shows much interest as yet in clothing, and neither could estimate how much she had spent on clothing in the past year.

"I like casual clothes," explains Joyce, a quiet but precise high-school junior who also reveals, with obvious satisfaction, that she's "been going steady for four weeks and one day" and that her bank account totals $309.47 "from a piggy bank I opened and some presents of money."

The teen-agers, of course, are in transition. This shows up in some startling ways, as with Judy, a quick-tongued, auburn-haired daughter of a butcher. Perched on the edge of a chair, arguing with some classmates, she talks with conviction about what makes a good high-school teacher—"The best teacher is one who makes you think, no matter how he teaches"—and philosophizes that, "If I had only one night to live, I'd spend it with those I love, including the boy I'm now interested in; I'd enjoy my friends." Less than an hour later, strolling along a dark street, she's whistled at by some boys in a passing car. "So I like your car," she shrills. "Just park it there and move on."

Or Anita, a dark-haired, solemn-eyed girl wearing a fire-engine-red blouse and tight black toreador pants. She talks about dating, revealing both childish pettiness and budding awareness of a different world.

"I don't care what a fellow spends," she relates, "if I don't like him I don't act nice and I just don't care. I didn't like the last date I had, so I'll tell you about the one before that. I went to a party given by some kids at college. It might sound strange but I just sat around for about three hours listening to them talk, about art, mostly, and listening to Tchaikovsky records. I really liked it."

It is interesting to speculate on the political awareness and interests of today's teen-ager—and what this may mean in elections of the 1960s and 1970s. Mike, Joyce, Judy and Howard and their friends very likely are more interested in politics than the high-school generation of the early 1940s, whose thinking was dominated largely by World War II and with wondering what military service of undetermined length would do to plans for job, college or family. (Military service is something these teen-agers accept, without any enthusiasm, but without much grumbling.)

But today's teens seemingly are less oriented to things political than the teens of the 1930s, who often sought in drastically different politics an answer to the economic problems that threatened their futures.

Mike, a husky high-school football player who wants to enter the diplomatic corps or teach political science, is more articulate politically than many a student who'll receive a college diploma this spring. But he's not isolated in being able to relate world affairs to teen-age life. A gabfest in Nancy's living room the other night switched abruptly from opportunities in the future to possibilities of war—just as it might have if her parents and their friends had been doing the talking while nibbling pretzels and fresh pineapple off trays on the coffee table. (And in fairness to the teen-agers, it must be said their observations, and lack of solutions, likely could be duplicated in more worldly-wise groups.)

"I hate to be an alarmist, but I think the thing we should worry about most is war," stated Marian, a soft-spoken, dark-haired girl wearing horn-rimmed glasses.

"Chances of war are going down," countered Howard. "The Russians aren't using such drastic measures. We believe what we believe is right, and they believe the same about their system. Someday there'll be two worlds."

"They have the A-bomb, too," offered Judy. "If anybody uses it, the whole world will be demolished. There might be civil wars, but there'll be no world war, or there'll be no race."

"Basically, they're different," chimed in Marian. "They're trying to convert the world, and a silly incident could start a war."

"Well," said nonworrier Shellie, "you don't sit around and wait for war to happen. Anyway, I don't."

Nor do the teen-agers sit around much of the time arguing the ways of an adult world. Friends, dates, hamburgers, Coke dates and "going steady" occupy a good share of a teen-ager's thoughts.

JAMES N. WALLACE

May 17, 1956

In Their Twenties

LOS ANGELES—The long, lean, serious-looking young man looks at you over his glass of beer and says: "I suppose you think I'm crazy. But I gave up that $100-a-week public-relations job in Sacramento just because I prefer to live here in Los Angeles."

Bill smiles wryly and adds: "I've got exactly $271 in the bank, and that's abnormally high for me." But he isn't worried: "I've never had any trouble getting a job, and I'm not in a dither about it this time."

A peek at Bill's job applications reveals two clues to this seeming complacency: age—26; marital status—single.

But the twenties, of course, is a marrying age. And the responsibilities of a family may crimp carefree attitudes like Bachelor Bill's.

Take two other 26-year-olds, Ruth and Roger R., married eight months now. Crew-cut, boyish-looking Roger draws $400 a month as a trainee for a consulting-engineering firm. "We're trying to save $80 a month. There are a few things we'd like to buy—a TV set, maybe—but with a baby on the way, we can't afford too much," says Roger seriously.

Another young couple here, Jim and Betty K., spend a bit more freely than the R.s. Jim is a soft-spoken, solidly built aircraft worker, born 27 years ago in Greenville, S.C. With total savings of only $400, he finds himself spending just about all his take-home pay—which, with overtime, averages about $100 a week. The K.s, who have two children, are buying a home and also making monthly payments on furniture and a car.

Despite some obvious differences in spending and saving habits of bachelors like Bill, newlyweds like the R.s and "old married folks" like the K.s, people in their twenties seem to share economic characteristics which set them apart from the older generations. No one knows how typical or untypical these folks may be. But a close look at Bill, the K.s and the R.s reveals certain likenesses.

They all agree that jobs aren't hard to get, and none can remember a time when it was really difficult to find work.

Bill was graduated from the University of Oregon in 1951 with a degree in journalism. "Before school was out I had two offers to work on newspapers. I took a job on a small-town daily in Washington for a few months until the draft caught up with me." When he got out of the Army in 1954, he landed his public-relations job "without any trouble."

When Jim K. was graduated from Greenville High School in 1947—finishing up after a year in the Navy—he was able to get work as a theater usher for a few months "until a job as a phone installer at the Bell Co. came through." In 1949 Jim left Greenville and the phone company for a job selling DeSotos and Plymouths in Jacksonville. Three years later Jim and Betty and their two youngsters climbed in the family car and headed for Los Angeles, after selling some furniture and a residential lot to finance their westward migration.

Jim reminisces about the ease of getting a job in Los Angeles: "We got here on a Friday about 3 P.M. At 8 A.M. Saturday, I hired in at Douglas Aircraft at $1.42 an hour, as a learner."

From 70 cents an hour as an usher, Jim has had steady increases in pay. Now he draws $2.50 an hour at Douglas, where he's an electrical inspector giving "Skyray" fighters a final checkout before the planes are turned over to the Navy.

Roger R., a U.C.L.A. civil-engineering graduate, has had similar good fortune in getting work. He went directly into the Air Force upon graduation, but was able to line up his present job while still in the service. He also paid for about 70 per cent of his college education by waiting on tables during the school term and getting summer construction jobs, which came his way "fairly easily."

The ease with which this "twenties" trio has found work probably reinforces their youthful feeling of confidence in the country and its economy. "The economy is good right now," says Roger, "and I don't think there's much downward trend in prospect over the next several years. The world situation will keep government expenditures high."

Jim agrees that times are good—and that Government holds the key to good times: "There's not much unemployment. People are making good money, and spending it. I'd say about 80 per cent of the workers at Douglas are like me—living from week to week off their salary." His only doubt about the economy: "We might have a depression if real peace came all over the world and we had a big cut in defense spending. Take my own job—it's strictly for defense."

Ask Bill about the country's economy, and he shrugs his shoulders and says: "I don't know what causes recessions, and I don't think Sumner Slichter does either. If the auto industry got into serious trouble, it might affect other industries, too. But I can't get too worried about it. Long-term prospects look good to me."

After tossing off this opinion, Bill absent-mindedly twirls his beer glass, tracing water circles on the bar table, and indulges in a bit of introspection: "Of course, I can't remember a thing about the depression. If I'd gone through that experience I might not be so confident."

Confidence—or complacency—about the country's future doesn't mean, of course, that young people don't have doubts and worries about their own future.

"The thing that bothers me most," admits Bill, "is not being quite sure of what I want to do. I'm capable of worrying about this once a day. I don't think I'm living up to my capabilities in PR work. Yet I'd never go to selling insurance or being a junior executive."

Engineer R. has definite ideas on what he wants to do, but he isn't sure where he wants to do it: "Within five years I hope maybe to go into business for myself, as an engineer and contractor. I don't know just where—maybe here in L.A. or in San Francisco—or somewhere in between."

The K.s are more firmly settled. "We figure on living in this house for at least ten years," says Jim. But he too has a hankering to go into business for himself: "I'd like to get a TV or appliance store with a service and repair shop so I can use my knowledge of electronics." But Jim isn't sure about going into business. "I'd need about $6,000 or $7,000 in hard cash," he estimates. "In a couple of years when we get everything paid for, except the house, maybe I can start saving $100 a month," he adds hopefully.

Bachelor Bill and the R.s are poor customers for many types of goods and services, because they haven't settled down yet.

Ask Bill what magazines he subscribes to, for instance, and he replies: "None, I don't dare to. I move so often I'd spend all my time writing change-of-address cards to circulation departments."

Neither Bill nor the R.s are in the market for a house.

"It's just as cheap to rent a place like this," Roger R. says, showing you the three-room apartment he and Ruth rent unfurnished in Hollywood for $70 a month. "We definitely won't buy a home for five years, or even ten years, unless a real good deal comes along on a house we could get cheap and fix up ourselves."

Apartment living restrains their buying appetite for home furnishings too. "We might buy a bed stand, dresser and end table this year, and that's about all," says Ruth.

Since their marriage last September, they have bought a few things for their apartment. But it's been no spending spree. They picked up a secondhand gas stove for $40, for instance, and also bought a used refrigerator for $85.

When the refrigerator went bad a week later, Roger returned it to the store and got his money back. "We were afraid to buy another secondhand one, so we bought this new Hotpoint for $200," he says, patting it fondly. Ruth, who kids her husband about his expanding waistline, says: "He thinks that's the best purchase we ever made."

Their only other major purchase for their apartment has been a queen-sized bed which they had specially made for $120. Roger says: "The fire insurance man came out here and estimated our belongings at $3,000. That's about it—and a good hunk of that is wedding loot."

Bill has even fewer possessions to impede his mobility: "You see that beat-up 1948 DeSoto out there? It holds everything I own."

Bill's wardrobe is really scant. He has two suits, "one good and one bad," one sports jacket, a couple pairs of odd slacks. "I hate to spend money on clothes," he explains. "I was ready to throw my present pair of shoes away a year ago, but I haven't bought myself a new pair yet." He does own a second pair of shoes—tennis shoes which he wears "just for sailing."

Bars do a little better at getting Bill's money than furniture and clothing stores. "I suppose I drop $30 a month in bars," says Bill, finishing off his beer and ordering another. "I'm a moderate drinker too, but the crowd I run with does a fair amount of barhopping."

While Ruth and Roger spend considerably less on liquor—about $10 a month—they are better customers for clothiers. Roger has three suits and two sports jackets and admits to "a weakness for Hathaway shirts." Ruth has no fur coat, but she does have a $75 formal, four "good suits" and five cashmere sweaters. "When I need clothes," admits Ruth, "I'm susceptible to high-priced goods."

The K.s' spending habits, unlike those of Bill or the R.s, reflect the needs and desires of people in their twenties who are already buying a home and raising a family.

Payments on their house, furniture and appliances make a big dent in the K.s' income. They pay $81 a month on their V.A.-insured, three-bedroom home in a big tract of 400 homes about five miles from Jim's plant. They moved into the $13,000 home last July after making a down payment of closing costs only.

Step inside the pleasant, one-story yellow stucco structure and you find an interior furnished tastefully in contemporary-style furniture. Tweed wall-to-wall carpeting which cost "slightly over $500" gives the living room and hallway an impression of warmth.

"We've bought just about everything you see here on time," says Jim frankly. The K.s are still paying for some things: $8 a month (for five more months) on a $350 Philco refrigerator, $12 a month (for 28 more months) on the carpeting, and $13 a month (for 22 more months) on their new TV set, a 24-inch Olympic console, which cost $409 with the K.s' 21-inch set as a trade-in.

Add to these monthly payments the $57.26 which Jim is still paying on the 1954 Plymouth he bought new, and you drain off $171.26 of Jim's monthly check. But Jim's a firm believer in buying on time "as long as you stay away from the loan sharks."

While the K.s' appetite for home furnishings is hefty, it is not indiscriminate. "We shopped over five months for the TV set," says Betty, "and almost as long for the carpet." She adds: "We believe in buying name-brand products." Jim admits he gets stung occasionally: "We got fooled on that desk you see over there. It was several months before we found out the back was real cheap plywood."

In contrast with the K.s, the R.s have never bought anything on time, "and I hope we never have to—except for a house," says Ruth. But the R.s' shunning of installment buying may be influenced by a considerable bank account which reduces their need for credit. Besides two checking accounts, each with about $1,000 in it, they have $20,000 in a savings account which draws 2 per cent interest. Mrs. R. inherited most of the money.

The K.s are modest spenders on themselves compared with the money they put into their home. Major items in Jim's wardrobe are limited to two suits, three sports jackets, four pairs of slacks and his work clothes. Betty has "lots of skirts and blouses and a couple of good suits." Her most expensive suit cost $50.

Entertainment expenses are at a "minimum"—mostly movies, dinner out about once a month, and people in for dinner "occasionally." Jim plays 10-cent-limit poker with five other Douglas workers once a month. Liquor expenses are low too. Betty doesn't drink; Jim drinks moderately and only at home. "Betty says I can import a bathtub full of it, as long as I drink it right here at home."

Autos seem to hold a strong fascination for the twenties.

Bill, the bachelor, with only one pair of shoes, has a hankering for another car to replace the 1948 DeSoto. "I've had it two and a half years and spent nothing on upkeep. I'm leaning toward a used MG, which is idiotic, I suppose. But I might as well indulge myself while I'm still single."

The R.s—conservative in most things financial—are a two-car family. Ruth drives a Volkswagen given her by her parents, while Roger has a 1953 Ford he bought just before he got married last year.

The K.s have "a car and a half," according to Jim. In addition to their two-tone blue 1954 Plymouth, they have a gray Chevrolet, vintage 1934. "I paid $60 for it, and it gets me to work and back," says Jim. But Jim's in the market for a new car. "We may get a new Dodge, a four-door sedan with radio, heater and automatic transmission."

Ask Jim K. about his hobbies, and he replies: "Being a union representative at the plant, I guess. That's where all my spare time goes." As an "area chairman"—a kind of chief steward—he's a spokesman for about 800 machinists.

"I spend about fifteen hours a week on my union work, mostly at the union hall after work attending committee meetings and so on." He's quick to tell you he has a diploma from the International Association of Machinists for night-school courses in industrial labor relations and chairman training.

Politically Jim is a Democrat, because he "believes the Democratic party is for the workingman and the Republican party for the employer." But he voted for Eisenhower in 1952 as "the better man." Betty is also a registered Democrat and says: "I guess I'll vote the same way Jim does."

Ruth, Roger and Bill are all nominal Republicans and all say they favor Mr. Eisenhower over any Democratic Presidential nominee. The G.O.P. can hardly afford to be smug about their Republican leanings, however. At the moment none is registered, and if their past voting history is any indication, it's unlikely they'll vote in November.

Failure to vote is common among young people who move frequently and don't have their roots firmly planted in the communities in which they live. But it may also reflect a contentment with things as they are.

Bill, for instance, says: "Unlike every barber I encounter, I have no desire to reform the world." Ruth came back from a trip to Europe two years ago "more sold on this country than ever. Europe lives in the past; America has a future." And Roger has a tolerant attitude about social problems: "Live and let live is my attitude toward gambling and liquor—even though some people go overboard on both."

Jim K. expresses similar ideas, noting that "since the beginning of time some people have been living a high life." He thinks "the churches are doing a good job" in keeping social problems in hand.

ED CONY

May 22, 1956

The Thirtyish C.s and Their Friends

The three couples in their mid-thirties stopped gabbing and picked up the poker hands. Mr. A., a $15,000-a-year engineer, winked across the table at his pert wife and advised: "Bet 'em like you owned 'em, kid. It's only money."

In the A.s' new $35,000 home in a fast-stepping New York suburb, the monthly poker game between the A.s, B.s and C.s thus got under way. It's a mild game of the penny-ante, three-cent-limit type and conversation centers more on diaper rash, the Cub Scouts and someone's new Buick than on poker. But financial conservatism ends with game playing for the A.s, B.s and C.s. All have taken high dives into fiscal folderol that might be considered dizzy by an earlier generation.

For by and large the three couples live by the rule of thumb outlined by Mr. A.: (1) "It's only money" (and there's plenty more in the future to match the ever growing bonanzas of the postwar years) and (2) today's income dollars can be pyramided through credit ("just like you owned them") to spend tomorrow's income now.

Living in a high style has its problems, to be sure. Near the end of last month, for example, Mrs. A. was unable to drive her new green-and-white DeSoto station wagon. "Mr. A. gets paid the first of the month, and the last few days we always run a little short—I had only a dollar, for emergencies, and no gas," Mrs. A. says with a little laugh.

Mrs. B., whose wardrobe includes original creations by Manhattan fashion designers, sometimes finds herself financially embarrassed, too. But she is handy with a home permanent set and has wriggled out of many a budgetary crisis by dispensing with the services of the woman who does the ironing. Mr. B. has his own methods of economy. For instance, he keeps two brands of Scotch on hand; one is served to guests of some importance, the other to neighbors and other close acquaintances.

Mr. C., a lavish spender and an apostle of full use of "credit resources," can lament: "The plumber we had in here last week demanded cash—and after all the business we've done with him."

No one knows how typical or how unusual the A.s, B.s and C.s may be. They have larger incomes than most people of their generation and their rise has been swift—from $3,000 a year to $17,000 annually for C. in a decade; B. at $13,000 and A. at $15,000 have had almost as dramatic rises.

The three families have other things in common besides fast-rising incomes and similar notions of how to spend it. Their money attitudes, in fact, may grow from the biggest similarity of all. Born in the half-dozen years following World War I, they were too young to experience the general economic debacle of the 1930s, except as children. For many folks of their generation, marriage and the beginning of careers were first delayed by World War II, then jet-propelled by the boom which followed.

The three families are rather typical of their economic generation in this respect. The trio of marriages took place in the waning days of World War II and in the year following V-J Day. A list of some of their possessions indicates something of the explosive impact of this generation on the postwar economy. Among current assets: nine children, three dogs, six automobiles, three dishwashers, four television sets, five club memberships—all this and much, much more on combined incomes for the three families of $45,000.

Liabilities are also impressive. The three families are paying off a total of 15 loans. Combined debts tower around $90,000. A ratio of debt twice income is considerably in excess of the national ratio, which currently finds that total consumer and mortgage debt for 1955 was about 0.4 times income.

Such comparisons have caused some economists to wonder if the early-postwar generation of family formations hasn't put more than its share of the steam in the national boom in private debt.

In some ways, the three families are hardly typical of their generation or any other. For one, all six of the poker pals have had at least some college training and two of the husbands have been to graduate school. For another, A., B. and C. have all succeeded better in their chosen lines than even most college graduates of their age.

It's interesting to speculate on what impact their attitudes—and those of other folks like them—will have on the nature of American business. As "middle-management" men in companies which believe in decentralization, all already are in positions where they can influence people at the policy-making level. And it is quite conceivable that A., B. and C. someday will be business policy makers themselves.

Plainly, A., B. and C. are harder-driving than most; their recent medical histories include two ulcers. The Mesdames A., B. and C. are equally ambitious, are prominent in church, club and school affairs. All three couples, born far from Manhattan in smallish towns of the West, South and Midwest, feel they have made their way in the Big City and are proud of it.

This, plus a feeling that they somehow haven't fully arrived in a town where older residents have lamented the cutting of large estates into quarter-acre plots, has bred a certain defiance in the families. Mr. B., a lanky junior executive for a well-known concern, probably speaks for his friends when he intones in his Midwestern nasal: "So what if a lot of the old-timers in this fawncy suburb do look down on us—call us the Nickel Millionaires? Well, I am a Nickel Millionaire and I know it. I'm not proud of it, but I'm not ashamed of it, either. It's just my way of life—and I've got a lot of company."

What of the future, if income including B.'s should plummet? Churchgoing B. quotes the Bible (slightly incorrectly): "Sufficient for today is the evil thereof," then switches to a little personal economic theory.

"No American Government," says B., "can afford to sit by and let another real depression come about." B., like his poker cronies, grew up during the New Deal days. Although he avers he has never voted for a Democrat, and can loudly lament New Deal and Fair Deal "interference with private enterprise," it's plain he counts on government measures to forestall any sharp downswing in general prosperity.

His friends echo the view that somehow reversals just can't take place. Engineer A., with a decade of seniority at a giant company, states: "Any financial catastrophe big enough to overwhelm me is going to shake this whole country so bad my debts will be the least of my worries—and that just won't happen."

A., a sales executive, has plainly done some soul searching about his way of life. Talk to him about depression possibilities and you'll find his talk studded with references to "when this house of cards comes tumbling down" and "this phony existence." But still he shows no signs of wishing any other. "I've got to live this way; I'm caught up in it and can't seem to let go," he says.

"I always tell myself when I find myself getting another bank loan: 'If that banker is a big enough fool to lend it, I'm a big enough fool to borrow it.' And in the end if it gets to the point where they want to take my house away from me, well, what is the bank gonna do with it?"

Mrs. C., a chic young matron with a detailed knowledge of the best-selling books and latest Broadway productions, chimes in: "You don't order your life against catastrophe."

For sure, the C.s haven't done that. After Federal and state income taxes, Social Security taxes and company-sponsored insurance, C.'s $1,400 monthly pay check has shrunk to $1,100. The rather complex C. budget—"We keep one, but don't pay much attention to it"—finds fairly fixed expenses account for all but about $35 of the $1,400 gross.

Against total assets of $15,000 ($12,500 of them the equity in his mortgaged house) C. counts debts close to $30,000.

It was not always thus with $17,000-a-year C. When he exchanged his Navy Hellcat fighter plane for a sales trainee's briefcase early in 1946, his first month's pay was $250 ($3,000 a year). And, C. recalls, "I was determined to stay out of debt. For one thing, I had been raised to believe that debt was almost a mortal sin."

For three years, C. played it cautiously, lived in an apartment "waiting for prices to come down" and steadfastly refused to sign an installment contract. About $3,000 accumulated from his World War II pay helped him marry, buy furniture and keep Mrs. C. and their first-born, a girl, in food and clothing. Steady pay hikes helped, too. By 1949 he was earning about $6,000 and added an auto to his possessions, a secondhand Chevrolet bought for cash. By 1950 he was making $8,000, had added a second child (a boy), more furniture and a spanking new Pontiac, still for cash.

In 1951 C. passed his original pay goal of $10,000 (before taxes) and bought a house. This home, a Cape Cod affair in a neighboring suburb, cost $18,500—and C. plunged into debt for the first time, with a $14,000 mortgage.

Shortly thereafter, Mr. C.'s boss suffered a heart attack and C. found himself a sales manager, at $12,000.

"At that point, we decided to do a little living," says C. In the next three years they bought a second car, new furniture, and another new car to replace the Pontiac. Installment financing helped lavishly.

When the third little C. was born the family started house hunting again. And last year the family made its move to the present four-bedroom, three-bath-plus-recreation-room-and-den, $37,000 ranch house. "We needed the room," Mrs. C. declares, adding: "And we were glad to get out of that development where all the houses looked the same."

Incomes generally run higher in the suburb the C.s now live in than in the one they moved from. "We enjoyed it in the other place when we lived there," Mrs. C. recalls. "But somehow we seem to have lost track of all our old friends over there. This is a much prettier town and, well, the people just seem more our kind."

Debt repayment takes the biggest single bite out of the C.s' $1,100 take-home pay—$437 a month. First, there's $230 to a savings-and-loan association—interest and amortization of the $25,000 mortgage on the $37,000 home, plus one twelfth of the annual real-estate taxes. Next, C. makes a $77 monthly payment on a $2,500, three-year personal loan which he arranged with a giant New York City bank to help cover his down payment on the home.

Three other loans take another $130 monthly. There's a $50 monthly payment on a 1955 Mercury station wagon. Mr. and Mrs. C. like to dance, so they signed up for 50 hours of instruction at Arthur Murray's studio to bring themselves up to date on the rumba, cha-cha-cha and merengue, at $500. This is being paid off in monthly installments of $50. Add in $30 a month payments on the wall-to-wall carpeting and the monthly debts are paid.

C.'s debts aren't out of line by most banker standards—one third of take-home pay usually is considered "high" but not exorbitant. And $130 of payments will be retired before 1956 is over if all goes according to C.'s plan.

"The first of the year I intend to start salting away that $130 in a savings bank or blue-chip stocks," says C., adding with a grimace, "if Mrs. C. doesn't press too hard for that new bedroom suite she's been hinting about." His present savings include about $1,000 in savings bonds, about $200 in a checking account and $2,500 cash value of insurance. C. borrowed the maximum lendable value—$1,500—on his G.I. insurance policy to help raise the money for the down payment on his home. He writes a $60 check to the Treasurer of the United States once a year to cover the 4 per cent interest; amortization of the loan is at C.'s option but thus far he hasn't exercised that option.

C.'s other "fixed" expenses, some of them variable in a pinch, include: Food, minor clothing and household, $260 (turned over to Mrs. C. every payday); $86 allowance for Mr. C.; $75 utility bills, including heat; $66.25 for life insurance; $17 medical bills for one of the C. children; $18 auto insurance; $15 country club dues and $10 to the C.s' church.

In addition, Mr. C. figures he averages another $72 a month for such relatively fixed expenses as milk and drugstore bills, miscellaneous doctor bills, major clothing purchases and entertainment.

How does he expect to replace his automobile, two TV sets, washer, dishwasher, dryer, furniture and other assorted bric-a-brac as they wear out? Or educate his children or meet some emergency?

"My income has gone up steadily for the past ten years, and I don't see why it shouldn't continue to rise," says C. "I'm not selling C. short."

April 26, 1956

The Slippered Years

JACKSONVILLE—In February 1954, after many years of hard work, Joseph and Bessie S. sold their candy store in a New York suburb for $6,500, retired and headed for an easier life here in warmer climes. But now, besides just resting in the Florida sunshine, Mr. S. finds, "You have to keep busy, keep interested. You're through if you don't."

Mr. S.'s discovery may be a nasty blow to less fortunate individuals still working for a living and looking forward to a good long loaf at retirement. But it's confirmed by other oldsters. Warns one: "You sit down to relax; then you lie down to rest a spell and, first thing you know, they're carrying you out feet first."

Inactivity after years of hurly-burly is only one of the problems faced by Mr. S. and his fellow members of the nation's fast-increasing older population. Among others: stretching a fixed pension to fit rising prices.

The S.s, friendly, cheerful people who live quietly in a comfortable little house here, are among the more than 14.1 million Americans who are over the age of 65. This group, now 8.6 per cent of the population, is becoming increasingly important to the rest of the country.

The Census Bureau statisticians figure that in 1955 one of every 12 Americans was over 65 years old. In 1940 the ratio was one in 15 and back around the turn of the century it was one in 25.

The trend, caused chiefly by the fact that we're living longer than we used to, is of considerable significance to young folks as well as old. For one example, it means the burden of caring for the senior citizens is bound to increase.

The life the S.s lead is placid and tranquil, probably much like that led by many other older couples. The dramatic turning points of their lives are past. Now a letter from their daughter in White Plains, New York, or their son in Madison, Wisconsin, is the high spot of the day.

Except for Friday, which is set aside for the dinner visits of a daughter who lives here with her family, evenings are spent reading or watching television. The arrival of a new grandchild—they expect their ninth shortly—is a major event.

In some ways the S.s are typical of their generation. In others, they plainly aren't. Many oldsters can't afford Florida retirement, and not all live so quietly.

Take Frank R., a big ruddy-faced man who says he's in his sixties and is about as active as men 30 years his junior. Mr. R., who lives alone at Jacksonville Beach, used to be on the professional stage. Besides vaudeville, he sang tenor roles in several Broadway plays, including *Blossom Time,* one of the top musicals of the 1920s.

Now he's a busy member of the Jacksonville Little Theatre Club and just finished a leading role in *The Remarkable Mr. Penny-packer.* The remarkable Mr. R. also manages a friend's apartment house in return for his room, makes costumes and other clothes, loves parties and has taken up oil painting to fill his spare moments.

"If I didn't stay active, I'd die of ennui," explains Mr. R. with a grin. "I've always liked that story about Tallulah Bankhead. You know . . . she asked someone how he did so many different things and the fellow replied, 'Superbly.' "

John W., a small, thin 79-year-old with a shock of gray hair, stays busy by trying to keep up with current events and maybe influence them a little. He rarely misses a meeting of the Jacksonville City Council. And he's an untiring letter writer. His targets: newspaper editors and members of Congress.

Recently he dashed off more than 90 letters, one to each Senator. The subject in this case, and in most others, was pensions. Mr. W. still firmly supports the depression-born Townsend Plan, which would provide government handouts for old people.

"Even if you could get along on your pension ten or fifteen years ago, you couldn't now because prices have gone up," says Mr. W. The former Philadelphian figures he covers all his needs on about $60 a month. "Except," he adds with a wink, "I like to be sociable and you can hardly meet a friend and be sociable without it costing you fifty cents or a dollar."

Another old-timer agrees with Mr. W., explaining with a worried frown, "I'm still getting the same pension I got ten years ago when I retired, and I'll bet prices have doubled since then. I can't ask for a raise."

In a study last year, the Social Security Administration figured that about two thirds of the men and women over 65 had incomes of less than $1,000 a year in 1954. Another 15 per cent were under $2,000 a year.

By dint of careful frugality, Joseph and Bessie S. are able to take care of themselves on his monthly Social Security check of $98.50. Actually, figures Mr. S., opening a large ledger bound in blue oil-cloth, their monthly expenses usually run around $88. The saving goes for trips to visit their children and for birthday presents.

A budget of this sort doesn't allow for high living. Running his finger down the neatly inked columns of figures, Mr. S. cites these typical monthly bills: the four-party telephone, $5.78; electricity, $7.79; water, $17.70. "That water bill was for three months," notes Mrs. S. quickly. "But it was a little high anyhow. We had put in new grass and we kept the sprinkler running all the time."

The S.s go to the movies occasionally, but their only other amusement expense is $6 each for season tickets for the Civic Music Association. Both love music; Mr. S. plays the violin and Mrs. S. the piano.

A few times a week they take the bus to the city's new Senior Center, a pleasant downtown clubroom where local oldsters gather for canasta and bridge. The club's motto: "Going Like Sixty."

"We don't own a car. For us that would be a luxury," says Mr. S. Once a week their daughter takes Mrs. S. on a shopping expedition. The rest of the week they use buses.

The couple do not have any rent to pay or mortgage to amortize. Their neat, white house is one of the estimated five million houses owned by oldsters, 80 per cent of them mortgage free. They paid $5,500 cash for it two years ago. "We'll never move from this house," predicts Mr. S. with a proud look around the comfortably furnished living room.

Food costs the couple only about $12 a week. Says Mrs. S.: "I'm very thrifty. We buy the kinds of food which take time and work to prepare. It's less expensive than ready-prepared food, but it's just as good if you take trouble with it. I have plenty of time."

For instance, Mrs. S. figures lamb shanks taste just as good as leg of lamb if they're cooked long enough. And a single serving costs only 28 cents instead of close to 50. "We never eat steaks or chops," she adds.

The Social Security check goes further in Florida than it would in New York, Mr. S. figures. But even at that, he's noted "a little increase" in their cost of living since they first retired.

The S.s have no debts and Mr. S. says he even has some savings left from sale of the store. "She won't be left without anything when I'm gone," he says, glancing at his wife of 42 years. Each has a $1,000 insurance policy, "to pay for our funerals."

They pay their bills quickly or else pay cash for their few purchases. "I'm not opposed to installment buying: it helps make the country prosperous. But I personally don't want the headache," explains Mr. S.

Mrs. S. adds severely, "My daughter has some friends. The husband is in the Navy and gets paid at the end of the month. Around the end of every month they come around to borrow cigarettes. Well, that same couple have a very fine record player, a motorboat, a dishwasher and a lot of other appliances and two cars. On payday they pay their installments and buy a lot of food to put in their home freezer. Then they have no money for the rest of the month."

CHARLES N. STABLER, JR.

April 30, 1956

BOARD ROOMS AND
ANTECHAMBERS

(*The Executive Life*)

———————————————❀———————————————

HOW THEY LIVE

Status Symbols

Every morning the president of a big Ohio paper products corporation carefully pilots his auto into the least desirable and least convenient spot in his company's parking lot—a place reserved for him at his own request.

At about the same hour the chairman of a giant Midwestern retailing company guides his conspicuously ancient Plymouth past the rows of gleaming 1957 models owned by his subordinates to his regular space.

These top executives are fighting a brave but losing battle. They're among the small minority of business leaders who are trying to downgrade that much maligned but omnipresent appurtenance of corporate power—the status symbol.

Almost wherever one turns the status symbol is on the rise. From the parking lot to the executive washroom, the special privileges denoting corporate rank are more prominent and more frankly acknowledged than ever before.

At an increasing number of concerns, the corporate caste system is being formalized and rigidified. Most Detroit auto makers have adopted strict management classifications for the purpose of doling out such privileges as the use of company-owned cars for both business and personal purposes. At top levels, executives not only get

75

"Nothing personal, Ralph, old boy. I just can't get used to you with a carpet."

more expensive models but also receive a second free car for the wife.

Gulf Oil Corp. divides its management personnel into five levels for the purpose of distributing special privileges. When it comes to company cars, Class I (division managers and the like) can choose between Cadillacs and Imperials. In Class V (which includes sales representatives), the employee can choose only from among the Chevrolet 150, Ford Custom and Plymouth Plaza.

Crown Zellerbach Corp. has been striving for more scientific stratification for three or four years. "Standardization will be in full force by the summer of 1959 when we move into a new twenty-story building," says H. W. Herzig, manager of the building and office services division. "We'll be able to arrange walls so that the offices for executives of equal rank can all be built to within a square inch of one another in size."

Status symbols are nothing new to the business world, of course. The early chief of one big Hollywood studio used to bring his two big boxer dogs to work with him every morning, housing them in a special kennel beside his office.

But not until more recent years have status symbols taken on such importance and formality at somewhat lower levels of the power pyramid. And this trend has presented companies with some severe headaches.

"Status symbol problems are by far the most ticklish internal difficulties of our management," confides the vice-president of a large international construction company.

The most common sources of interoffice rivalry over status symbols involve such obvious executive trappings as the size of the desk, the quality of drapes and carpets in private offices, the number of windows and the over-all nature of the office furnishings.

Warfare recently broke out at the offices of a Boston-based utility company when an executive fell heir to a fine red leather couch. Says the executive: "The vice-president next door began coveting my couch, even claiming his doctor ordered him to take midday naps. I finally told my secretary, 'You decide.' She told me not to give it away."

Collectors of status symbols vie for the little "extras" in office furnishings. Witness the Madison Avenue executive who had his office relaid in pigskin tile at company expense (at something like $5 per square foot). One former president of a Chicago food processing concern put his desk and chair on a raised platform so that he could look down on employees who dropped by his office.

For many years at Standard Oil Co. (Ohio) a brass spittoon symbolized authority. But more recently a water carafe and tray have replaced the spittoon in the offices of top brass.

At Cummins Engine Co. in Columbus, Indiana, another new symbol of executive caste has appeared. Top management personnel have been awarded aides—bright young assistants fresh out of Harvard Business School.

Secretaries play a key role in the status symbol game. One Eastern manufacturing company calls the secretaries of department heads "executive assistants," while ladies performing identical chores for lesser personnel are merely "stenographers." At a major broadcasting company an executive's stratum is given away by a look at his secretary's typewriter—only the offices of higher-level officials get electric models.

To attain two secretaries is the goal of many a rising executive. But this achievement can bring problems. After a department manager for a western Pennsylvania oil company finally managed two secretaries he found they couldn't get along together. The possibly temporary solution: He induced his company to construct a wall between his warring secretaries.

Some status symbols have been snatched—before being awarded—by ambitious young management climbers trying to better themselves. In many companies, for instance, only members of top management are permitted to include their wives in their expense accounts on corporate junkets. This has led some men on the make to bring along their wives at personal expense just for show. And the widespread practice of corporations footing the bill for country club memberships for key executives has led many newcomers to pay their own way into the clubs just to pal around with the brass.

Such maneuvers can be dangerous for the practitioners, of course, if they stir their bosses' resentment. They also have contributed to a minor revolt against the more blatant aspects of the caste system.

"You can spend lots of money on status symbols—false rewards is what we consider them," observes an official of a Los Angeles electronics firm. "But real rewards for a job well done, let's face it, should be largely financial—higher pay, bigger bonuses."

"Status symbols only help to feed office jealousies," says the president of a West Coast communications equipment concern.

Some companies have sought to cut down on some of the more obvious trappings of rank. At International Minerals & Chemical Corp.'s new Skokie, Illinois, headquarters—to be completed next summer—the dimensions of offices will be standardized. And there will be less than usual rivalry over windows because, as Thomas M. Ware, administrative vice-president, explains, "The walls are all window." There will still be competition for corner offices of course.

Similarly, Du Pont is slowly but surely doing away with executive washrooms on the pretext that "there's a premium on space."

Monsanto Chemical Co.'s new St. Louis headquarters has eliminated competition over water coolers by installing only permanent drinking fountains in the hallways.

One of the most sweeping status symbol upheavals took place when young Henry Ford II took over the reins of his company. As is widely known in Detroit, he lost little time in chopping away all the so-called "fringe benefits" that had arisen during the Harry Bennett regime. In their place he introduced a highly formalized system of status symbolism which, among other things, drastically reduced the number of free autos given Ford officials.

Under the current setup at Ford, which the company refuses to discuss, status symbols are awarded in accordance with a set salary scale. Here's the way one former Ford man describes his trek up the ladder: As his position improved, his office grew larger, his furniture fancier, his name went on the door, he received a rug for the floor and a spot in the indoor garage. Then came keys to the executive washroom, country club membership at company expense and finally the free car.

These various rewards, he recalls, did more than merely bolster the ego. The executive washroom to which he gained admission offered showers and electric shavers, as well as cologne. And the indoor garage proved particularly helpful during midwinter freezes.

A number of personnel experts rationalize the entire matter of status symbols in terms of alleged "practical benefits" accruing to both company and individual executive. Nearby parking lots and washrooms, they argue, save time and energy for high-salaried officials and hence save money for companies.

A Portland bank executive claims that a certain amount of "window dressing" is needed to please customers. Bank officials need fancy titles and elaborate furnishings, he reasons, to make clients believe "they're talking to big wheels."

In a similar vein, a former soap company president used to explain away the immense fireplace in his office by claiming it "put visitors at their ease."

Some corporate leaders also defend status symbols as being important to a company's discipline and operating efficiency. They serve to underscore the lines of authority, goes this argument, and remind employees where the power actually resides. Moreover, status privileges sometimes are used as "fringe benefits" in lieu of pay boosts or bonuses.

Many skeptics, of course, take a dim view of all this. To them the status symbol is mainly a device for flaunting one's power, and any practical justification is largely accidental.

The wives are as responsible as anyone, says a top official of a Western power company. "The company wife can't brag that her husband makes so much money, but at least she can boast about his new title or bright new office," he remarks. "Company wives need a way of displaying their husband's importance."

"If a young junior executive becomes preoccupied with symbols," says Dr. J. Elliott Janney, a Cleveland psychologist and management consultant, "you will find a pattern of other things that will show he's self-centered. Subordinates and superiors both will become distrustful of his motives and lose confidence in him.

"But," Dr. Janney concludes, "status symbols to a large degree are just part of human nature."

For lesser brass, railway cars, sun lamps and hilltop mansions usually are out of the question. Lower-level executives must settle for smaller fringe benefits. The distinctions sometimes seem trifling. At a major Midwest oil company, vice-presidents get private washrooms just like the boss, but theirs contain no toilets. At Campbell Soup Co.'s new headquarters at Camden, New Jersey, the presidents must double up on their adjoining washrooms. Below the vice-presidential level, executives are completely barred from the bathroom aristocracy and must walk to the regular facilities.

October 29, 1957

Expense Accounts

Federal tax men are forcing some profound changes in the workings of that trusty old corporate companion—the expense account.

The revenuers are insisting that taxpayers with expense accounts report and itemize reimbursed business outlays as income on their 1958 tax forms—and then deduct the money actually spent for business purposes. The precise requirements haven't yet been formulated.

Whatever the tax men decide, it's apparent their campaign already has produced, in addition to confusion, some noteworthy results. A major change: Corporate managers are going to some effort—and expense—to keep closer track of expense account spending. So are the spenders. Another innovation: Many a company is issuing credit cards to executives and opening new charge accounts. By having items charged directly to themselves, companies hope to limit the impact of the ruling on their employees.

Because of the confusion over exactly what the Revenue Service wants, many concerns merely have advised their employees to keep duplicates of expense account vouchers. But even this approach probably won't end the matter for corporations; executives admit they almost certainly will have to provide expense summaries to employees who come around next year and ask for them.

Tax authorities, who say they're out to crack down on expense account situations which are "open to abuse," insist they do not want to "harass" taxpayers or companies by making them itemize every little phone call or taxi fare. But talk with corporate officials, businessmen who have expense accounts and even tax experts and this pronounced intention often is answered with an angry explosion.

"It's the biggest bunch of baloney I ever heard," grumbles an official of an auto parts company in Detroit. "You'd think the Government would realize people like me aren't handling personal money. It's company money," he contends, "and we're just passing it along."

For some businessmen, the expense account has become, willy-nilly, an adjunct to salary. In some cases, high officials may draw flat monthly sums for "expenses" without ever having to account for the dollars they spend. These undoubtedly are the cases in which the tax men are most interested, but anybody who has ever tried to explain exactly where he has spent a company dollar in the line of business knows the difficulties—and the temptations—involved.

"Let's face it," blurts a traveling salesman in the lobby of the San Francisco Merchandise Mart, "when it comes to expense accounts we're all crooks. That 'entertainment' column is the rough one. If somebody takes Betty So-and-So out because she's a big buyer, he's not going to ask her to sign an affidavit that it's a legitimate business expense. So how is he going to prove it to the Government?"

A Portland, Oregon, insurance adjuster muses: "It looks like my family will have to get along without the little luxuries from now on. The little extra cash my expense account used to bring in was just enough to pay off those minor monthly bills, leaving at least part of my salary free for extras."

February 14, 1958

The New Executives

As a young man on the way up, Larry C. has his problems. He has just been promoted to assistant personnel director of a major food processing company, but the new job entails some basic decisions.

There's the matter of the car. "I'm not ashamed to ride my boss around in the old, beat-up car; I refuse to build my whole life around pleasing the company," he says, planting a foot atop his shiny new desk. After a moment's reflection he adds: "Of course, I'm kind of looking forward to buying that new station wagon we can afford now."

And as this earnest young executive in brown tweeds talks on, he concedes this about his selection of a new suburban home: "We had to eliminate a few places that were pretty good simply because I knew they were poor addresses for a management man in our company."

A good many newly appointed executives like Larry C. find themselves torn between two basic drives. On the one hand they're ambitious and want to do "the right things" to further their careers. On the other, they instinctively rebel against being forced into a corporate mold.

Most newly promoted executives vigorously deny that company considerations shape the way they live, dress or think. But often the very firmness of their denials betrays the inner conflict.

Rationalizes one new executive: "You can divorce business completely from your private life. But I think you'll find the private life you choose still will be in the best interests of the company. The people I find intelligent and attractive usually turn out to be the same ones who are 'comers' in the company."

Another young management man, recently named a sales executive, argues, "I'm not one of those organization men who just live for the company." Later he adds: "My wife and I decided a long time ago not to waste too much of our leisure time with casual entertaining. When we have people out to the house, it has to be those who may be important to me as contacts."

These reluctant admissions that corporate careers bring changes in the private lives of executives tell just part of the story. Almost as soon as any corporate worker learns of his rise to the executive level, he appears to begin wondering how he'll perform those unspoken, but frequently important, duties of his position.

The often touchy adjustment problems are all the more noteworthy today as growing numbers of young businessmen are thrust into key corporate posts. Lower retirement ages, postwar business expansion, the increase in mergers—all these factors have contributed to a sharp rise in the number of executive opportunities.

Should the new executive try to "live up" to his new position, or should he try to preserve his former mode of living? How can he step gracefully into the management circle without offending its older members?

One new executive, impressed with his promotion and already bucking for another, still better job in the company, adopted an elaborate and costly front to impress his superiors. He bought a fancy car, had his suits made to measure, and talked his way into an exclusive country club. Finally, after his extravagant display failed to snare him another quick promotion, he hastily accepted another job elsewhere to support the expensive front he had adopted. "The sad thing is," reports a close associate of this executive, "J. had such a better future with the company he left in such panic."

Many a new management man finds that, even without an overt display of wealth, his promotion can bring on some budgetary problems.

"You know, I proved on paper that I lost $5 a month by being promoted and moved from a branch operation," says George C., who now is vice-president in a machinery company's New York headquarters. "I had to move here from a small town. That's one of the ways I lost money.

"And, of course, that figure doesn't take into consideration that I live in a better house and have nicer furniture. I feel sort of an

obligation to live better now; that's part of the promotion," declares
George C.

After 26 years with the Chock Full O' Nuts restaurant chain,
graying Herman Kleeger recently was promoted from store manager
to field supervisor. He now oversees the work of many store managers.

"I can't live as a store manager any more," says he, sitting by the
counter of one Manhattan restaurant unit, this time on the customers' side. "I have to sort of live up to the position." For Mr.
Kleeger, living up to his new job means a new home on Long Island,
a part-time maid, a new company car and, of course, spending his
larger salary. It also entails some social adjustments.

"I don't think it's a good policy to socialize with the managers
under me," declares ex-counterman Kleeger. "It might give the
wrong impression, maybe suggesting I would play favorites when
good openings come up." Mr. Kleeger is equally dubious about hob-
nobbing with his superiors: "Most of the higher officials live in
Westchester; I don't feel comfortable up there."

George C., the new vice-president, has some different thoughts,
however: "Naturally you have pride if you're socially accepted by
your superiors. It does you an awful lot of good. You can have a
wonderful personnel system, but the thing that determines where
you go in the company is personal contacts."

John F., who recently was named chief of his company's marketing
department, recalls some early attempts at socializing with his immediate superior. "I asked him out a few times. Nothing happened.
It soon became clear he didn't want to come. We get along fine at
the office, and that's enough for me," he says.

Larry C. reluctantly joined an executive eating club within the
company "because the boss is club president this year and I thought
it was expected of me." But as soon as the year for which he paid
dues is over, he's going to quit. Why? "It's dull as dishwater."

LOUIS KRAAR

February 10, 1958

Throat Cutting

A vice-president of one Eastern corporation not long ago plugged
the carburetor in the auto of a new rival to make him late for his
first executive meeting.

A high executive of a conservative Pennsylvania corporation planted rumors that his principal rival had "fallen for a New Dealish line," thus ruining his chances for the presidency.

An elevator company executive waited for his rival's special project to flop, then submitted to the boss a series of memos (carefully backdated) to show he'd opposed the project all along.

These businessmen were practicing that most delicate of all the arts of self-advancement—throat cutting. Most of the techniques of throat cutting have changed little with the years. The rewards for the skilled practitioners of the art remain high—and so do the risks for the inept.

One man who gambled and lost was a salesman for a rubber company. Scrambling for a vacant job of assistant sales manager, he spread rumors of his rival's addiction to wine, women and song. As he expected, these tales reached the ears of the boss. But they backfired; the boss, who liked to dally a bit, too, handed the job to the high liver. The more circumspect salesman, who had been careful to stress his own purity, fell from favor and eventually was fired.

More than 50 executives interviewed by *Wall Street Journal* reporters in twelve cities agreed that throat cutters nowadays meet with disaster almost as often as with success. Still the alluring example of those who are successful is keeping the art very much alive.

Throat cutting isn't the only route to promotion, of course; some executives advance simply because they're skilled at their jobs. But one leading San Francisco management consultant maintains, "The man who is competent and ruthless and combines this with skill at throat cutting will probably win out over the man who is just competent."

Most executives—after they think it over—concede the existence of throat cutting within their companies.

"There's no throat cutting around here," avers an officer of a big Southwest oil company. But after a moment's reflection he adds: "Of course, some people in this company will do just anything to get promoted." He claims one high official hired a staff of talented assistants to do all his work so that he could devote more time to office politicking.

Among the basic weapons of throat cutting the verbal scalpel ranks high, whether applied at the conference table, in the executive lunch room or right in the boss's office. The interoffice memo is another traditional vehicle for demolishing a rival. Of more recent vintage: introduction of an "objective" management survey to undermine an opponent's project. Pacts with customers or competitors to do in an executive are not uncommon. Some overeager throat cutters have even placed bribes and rifled files to achieve their ends, but these coarser methods are scorned by the *cognoscenti*.

Most of these techniques have stood the test of time. Historians say underlings managed to bounce president Charles Schwab of U.S. Steel from his job 54 years ago by spreading tales of Schwab's Monte Carlo gambling expeditions. Chairman Elbert Gary, something of a moralist, started restricting the president's jurisdiction, so Schwab stormed out of the company.

What troubles many business leaders is that a surprising number of younger corporate recruits have taken a liking to these well-worn techniques. One Detroit business official says he's noticed many youngsters just embarking on corporate training programs who already are trying out their carving skills.

"It's the younger man who thinks his superior is not doing his job who comes to me with a complaint," says the executive vice-president of a Dallas manufacturing company.

Another point of agreement among executives: Throat cutting appears to be more prevalent in large companies which have achieved predominance in their fields than it is in smaller, still growing enterprises. "Internal warfare is bound to be greater in a mature organization which isn't growing very rapidly," says one veteran manufacturing executive. In small, fast-expanding firms, he says, there are always new opportunities for meritorious young men.

In large companies, the corridors sometimes can become cluttered with throat cutters. In one concern, an attorney thought he saw a long-awaited chance to nab the president's job, and he took dead aim. The company was being sued by an inventor over the use of certain key patents. In an effort to show that he could get the company out of the mess into which the president had led it, the attorney paid an outsider to rifle the inventor's files and steal some vital evidence. But another company official, in turn, was after the attorney's throat; the file-searching incident was made known to the president and the attorney was fired.

"Throat cutting frequently occurs in places where people don't have very much to do," says one veteran vice-president of a major West Coast manufacturing concern. "I spent five years in Washington—that's where the pros are. In any other spot you merely see minor-league stuff."

There also are plenty of pros operating in the ranks of corporate management, of course. And the game is played at the uppermost rungs of the corporate ladder. "The higher the monkey climbs on the pole, the easier it is to shoot him down," quips one Boston banker.

One personnel executive for a major broadcasting network claims some officials on the business side of the company carefully doctored cost estimates in order to sabotage the career of the network president. "The president would ask for an estimate on the cost of a new television show, and they'd say $500,000, knowing darn well it would come to $750,000 or more. This meant the guy would really catch it from the powers above for consistent overspending," explains the personnel man.

Eventually the president was dismissed, but his successor lost no time in cleaning out the men who had come up with the wrong estimates.

Another favorite Madison Avenue trick: When a new vice-president moves in, his rivals get him credit cards in the company's name for many of the more roisterous restaurants and bars about town. They then spread the word that the new executive is a heavy drinker and therefore something less than dependable.

It's naturally much easier for the president of a concern to slice up a subordinate he considers a threat to his position than for underlings to knife the top man. But in the case of a vice-president who wishes to do away with a rival vice-president, subtler methods must be sought.

One favorite device: bringing in an "unbiased" management consultant firm. Such a survey was arranged by a vice-president in charge of supply and distribution for a major Midwestern oil company in his feud with the sales vice-president. The supply v.p. wished to enlarge his department by appropriating some of the more important functions of the sales v.p. The motive: If his department expanded, his claim on a still higher post would be enhanced.

The survey was made, and it supported the proposal of the supply vice-president. "Surveys often are slanted in favor of the man who requests them," observes another official of the same company who watched this duel with great amusement. But despite the survey, higher-ups looked askance at the proposal and no changes were made.

Veteran throat cutters have learned to shrug off such disappointments. There's the case of two such veterans, the controller and the head of the legal department of a big Midwest corporation, who both were running hard for a vacant vice-presidency. Their rivalry reached its climax in the composition of the president's letter for the concern's annual report.

Says another officer: "Both men drafted a copy and took it to the president. They spent more time criticizing the other's letter than trying to sell the virtues of their own. Finally the president called in both men and said he was disgusted with their jockeying and if it continued he'd fire them both."

On rare occasions the victim of throat cutting returns to haunt his tormentors. An executive of a Pacific Coast concern was put upon not long ago by his colleagues—they hacked away at his prestige, his salary, and finally got him fired. A short time later, the victim suddenly reappeared as an executive of his original company's biggest customer. In his new position he could decide whether to buy from its competitors. Since he was not a man to forget a grudge, his decision was fairly obvious.

November 20, 1957

"*Due to our profit-sharing agreement, you each owe the company $137.50.*"

Option Opulence

The bull market is bringing huge "paper" profits to executives of many a U.S. corporation.

In the past five years, nearly 500 major companies have granted employees options to purchase stock; in most cases, the privilege has been restricted to officers and other "key" employees. The avowed purpose: to increase employee incentive.

The list of option granters includes well-known firms, such as American Airlines, Gulf Oil, Republic Steel and Westinghouse Electric. The option pace shows no sign of slackening. Last year, 74 companies listed 13.6 million shares with the New York Stock Exchange for employee plans, compared with 72 companies and 9.2 million shares in 1953.

Congress, in passing the 1950 Revenue Act, opened the gates for the big stock option rush.

Before that act was passed, an executive who exercised an option to buy stock in his company at a price below the market generally had to report the difference as additional income. He had to pay taxes on it at ordinary income rates. It didn't matter when he sold the stock or if he ever sold it; his "paper profit" was considered to be additional income.

Under present law, if the stock option and its use conform to certain restrictions laid down by Congress, this rule is changed and an executive buying stock under an option receives two tax benefits:

He is not considered to have received any income when he buys the stock. If he holds the stock for more than two years from the date he obtained the option, and for more than six months after he received the stock, any profit on the sale of the stock may be treated as a long-term capital gain, taxable at lower rates than ordinary income.

Few option recipients anticipated the market's meteoric rise, of course. As recently as late 1953, bull market prophets were in the minority.

An executive can win with options, but it's difficult for him to lose. He can buy stock at a fixed price, regardless of how high the market price has gone when he exercises the option.

He can lose if the market price drops below the option price before he sells the stock. If he borrows from his bank to buy the stock, as many executives must, any break in market price may cause him trouble. Since his stock usually would serve as collateral for the loan, a drop in price would make it necessary for him to provide additional collateral—or possibly sell some of the stock without the advantages of capital-gains-tax treatment. These risks can be minimized by delaying exercise of the option until the spread between market price and option price is wide.

Some option holders have been disappointed, to be sure. Textron, Inc., in 1951 granted chairman Royal Little and other officers options to buy stock at $25 a share. Textron stock now is selling at about $14 a share, after sinking as low as $6.25 in late 1953. For obvious reasons, none of the options have been exercised.

American Viscose in 1950 granted 34 officers and key men options to buy 59,400 shares at $60.50 a share—the market price at that time. The stock now sells at about $42 a share, after dropping to $30.62 in 1954. Only one Viscose executive exercised his option; he's still doggedly holding the stock.

While stock option plans have been overwhelmingly approved by stockholders, they are nevertheless a source of wide differences of opinion. Almost all companies claim their plans have worked well.

"We are extremely well pleased with our plan," declares a spokesman for Brown Shoe Co. of St. Louis. "It is a very great asset in boosting employee morale and makes a good selling point for obtaining new executives."

"I believe that in a couple of instances individuals have been at least partially influenced by our stock option plan in deciding to join the company," says Arthur Cahill, treasurer of International Minerals & Chemical Corp., Chicago.

"The plan has worked out to the complete satisfaction of the board of directors," remarks Walter Tuohy, president of the Chesapeake & Ohio Railway. Another C. & O. executive says options have helped the road retain its executives, since "railroad executives generally are underpaid in comparison with executives of other big firms."

Most opposition to options has come from small but highly vocal stockholder minorities. Stockholders unsuccessfully went to court in an effort to overthrow option plans of such concerns as C.I.T. Financial Corp., Standard Oil Co. (New Jersey) and United States Steel.

Stockholders opposing the stock option plans have three chief objections:

Increasing the common stock outstanding reduces the company's earnings per share. Stockholders, other than the employees eligible under the plans, have no right to buy any of the new stock so that they may continue to own the same proportionate share of the company. Officers and key employees already are getting enough compensation for their services.

Few companies have a harsh word for stock options, whether they've adopted plans themselves or not. But many concerns obviously are yet to be convinced of the option's value; some two thirds of the corporations listed on the New York Stock Exchange have avoided option plans.

Many a company is reluctant to discuss its option plan, claiming stockholders will "misunderstand." Says one official: "They'll blame us for the bull market." Goodyear Tire & Rubber, which adopted an option plan four years ago, won't talk about it at all.

There's little doubt options have helped to woo many executives from one company to another. When Laclede Gas adopted an option program at last week's annual meeting, president Robert W. Otto declared: "We found we were running a training school for other gas companies." He told stockholders one executive recently moved to another company simply because he was offered an option to buy 10,000 shares of stock.

Most companies take steps to make sure the option plan holds its executives, for a time at least. C.I.T. Financial, for example, requires a two-year-employment agreement from participants under its plan.

Employees often cannot exercise options until two years after they are granted. One West Coast manufacturer belatedly discovered the advantage of such a provision; an executive was granted an option, exercised it and quit the next day. After the company had to go to court to recover the stock, the two-year rule was inserted in its plan.

Although some companies, such as Bridgeport Brass and Pittsburgh Plate Glass, permit employees to pay for stock through payroll deductions, most plans require a single payment. So employees often must secure substantial bank loans to buy stock.

"The trouble with option plans, by and large," according to Textron's Mr. Little, "is that they're only good for rich men who don't need them. How else can a man afford to exercise them?"

February 1, 1955

HOW THEY WORK

Brainstorming

A group of salesmen from Christmas Club, a corporation engaged in promoting a bank thrift plan, gathered at a suburban country club the other day for an unusual type of business session.

The salesmen had been asked to think up new ways for banks to use the Christmas carol books the corporation distributes. They did it by "brainstorming" the problem—a technique that growing numbers of companies are finding useful in hatching ideas for such things as new sales methods, new products and new product uses.

Brainstorming, a creation of an advertising man, represents another mating of the Age of Freud with the Century of the Salesman. The approach to a brainstorming session is semievangelistic, with stress on getting the participants in a "positive" mood. The brainstormers are seated around a table and the problem is stated. Then recourse is had to the "subconscious" of the brainstormers. In an atmosphere of "anything goes," the participants throw out whatever ideas come into their heads. The theory is, some good ideas will come out this way; and even some outlandish ones will trigger good ideas. A stenographer transcribes the proceedings, and later the ideas are examined by policy makers.

These sessions differ from more conventional idea-hunting systems in other ways. To avoid inhibitions, participants generally are of nearly equal rank. Often the meetings are held at lower levels in a company hierarchy than the usual policy-making discussions. And criticism of ideas is flatly barred so long as the session is in progress.

At most sessions, "killer phrases" (such as "That won't work" or "It's been done before") are blocked by a leader who usually rings a bell or flips a red disk on a flannel board. This frequently provokes laughter, which is supposed to relax the group and get participants back into a free-wheeling mood.

U.S. Steel has used brainstorming to attack administrative problems. Reynolds Metals used it to develop marketing plans for new products. Ethyl Corp. turned up 71 ideas in 45 minutes on a new booklet on employee benefit plans. One brainstorming session at

91

General Motors' AC Spark Plug Division produced more than 100 ideas on how to finish off a casting.

Most of these ideas, it's true, wind up in the wastebasket. "There's a lot of fluff in any brainstorm session, but, after all, new ideas are hard to come by," says Edward F. Dorset, president of Christmas Club.

Brainstorming businessmen generally expect only about 6 per cent of the ideas from any one session to be practical. Dr. Dorset, however, is much more optimistic: He figures 90 per cent of his salesmen's ideas could be used. "Even more important than the ideas," he contends, "is the stimulation the experience gives to salesmen to use more imagination instead of an old stereotyped line of chatter."

Christmas Club salesmen at their recent session were introduced to brainstorming by an expert from another company, who started with a "warm-up" period on this question: "How many ways can you think up to improve a suit of men's clothes?" In this trial run the salesmen came up with 104 ideas in 17 minutes.

The salesmen then concentrated on carol books for 30 minutes, coming up with 75 ideas. Samples: bank-sponsored carol singing at railroad stations, with free carol books for persons attending; a helicopter that would circle a town, broadcasting carols through a loudspeaker, and then land in a bank parking lot with a Santa Claus, who would step out and distribute free carol books.

The products of brainstorming sessions—even those that are accepted—are often so simple that any employee might conclude, "I could have thought of that." But the point is, according to brainstorming's advocates, that few employees do present such ideas. The sessions permit management to collect a mass of possible solutions to a given problem, narrowing the chances of overlooking the best solution.

The creator of brainstorming as a systematic technique is Alex F. Osborn, a 66-year-old advertising man and cofounder of Batten, Barton, Durstine & Osborn. Mr. Osborn began using small groups of that ad agency's employees many years ago to brainstorm such things as new product names and sales slogans for clients.

About two years ago the agency organized brainstorming as a regular service for all its clients. In the past year it has trained about 40 panel leaders in its offices to conduct sessions. Participants usually consist of a permanent chairman, an "idea collector," five "core" members known for creative ability but not working on the account whose problem is discussed, and five guests from within the agency.

B.B.D. & O. sessions in New York are held in an informal, pine-paneled room especially designed for this purpose. On one wall hangs a poster displaying the rules; on shelves and tables are scattered products for which ideas have been developed at previous brainstorm sessions.

After a one- or two-hour session, usually punctuated by a coffee break or lunch, panel members are asked to continue thinking about the problem for 24 hours; the chairman later phones them for any extra ideas which have occurred to them overnight. The five core members then screen the ideas, and the chairman, the account executive and a vice-president start discussing ways to put the ideas to use.

December 5, 1955

The Managerial Art

If you were handed the job of putting large numbers of men and a lot of money and materials together into a working enterprise, how would you go about doing it?

The question is, if not as old as the hills, at least as old as human society. But in past times big organization has largely been a problem pertaining to armies, or universal churches, or the political state. It is only with the rise of large-scale industry, a phenomenon of the past 30 years, that the question has forced businessmen into conducting an organized search for the principles underlying the answer.

Time was when the businessman considered the whole thing to be a self-evident proposition, even in the relatively big company. The boss, usually a member of an owning family or the representative of a few large stockholders, set the day-to-day objectives of the company within the wider policy imposed by the board of directors. The boss ponied up the payroll, told the foreman and salesmen what to do, and talked directly with board members about expansion.

But today, even in closely held big companies, problems are no longer that simple. Management ideas that were once considered axiomatic seem more and more inadequate to the complexities of the modern company which makes many different products and markets them from New York to Hong Kong, or from Chicago to Timbuctoo. The history of modern corporate management is one of a steadily increasing search for ways of avoiding the bottleneck of one-man rule.

The main reason for the search, which extends to medium-sized companies as well as to the corporate giants, is the ever changing nature of the industrial landscape; it is one of increasingly complex diversification of product within the confines of single corporate shelters. To some extent the merger movement is responsible for it—but more importantly the quest grows out of the unpredictable thrusts of modern technology, which can take a company almost anywhere in no time flat.

Oil companies which once dealt solely in liquid fuels now find themselves in the huge tangle of petrochemistry. Steamship lines to South America discover they must take a hand in developing local economies if they are to make money—or to employ profitably the money they make. Concerns which once sold gunpowder to the Army learn that nitric acid can be put into creative forms as well as destructive.

Electrical manufacturing companies suddenly wake up to the fact that there is a world of market difference between giant turbines and atomic submarines, or between washing machines for laundries and toasters and light bulbs for private homes. Hence the need for divisionalization—and hence also the need for decentralizing the power of decision to the point where it must be applied.

Sheer size alone can also increase the complexities. Even a company that sticks to its main product can get so large that it is too unwieldy for one-man management. The "boss" becomes a bottleneck.

The search for ways of eliminating bottlenecks in decision making inevitably involves a paradox. Clearly the boss must rule in certain instances if cohesion and integration are to be maintained. But the boss can't possibly know enough about detail in a General Motors or a Borg-Warner or a Du Pont to make any but the broadest decisions unaided. Clearly some sort of group leadership is necessary, with the boss serving as team captain, not as dictator.

When Rome was master of the world, it had the problem of the provinces—and it frequently had to leave things to the proconsul on the spot. In the Roman Army the general in charge of the legions in Britain was answerable to Rome itself—but he needed a free hand when chasing the Picts and the Scots back across Hadrian's Wall. Julius Caesar did what he liked in Gaul, but when he chose to "cross the Rubicon" it meant that he was getting out of his own bailiwick—and out of hand. As for the Catholic Church, though it is headed by a Pope, it leaves the bishops a lot of latitude, and the bishops in turn do not unduly interfere with the parish priests.

In developing its patterns of decentralization, the modern American corporation has, often unconsciously, borrowed from the forms of politics. Such diverse responses as the limited monarchy, parliamentary rule, states' rights and the British Commonwealth of Nations have offered many models for imitation.

The United States Steel Corporation, which is "two-thirds centralized, one-third decentralized," is a prime example of an organization which sticks essentially to a chain of command, like an army. But it allows certain subsidiaries such as American Bridge or Tennessee Coal and Iron the autonomy of army task forces.

More often modern "divisionalization" takes the pattern of the limited monarchy—a king subject to check by his nominal subjects —as in General Motors, General Electric or General Foods. These companies combine the principle of "federal decentralization" with the principle of cabinet and top-executive rule.

Rule by committee vote—which suggests, roughly, the parliamentary form of government—is rather rare in big industry. But the huge Du Pont Company reaches its decisions in accordance with the majority preference of an executive board of nine vice-presidents and a president.

As for the states' rights analogy, there is the successful experiment being conducted by General Robert Wood Johnson of the New Brunswick, New Jersey, pharmaceutical firm of Johnson and Johnson. General Johnson's firm is split up into a number of autonomous subsidiaries which are actually legal entities of their own.

Naturally, the search for a way to blend authority with the flexibility of the small, autonomous unit results in interstices where control goes according to personal ability to take and hold power. No analogy from the political world can wholly explain a G.M. or a Du Pont or a Johnson and Johnson. But a body of material is accumulating which makes possible an art, if not a science, of industrial organization. And this body of material is worth pondering in detail.

JOHN CHAMBERLAIN

December 17, 1957

Flexible Formula

The commonly accepted "chain of command," or straight-line, formula is the oldest method of organizing people and economic resources for a common undertaking. It worked for single automobile companies. But when W. C. Durant put a whole complex of separate automobile companies together into General Motors, something else was needed.

Seeking a solution back in 1920 for the General Motors problem, Alfred P. Sloan, Jr., sought refuge in a paradox—he would centralize and decentralize at the same time. It was a neat trick, but Mr. Sloan pulled it off.

The form which Mr. Sloan evolved—a complete divisionalization of G.M. products into what might be termed the "line," plus a grouping of corporation-wide services into "staff" units which were available on equal terms to all the divisions—was highly original in his day. Under the Sloan conception the members of the "line" (Pontiac, Chevrolet, Fisher Body) marched abreast, each a coequal, each reporting to a divisions group (car divisions, accessories). The divisions groups were responsible for general policies to an executive vice-president who in turn reported to the president.

During the past three decades the G.M. formula—"centralized policy, decentralized administration"—has been imitated widely. It has proved its staying powers and its flexibility for all sorts of companies, both large and medium-sized, which have variegated product groupings and multimarket customer problems. For purposes of simplification it might today be called the formula of the Three Gs, for its most successful contemporary exemplars are General Motors, General Electric and General Foods.

Cut into any one of these companies, from huge G.M. to merely big G.F., and you find the same thing: semiautonomous "line" divisions which have access to common "staff" services, either by direct solicitation or through an over-all executive organization at the top. In G.M. the Pontiac division will make and market its own cars, but for styling, research, legal advice and investment in expensive automation machinery it must normally consult vice-presidents in charge of such things for the whole corporation.

Should a Pontiac problem involve a showdown with Oldsmobile over allocation of limited "staff" resources or company investment funds, or over the use of a distinctive Oldsmobile feature, G.M. president Harlow Curtice himself might have to step in. But otherwise the decision would be made down the line, without going all the way to the top.

Reduced to organization charts, the "Three G" formula looks rather austere. On the General Foods chart, for example, the "line" divisions—Birds Eye (frozen foods), Maxwell House (coffee), Post Cereals (breakfast foods), Perkins Products (Kool-Aid), and so on—are connected with various "staff" vice-presidents in charge of interunit services through an executive vice-president and other officers.

But the chart, which implies a cumbersome routing of requests upward "through channels," does descriptive violence to the actual crisscross of co-operation between line and staff components.

How does this co-operation—and the accompanying decision—work out in practice?

Let us suppose, for instance, that the advertising department of the Post Cereals division, which manufactures in Battle Creek, Michigan, wants to use a television series on cadet life at West Point to sell a breakfast food. Within limits it could do so on its own. The cost of such a show, however, comes high—perhaps too high for the limited advertising budget of Post Cereals. The problem would naturally be one for the General Foods "staff" vice-president in charge of advertising and consumer relations, who connects on the organization chart with Post Cereals by a roundabout circuit involving a couple of general vice-presidents, an executive vice-president and a President's Council.

Actually, the General Manager of Post Cereals might crosscut the chart—pick up the telephone and get into direct touch with the v.p. in charge of G.F. general advertising. Conning the situation, the v.p. might see some objections to using a West Point series to sell other General Foods products. After all, a program with an obvious teen-age appeal, while it demonstrably can sell cereals, could be of lesser use in marketing such things as Gaines dog food, soluble coffee and Birds Eye fish sticks.

So it might look like the sort of impasse which normally demands a high-level executive-group luncheon or a buck-passing job to the President's Council which meets twice a week at G.F. headquarters in White Plains, New York.

Just as he is about to hang up the phone, however, a bright idea might assail the v.p. in charge of advertising. Maybe it would be good to precondition adolescents to accepting Maxwell House coffee. Maybe they should know about Minute Rice. And—a further thought—maybe the West Point series has a good rating with adults, anyway. Eventually parceled out among three subsidiaries, the West Point series would thus be brought within the advertising budgetary purview of General Foods Corp. as a whole. And so the problem could be decided, with a minimum of reference to high-level luncheons or to the office of president Charles G. Mortimer and his advisory Council.

In well-run companies the crosscutting of the chart as between "line" and "staff" components is taken as a matter of course. Without such horizontal motion everything would become bogged down in "channels." The bottleneck to the president and his top-executive team would bulge with unsolved problems. Worse still, neither the president nor his aides would ever have any time for thinking about company problems as a whole. They would be perennially occupied with cleaning out the bottleneck.

In General Electric, decentralization of decision making into operating and service components is consciously used as a device to "free up" the time of a large group of top executive officers.

G.E. has about 100 independent operating departments, tied into 22 divisions. Each department is engaged in a business simple enough for "one man to get his arms around." The Office of the President, which keeps a weather eye on the departments, consists of president Ralph J. Cordiner, board chairman Philip D. Reed, and five group vice-presidents, all assisted by 10 vice-presidents in charge of the Service Divisions.

Service vice-presidents (manufacturing, engineering, public relations, etc.) are charged with spending half their time on long-range plans; for the rest, their authority is one of transmitting new methods to divisions and departments. Each of the seven members of the Office of the President has the authority to assume "the posture of the president" when the Office is not meeting as a group.

While the authority of G.E.'s president is final (subject, of course, to permission or check by the board of directors), the company adds a specifically liberalizing footnote to its organization chart: "While the organization structure and chart define lines of responsibility, authority and accountability, they do not indicate or limit channels of contact, or flow of information . . . policy permits and expects the exercise of common sense and good judgment, at all organization levels, in determining the best channels of contact for expeditious handling of Company work."

Thus goes the practice in the group of companies which have chosen the way of the limited, or constitutional, monarchy in dispatching their business. "Federal decentralization" permits the "provinces"—or, in common industrial parlance, the "line"—to run their own affairs. "Functional decentralization" of services gives the "staff" its own comparable freedom of movement. And the "king" or president at the top has his own council of state, which watches over the provinces to see that revolt does not take place.

Normally it is enough for a "province" to consult with a staff man or a councilor of state to deal with a specific problem which is not covered in the charter of responsibilities. Needless to say, however, the king has the final say where authority is not specifically delegated.

And the king is always beholden to the kingmaker—in corporate terms the board of directors. He cannot pretend to absolute prerogatives unless, as rarely happens, he is also a majority stockholder with a decisive board-of-directors vote. The absolute tyrant is practically gone in large American industry, and the "team" has taken over.

JOHN CHAMBERLAIN

December 21, 1957

Efficient Bigness

The development of American industry has proceeded by shattering rule after rule—or, to put it more accurately, myth after myth. From the idea that profits come out of the hide of the worker to the "law" that increasing populations must compound the amount of misery in the world, the ground is littered with the broken fragments of beliefs once thought to be "immutable."

Along with the other shibboleths, the idea that Bigness and Efficiency don't go together has also been dealt some stunning blows. Just as American industry has created complex machine tools and discovered ways of bringing luxury markets to the masses, so it has evolved new tools for breaking down complex management issues into simple forms.

For 20 years and more it has been experimenting with methods for giving down-the-line managers increased responsibility and scope. Along with this it has ceased to regard the individual worker as a machine. The idea has been to treat employees as separate, human personalities, and to organize them into small, compact teams in which they can feel creatively at home.

There is, indeed, a whole new literature devoted to explaining how big companies can be "divisionalized" in accordance with something which the sociological doctors call the "span of control," meaning the number of people a man can handle without losing touch. Management consultation companies stand ready to elucidate, annotate and provide glosses on the literature. And there is hardly a big company which does not maintain resident philosophers who spend most of their time studying human "span of control" problems.

A General Electric has its "management consultation" and its "organization consulting" services; P. E. Mills, one of its resident philosophers, keeps a whole book of commentary on Peter Drucker's provocative *The Practice of Management* in his desk. A General

Motors hires the same Mr. Drucker to do a book on its divisions, *Concept of the Corporation*. Company presidents, including Cordiner of G.E. and Curtice of G.M., take time away from busy affairs to lecture and write on decentralized management. And the American Management Association serves as a clearinghouse for the literary production of all its members on every conceivable aspect of the topic.

The movement toward efficient organization of big industry is, of course, as old as the "scientific management" concept of Frederick Taylor, whose experiments and writings date back to the late nineteenth century. Oddly enough, however, the concept of practical modern divisionalization never got anywhere until Taylor's "scientism"—the idea that man was a machine who could be "engineered" into efficiency by making him a time-motion-study guinea pig—was thrown into the discard.

In Taylor's heyday "scientific management" meant breaking down the motions of men into their simplest and most time-saving elements. The long assembly line for the product, the relegation of men to mechanically repetitive tasks, the integration of the product (raw materials, transportation, processing, assembly and sales) into straight-line relationship—these, if mastered, were deemed sufficient to the day by an older school of "scientific" managers.

The big break from the notion that workers are machines came when Elton Mayo discovered that the efficiency of men was bound up not so much with mechanical simplicity of motion as with their feeling that they were embarked on team projects in pleasant association with other men. Mayo showed by experiment that men worked more effectively when they had a hand in following something through from beginning to end.

The Mayo studies had nothing to do with divisionalization as such. But if the smaller team was more efficient than fragmented, isolated man within a given factory, it was only logical to suppose that a big company would do better if it were split into divisions according to region, product or customer appeal.

The modern "team" organized to carry a project through from beginning to end may utilize the Taylor principles of time-motion simplification. But "automation"—or the relegation of mechanically repetitive tasks to automatic machine operation—is making Taylorism obsolescent, if not obsolete, as applied to human beings. The notion of "scientific management" has been giving way to the idea of management as an art.

True, the lingo of "scientism" is still used by businessmen to describe divisionalization, but Mr. Mills of General Electric now speaks of decentralization as having "a kind of poetic rightness" because it "touches directly on the 'spirit' of men." "The decentralization of true authority," says Mr. Mills, "answers the need of all normal individuals in society to have a responsibility for some part, or some kind of, meaningful and lasting contribution to the betterment of their environment—in other words, personal purposefulness."

This is the language and the sentiment of "belonging"—and, in its own turn, the new concept is giving rise to some new fears. Thus William H. Whyte, Jr., in a recent book called *The Organization Man,* holds that "company men," living and working in small, homogeneous communities for large concerns, are losing contact with the older individualism that was born of struggle. The modern employee, says Mr. Whyte, is encouraged to "adjust," he is lapped in "beneficence" (profit sharing, pensions, etc.); and, "imprisoned in brotherhood," he ceases to fight for his own ideas as against those of the "team." This sort of criticism is a far cry from the day when the big organization was condemned for treating the employee as a soulless automaton.

But even if "belonging" contains hidden dangers to individualism—and to the originality which gives rise to new ideas and products—it is something that pays off in immediate productivity. It has immediate "survival value," for the companies which have encouraged it are doing better than the ones which stick to older patterns of organization.

The difficulties standing in the way of new team methods of "divisionalizing" are mainly technical. Knotty questions arise—such as whether to maintain separate sales forces for separate product divisions in a loosely related field; or how to arrive at fair cost figures when products are transferred from one division to another; or when to subcontract to another division; or how to contain small and large divisions within the same company; or when to spin off a product into a new subsidiary. But these are matters of detail.

The main thing is that the modern corporation is discovering ways of putting large aggregations of men, money and material together and making them work efficiently. Moreover—and this is the key to efficiency—it is doing this without turning men into automatons or ignoring their human problems. The principles of the new methods of organization may still be fuzzy at the edges, but the "art" of applying them—as distinct from the "science"—is becoming more and more understandable to all.

JOHN CHAMBERLAIN

January 7, 1957

Who Rises in U.S. Business and Why

What are the prerequisites for business success in America?

There are many who think the lines of advancement have become more and more constricted with the rise of the big corporation. But the facts are quite at odds with this popular supposition. Instead of hardening into stratification, American economic life has become more and more fluid in recent years. And the poor boy from the wrong side of the tracks has a better chance of becoming a top business executive now than he ever had before.

Such is the conclusion which leaps to the surface of two contemporary studies, *Big Business Leaders in America*, by W. Lloyd Warner and James Abeggien, and *The Big Business Executive*, by Mabel Newcomer.

Of course, it isn't as simple as all that; social position helps, money helps, education helps, and luck is always a factor. But the main point to be gleaned from the study of relevant samples in these two books is that "upward mobility" (to use Lloyd Warner's favorite phrase) has not been closed off by such things as the disappearance of the frontier. "The over-all difference is clear," say the Messrs. Warner and Abeggien. "The present-day business leadership includes more men from lower-level occupations. While both in 1928 and in 1952 most business leaders are sons of businessmen, the proportion is smaller now than a generation ago."

Both the Warner-Abeggien and the Newcomer books have the aesthetic and dramatic shortcomings of any literature that consists of prose woven about the manipulation of statistical samplings. Much of the writing is inevitably devoted to explaining the methodology of statistical interpretation. But if the structure of these books makes for dullness, the conclusions do not. Some of the conclusions are merely titillating, but others are little short of astonishing, at least for the single moment of initial impact.

Take, for example, the Warner-Abeggien conclusions about the opportunities open to the sons of white-collar workers, laborers and professional men over the course of a half century. According to the Warner-Abeggien statistical samplings the proportion of sons of white-collar workers in business leadership had virtually quadrupled during the period. The top-job chances of the son of a laborer doubled in 30 years. On the other hand, the chances of a son of the owner of a large business declined by a little more than one half.

With the sons of "major executives," there was neither progress nor retrogression; their opportunities in 1950 remained the same as they had been at the turn of the century. As for the sons of farmers, they have dropped in "business elite representation" in 30 years. But the number of farmers also declined during this time span to the point where statistics on the subject of "elite representation" by farmers' sons became meaningless.

The Warner-Abeggien team and Professor Newcomer manipulate their statistical samples in such a way that a vast number of curious and interesting psychological facts come into view. It would seem, for example, that to become good executive material it pays to have a shiftless father—provided that you have a determined mother "of the old school."

On the other hand, dynamic fathers tend to have undynamic sons; simply because the "old man" has solved the economic problem, the son takes it easy. It's all very obvious when you think it over—just as obvious as the fact, observed long ago by Branch Rickey, that "hungry" ballplayers tend to make better World Series competitors.

To rise in business it helps definitely to have gone to an Ivy League college. It helps most of all to have studied at Harvard or at Yale. But before you begin to make generalizations about Ivy League "snobbism" as a key to big-business "elite recruitment," stop and reflect upon a couple of facts.

One reason why Harvard figures so heavily in the statistics of business leadership is the opportunity offered by its fine graduate school of business administration. As for the "availability" of Yale men, that traces back to the job recommendations provided by the engineering courses of the Sheffield Scientific School. If Podunk U. had comparable facilities for training incipient business leaders, Podunk would rate with anything in Ivy League circles.

This matter of education, indeed, is a curious thing. According to Warner and Abeggien, certain big mail order houses actually discriminate against the Ivy League. They prefer to recruit their potential leaders from state universities "where they find men who have not lost touch with the vast masses of the people whose hopes and desires create the greatest market of all."

Do considerations of nationality, religion and racial origin keep people from rising in business? The only valid conclusion to be drawn from these books is that, to the extent such considerations play any part, different traditions govern different industries. If you want to rise in the railroad or the public-utility world, for instance, it does not hurt to be Irish—and a Roman Catholic. The reason has to do with the history of immigration; when the railroads and the utilities were abuilding, lots of Irish Catholics went to work for them and rose to the top in the course of time.

Professor Newcomer comes up with the interesting statistic that "Episcopalian membership among the executives is . . . ten times as high as it is in the whole population." Jews figure as leaders roughly in proportion to their numbers in the population, but an analysis of data shows that they are "heavily concentrated in the merchandising, entertainment and mass-communications fields."

There would seem to be no discrimination in American industry in general against foreign birth as such. Says Dr. Newcomer, "The proportion of foreign-born among the executives is lower than the proportion in the total of the United States population, but in view of the many handicaps of this group it is surprising to find it as high as it is." Canadians, in particular, do well in American industry: "the proportion of Canadians . . . far exceeds the proportion of Canadian-born in the total population."

To sum things up, the statistics of business leadership derive from an interaction of chance, propinquity and the presence of internal drive in specific individuals. Education plays an obviously important part but since education in America is open to practically anybody who wants it, it is the person with internal drive who tends to make the best use of it. Geography can be a limiting factor (Southerners, being traditionally far away from the centers of industry, are under-represented in the statistics of leadership), but it is bound to be less so as industry decentralizes itself.

In short, everything in America conspires to make "upward mobility" more and more possible for more and more people rather than less. Before they go making any more speeches about the narrowing of opportunity under capitalism the Messrs. Khrushchev and Bulganin might well take note.

JOHN CHAMBERLAIN

February 23, 1956

How to Get Fired

Top executives are finding it tougher and tougher to get fired these days.

Some do, of course. Plant managers, vice-presidents, presidents, even board chairmen occasionally are getting the gate. But it sometimes requires special effort. Those who lack the knack of getting sacked in style may find themselves suddenly shoved aside—or kicked upstairs.

Seldom before in the world of business has the power to fire been

more cautiously practiced. And with good reason. In this era of unprecedented corporate growth—and consequent dearth of mana-
gerial talent—enough men with executive ability are hard to find.
Then, too, there's a growing conviction in corporate counsels that
the outright firing of a key executive is more likely to sully a company's reputation than to strengthen it.

As one corporate official puts it: "The day of the hard-hitting
empire builder who fired an executive because he didn't like his
looks, or dismissed them wholesale because he was in bad humor, is
gone." Another observes: "There aren't many top-level executives
who've been fired in the past 10 or 15 years—too many safeguards
have been placed around management decisions these days for all
the blame to fall on one man."

To get an idea of how far companies will go to avoid firing an
executive, consider a couple of actual cases.

James C., an amiable chap, managed a plant for an electronics
parts producer in the Chicago area. This interfered not at all with
his sideline as an amateur radio operator. He turned an upstairs
storage room into a radio "shack" and put a transmitter tower atop
the factory roof. Mr. C. sloughed off his corporate duties every
chance he could and shambled up to his shack to chat by radio with
other ham operators the globe over.

For six years Mr. C. thus mixed his play and work. Eventually,
of course, the word was wafted on high. Was Mr. C. canned? No,
indeed. He was appointed "assistant to the president" and assigned
duties requiring less direct supervision. It helped, of course, that
Mr. C.'s superiors, like himself, were amateur radio addicts.

A farfetched example? Perhaps. But take Victor H., a meek, unobtrusive fellow who generally did what he was told to do as district
sales manager in precise, unquestioning manner. At last year's company Christmas party, Mr. H. got in his cups and became quite
loquacious. Thus fortified in spirits, he buttonholed the company's
executive vice-president and declaimed for all to hear that his policies were "ridiculous to say the least!" Curious to tell, Mr. H. still
works for the company, in his quiet, unassuming fashion.

Few who know the details behind firings of upper-echelon personnel are disposed to disclose them. "I don't even discuss them with
my own partners, they're that personal," exclaims a senior member
of a large consulting organization. However, more than a score of
top company officials—including this one—did provide *The Wall
Street Journal* with close to a hundred tales of executive firings.
They stipulated only that identities be disguised. They have been,
but the essential details of the firings are unchanged.

These stories—fascinating reading in themselves—also can be useful by alerting executives to possible pitfalls ahead, by staking out some danger areas and, generally, by turning the spotlight on an important area of employer-employee relationships that for the most part has been long left in the dark.

Foreknowledge, on the part of management or the executive involved, might have spared the brilliant manager of an Eastern factory who had helped turn his plant into a model among the company's producing facilities. His plant was a source of pride to directors of the firm. Several, who lived nearby, often took guests through it. During these tours, plant manager Alan G. came to know many of these people. He was invited to spend weekends in country homes, join hunting trips and otherwise hobnob with a social set new and exciting to him and his wife.

Little by little Alan G. began to lose touch with the operating people. He postponed a crucial decision, for example, when he had to catch a train to make a theater party. One day he was photographed at an elegant affair with some of his new friends by a national magazine and identified, quite accidentally, as being in a higher company position. Alan G.'s bosses, who already had some indications he was beginning to neglect his duties, had enough. They ordered him transferred to another, smaller plant some distance away—the equivalent, as far as he was concerned, of an invitation to depart from the organization. So he did.

Alan G., of course, was not entirely responsible for the events that led to his parting. But few executives are. As one management consultant puts it: "No executive firing is 100 per cent justified. Even alcoholism may be due to tensions the company has created. Or maybe unnecessarily frequent assignments away from home with heavy entertainment responsibilities contributed to it."

A man who manages to rise to a high position, most management experts agree, generally has the qualifications to keep him there— if his firm is willing to help him through special training or by providing him with the right kind of assistance. If an executive does flop, they suggest, he usually can be switched to another position within the company advantageous to both. "Seldom," says another consultant, "is it warranted to wash executive experience down the drain."

MITCHELL GORDON

February 25, 1957

The Organization Woman

The Lord created man, and industry came up with the organization man. Now Richardson, Bellows and Henry, a New York management consultant firm, is testing wives of organization men to see if they meet the proper standards for an organization woman.

So far the tests are confined to wives of organization men whose companies send people overseas. The general idea is to find out how this or that wife fits in. One troublemaking wife, the consultants know, can upset a whole community of organization men and women. And the wife who can't adjust to the food or the surroundings, or who doesn't like foreigners anyway, could cause the sheik to close down the pipeline.

To find out the chances of such happenings, the wife of the organization man is asked to fill out first a complete history, including age, though whether this will turn out to be useful as a gauge of accuracy or of imagination the firm isn't sure. She is asked to tell what adults she admires, and why, as well as what books and magazines she reads. She is given an oral intelligence test, a Rorschach blot test, and asked the difference between Botticelli and vermicelli. She will sort out blocks and squares and tell whether she'd rather collect butterflies or autographs. After that there's the psychoanalyst, and about time, too.

"When we're through," an official of the consultant firm explained confidently, "we have a complete picture of the woman."

Well, we wouldn't be quite so confident as Messrs. Richardson, Bellows and Henry seem to be. Friends of ours who think they know something about the ladies claim there is nothing a woman likes less than for anyone, including her husband, to have a complete picture of her. One of the enchantments of women is that they are, and ought to be, unfathomable, and most of them know it.

Further, some mysteries are best left unsolved. Life would be pretty dull for a man who really knew what makes the little woman tick, and it could be pretty dangerous for the man who acts on the assumption that he knows. In fact, it could completely disorganize the best of organization men.

EDITORIAL

September 29, 1958

Women Executives

Time was when women's place was in the home and the workplace was a masculine sanctuary. But that was before the Nineteenth Amendment, Emancipation, and Equality. Now, as Margaret Cussler reminds us in her *The Woman Executive* (New York: Harcourt, Brace, $3.95), even the executive suite is no longer safe from the rustle of skirts and the fragrance of perfume.

Dr. Cussler, herself a woman executive (the president of a documentary-film company and the partner of a motivational-research firm), looks upon the female invasion with a reasonably prideful eye and, happily, she has none of the suffragist militancy of a Carrie Chapman Catt or a Susan B. Anthony. Yet she observes that women executives still believe they have to struggle to win status, and that they still get various snubs from their male colleagues.

There are little snubs and big snubs. Little snubs may lie in a lack of status symbols—private offices (with window), secretaries, telephones, entree to the executive dining room, ghost writers for public pronouncements, committees and conferences, wall-to-wall carpeting. One woman executive told the author she was "furious" because her male colleagues rarely talked shop to her but only complimented her on her attractiveness and her "pretty dress."

Not all the snubs go with the workplace, however. Unmarried women executives on vacation, the author notes, long "to share the beauties of a trip through the Pacific Northwest with someone other than the waiter of the hotel, and dread the familiar query: 'Why haven't you ever married?' "

The big snub is financial, what Dr. Cussler calls "the root of all evil." That's the snub to the pocketbook—the absence of equal pay for equal work. The author says many women are sensitive to being sensitive (we never found them that way) and take salary discrimination without even grumbling. The trouble is, as the National Federation of Business and Professional Women, the sponsor of Dr. Cussler's study, has found out, women executives, though frequently "single women," nonetheless have dependents to support in many instances.

WILLIAM H. PETERSON

"I'm prescribing golf twice a week—fourteen clubs, no caddy, no scooter!"

HOW THEY PLAY

Living It Up

Deep in the thickly wooded mountains surrounding Portland, Oregon, there's a $60,000 hunting lodge staffed with a cook, a gardener and two other servants. The plywood firm that owns the place spends $10,000 a year on its upkeep alone, yet the hideaway's hunting and fishing preserves, skeet-shooting range and liquor supplies are all free to fortunate guests.

"Our top executives use this secret hangout for poker parties and general relaxation," says a company vice-president, "and its existence is unknown to most of our stockholders and lesser executives. A key to the lodge becomes sort of a reward upon elevation to a higher standing within our firm," he adds.

Hidden hunting lodges are one of the "fringe benefits" awaiting officials who succeed in working their way up to the executive suite of a good many U.S. corporations. Other impressive prizes: sharing use of yachts, private planes and railroad cars, jaunts to exotic watering places and spectacular soirees—all paid for by the corporation.

Companies maintaining private retreats, planes and other facilities for fun or luxurious traveling generally report they are necessary to the conduct of their business. They are used for entertaining important clients, for example, or for speeding executives' travel and getting the most efficient use of their time.

This undoubtedly is the prime reason for some companies maintaining such facilities, though perhaps not for others. Even in the former case, executives generally manage to get considerable enjoyment from their firms' luxury properties, sometimes in the company of clients and sometimes when the facilities are not needed for strictly business use.

In this way, a good many executives whose fortune-building efforts are impaired by today's high taxes still are enjoying the frills enjoyed by the Mellons, Morgans and Baruchs.

Bernard Baruch entertained business associates at Hobcaw Barony, his 17,000-acre duck-hunting estate in South Carolina. (He now entertains friends at a smaller South Carolina retreat, Little Hobcaw.) But officials of Minnesota Mining & Manufacturing Co., Olin Mathieson Chemical Corp. and Continental Motors Corp. come close to matching Mr. Baruch's hospitality at company-owned retreats. Andrew Mellon and Cornelius Vanderbilt relaxed amidst their fabulous art collections, but officials of International Business Machines Corp. and House of Seagram, Inc., can take their ease encircled by corporate-owned art works. J. P. Morgan cinched some of his biggest business deals aboard his luxurious yacht *The Corsair,* but corporate pleasure craft for executive use are so common today that Lloyd's *Register of American Yachts* lists 15 corporate owners under the A's alone.

Anheuser-Busch, Inc., has its own air-conditioned railroad car equipped with observation lounge, four bedrooms, two showers with germicidal lamps, a dining room that seats 10, three conference rooms, a telephone, a TV set, two servants, and a special tap for serving draught beer. "We have breweries in St. Louis, Los Angeles and Newark, and branch offices in twenty other cities, and we need this car so that our officials can visit these areas," a company spokesman explains.

A Texas oil company is so anxious to have its chief executive travel in comfort that it has supplied him with a richly appointed Boeing Stratocruiser that requires 2,000 gallons of expensive aviation fuel for a single filling of its massive gas tanks.

The eagerness of some corporations to supply their highly placed executives with the finest is recognized by a group of businessmen who cater to such demands.

Chicago's Conrad Hilton Hotel reports a "growing demand among top-level corporate executives" for its two Imperial suites that cost $600,000 to build and rent for a staggering $300 per day. This stiff tab entitles executives to a 2,000-square-foot living room complete with wood-burning fireplace, baby grand piano and color television set, plus a brace of bedrooms featuring wall TV sets controlled from beds made up with satin sheets and cashmere blankets.

Not all corporations are flooding their top executives with luxuries, to be sure. General Dynamics Corp.'s Convair Division is one of many concerns that profess to shun such "fringe benefits."

The recession also is cutting into corporate bounty. Tough times recently prompted a Southwestern manufacturer to order its traveling vice-president to eat in hotel dining rooms instead of taking his breakfast in bed. A steel company famed for the parties it throws at petroleum industry conventions has ceased offering oilmen a chance to win the companionship of two pretty girls for an "evening on the town."

Even when business is booming, corporations must be on the alert lest impulsive executives fall overboard in pursuit of the good life. Not too long ago, for instance, a Midwest manufacturing firm's chairman, its sales vice-president and a company director chartered a plane at company expense, loaded their wives aboard and headed west, ostensibly on a morale-boosting tour of select company dealers. Several dealers were instructed to show up at their local airdromes at specified times, and when the plane touched down the officials gave the dealers a half-hour pep talk while the ladies powdered their noses. After a day or two of this, according to the way other company executives tell the story, the officials turned the plane's nose toward Canada's scenic Lake Louise, and spent the rest of the week living it up. When word of the outing reached the company's distraught bankers and board of directors, the junketing officials got the old heave-ho.

March 18, 1958

Clubmen

In the rambling, high-ceilinged library of New York's University Club—a room built on the grandiose design of the Sistine Chapel— an elderly, white-maned member dozes peacefully in an oversized leather chair.

In Chicago's 12-story Illinois Athletic Club, several score members cluster around 14 billiard tables at the noon hour, while others dine nearby amid the din of clicking billiard balls and sporting banter.

To the casual visitor, the ways of urban clubdom may seem remarkably resistant to change. The athletic fraternities retain their aura of clamorous conviviality; the aristocratic old-line clubs still look as if J. P. Morgan himself might suddenly appear at the door.

Like many casual impressions, however, this one is largely illusory. Club life in the U.S. is indeed undergoing some basic changes.

For one thing, the typical old town club is changing in character from a social meeting place to a more business-oriented institution. At lunch hour the handsomely furnished dining halls resound with talk of stock yields or steel prices, while the cardrooms, libraries and lounges, once alive with activity, often stand almost deserted throughout the afternoons and evenings. And new clubs are arising designed specifically for the luncheon trade.

Moreover, business prestige rather than family lineage more and more determines one's chances for admission. High-ranking corporate officials, in fact, are becoming the "prize catch" of clubdom: Revenues from business entertaining provide the principal means of meeting ever mounting operating costs at many proud old clubs.

"This club will never again be what it was in the old days," declares an elderly member of New York's baronial Metropolitan Club, whose president in 1891 was Mr. Morgan himself. "Today's members don't seem to have the time or the inclination to devote themselves to club life. The cardrooms, which once were crowded during the day, now are empty, and the entire club is dead many evenings and weekends." Strolling across the club's sacrosanct Governors' Room—a chamber dominated by red leather chairs, huge gold-framed oil paintings and countless shelves of elegantly bound volumes—he adds: "And have you seen all the women running around these old halls? We never permitted that in the old days."

The Metropolitan, which is housed in an immense marble palace on Fifth Avenue and 60th Street, boasts such members as General Douglas MacArthur, shipping magnate Stavros S. Niarchos and I.B.M. president Thomas J. Watson, Jr.

What's responsible for the changes in city clubdom? Many factors enter in, of course: the trek to the suburbs (which has spurred the growth of country clubs); the growing popularity of outdoor activities (which has boosted the number of yachting and fishing clubs as well as golf clubs); the democratization of social values (which in turn stems from a similar democratization of prep-school and college life); the quickening pace of business; the rise of the income tax—and of the expense account.

"The old clubs still are important to lots of people, but they just don't represent a way of life any more," explains one New Yorker who belongs to two of the "best" clubs. "You have your business schedule in your left pocket along with your schedule of civic obligations, and your commuting schedule in your right pocket—I guess town clubs are monuments to a more leisurely age."

There's another factor, too, which is changing the club landscape: namely, economics. Despite repeated increases in dues and prices, total revenues of city clubs have risen 19 per cent over the last five years while payroll costs alone have soared by 25 per cent, according to a recent survey by the accounting firm of Harris, Kerr, Forster & Co., which numbers many top clubs among its clients.

To be sure, most business corporations have experienced similar cost increases over this five-year period. But clubs are not run as profit-making ventures and thus, in times of stress, cannot merely absorb rising expenses in reduced earnings. Further, many clubs are restricted in their efforts to turn up fresh sources of revenue. They can sharply boost dues only at the risk of disheartening young members; they can increase food and bar prices only at the risk of inhibiting use of club facilities; they can turn to the waiting list and admit scores of new members only at the risk of overcrowding the house.

Of course, not all clubs face this financial squeeze. "The healthiest clubs financially generally are the men's city luncheon clubs," observes one expert in club economics. "They can prosper on business entertaining (much of it on the expense account) and still keep down operating costs by remaining closed most of the day." This expert notes that while luncheon clubs have continued to multiply in many cities, the number of all-purpose social clubs has remained fairly static over the years.

Among the older and most revered luncheon retreats are Pittsburgh's elegant Duquesne Club, Chicago's high-perched Tavern Club and Boston's patriarchal Down Town Club, but these old-timers are being joined by some plush newcomers.

One of the best financed upstarts, for example, is the 675-member Pinnacle Club, perched atop the Socony Mobil Building on New York's East 42nd Street, and commanding a breathtaking view of Manhattan.

The Pinnacle was organized by a band of top-level industrialists including Charles S. Munson, chairman of Air Reduction Co., B. Brewster Jennings, president of Socony Mobil Oil Co., and Howard C. Sheperd, chairman of the First National City Bank of New York.

Despite a total admission cost of $1,875 (including taxes and initial dues) and an average daily luncheon bill of from $5 to $7, the

Pinnacle Club has a lengthy list of executives seeking to gain entry. "You get just about the best food and the best view in New York, and your company foots the bill," says one of the Pinnacle's original members.

The Pinnacle is geared strictly to the luncheon trade. Its facilities consist of a spacious modern dining room, an intimate bar which rarely dispenses anything but martinis and Scotch, and several small private rooms for business meetings.

One wall of the Pinnacle bar consists of a large one-way mirror which permits its occupants to look across a hall to big windows opening on a panorama of Manhattan's skyscrapers. At the same time, the trick wall permits other members on their way down the hall to the dining room to survey themselves in the mirror. One very celebrated New Yorker, known to all Americans (he shall remain nameless here), not long ago tarried for some moments at the mirror to fix his tie and adjust his stuck zipper—unaware that his actions were being viewed with great amusement by the bar occupants within.

Visit the Pinnacle on a typical weekday and you'll see members tackling jumbo steaks and chops or such specialties as *gevulde kalborst loftschotel* (a Dutch veal dish). When greeting diners, waiters are careful to give the host a gold-tasseled menu—that's the one with the prices—while guests get gray-tasseled menus unmarred by statistics.

Of course, the typical city club has neither the affluence nor the novelty of the Pinnacle. Its chief assets, in fact, often are its traditions and its "house"—both of which may actually be distinct liabilities in many ways. Its house, for example, which may have been built six or even seven decades ago in keeping with the noblest standards of Victorian elegance, may be extremely costly to maintain in this era of the $4-an-hour carpenter.

Its customs, too, may threaten the club's solvency. Says the scion of a distinguished family who belongs to several clubs around the country: "There are some fine clubs whose old-line members are fast dying off and whose only hope is to recruit promising younger men who have made a name for themselves in industry. But the old-timers hesitate—they still cling to the idea that only the bluebloods, the sons of the founders and so forth, deserve membership. They fail to see that the so-called social aristocracy has long been on the wane, that the business aristocracy is in the ascendancy."

As a result of these and related problems, some distinguished clubs recently have experienced troubled times. Even New York's elite Knickerbocker Club, which has a private "angel" in Governor Nelson Rockefeller, not long ago was considering a merger with the

Union Club as a partial cure for its financial ailments. In addition to membership problems, the Knickerbocker also was faced with a towering debt. Says one officer: "Things looked pretty black."

In recent months, however, the Knickerbocker has made a comeback. "We settled our $200,000 bonded indebtedness to certain members by paying ten cents on the dollar, and we managed to raise over $100,000 to build up a reserve fund," says an officer of the club. Moreover, the Knickerbocker has been busily recruiting younger members; those under the age of 30 need pay dues of only $100 a year, compared with $325 for senior members. The club, whose first president was Alexander Hamilton, now includes Winthrop Aldrich, John Jacob Astor and Nelson, Laurence and David Rockefeller.

Despite its patrician past, the Knickerbocker is rather plain in appearance compared with the neighboring Metropolitan or Union clubs. Its ceilings are unadorned, its dining rooms small and routinely, if comfortably furnished; its bar has almost a fraternity house air about it, with well-worn leather chairs and tables and a vague scent of spilled inebriants.

The Knick, too, has modified its customs with changing times. Its governors, for instance, now wear ordinary tuxedos to their monthly dinner meetings—quite a comedown from the regal days when top hat and tails were the only acceptable attire.

PETER B. BART

December 24, 1958

HEADACHES, HEARTACHES...
AND SOME HAPPY TIMES

WARS, COLD AND HOT

December 7, 1941

War with Japan means industrial revolution in the United States.

The American productive machine will be reshaped with but one purpose—to produce the maximum of things needed to defeat the enemy.

It will be a brutal process.

It implies intense, almost fantastic stimulation for some industries; strict rationing for others; inevitable, complete liquidation for a few.

War with Japan will be a war of great distances.

Thus, certainly in its preliminary stages and probably for the duration, it will be a war of the sea and the air.

This means unlimited quantities of ships and shells, bombers and bombs, oil, gasoline.

Eventually, it also means an Army dwarfing the present military establishment—5 million, 8 million. It's a guess. But that will come later.

These are the dominant factors which will channel the production of American factories, mines, farms and forests into the prosecution of a Far Eastern war.

The general outlines of the coming industrial revolution are visible in the shaping of the defense effort during the past year and a half.

The materials which already are scarce or hard to get will become just about nonexistent for civilian use. This applies with dead certainty to steel, alloys for steel, copper, tin, zinc, aluminum.

Now, and in the fairly immediate future, it will be necessary to add other products to this list. These will be materials and products which have come to be regarded by Americans as everyday necessities.

An oil shortage, with civilian oil rationing (gasoline, fuel oil), is inevitable sometime in 1942. It was expected before, it is a certainty now. (However, the chances are that both heating-oil and coal supplies are relatively safe for the winter.)

Textiles, wool and cotton goods, will become scarce. Mills now are laboring under their heaviest load of orders; their problem, and the problem of civilian clothing, will grow in direct ratio with the increase in the armed forces. But sometime next year civilians are going to stop being choosy about shirts, blankets, sheets, suits and dresses.

Leather, sooner or later, also will be added to the list of scarcities.

Then there are the important commodities which must travel the now dangerous trade routes from the Far East. Primarily, these are rubber and tin. Secondarily, there is coconut oil, tungsten, chromium, copra, tung oil, palm oil, manila hemp, jute, graphite. Sugar, too, comes from the Philippines, but there are ample supplies available from the West Indies and the continental United States.

Thus, American industry now divides itself automatically into war-useful and war-useless categories. And, again, particular emphasis must be placed on the modifying geographical character of an American-Japanese war.

Because such a war puts great stress on planes and ships many industries will work to the limit of their capacity, expand and expand again. These include: steel, shipbuilding (warships and merchant vessels), aircraft (emphasis on long-range bombers), ordnance machine tools. Plus, of course, all the now familiar list of supplying and complementary industries.

WILLIAM F. KERBY

December 8, 1941

Civilian Front

WASHINGTON—Price Administrator Prentiss M. Brown announced relaxation of the pleasure-driving ban in the 12 northeastern states to permit one vacation trip this summer.

Mr. Brown said that the Office of Price Administration will permit such trips, however, only where motorists have enough gasoline in their existing ration books, and will not grant any additional gasoline for the purpose. All other provisions of the pleasure-driving ban remain in effect. Thus, it will be illegal to take the family out for a Sunday picnic in a nearby park, while it will be legal to make a trip to a distant resort.

July 7, 1943

Ice Cream

CHICAGO—The average American will have to be satisfied with 9½ pounds of ice cream this year.

Translated into consumer language, that means less than a dish a week, or, by juvenile standards, approximately 95 ice cream cones a year.

This represents a tremendous slump in the country's favorite dessert. Last year the figure was 15.2 pounds, but for the four-year period of 1935–39, a period that government statisticians are inclined to regard as "normal," it was only nine pounds.

Wartime shortages of sugar and milk are largely responsible. Demand for ice cream, some manufacturers guess, is running as much as 60 per cent above a year ago, but they can't come anywhere near supplying it. The reason is that the Government, while regarding ice cream as a basic food, has limited the manufacturers to 65 per cent of the amount of milk solids they used in 1942 and to 70 per cent of their consumption of cane sugar in 1941. The use of natural flavorings has also been hit, because the manufacturers of these flavorings in turn have been hurt by reduced sugar supplies.

August 3, 1943

Pawnshop Slump

Manhattan pawnbrokers are complaining of hard times.

Business is off "almost 50 per cent" since 1941 and loans are fewer than in any year since the late 1920s, most of them say.

In dingy Bowery shops, reeking of moth balls, proprietors report that "international seafaring" customers don't give them the business they used to. They're "not in town long enough." And the best neighborhood clients, men between 18 and 30 who habitually "lived too fast" and pawned the same wrist watch several times a year, have gone into the Army.

Failures are still rare. (There are only 13 fewer licensed pawnshops in the five boroughs of New York than during the depression depth of 1933.) But this is partly because it is so hard to get out of the pawnbroking business. If you stop loaning on the first of one year, you have to stay in business until 30 days after the first of the next, to give pledgers time to redeem.

August 5, 1943

Shift to Peace

WASHINGTON—Government controls which have guided the day-to-day activities of individuals and businesses will start to disappear now that the surrender of Japan is a fact instead of the imminent possibility of the past week.

First to lift its regulations was the War Manpower Commission. It announced last night that all manpower controls were removed. "Bill Jones" the factory worker and "Joe Smith" the office worker now can make a change in jobs without government approval. Employers are permitted to expand their working force without official sanction.

Ration books, the housewife's most cherished possession, soon will lose much of their importance. With the exception of sugar, meats, fats and oils, foods shortly will become point-free.

Those who would travel will be able to get their car tanks filled with coupon-free gasoline, probably within a week. But space on the railroads, airlines and motorbuses will remain tight for a few more months as the military services speed demobilization.

Industry, rigidly controlled as to what and how much was produced during the war, will begin regaining its freedom.

The War Production Board has what it calls a "master" plan for reconversion after V-J Day. Under this program most controls will be dropped. Some will be kept for a while—those considered necessary to supply the continuing, but greatly reduced, needs of the military, and those needed to make certain that scarce materials go into the most essential goods.

The prospect is that within 60 days makers of such consumer durable goods as passenger automobiles, refrigerators and washing machines will be free of W.P.R. production controls. Quotas now imposed on their output would be lifted.

Taxes will move down from their wartime peaks, but these first cuts, planned for enactment by Congress this fall, will not become effective until January 1, 1946. The outlook is that Congress will lighten individual income taxes and ease the load on corporations by cutting the excess-profits tax.

Wage and salary controls, which are a part of the over-all economic-stabilization program, will continue on the books for a while yet. But there may be some immediate relaxation to permit wage rate boosts to partially offset the loss in take-home pay which will result from the return to a 40-hour work week.

But the shift to the ways of peace will not be without its problems—problems for individuals, for business and for Government.

The end of the war, months earlier than had been expected until a few days ago, will be followed by a flood of orders cutting back and cutting off war contracts.

Many workers—they will be numbered in the millions—will be thrown out of work. Some will move quickly into other jobs. But until reconversion has been pretty well completed and industry is fully ready to start turning out goods to meet a huge demand piled up during the war, many will be unemployed.

GEORGE B. BRYANT, JR.

August 15, 1945

Germany's Future

FRANKFURT-ON-MAIN—Given the opportunity and means, the German people are likely to achieve economic reconstruction as soon as, if not sooner than, any other nation in Europe.

The Allies have to face that probability. They have to decide whether to put the brakes on reconstruction and, if they are to be put on, to decide how hard. If they are unable to decide within the next few months, it is fairly certain that the Germans will decide for them. It is not certain whether, even if an attempt is made to put the brakes on, the Germans won't foil it.

Today, all Germany is "anti-Nazi." All Allied officers in touch with employers and workers tell the same tale about their eagerness to co-operate and collaborate. An American textile leader who has just toured German mills said the outstanding impression left on his mind is the intensity of the desire of manufacturers to get their plants working again.

The Britisher mainly responsible for the operation of Ruhr coal mines asserts every mineworker is offering the hand of friendship. The *Oberpräsident* of one of the Rhine military districts, upon entering office, launched the slogan "Friendship and Work." On their

own initiative cities are changing all the names of streets commemo-
rating Nazis. The burgomaster of one town, finding ruins still un-
cleared, ordered all able-bodied male residents to work ten hours
daily seven days a week under threat of fine for the first offense and
prison for the second. In various rural districts children have been
mobilized to make war on the Colorado beetle.

To prove the German has not lost his taste for work you might
add the tributes paid to German war prisoners already employed in
Allied countries, so long as they are left to work by themselves. The
German has not lost, either, his genius for organization, based on
sense of discipline.

It is remarkable, for instance, that Allied authorities ten weeks
after the unconditional surrender can find no trace of a breakdown
of price controls, or growth of a black market, despite the disorganization of central, provincial and local government, including
police. Nor is there any tendency to withdraw money from the
banks, despite the disorganization of the entire banking and monetary system of the Reich and the inevitable deterioration of its
financial structure.

Amid all the confusion there has not been an increase in lawless-
ness among the German population. Occupying troops haven't encountered serious acts of aggression. "We want ourselves to keep
order and avert military measures," said one of the German officials
already quoted.

To make the Germans themselves responsible under supervision
for maintaining order, public services, food supplies and communications is an accepted principle of military government as con-
stituted in the American, British and French zones, as also probably
in the Russian, though little or nothing is known about Russian
methods or plans outside Russia. It is the only practicable basis on
which to establish the occupation.

A little band of officers and enlisted men can be found in each
city supervising law courts and police, public health, transport,
water and power, food rationing, housing, organization of labor exchanges, reopening of banks and schools, revival of agricultural and
industrial production, as well as the movements of displaced persons.
The network extends throughout the western half of the Reich. For
want of trained personnel it is not always perfect. But it seeks to be
fair and just, to avoid tyranny and inquisition.

This system is on trial. It is well adapted to present conditions in
which each locality is isolated from its neighbor as well as from
larger grouping of localities and provincial and central government.
What links there are must perforce be through Allied military organization. And if little by little administrative organization is

extending into larger and larger areas, it has yet to be seen whether or to what degree the old centralization in one capital can or should be restored.

Today, Germany is split into a thousand and one little pieces, themselves tending to group under the four military zones of occupation. The degree of collaboration, co-ordination or consolidation of these four zones has yet to be determined. All that seems certain is that some sort of uniform administration must be worked out in certain fields, notably communications, commerce and finance.

But, even when that is decided, the larger question remains: Just what is the economic role that the Allies shall assign to Germany in the postwar Europe?

On that point three of them, occupying the western half, know each other's views—and they are not necessarily identical in all respects. Even if they were, they would not attempt to formulate an agreement before learning and discussing the views of the fourth, Russia. Nevertheless, at the forthcoming meeting in Berlin, intended to coincide with the coming into operation of the Allied Control Council for Germany, that great question must be decided.

CHARLES R. HARGROVE

July 9, 1945

Sweating It Out

WASHINGTON—The Truman Administration got into the Korean War in a moment of inspiration and now it is relying on perspiration to get us through.

The President made the momentous decision to fight in Korea as a "calculated risk." But so quickly was it made, his advisers are only just now beginning to calculate all the risks and think of what to do to meet them. Each new decision is sweated out as another new decision is forced upon them.

There are at the moment no plans for carrying on a war with Russia in the unlikely event that one should develop. Plans have just begun on what to do if—as is more likely—Russia stays out but the "limited warfare" still fails to save the South Koreans. Neither the diplomats nor the military have buckled to the problem of what to do if the little war turns into a long stalemate.

This simple fact of the improvisation of Korean policy does much to explain the confusion and contradictions in the reports from Washington—the fact that everyone admits we have taken a desperate gamble—and yet Congress intends to leave town for a holiday.

What seems to be an attempt at calmness is just a product of uncertainty. Nobody knows what's coming, much less what to do about it when it comes.

The decision to fight in Korea was made personally by the President, and it was as much a surprise to some of his closest advisers, diplomatic and military, as it was to the public. The haste in which it was made obviously precluded any but the most rudimentary calculations about the moves ahead on this complex chessboard.

There is good reason to believe that the President decided to fight, in his own mind at least, as early as last Sunday even though the decision was not confirmed until Monday.

White House intimates, with the perception of hindsight, recall that after the President returned hastily from Missouri on Sunday he remarked that the Communist march in the Far East could no longer be "ignored" and spoke strongly of the need for "vigorous action." But at this point no one took the words to mean we should shoot in Korea.

Their significance was overlooked because up to that moment the Administration's announced, and apparently firm, policy was to "draw the line" through the Philippines and Okinawa. Formosa was to be written off, and Korea was thought not worth the gamble of war. Secretary of State Acheson was (and still may be) opposed to a fight for Korea.

The decision to reverse this policy was made on the spur of the moment. There can be only guesses as to why this moment and this place were picked for the reversal, but one important factor was an intelligence report from the military that, if the Russians stayed out, the Communist Koreans could be halted.

In any event, late Sunday the State and Defense departments were ordered to discuss ways and means of taking the "vigorous action." By Monday afternoon, as is now generally known, the concept of limited warfare was developed, and that night it was approved and sent to General MacArthur.

The point is that this fateful decision was made by President Truman himself, possibly even before he had talked with his advisers and certainly against the previous advice of his Secretary of State.

The actual thinking about ways of implementing the decision, of its costs and risks, was in a time span of less than 24 hours. The decision itself marked a complete and unexpected reversal of the Far Eastern policy. Indeed, many key officials had no inkling that it had been made until it was publicly announced on Tuesday.

Under such circumstances, there could be no careful calculation of all the risks. Apparently only one risk—the risk of open war with Russia—was seriously debated because of the military's confidence it could clean up the "local" situation quickly. This Russian risk was taken because of other intelligence reports that said Russia "isn't ready."

Nor, under such circumstances, could there be anything more than the most cursory planning on how to carry through even if the Russians stay out. With the main decision made on Monday, the conferees adjourned to think about the other problems tomorrow.

They are just now beginning to think about the alternative risks. An open war with Russia, tragic as it would be, would at least make decision easy. War itself is so big a problem it sweeps little problems away. But the mire of a half war makes decision difficult.

How much blood and tears is Korea worth? Do we make a token effort or do we go all-out for this remote peninsula? Do we send ground groups and risk another Bataan in a second gamble to back the first gamble?

Korea is worth nothing except as a symbol. We went into this shooting war to wage a political fight against the Russians. Today it looks like the shrewd Russians may simply ignore the challenge, neither backing down nor openly fighting. As in Greece and the Berlin airlift, we may be left to expend our energy while the Russians rest.

Thus we may be drawn deeper into a war against a little man who isn't there. Are we willing to expend the wealth of lives and material that may be necessary to win a prize of uncertain value? But, having committed ourselves this far, can we afford to quit?

These were the questions not talked out. The decision was made on impulse, on the feeling that it must be sometime and might as well be now, and in the faith that the Army that won a big war could easily win a little one. These unanswered questions have the diplomats and the soldiers sweating in the morning after.

VERMONT ROYSTER

June 30, 1950

Warmongering

Soviet propaganda has long maintained that "Wall Street monopoly-capitalist imperialists" are getting ready to start a new war.

You can find this warmongering accusation in almost any Russian newspaper or magazine of the last three years. It appears constantly

"We can make a lot of new records with this baby, but let's wait until the Russians pull off some new stunt."

in the press and radio of the satellite nations, in Soviet-sponsored books and pamphlets in Berlin. It has been heard at diplomatic conferences and in the United Nations. It is a cry frequently raised in America, by no means exclusively by Communist tongues.

The argument goes something like this: American "monopoly-capitalists" made tremendous profits from the last war. Therefore they like war and want more of it. To this unseemly lust is added necessity, for the American economic system would break down under peace conditions.

Stated thus baldly, the charge sounds ridiculous. But the Soviets have carefully developed and embellished it, using as a basis the economic theories of Marx and Lenin, according to which capitalist society is subject to recurring and ultimately destructive crises; to stave off its own destruction, capitalism becomes imperialist and resorts to wars.

The one (and once pre-eminent) Soviet economist—Varga—who suggested that the postwar economy of the United States could endure for a number of years without a major depression, and hence without having to go to war, had of necessity to be denounced. Not only was his view heretical; it also tore the heart from the charge that United States business interests are preparing a new war to save themselves from economic collapse.

This idea of American warmongering is perhaps the most stock-in-trade of Soviet propaganda. A devastating charge in itself, it provides a convenient springboard for attacks on the Marshall Plan, the Truman program for technological assistance to underdeveloped areas, the Atlantic Pact and practically anything else the Kremlin happens not to like.

But its best service is performed as a red herring, a deflection of interest from what oneself might be up to. If a country has aggressive intentions it can best mask them by accusing some other country of having them. To suppose the Soviet charge against American business is without effect on a great many people in many parts of the world is to overestimate human resistance to hammerlike repetition as a means of thought conditioning.

Let us look first at the war-profits part of the accusation. According to *Izvestia,* "monopolistic capital in the U.S.A. pocketed $52,-900,000,000 between 1940 and 1946, after taxes."

It is hard to tell what the Soviets mean by "monopolistic capital"; they never define it. Assuming they mean corporations, of which there were just under 425,000 in the United States in 1945, their figure is not far off; total corporate profits after taxes for the six years 1940 through 1945 were about $55 billion. That, of course, is not at all the same as saying this figure represents war profits. It represents total profits of nearly half a million corporations for everything they produced, including the implements of war.

Even if this figure were all war profits, it would scarcely prove the Soviet contention that war is more profitable for American businessmen than peace. In the most "profitable" war year, 1944, total corporate profits, after taxes, were $10.8 billion, or not a great deal more than in the peace year of 1929, when they were $8.4 billion. Indeed, for the war year 1945 they were only $8.7 billion. And 1944, the "best" war year, compares very unfavorably indeed with the peace year 1947, when total corporate profits after taxes exceeded $18 billion.

All of which is to say nothing, of course, of the fact that since war destroys capital, it would be somewhat idiotic of capitalism deliberately to seek to destroy its own subsistence.

If the Soviet charge that war is profitable for American business is demonstrably false, what of the capitalist economy's "need" for war, its incapacity to endure the conditions of peace?

The approximately 50 years from the end of the Civil War to the beginning of the First World War saw the greatest expansion, industrially and otherwise, in United States history. Factories sprang up, the nation was bound together by rail—200,000 miles of track by 1900—and trade flourished as never before. With economic growth came scientific advance—four million patents issued between 1890 and 1900—and phenomenal extensions of education, with the fruits of capitalism endowing libraries and universities.

These are facts well known to any high-school student. What is relevant here is that this half century of growth which formed the basis of the present American capitalist economy was also—with the exception of the brief and, from the viewpoint of military comparison, insignificant Spanish-American War—an era of peace.

Far from coincidence, that growth would literally not have been possible if the United States had been entangled in the European wars of the time, much less in anything comparable to the mass destruction of the two world wars of the twentieth century.

But perhaps American capitalism underwent some mystic change after those 50 years of development; perhaps, for some obscure reason, having grown on peace, it suddenly required war to sustain it. If that was the case, it is surprising it did not provoke wars instead of having to be virtually dragged into both world wars after, in both cases, years of nonbelligerence.

Who were those Wall Street monopoly-capitalist imperialists who forced the United States into the Second World War? It is difficult to recall any who were prominent in the ranks of the interventionists in 1938. It is even more difficult, in 1949, to find any urging an attack on the Soviet Union. Except, of course, in the imagination of the Kremlin's propagandists.

JOSEPH E. EVANS

April 4, 1949

Knocking Oneself Out

Mr. Ray Robinson is not the first nor the last to knock himself out and topple before a lesser foe.

Mr. Robinson, as those who read the sports pages will know, took on a Mr. Maxim, a slow, plodding sort of fellow, for the light-heavyweight championship of the world. Mr. Robinson was by far the best fighter; skillful, determined and courageous. As a matter of fact, he walked right up to victory and then fell prone on the face.

Mr. Robinson was a victim of too much effort too soon, of planning a short fight when he had to fight a long one. What failed him was not courage but staying power. Mr. Maxim won by the simple device of shuffling along while Mr. Robinson wore himself out in the heat.

It is an old, familiar story, among nations as well as gladiators. It was the Pharaohs who knocked out the Egyptians and Rome that licked the Romans. The barbarians just shuffled up and pushed.

Mr. Stalin is not the first ruler who, by accident or design, has just plodded along in his campaign for conquest while waiting for a great opposing nation—one skillful, determined and courageous— to knock itself out.

We don't think anyone—including Mr. Stalin—has the slightest idea that Russia could now defeat this country in a fight. A war, a World War III, would be bloody and horrible and it might leave us with an empty victory. But no one doubts that in the end we would have that victory.

The only real danger to the United States is that it will wear itself down and knock itself out.

Russia is not beating its brains out in Korea. It does not have the bulk of its army tied down there in an endless and almost hopeless fight. It is not sapping its manpower or burning up its resources. It is we who are wearing ourselves down with the sparring and the clinching which even though it wins points will not end the bout.

It is we who are gearing ourselves up for a fast pace; the Russians who are shuffling along.

It is we, not the Russians, who are undertaking to support and arm not merely ourselves but the whole world and for a time we know not the end of. It is we who are pouring out our substance, beating ourselves down with taxes, paralyzing ourselves with controls, sapping our strength with inflation.

Sure, say we swaggering, we can lick the Russians just like we licked the Germans and the Japs. Sure, we are the mightiest industrial nation in the world with great reserves of economic strength to back up our skill and our courage and our determination.

But if we keep wasting our substance, frittering away our strength, what are we doing to our staying power? Is our strength so limitless that we can never wear it out?

Mr. Ray Robinson is not the first nor the last to knock himself out and topple before a lesser foe.

EDITORIAL

June 27, 1952

The Value of Geneva

The meeting at the summit seems to have ended pretty much as it began—as little more than a breaking of bread between adversaries who will agree on nothing except that they would like to agree.

This has given to the Big Four meeting an air of futility. When the statesmen departed over the weekend, nothing was settled. Germany is still dismembered. The satellites are still under the Russian thumb. NATO and the Warsaw pact nations still face each other as opposing military alliances. The armaments, East and West, are being piled up as rapidly as before.

And this is bound to make the return of the statesmen something of a disappointment. For in spite of all their efforts to caution against hope—in Premier Bulganin's words it was "naïve to look for settlements"—some hopes nonetheless had been raised that when the statesmen did sit down face to face perhaps something could be done. Nothing was. What was proposed by one side was disposed of by the other. On any tangible scoreboard, the score was zero.

Nevertheless, we think, there was an accomplishment in the meeting at Geneva. And the fact that it is largely intangible does not make it less something of value.

There are three things we might have found at Geneva.

We might have found the Russians actually ready to agree. Or we might have found them as belligerent as ever with no desire at all to agree on anything. The first would have been a miracle; the second would have at least had the virtue of removing uncertainty.

Finally, there is what we did find—Communist leaders apparently desirous of agreeing on something, for their own private reasons, but unwilling to do now any of the things necessary to make agreement possible.

This may seem like no gain at all. Of what earthly use is agreeableness that comes to no agreement? Does it not lead to an even more frustrating kind of futility than more straightforward obstinacy?

We do not think that is necessarily the case. Whenever an adversary in a struggle finds the struggle oppressive or frightening and wishes to lessen it, it does not follow that he will promptly yield everything. He will still seek the most favorable bargain. He might not yield at all because he may think yielding worse than the struggle. But certainly a gain has been made when he once reaches the point of considering how he might settle. Then there is a chance which before did not exist at all.

Geneva showed the Russians in this mood. They would agree to none of our proposals on Germany. But it was not so long ago they considered East Germany their permanent domain and the price of unification was adding West Germany to it. Today they demand all sorts of impossible conditions, but they have got around to talking about a unified Germany as a distinct nation. That the Russians would do this was unthinkable not so very long ago.

The pattern was alike on other subjects. They were seeking hard bargains. But they did propose—and counterpropose. They were seeking, nonetheless, to bargain.

The reasons for this are obscure. But we will venture two possible ones that have nothing to do with a change in Russian ethics or goodwill.

One could be an awareness that the cold war has been going against them; that Communism, while perhaps still undaunted, is not, after all, the swift wave of the future. Men experienced in power have taken the measure of opposing power.

The other, and the one to be most devoutly hoped, is that these men may have taken the measure of modern war and found in it no victory. They would not hesitate to murder, slaughter or enslave. They pause before a war that could gain them nothing and lose them all.

Indeed, the most heartening thing to be found at Geneva is the feeling buried among the debris of words that a world war no longer offers to conquerors even the promise of a prize. This may not banish wars, for there are other roots to them than greed. But it does hold hope that wars have ceased to serve as instruments of ambition.

It would have been happier, it is true, to have the statesmen come home from Geneva with the deeds all done. And it is true that the peace we reach for still lies beyond the grasp. But surely there is some value in finding, after all these years, that the reach can be extended.

EDITORIAL

July 25, 1955

What's in a Crime?

HONG KONG—So many confusing anti-Communist sins and crimes are being proclaimed in Red China's anti-"rightist" crusade that a simplified glossary of Communist jargon seems to be in order.

Here is an attempt, then, to define simply the more grievous deviations and offenses ascribed to the reactionaries and "rightists" now under arraignment and denunciation throughout China:

Commandism. Throwing your weight around without first consulting the top party man who has a say in, or can be personally embarrassed by, your promotion. This sin is often committed in rural areas by young cadres who try to teach old peasants how to suck eggs without getting their formula, right or wrong, approved by their superior.

Cosmopolitanism. Any suggestion that Western culture is superior in any aspect to Communist culture, that the Empire State Building is taller than the Temple of Heaven, that Aylesbury duck is fatter than Peking duck, that Cromwell had a bigger wart on his face than Mao Tse-tung has.

Dogmatism. Officially (and piously), "uncritical acceptance of Communist doctrine without considering the conditions of its application." But, in practice, of course, it all depends on who does the considering and the accepting.

Economism. Preferring the arguments of economists, scientists and experts to those of party political leaders.

Equalitarianism. The absurd notion that a Yangtze peasant should earn as much as a Shanghai factory worker, or that a Shanghai factory worker should earn as much as a party functionary; the equally absurd notion that the "incentive" system of paying bonuses and rewards to more industrious workers, while palpably vicious in capitalist countries, should at least be considered undesirable also in China.

Formalism. The decadent aspiration of art for art's sake; setting more store on artistic technique and style than on the party "message."

Naturalism. A writer's offense when he describes life and events as they are instead of as they ought to be.

Objectivism. Officially, "to adopt an impartial and natural manner, under a pretended theoretical absence of party spirit." In other words, to consider the arguments on the other side.

Particularism. To try to put one's own particular and personal interests above those of the party.

Personality Cult. Mao Tse-tung is, of course, the omniscient exception to this rule; but it is naturally counterrevolution most foul and foolish to whisper "personality cult" at any hero-worshiping rally which Mao attends.

Practicism. In theory, "to work pragmatically without considering the Marxist theory behind the practical result." In practice, the sin of a scientist who tries to solve a laboratory problem without considering whether the solution harmonizes with the interests of state and party.

Reformism. The heresy that capitalism can be reformed by working honestly with socialist or leftist parties in capitalist countries—although the party line may expediently direct this course as a dishonest and temporary stratagem.

Sectarianism. Refusal or reluctance to switch back from the left (as above in reformism) to the right, in accordance with another expedient turnabout in the party line. A faithful party member who has escaped the crime of reformism by "pretending" to be a "reformist" may thus, in some bewilderment, find himself guilty of sectarianism by forgetting which side is which. This is definitely a trap for young players.

Social-Democratism. Placing petty-bourgeois patriotism above the opportunity for treason and world revolution in time of war.

Spontaneity. Letting the people make up their minds spontaneously about their future.

Subjectivism. The archheresy and unforgivable sin (which really is a blanket cover for all the crimes in the Communist code)—to think for yourself instead of as the party tells you to think.

RICHARD HUGHES

March 20, 1958

Drawing the Line

WASHINGTON—President Eisenhower yesterday served notice the U.S. is ready to go to war in the Mideast if necessary to prevent the overthrow of any more friendly governments in that area.

His notice serving—in the form of ordering U. S. Marines to land in beleaguered Lebanon—was directed at Arab leader Nasser and other anti-Westerners in the Middle East. It was an attempt at a final drawing of the line in an effort to hold onto what's left of Western influence in the Mideast.

Any future coups that come as swiftly as Monday's Iraq upheaval may make U.S. intervention even more difficult than in Lebanon, where the pro-Western government has been able to hold out for some time against rebel onslaughts. But the U.S. hope is that its armed intervention in support of the Lebanese government will deter revolutionaries in other lands.

Despite Mr. Eisenhower's statement that the Marines' landing wasn't "any act of war," the possibility of war is definitely present—and it is clear that the President thinks it is a risk worth taking to keep Lebanon and other friendly governments in the Western camp.

In a special message to Congress late yesterday, the President acknowledged that the Marines' landings "may have serious consequences." But he said he had decided that "despite the risks involved this action is required to support the principles of justice and international law upon which peace and a stable international order depend." And Mr. Eisenhower said the U. S. would increase the number of troops in Lebanon "as required."

It was far from clear, however, just what the Marines were to do in Lebanon. They were given the immediate mission simply of securing the capital city of Beirut and the nearby airport. It was not planned to use them to seal off Lebanon's border with Syria to bar infiltrators.

The question arose immediately as to what the Marines would do if they were attacked by the Lebanese rebels, some of whom are barricaded in Beirut. Would the U. S. troops fight? No one in Washington was answering this question directly. But a Pentagon spokesman said the Marines had orders to shoot if necessary. One military official said the Marines would "have to play it by ear."

JOHN R. GIBSON

July 16, 1958

Mideast Crisis: Eisenhower Legend Tested

OTTUMWA, Iowa—The heroes of Greek and Roman legend often made mistakes. But America's legendary heroes are almost always perfect: Lee failed only because of Gettysburg, Lincoln stumbled in his early Presidential years only because of bad generals, and Franklin Roosevelt made foreign-policy blunders only through illness and foolish advisers.

Much has been said of the Eisenhower legend and of the great hold the President has on the hearts of his countrymen. In the current Middle East crisis this is once again being demonstrated. Talks with dozens of people in six states in the East and Midwest give one the impression that while there is widespread disappointment in the President's regime, he himself remains highly popular. If anything, his intervention in the Middle East has heightened this popularity.

That could change, of course, if the present dangerous trend of events leads to a bloody explosion. Something like that happened to President Truman as the Korean War dragged on. But he never had the deep veneration so many hold for Dwight Eisenhower.

Here in Ottumwa, for example, a leading businessman recently said: "The President is a very great man. He is one of the three greatest Americans in history. I was not in favor of what he did in the Middle East, but no one is better qualified to make such a decision than Eisenhower. Therefore, I accept it."

This man, to be sure, is a Republican. But one hears much the same thing from an Indiana Democrat of New Deal persuasion. And listen to S. N. Glassman, interviewed in Newark, New Jersey, who is proud of his independent-voter status. He uses almost the same words as the Ottumwa Republican: "Eisenhower is a very great man," and adds: "What he did in the Middle East is what any decent man would have done to preserve liberty."

However, Mr. Glassman has apparently had a rising sense of disquiet as events have progressed, for he also says: "If there had been more time, perhaps the President would have acted differently. You know, he has to depend on his advisers, and sometimes they let him down."

Over and over one hears this belief—that if there have been mistakes by the Administration and most voters will acknowledge there have been many, they are not really President Eisenhower's fault.

"Foreign policy has too often lagged behind the events," says an Ohio traveling man, "but that is mostly the fault of Dulles; he doesn't seem to know what he is doing much of the time." There is little suggestion in this man's views that the President is responsible for Mr. Dulles, and when this is pointed out, he notes that the President has not been well much of the time, that "it is the duty of people like Dulles to take some of that responsibility off of his shoulders." This man, incidentally, describes himself as a Democrat.

The same blaming of the advisers, rather than the President, is heard for troubles other than those in foreign relations.

Here in Iowa, and in Illinois also, one hears the farmer and the farm town merchant blaming Ezra Benson for lower price-prop difficulties rather than the President. "Ike's no farmer; he's a military man and depends too much on Benson," said a merchant in Donnellson, Iowa, a town of less than 1,000 population.

A Pennsylvania textile man believes the President has been "ill-advised" on tariff policies, which have let foreign textiles into the U. S. An Indiana banker blasts "monumental spending" but blames it on "the military." Almost everywhere there are dark references to Sherman Adams letting the President down.

This is not to say that one doesn't run into a minority of people who take pot shots at the President himself. For example, in Huntington, Indiana, a former Taft supporter bangs his fist on the table and declares: "I'm confused. Eisenhower ought to know more about this Mideast thing than it seems he does. But the whole picture on that side of the world is a mess. I can't help but contrast it with Japan, where MacArthur told the Russians where to head in. Eisenhower was in charge in Europe, you know."

The feeling of some disappointment in the Administration comes through even in talking to the staunchest Republicans. Consider a trio of such voters interviewed on the streets of Newark.

Ruth Goodger, a businesswoman, says she used to be a "radical Republican" but is not so much so now. Why? There is nothing specific, just a feeling that things generally haven't been what she had hoped. Yet, she too tends to blame advisers, rather than the President.

Or listen to Robert Pope, a strapping young Negro postal employee who has obviously studied most of the big issues of our times. He has never voted anything but Republican, and while he thinks the President has generally done a good job in the face of very great problems, he feels there has also been a lack of push. "As a Negro, I may be overly conscious of the civil-rights issue, but I think there have at times been retreats as well as advances," he says. But he goes on to say that he admires the President for the way he has faced criticism—"much more like a President should than his predecessor did."

Or to Vincent Radice, a maintenance man who is a Democrat but voted for Eisenhower in the last election. With him, the disappointment was in the recession, but he believes that is proving temporary and is glad, over all, that he voted for the President.

And in one's travels the reporter comes across other, less concrete, attitudes toward the President that enhance the picture of a man who personally can do almost no wrong as far as many Americans are concerned.

Besides the Republicans who see him in this light, and believe rightly or wrongly that he is reviving their party and principles, there are the Democrats who will strike at everything his Administration has done and has not done. But will say little against the President himself; who will cite instead his ailments, his massive problems—and his advisers. It is almost as if President Eisenhower has managed something that Lincoln, Lee or even Washington were unable to do—become an untouchable legend in their own lifetime.

And there is the feeling one gets—sometimes expressed but more often to be read between the lines in attitudes of the people—that there is a belief that the sudden Middle East action shows that the President has regained his health. That he is once more the man who led the crusade in Europe in World War II.

And one feels that picture has never really died in the minds and hearts of most Americans—of the hero that could do no wrong in one great war; who stopped another one in his early days as President, and now will lead them as of yore through the new valleys of darkness in the Middle East.

JOHN F. BRIDGE

July 25, 1958

War Correspondent, 1958

BEIRUT—If somebody wants to start a war there are a lot worse places than Beirut, Lebanon, for staging the fracas. Beirut is a sunny city on the blue Mediterranean with pastel houses which cling to the sides of hills rising in folds to high mountains and with a people who cling to folding money with the trading instincts of generations.

The most important feature about Beirut is the fierce determination of sharp-trading Lebanese to do business as usual no matter what the circumstances. For the newspaper correspondent this has potent meaning. In this "war" you encounter none of the privations and discomforts usually associated with exploding shells and bursting bombs. If one will pay the price, almost anything can be obtained.

Even as bombs were being tossed indiscriminately into shops and government buildings, during the "height" of the rebellion, the Lebanese still found time for swimming daily at the rocky beach of the swank St. Georges Hotel. Night clubs operated surreptitiously for the benefit of those newsmen who had curfew passes. Restaurants somehow managed to stock larders with choice steaks, the juicy shrimps of the eastern Mediterranean, and sparkling wines.

On the terrace of the St. Georges Hotel, with its red-painted chairs, there is always to be had a bottle of Löwenbräu or a cool gin-and-tonic; one can relax and listen to the crackle of bullets in town. Sometimes the firing is only a few blocks away and sometimes there is worry about strays; but only a little, for there is an atmosphere of unreality about that firing.

But a visit to any government building, such as the post office, can sometimes bring the "war" uncomfortably close. A rebel attack may trap everyone in the thick-walled building for an hour or so. But the cable clerk continues taking messages.

Outside, farther down the block, a cab driver waits for his passenger, lying down on the pavement between the curb and the car wheels. As soon as the firing stops, he rises, brushes off his clothes and then opens the car door as the passenger dashes hurriedly from the post office's main entrance. Perhaps he drives rather rapidly from the area. But he probably would have been surprised had anyone suggested that this might be a better time to loaf at home.

After one such trip, when three hand grenades exploded uncomfortably close, the driver patted the windshield of his cab saying: "I was very worried for the windshield."

Then he casually quotes a cab fare six times the usual peacetime rate, apologetically mentioning that he has to allow for the future possibility of a smashed windshield. His passenger admits that though it would be a tragedy indeed to lose the windshield, it would be a bigger tragedy to lose the passenger. The driver shrugs. "What will be will be." The impression is unmistakable that if he really thought he were going to lose a passenger, he would ask for his fare in advance.

Newsmen never have to worry about story material. If the day's happenings are dull one can always phone Saeb Salam, the rebel leader, and ask for an interview. Along with some fiery quotes, he also serves up some syrupy Turkish coffee and some cakes that probably were baked that morning in the government-controlled section of town.

Machine-gun-toting guards at the barricades of the rebel area get to know most newsmen by sight, if not by name. They know who smokes Luckies and who prefers Camels and who doesn't smoke at all. It becomes rather difficult to turn down requests for cigarettes from somebody lugging a loaded gun.

If anybody encounters any trouble covering this pocket war, he really needs only call on Joseph, the always smiling, neatly groomed concierge of the St. Georges. A passport visa expiring? Joseph can have it fixed for a fee. Airline space to Amman on a plane with all seats sold? Ask Joseph after slipping the right-sized banknote into his palm. A driver willing to risk the trip over the mountains to Damascus through rebel territory? Well, Joseph knows just the man, though the fellow naturally expects the pay of an executive.

Only the weather is really un-co-operative. But it never is very pleasant in Beirut in July and August. Stifling heat keeps most newsmen in the air-conditioned bar through the height of the day.

As for the Lebanese, nobody can say they don't try to keep newsmen happy and well supplied with copy—at a price. And among newsmen there is a suspicion that the war is petering out not because of any political changes, but because expense accounts are running low.

RAY VICKER

August 20, 1958

The Big E

Sentimentalists will shed a tear at the passing of *U.S.S. Enterprise,* which shipped her mooring lines for the last time the other day. She left Brooklyn Navy Yard for Lipsett's junk yard.

A lot of nonsense has been written, and will be still written, about how Tokyo Rose's prediction finally came to pass and how Mr. Lipsett will finally do what the Hiryu, the Soryu and the kamikazes couldn't do—which is, bluntly put, destroy the most famous U.S. Navy ship of its war and maybe some other wars to boot.

Planes from *Enterprise* fought in the Pacific from the attack on Pearl Harbor to Okinawa. She was listed officially by the Japanese seven times as sunk—and many times she almost was. She was Admiral Halsey's flagship for a time, and Admiral Radford's, and from her decks Butch O'Hare was lost in the first night fighter battles on record. She was good, she was lucky, she was proud.

But she was also old. Time and science put her out of joint. If she had been saved, as some of her officers and men wanted her saved, as a memento or maybe a museum, she would have ended up a quaint curiosity, embedded somewhere in concrete, with a proper guide reciting her victories in monotonous rote and describing her dimensions, broad as the Pacific, in square and linear feet.

This is not the end, we're sure, that the men who fought aboard her would wish for the Big E. It is better that she go, and she has no need for sad requiem or sentimental tear. Lipsett's torches won't destroy her.

EDITORIAL

August 25, 1958

An Appetite for Frigates

There's an old military saying, whose ancestry probably reaches back to Hannibal, that the general always needs two more cavalry troops and the admiral two more frigates.

There's some truth in it. There never yet was a war in which the size of the contending forces did not have its influence on the outcome, and when you consider the importance of the outcome to the nations involved it is not at all unreasonable for commanders to want to go to battle with the largest possible force.

But the point of the saying is that this military appetite, being always insatiable, cannot possibly be satisfied. The problem is to decide what is a reasonable and supportable number of horsemen and frigates; many a commander has sadly learned that sheer numbers is not the secret of success. Impoverishment lies around the corner for the king, dictator or republic that tries to meet some absolute standard of military science.

This, we think, is what General Nathan Twining, chairman of the Joint Chiefs of Staff, had in mind the other day when he read the Army a little lecture about its future size and growth. What he had to say gets an added sharpness from the fact that it comes from a top military man who has something more than a military mind.

The main Army complaint, the General wryly noted, is that "we need more airlift; we should have more divisions; we need more air defense; we need more strategic offense; we need more ships . . . and, of course, everybody wants lots more missiles." The Chief of Staff replied, in effect, that this was pretty unrealistic and not even very sensible.

"First of all," he said, "we must face up to the fact that the personnel strength of the Army, and of our armed forces as a whole, is not likely to increase. Consequently, your plans with regard to organization and deployments must be made accordingly."

And the General plainly suggested that he did not think this facing up to the facts was a bad thing. The necessity to plan "within resources and funds available" might compel a wise reassessment of priorities and the allocation of forces. For example, he questioned some of the effort going into airlift power and into most Army missiles of today—the latter, he noted, "are not really mobile in the sense of rapid movement in a battle area."

As if this were not startling enough, the General threw out another challenge: "I think we should look closely at some of the noncombat activities of the Army." In a day when all manner of things are lumped under the military budget, this surely offers a wide field for looking.

General Twining, no doubt, has started a lively little battle of his own. He is, one may be sure, no blind apostle of military penury, yet with the 1960 budget now being put together the various military departments, already asking for more, are not going to take kindly to his "few suggestions" for eliminating "waste and misdirected effort."

Yet the General has, we think, said some things the rest of the Government—and the country—should heed. Military defense is the most important demand on the nation's resources. But that only makes it more, not less, imperative that there be a searching scrutiny of those resources and how they are applied.

Otherwise we will not be the first people to learn that safety and security cannot be bought by endlessly feeding an insatiable appetite for frigates.

EDITORIAL

October 23, 1958

"Say, I'm in pretty good condition at that! I couldn't carry twenty dollars' worth of groceries when I was just out of college."

CHEAP MONEY

People and Prices

"Inflation is inevitable. There's not too much an individual can do about it, except to try to protect himself. And, if prices show signs of getting out of hand, the Government should step in and impose price controls."

That's the prevailing sentiment of a wide cross section of the population interviewed by *Wall Street Journal* reporters in 12 cities. There has been a rash of predictions recently that the country was headed for another round of inflation. The reporters solicited citizens' views on this possibility—and what, if anything, they were doing to adjust their personal affairs to their estimate of the economic outlook. The majority view was one of fatalism and resignation. "Inflation is just a fact of life. You have to accept it and live with it," says an American Motors executive, typically.

"We're going to have inflation in this country because Americans

142

like to feel more money in their pockets regardless of whether they can buy any more with it," predicts William E. Umstattd, president of Timken Roller Bearing Co. of Cleveland.

Although most of the persons interviewed regarded continued inflation as undesirable, many were unconcerned. Some even welcomed it.

Kirk Frazier, a Jacksonville insurance salesman, looks at the declining value of the dollar this way: "It's really just conversation. In the long run, everybody's standard of living is rising. Purchasing power is going up while the value of the dollar is going down. Everything is relative. The important thing is what you can buy, not whether you make ten dollars a week or two hundred, and most people can buy more now than they used to be able to."

"I think we can stand quite a bit more inflation," says Earl Reed, who owns an appliance store in Atlanta. "People in debt need inflation to help them get back to normal." In Los Angeles, Jerome Rose, proprietor of Jerry's Juice Bar, smiles amiably at his interrogator. "It's no concern of mine," he says. "As long as the present equilibrium is maintained and everybody has more dollars, nobody is going to get hurt."

A young Clevelander, striding to work along East 9th Street, echoes a similar view: "This recession has been hard on our place. I'm still too concerned about keeping my job to worry about inflation yet. Anyway, as long as my salary goes up as fast as inflation I'm not going to complain."

Kenneth Barnes, 43-year-old St. Louis plumber, comments: "At least during inflation everybody's got a job. They can eat. But in a recession, there's no work and everybody suffers."

A portly, bluff Bostonian in his late fifties, who says his job is handling his family's investments, welcomes the idea of inflation. "It gives you more opportunity to make money," he says.

Most Americans, however, are anything but pleased by the possibility of a new wave of inflation. "We've already cut down on almost everything," says H. M. Cowser, a Dallas bus driver. "We don't eat meat every day any more. I haven't bought a new suit in four years."

"I'm plenty worried about inflation," says a Los Angeles tax accountant. "I find it difficult to raise my professional fees as an accountant, but my costs are going up all the time."

A majority of the persons interviewed declared there was little they could do about inflation—other than cutting their personal spending.

But many persons believe that they are clever enough to come out ahead in the game of constantly rising prices. Many are planning to protect themselves against future inflation by taking steps that paid off in the inflation that followed World War II. There is no guarantee, of course, that the conditions of any future inflation will exactly duplicate those of the past, or that the same safeguards will work.

Yale Brozen, economics professor at the University of Chicago, looks upon the postwar years with satisfaction. "My salary is fairly fixed, so I have myself hedged. I saw this coming back in 1945, and I got myself in hock so bad to buy a house, apartment building and common stocks that I thought I would never see daylight—but now on the apartment alone I'm making a 30 per cent return on my investment."

"It seems the smart guys are the ones who go 'way into debt and buy something they can't afford," says an executive in an appliance firm, who tells of a colleague "who is buying a $32,500 house when he should be buying one for about $22,000. He's pushing himself just as far as he can go because he figures by the mid-1960s his house will be worth $15,000 more. What has he got to lose?"

Darwin Martin, a young Detroit advertising man who bought a house this year, admits that inflation was a factor that "influenced us to buy as early as we did." In Pittsburgh, the vice-president of a medium-sized manufacturing company (sales of $20 million a year) thinks he has the problem licked: "I'm borrowing all I can and buying securities and real estate. I don't see how I can lose." Cleveland manufacturers' agent Ned Gross puffs a long cigar as he says, "I've got $40,000 in the stock market and I'm keeping it there. I may lose a little, but whatever happens I'll never lose as much as if I'd bought government savings bonds."

Not all businessmen are as happy about the possibility of inflation, however. L. S. Hamaker, general manager of sales for Republic Steel, says, "My pension rights looked a heck of a lot better eight or ten years ago than they do now. I'll have plenty of dollars coming in when I retire five or six years from now, but if the fifty-cent dollar has become a thirty-cent dollar by that time, I may have to make some adjustments. Moving out of my $550-a-month apartment, for one thing."

Mr. Hamaker says he has been attempting to cope with the situation for about 10 years "by putting all my extra nickels into common stock."

The rise in property values has its drawbacks, too. Charles Hobbet, a Chicago credit man, complains, "I bought a bungalow out in Glen Ellyn (a Chicago suburb) in the mid-1940s for $7,000 and now it is worth $15,000. But when I bought it, the property tax was $84 a year. Now it has gone up more than three times to $303 and will probably be $350 next year. I don't know if it is worth it to hold on and pay the property tax or sell and pay a big capital gains tax—it doesn't make sense."

Inflation's effect on the educational planning of fathers was cited many times by persons interviewed. A Philadelphia executive says he has had to increase his annual contributions toward his son's college fund 25 per cent in the last four years and lately "I've had to take a fresh look at it about every two years." The next step, he says, will be to take the fund out of a savings bank and place it elsewhere. "Even though interest rates are high, they are hardly enough to keep up with inflation."

The safety of common stocks as an inflation hedge is questioned in some quarters. "I'm not putting money into the stock market because stocks are high enough," says Ben Wooten, president of the First National Bank in Dallas.

The level of the stock market, "with stocks showing little relation to their yields," also bothers a Dallas oil company official, whose favorite anti-inflation tactic up to now has been to buy stock in his own company.

Who's responsible for inflation? "Me and everybody else," says John L. Briggs, vice-president of Dallas-headquartered Southland Life Insurance Co. "It's our desire for a higher standard of living and things we enjoy but don't necessarily need that made inflation," Mr. Briggs says, adding that another factor is Federal deficits and defense spending. "If we had gone ahead and challenged the Commies right after the war, maybe there wouldn't be any need for this big Federal spending now."

"The fault probably lies primarily with the Government," says A. H. Tibbits, a San Francisco attorney, "but everyone must share some part of the blame. If there were more public sentiment against it, the Government and labor and management would move a lot faster to do something about it. As it is," he adds, "I don't think most people really care about inflation."

Dr. Julius Grodinski, professor of finance at the University of Pennsylvania, says the current inflation trend is "unique in the history of the civilized world." He adds, "In a classic inflation, prices rise first and wages lag behind. But in our inflation, production costs are rising first and prices are following."

Money managers, Dr. Grodinski says, could stem inflation by refusing to finance it, but this in turn leads to a great debate: "Is it better to have price stability or to have full employment?" Dr. Grodinski indicates you can't have both.

September 30, 1958

Troublesome Currency

When the United States took the lead right after World War II in creating the International Monetary Fund, one of its chief concerns was to help stabilize the "soft" currencies of the world.

In those days the U.S. dollar was almost the only "hard" currency. The British pound, one of the chief moneys used in international trade, had been buffeted by the war and was soon to be abused even more by the economic policies of the Labor government. The German mark, of course, was a shambles, as were the Italian lira and the Japanese yen. Most of the European currencies, such as the French franc, were very dubious. Certainly few were "sound as a dollar."

Well, the other day Mr. Per Jacobsson, director of the Monetary Fund, was able to report quite a lot of progress. The German mark has long been a dependable money. The British pound has been strengthened within the last few years until it is once more a general currency of international trade. The lira and the yen have at least begun to command respect, and even the poor French franc has lately begun to revive with the promise of a return to stable government.

So Mr. Jacobsson could give most of the world a fine financial bill of health. "I think we will reach the conclusion, perhaps with some astonishment, that the results in the end have not been too unfavorable."

But there was one currency that troubled some of the delegates. And surely some of them must have noted the little irony in the fact that this time as they talked of "dangerous inflationary pressures" they were furrowing their brows over the good old United States dollar.

October 9, 1958

EDITORIAL

$1,000 Bill

Poor Mrs. Brkljacic had her troubles not because she was an innocent immigrant but because she had become too wise from too much
experience in the ways of the world.

Poor Mrs. Brkljacic, you remember, is the lady from Yugoslavia
who arrived on the boat with a $1,000 bill and found herself in her
new country unable to buy a cup of coffee, ride in a taxi or make
a phone call.

It wasn't only the cab driver who rejected the $1,000 bill. Hotel
managers and the vice-presidents of two banks shied away from it.
So poor Mrs. Brkljacic had to be sheltered by the Travelers' Aid
Society until she could be succored by the Federal Reserve Bank of
New York.

And everybody got a chuckle out of the naïve little lady who
would innocently tender a $1,000 bill for a plane ticket to Detroit.

The story does make an amusing vignette, but after a while we
began to find a little meditation mixed with our amusement.

You see, Mrs. Brkljacic has lived and passed through the part of
the world where counting money in units of a thousand is too commonplace to be noticeable, and at times too cruel to be amusing. A
thousand Yugoslav dinars, for instance, is about like a two-dollar
bill and a couple of silver quarters—a ride for two people from airport to town.

The casual use of thousand-unit notes is not rare for European
travelers. A thousand French francs is less than three dollars and a
thousand Italian lire not much more than a dollar and a half. Ten-
dering a thousand Spanish pesetas is about like passing over a
twenty-dollar bill.

These, of course, are the "little" currencies, and American tourists
last summer tossed them about with amused disdain. But what
spoils our amusement is the fact that they were not always so care-
lessly tossed.

Take the French franc. To the doughboys of World War I a
thousand-franc note was still worth nearly $200, hardly a bill to be
handed to taxi drivers or used to pay luncheon checks. Indeed, it
was not the war itself but the fiscal foolishness of government in the
1920s that sent the franc skidding.

In 1918 the franc was the equivalent of 18 cents. By 1922 it was worth nine cents. By 1926, two and a half cents. By 1940, barely two cents.

Today, if you wish to be technical, the franc is worth $0.0028$11\frac{1}{16}$, or less than a third of a U.S. penny—and those U.S. pennies themselves are not worth what they were ten years ago. And a thousand-franc note will barely buy your dinner in a first-class Paris restaurant.

Of course all this is in old countries far across the sea, and it was amusing of Mrs. Brkljacic to think the New World as foolish with its money as the Old. This is the United States, and the United States Government stands as guardian of the United States dollar.

We would feel more amused if yesterday at lunch we had not spent two dollar bills to do the work one would do a decade past. We would be more amused if we were sure Mrs. Brkljacic was naïve rather than, out of her wiseness in the ways of the world, unknowingly prophetic.

February 7, 1951

EDITORIAL

On the Treadmill of Rapid Inflation

Probably the word most often used nowadays in writings about business or securities is "inflation." That this nation is on a treadmill of even more rapid inflation than experienced so far in the war and postwar periods is an article of faith accepted and loudly repeated by all. A unanimity so nearly complete—almost as complete, for instance, as the "new era" thinking of 1929 just before that year's stock market crash—ought to be examined to see if inflation is the major cause of the recent stock market boom.

One example is current talk about the rise in stock prices since last winter. Because earnings are down sharply from last year's and as yet show few signs of upturn, most commentators say flatly that fear of inflation lies at the root of the rise. Yet there are two reasons for questioning this explanation.

One is the kind of stocks that rose first. The advance was led by the utilities, which are among the stocks least likely to benefit from inflation, and by drug shares, which are not traditional inflation hedges. Later other groups joined in, but still not those regarded as true inflation hedges. For instance, the steels rose at a time when their costs were going up and their selling prices weren't, and went up further when the price advances came even though these proved to be far smaller than the cost increases. Steel, in any case, is not a good inflation hedge because it is such a universally used product that its price advances usually run into heavy political as well as consumer resistance. Meanwhile, the stocks normally sought for protection against inflation, copper and domestic-oil shares, did share in the rise, but were laggard until this summer.

The other reason for doubt is that a stock market rise almost always precedes a business recovery from recession. Careful studies by economists show that such stock price advances have in the majority of recessions started while business was still on the way down, sometimes preceding the start of recovery by half a year or more. Thus it is not necessary to cite inflation as the cause in this instance, if one accepts the widespread judgment that the recession is at or close to bottom.

The reason why everyone expects inflation, of course, is the rapid increase in the Federal deficit. That such governmental red ink tends to rot the value of the currency admits of no discussion or disagreement. Furthermore, that our system of government—indeed almost any system of government—has a built-in bias toward deficits and inflation is also just about unarguable.

However, the sizes of deficits do matter. Inflations of the most extreme kind, such as the one in Germany after World War I, come from deficits that double or triple year after year. The much milder inflation we have suffered in this nation since World War II came principally from deficits that ran above $20 billion a year for five war years, and above $50 billion a year in three of those years. The current fiscal year's projected deficit, at $12 billion, is by no means as big as those wartime figures.

The economic background also makes a great difference. In the past year private debt has shown very little gain, in contrast to the huge increases which helped finance the boom of 1955–56. Furthermore, a $12 billion Federal deficit is less than 3 per cent of the nation's over-all output of goods and services. The deficits of the 1930s, which mostly varied between $2.6 billion and $4.4 billion (the sole exception was 1938, when the figure fell to $1.2 billion) were proportionately somewhat larger, ranging around 4 to 5 per cent of gross national product. Yet they produced no appreciable inflation after the initial rebound in the general price level in 1934–35 from the extremely low levels of 1932–33.

One reason why the deficits of the 1930s had so little inflationary effect is that the nation's productive capacity was not being used fully. There was room for more production than the market demanded, so that price boosts were not needed to stimulate the creation of added capacity.

In contrast, for a good many years after World War II there wasn't enough capacity here or in the rest of the world to produce the goods the market demanded. Under such conditions price advances were needed to stimulate the building of added capacity.

Today that situation has changed radically. The producing rates in steel, copper and aluminum testify to the fact demand is now below capacity. And that's not just because of recession. Indications are that even after recovery has taken place, there will be enough of most goods to go around.

That's true not only here but abroad. The Russian offerings of aluminum, tin, gold and other metals in world markets are often given dramatic names such as the "ruble war" or the "Communist economic offensive." More probably the Russians too have reached the stage where in spite of the needs of their people they have too much of some primary products. For instance, their switch toward missiles from airplanes may have helped bring about a surplus of aluminum there just as here.

These conditions have already found reflection in prices, although advances in the broad wholesale and consumer indexes generally in use, which contain a large element of labor cost, have tended to conceal the fact. In contrast, the Dow Jones spot price index is now, and has been for many months, down around 160 per cent of its 1925 base compared with a 1951 Korean War high of almost 225. A Department of Commerce index of raw-materials prices (not published regularly in this paper) has fluctuated in the past year between 84 per cent and 90 per cent of its 1947–49 base, down even more from its Korean high above 135. The kind of inflation we are experiencing is not a one-way street.

GEORGE SHEA

August 18, 1958

Lone Ranger to the Rescue

The way the dollar's disappearing, someone was bound to suggest it sooner or later. The Lone Ranger is riding to the rescue of the Treasury.

Tonto and Silver will storm with him across the nation's TV

screens this fall rounding up dollars for Uncle Sam as well as assorted scoundrels. They have agreed to induce the nation's small fry to buy U. S. Government savings stamps to be turned into Series E Savings Bonds.

The way the Lone Ranger and Mr. James F. Stiles, Jr., head of the Treasury's Savings Bond Division, have worked things out, each buyer of a savings stamp will be entitled to a picture of the Lone Ranger and membership in the Lone Ranger Peace Patrol. On his TV program, the Lone Ranger will push the sales of savings stamps through the Post Office and the schools. The idea is to get American youngsters to contribute their dimes and quarters to "build the economic and military strength required to preserve our freedom and insure the peace."

The dimes and quarters go into little booklets and after there are enough of them the small fry turns the booklet in to a post office or a bank and receives for $18.75 a U.S. savings bond. After eight years and eleven months, the bond is turned in and Uncle Sam hands the fry, no longer so small, $25, no longer worth $25, unless things change in a hurry.

In fact, the way the dollar's been going for some years now, the $25 bond the small fry gets may not be worth the $18.75 the youngster put into it in dimes and quarters, and when the kids find out they've been dry-gulched at his urging we'd hate to be the Lone Ranger.

We don't want to seem unpatriotic about this matter, but after all the Lone Ranger strikes us as a man as sound as the dollar used to be, and we hate to see him walk into such an ambush without warning.

The fact is, the Lone Ranger's on the wrong trail in trying to rescue the Treasury this way. There's only one way to do it, really, and that's to rescue the dollar, as distressed as any damsel he ever came across. But even the Lone Ranger, Silver and Tonto, resourceful as they are, can't round up a whole Government.

September 10, 1958

EDITORIAL

Anatomy of Inflation

Anyone discussing inflation does well to begin by defining the word.

Inflation occurs when an increasing number of monetary units is brought to bear on a supply of goods which is diminishing, stationary or not increasing in the same proportion as the increase in the monetary units.

There may be those who will declare this definition is too narrow and others who will regard it as too broad. Any such argument would be academic because the definition suffices for the purpose of this article.

There is inflation when a government finances large and continuing deficits by printing money outright or by creating money through the central banking machinery, as did our own Government during the two world wars. More dollars are then set to purchasing fewer goods and each unit of goods must absorb more dollars, which is another way of saying that prices go up.

Previous to the spring of 1951 the Government was feeding inflation not so much by incurring current deficit as by monetizing the evidence of past deficits. The bonds issued during the war could be carried to the Federal Reserve System and there cashed for par or better. When that policy was abandoned inflation was abruptly checked.

In testimony before a Congressional committee the other day William McC. Martin, chairman of the Board of Governors of the Federal Reserve System, spoke of the danger of inflationary pressures getting out of hand. He sees this danger in a period when the Government is not running a deficit, when its cash receipts for a fiscal year are likely to exceed the cash outgo.

The danger Mr. Martin foresees is that in certain lines the supply of goods already is bumping a ceiling. The facilities of production are already working at their maximum; also additional labor is not available. Mr. Shea already has called attention to that situation in this newspaper and he has mentioned steel and newsprint as among commodities where capacity production cannot fill the demand.

What may happen in a case like that is that buyers begin to bid against each other for the available supply. Consumers begin to accumulate abnormally large inventories to protect themselves. In other words, they begin to hoard and so aggravate the shortage. Also speculators begin to get into the picture. They buy, not for consumption, but for hoarding in the belief that the subsequent higher prices will return them a profit.

These operations, when they take place, are financed by bank credit. Mr. Martin says that "to meet these demands by creating new supplies of money through the commercial banking system with Federal Reserve assistance would invite dangerous inflationary repercussions."

The Federal Reserve can—and there are those who would have

it do so—operate to give the banks ample lending power and thus encourage them to lend freely for the accumulation of goods priced at levels which disregard costs of production and what people in the long run will be willing to pay. Or the Federal Reserve can—as Mr. Martin says it intends—act to discourage such lending.

The situation against which Mr. Martin warns would be marked by an accelerating spiral of prices, first in raw materials and then in finished goods. In fact Mr. Martin noted that higher prices for consumers were already showing up.

The aftermath would be a quick descent of prices. Supplies would begin to catch up with demand. People might refrain from buying at high prices—a buyer's strike—and thus decrease demand. Even without that, production might increase just enough to bring supply and demand into balance. At the first sign of that, those who had been stocking up with goods would cease to buy and demand would be falling at the same time supplies were increasing. The speculative holdings would be dumped for what they would bring, thus artificially increasing the supply just as they had previously artificially stimulated demand.

At any time the line between a shortage and a surplus is very thin. A hundred widgets offered to 99 buyers is a surplus. The same hundred offered to 101 buyers is a shortage.

A swift change from shortage to surplus would find retailers, wholesalers and manufacturers loaded up with high-priced goods which they could not sell at a profit. High-cost inventories which could not be moved in the form of finished products might very well lead to bankruptcies. And if one bankruptcy should set off two and those two set off four, we would then have with us a full-scale depression.

All of this is not—most distinctly not—a prediction of dire future consequences. With the economic erudition that marks the present day and age people would have to be very foolish indeed to invite the bust by inflating the boom. Also the monetary authorities seem to have the courage to speak plainly and so far to act.

However, it will certainly do no harm to point out what inflation is, what makes it and that its consequences can be very uncomfortable.

And it is a better time to lift the foot from the accelerator now than to wait until after we have rounded the next corner.

WILLIAM H. GRIMES

December 6, 1955

BIG TAXES, MORE AND MORE

First Income Tax Regulations

WASHINGTON—Instructions have been issued by the Commissioner of Internal Revenue as to the method of filing income tax returns by individuals. The instructions are as follows:

> This return shall be made by every citizen of the United States, whether residing at home or abroad, and by every person residing in the United States, though not a citizen thereof, having a net income of $3,000 or over for the taxable year, and also by every non-resident alien deriving income from property owned and business, trade or profession carried on in the United States by him. . . .
>
> The normal Tax of 1% shall be assessed on the total net income less the specific exemption of $3,000 or $4,000 as the case may be. . . .

January 7, 1914

Is the Income Tax Constitutional?

Henry Wynans Jessup writes to *The Wall Street Journal* some pregnant thoughts on the income tax and its constitutionality. There is no lawyer whose opinion is entitled to more earnest consideration:

> I have been much interested in the various articles in your publication on the income tax. There is one feature of the tax bearing upon its constitutionality that I have not seen covered in any of the newspaper discussions, and that is that: The scheme of collecting at the source appears to be unconstitutional in that it imposes upon persons or corporations, in no manner connected with the Government, governmental duties or functions. Take the case of the burdens imposed upon banks and trust companies

acting as the intermediaries for the collection of coupons. If I am correctly informed, the scheme of the new law imposes upon these companies bookkeeping expenses amounting to thousands of dollars per annum in each instance. They are charged, therefore, with a burden of expense amounting in effect to a tax in excess of the return to the bank or trust company in the business out of which this expense arises.

A collector at the source is impressed with the duty of assessing and collecting the tax for the Government, although not in any relation to the Treasury Department or the Internal Revenue Bureau, and in this respect it seems to me the income tax provisions are open to serious attack. Assuming the willingness of a particular corporation or persons to exercise this duty of assessing and collecting the tax upon a rent payment, or interest payments, or on wages or salaries, has not that individual or corporation a right to insist preliminarily on being indemnified by the Government for the expense to which he or it will be put in exercising these governmental and administrative functions? Why should I be charged with a duty and an expense in connection with the tax of a third party?

There is another feature of the system, i.e., its onerous working. I have in mind the case of three missionaries living abroad, who are jointly interested in a $300 bond. The income from this bond, added to their munificent salaries of $800 a year, of course, entitles them to exemption, but in order that this exemption may be secured, certain papers of attorney executed abroad amount in the first instance to more than their joint tax on the income coupon, and the same red tape in regard to the making and filing of certificates with the bank or trust company with whom the income is deposited has to be resorted to as in the case of the depositor of thousands of dollars' worth of coupons per month; that is to say, the expense in the case of a very poor person of securing exemption is almost equal to the tax, and amounts in itself to the tax and is unjust and oppressive.

In the third place, we have not yet reached the inquisitorial stage of the administration of an income tax law. If the patience of the people is not exhausted by this preliminary red tape, it may well be expected to be exhausted when the collectors commence the verification by inquisition of returns claiming exemption. The powers that they will enjoy extend to a method of inquisition that is totally hostile to the Anglo-Saxon theory of government, and it would not be too far-fetched to predict that it will provoke a revulsion of feeling all over the country that will lead to the repeal of the law.

January 8, 1914

The New Tax Bite

First bite of the withholding tax into worker incomes came for millions of Americans this week, but almost all took it in stride.

There was some grumbling, there were a few isolated instances of men and women who quit their jobs (or threatened to), and there was much speculation on what this 20 per cent slice from net income would mean to retail trade, war bond buying, and wage demands in the weeks ahead.

But what trouble there was seemed to develop in small business establishments where there had been little if any organized effort to prepare the workers for a tax deduction which had the effect of a major wage cut. In huge arms plants personnel men had spent many hours preparing notices, writing stories for company papers and otherwise getting their men and women ready for the blow.

July 17, 1943

Tax Havens

NEW YORK—One day some weeks ago an agent for the Honduran government put in a long-distance call to Chicago's International Harvester Co. He offered a simple proposal: Set up a farm machinery plant in Honduras and we won't tax you for 30 years. At last report, Harvester had not accepted the offer.

There's nothing particularly new about this proposal—except for the country making it. Until recently, the tiny Central American nation had not been making such offers. Several other nations are joining Honduras in bidding for business concerns with tax inducements. A partner in a New York City law firm that delves deeply into foreign tax subjects can hardly contain his enthusiasm: "We've never had so many wonderful places to offer clients trying to protect foreign income against depletion by taxes."

Other newcomers to the bidding for new businesses include the Bahamas and the Netherlands Antilles in the Caribbean and, farther north, Bermuda. They're joining a group of somewhat more venerable but increasingly active tax havens such as Puerto Rico, the tiny

"I only want to beat the government out of what I'm entitled to."

European principality of Liechtenstein, the internationalized North African port of Tangier, the Central American republic of Panama, and the West African republic of Liberia.

As the number of potential tax havens rises, more and more U.S. corporate executives are showing interest. Walter Diamond, editor of *Foreign Tax and Trade Briefs,* a bimonthly report on the tax laws of some 73 foreign nations, explains: "The American firm that wants to expand its operations abroad can shop around for a place to suit its needs more closely—and one which will give greater semblance of reality to its operations there."

Tax havens are of interest to companies entering or expanding foreign operations. If a company treads carefully, it may be able to put off paying taxes on foreign profits until those profits are returned to the U.S. In the meantime, the company's profits can be used to build up its business overseas. Any levies imposed by the tax haven nations are small, when compared with U.S. taxes.

As Mr. Diamond emphasizes, the look of reality is important. Uncle Sam may require a company to prove its foreign affiliate serves a business purpose other than postponing taxes. If the company fails to prove its case, it may be slapped with a big U.S. tax assessment. Foreign tax law is complex and the pitfalls are plentiful; capable legal advice is a necessity for any company contemplating foreign operations.

Use of tax havens is almost a must for companies in some industries, according to John J. Powers, vice-president of Chas. Pfizer & Co., Brooklyn producer of antibiotics and other drugs. Pfizer's affiliate in Panama has proven of "decisive importance" in helping the company meet competition in overseas markets, Mr. Powers says.

Remington Rand, Inc., now a division of Sperry Rand Corp., a few years ago created "The French Co. of Western Africa" in Liberia to distribute its typewriters, adding machines and other office equipment abroad.

Dresser Industries, Inc., Dallas producer of oil and chemical industry equipment, three years ago set up a subsidiary in Liechtenstein to license European manufacturers to use its patents; the royalties soon will help Dresser build a few factories of its own abroad.

Late last year a New England engineering-consultant firm specializing in textile-making problems set up a Liberian affiliate. Its experts now advise textile producers in Europe and Latin America. Fees for these services are used to expand operations of the Liberian company or to invest in foreign enterprises—chiefly those they've helped to rejuvenate.

An American construction company some months ago walked off with a contract for a highway in Arabia; the bid was filed by a Panama affiliate set up for that job. The parent company plans to bring the profits back to the U.S. at a time when its other income is lower.

Why are the tax haven nations trying so hard to attract new businesses? Some, such as Honduras, are interested primarily in building up industry. Others, such as Liechtenstein, are chiefly interested in collecting their own relatively light taxes and corporate fees.

Movie men believe they have found a way to cut total taxes on foreign income. The formula: Accumulate foreign earnings in a subsidiary in a tax haven country. Once the statutory limit of three years has elapsed, dissolve the subsidiary and bring back the profits as a capital gain, taxable at a maximum 25 per cent rate, compared with the 52 per cent rate on ordinary corporate income.

U.S. companies with manufacturing or sales subsidiaries in more than one country are using tax haven affiliates to maximize tax credits. Uncle Sam allows credits against U.S. taxes for taxes paid to other nations—up to a maximum of 52 per cent, the top U.S. rate. But some foreign tax rates exceed 52 per cent. Here's how some companies avoid partial loss of credit for the over-52 per cent taxes:

Suppose a U.S. company has plants in countries X and Y, each of which showed a profit of $1 million in 1955. Country X levies a 62 per cent income tax, while Y contents itself with 42 per cent. The U.S. company channels its aftertax profits through a holding company in a tax haven nation. Lumping together the $620,000 tax paid in X and the $420,000 levy paid in Y, the holding company comes up with a total payment of $1,040,000—or 52 per cent of the $2 million total income of the two plants. So, when the profits are brought back to the U.S., the American company is allowed full credit for the taxes paid to both X and Y.

Tax havens offer attractions that have nothing to do with taxes. Most offer easy rules for setting up new companies. In Liechtenstein, for example, a corporate charter may include little information other than the company's name, its address and its line of business. A Liechtenstein lawyer may represent a number of companies. If necessary, he can conduct one-man annual meetings.

Most tax havens have long records of political stability, a factor not to be taken lightly by any businessman contemplating foreign corporations. In general, the tax havens also offer a greater degree of exchange freedom than other nations, making it easier for a businessman to transfer funds from one country to another or from one currency to another. But the chief attraction, of course, is low taxes.

Few tax haven nations levy any income taxes at all. Instead, most of them levy a tax on the haven-seeking company's capitalization. The rates are very low. Liechtenstein, for example, charges a flat one tenth of one per cent a year. The principality in some cases will sign a tax contract, guaranteeing companies a tax assessment of as little as $95.25 a year for the following 30 years.

MITCHELL GORDON

February 7, 1956

Taxes, Taxes, Taxes

NEW YORK—Where does the money go?

Arthur F. and Peter B., two young and conscientious New York City accountants, last year set out to answer that oft-asked question for themselves. Mr. F. and Mr. B., and their somewhat less than willing wives, during 1956 scrupulously noted down each of their expenditures, no matter how trivial.

When Mr. F. and Mr. B. burned the midnight oil the other

night over their staggering mass of figures, they reached some totals that to them seemed mildly astonishing.

Peter B., a slim, nervous 30-year-old who's rising fast in his firm, found he had spent $235 to have coffee brought in to his desk. "Do you realize," he asks in an anguished voice, "that that's nearly a hundred gallons?"

Arthur F. was equally dismayed to discover that he and his wife, who do a lot of their traveling by subway around this traffic-bound metropolis, had shelled out nearly $300 for carfare. "That," says Mr. F. with an awed expression, "comes to close to two thousand trips."

Surprising to both Mr. B. and Mr. F. were the amounts they had paid in taxes—to the Federal Government, New York State and New York City. More surprising: They paid almost as much in "hidden" taxes—corporate taxes that businessmen pass along to consumers in the prices of the goods they sell.

Like most Americans, the two accountants never saw most of the money they paid Uncle Sam, even their direct payments. Their employers took over that responsibility, deducting their taxes from their checks—$534 for Mr. F., $1,429 for Mr. B. When the Messrs. F. and B. sat down last week to fill out their 1956 Federal income tax returns, it was little more than a formality. Mr. F. had to enclose a check for an additional $13.02; Mr. B.'s balance was only $6.87.

By midnight tonight some 60 million other Americans will have settled their 1956 tax debt to Uncle Sam. What's more, they're anteing up additional billions to state and local governments throughout the year—enough to push per capita tax payments to the highest level in history.

In the year ending next June 30, Americans—corporations and individuals—will pay more than $100 billion in Federal, state and local taxes. That's an average of $636 for each man, woman and child, compared with $607 in 1956.

John Q. Taxpayer's burden includes taxes he's only vaguely aware of, such as Federal excise taxes added to the price of many products he buys, and many levies he's not conscious of at all. The latter are the "hidden" taxes.

Stocky, 32-year-old Mr. F., who in the past 10 years has progressed from a $2,500-a-year clerk to a $7,349-a-year accountant, paid $1,217.48 in direct city, state and Federal taxes in 1956. But that's something less than half the story. Hidden taxes pushed Mr. F.'s total burden up to a total of some $2,500.

Mr. B. last year earned $9,989, more than five times his take in 1949, his first full working year after four years in the U.S. Navy as a storekeeper. His direct tax payments in 1956 came to $1,997, but hidden taxes lifted his total burden at least to $3,500.

It's impossible to figure hidden taxes precisely. Consider a suit of clothes. Income taxes are imposed on and paid by the manufacturer. The manufacturer then can try to pass along the tax to the retailer through an increase in price. Or he can, in effect, try to pass the tax backward by purchasing less expensive raw materials or by cutting his production costs in other ways. Or, if his market is highly competitive, he may be forced to absorb all or part of the tax himself. The final, and most likely, course is a combination of the first three.

But that's only part of the problem. To determine the impact of income taxes on the average men's suit maker, it would be necessary to know where the suit was produced (some states impose income taxes and others do not), when it was produced (tax rates vary from year to year), and which manufacturer produced it (a manufacturer operating at a loss would not pay an income tax).

Even these difficulties conceivably might be surmountable if it were not for the bewildering multiplicity of taxes. The Tax Foundation, a private, nonprofit research organization, estimated that at least 116 taxes figure to some extent in the price of a man's suit, 100 taxes on an egg, 150 taxes on a woman's hat and 600 taxes on a house. The taxes on the suit include the levies on the businessmen who handled the product and those on the raw-material suppliers.

Despite these awesome obstacles, tax statisticians by making numerous assumptions are able to estimate roughly the tax burden—direct and hidden—on spending units at various income levels. Here are figures prepared by the Tax Foundation:

Income	Tax Burden
$3,500	$1,031
4,500	1,358
8,000	2,680
17,500	7,209

April 15, 1957

*"It could be just a coincidence, I suppose—but sometimes I
wonder if it's the government's way of rubbing it in."*

Tax Chiselers

Growing numbers of Americans, angered by high Federal income
tax rates and rising state and local levies, are turning into tax
cheats.

With the Federal tax deadline just a week away, *Wall Street
Journal* reporters interviewed tax lawyers, accountants and a lot of
ordinary taxpayers in 15 major cities around the U.S. The findings indicate not only that the number of tax chiselers is growing
but also that evaders make up a sizable proportion of the population—considerably bigger than the one per cent estimate offered
by the Internal Revenue Service.

Among the ordinary taxpayers, two of each five, after first carefully getting assurance of anonymity, admitted they cheat on their
taxes. These were not people who merely sought to take advantage

of every legal loophole in the tax laws, or who gave themselves the benefit of the doubt when it came to figuring how many deductions they could take. These were people who knew what they owed Uncle Sam, and then shortchanged him. And while the survey made no pretense at being scientific, it did offer some idea as to the way many a citizen has come to regard his tax obligations.

In Boston, a 30-year-old electrician says, with a grin, "I dodge my taxes whenever I can. It's kind of like a sport to see if you can't make a buck here and there."

In Detroit, a young businessman, who says he "plays the stock market," comments that he isn't "finicky" about complying with the "fine points" of the tax laws—he skips reporting his capital gains, for example, and ignores "some other formalities."

A well-dressed middle-aged man, waiting for a bus in Philadelphia's terminal, snaps, "Sure I cheat. It's not my obligation to pay every nickel."

And in San Francisco, a burly bartender sunning himself in verdant Union Square asks, "What am I going to do? Lots of times I'll put something on the cuff for a customer when I know I'll never get it back. So maybe I claim a $20 donation to the Community Chest when I only gave $5. And tips in my joint—if I get $5 a week I'm lucky. I don't list a dime that isn't part of my salary, and nobody's questioned me yet."

Officially, the Internal Revenue Service says tax evasion is not increasing. The service estimates that only one per cent of the 60 million people who file Federal income tax returns deliberately make out false reports. Asked recently what he thought was the present extent of tax evasion, Commissioner Dana Latham replied, "We do not believe it is any worse today than it has been in the last ten years."

But privately other I.R.S. officials concede evasion is a growing problem. They note that in the last few years it has become more profitable to avoid paying Uncle Sam his due. "When the tax rates were low, there wasn't much to be gained," comments one aide. "But there's no doubt that the higher tax rates have made it a more attractive risk to some people."

Many nongovernment tax experts also think evasion is growing. M. L. Rachlin, a New York City certified public accountant and a specialist in tax matters, says there has been a "marked increase" in tax evasion recently. Adds a Portland, Oregon, attorney: "I'm handling nearly twice as many tax suit cases now as compared to five years ago." Observes a Jacksonville tax lawyer: "There's been a definite lowering of moral standards as far as paying taxes goes."

Although I.R.S. figures indicate that there was a decline in the number of tax evasion cases last year, Commissioner Latham says the statistics don't give the true picture. In calendar 1958, 1,635 cases were recommended to the Justice Department by the I.R.S. for prosecution, down from 2,062 a year earlier. Of the 1,635 cases, 974 individuals were convicted, a drop from 1,276 in 1957. Back taxes and penalties recommended amounted to $146 million, down from $167 million in 1957.

But Mr. Latham explains that the statistical decline came about because the service now is putting emphasis on picking out important cases from the standpoint of revenue involved "and deterrent effect on other potential cases." One aide sums up the program in this way: "If the word gets around that we're looking at a particular group of returns—and believe me, it gets around—then that helps scare off any others who had an idea they might do some evading." Says another revenue agent: "When a prominent doctor is prosecuted on charges of tax evasion, it's amazing how his colleagues show terrific rises in income the following year."

Tax evasion schemes take a variety of forms. One of the simplest merely involves boosting by a few dollars the amounts claimed as deductions for charitable contributions, state and local taxes, medical payments or other outlays. More venturesome taxpayers may claim fictitious dependents; a Philadelphian once listed Poncho and Sanchez, two Mexican burros, as members of his family. Still other schemes are far more elaborate; some individuals, for example, may claim business losses from nonexistent companies.

"There seems to be no end to the ways taxpayers seek to defraud," says H. Allen Long, Chicago district director of the I.R.S. Adds B. Frank White, I.R.S. district commissioner in Dallas: "I'm sure a lot of people stay up nights thinking up new ways to beat their taxes."

Although I.R.S. officials won't say what particular category of the taxpaying public causes them the most trouble, one official notes that "anywhere you have anyone handling a largely cash business, where he doesn't have to make a detailed accounting to anyone else, the temptation for tax evasion is greater." And he adds: "That way, it's just between him and the Government, without a lot of other people looking over his shoulder." Mr. Long of the Chicago I.R.S. office observes that "the most frequent instances of fraud appear in the case of owners of moderately sized businesses and in the case of professional people."

Taking payments in cash and then not reporting them, and deducting personal expenses as business costs, seem to be the specialties of some professional men and the small businessman, tax experts say. Washington I.R.S. officials cite the case of the doctor who didn't think he should be taxed on the night calls he had to make; he was sentenced to eight months in prison for understating his income over a four-year period by $80,000. A Boston undertaker understated the number of funerals his establishment handled, claiming an annual profit of only $5,000 to $6,000. But by culling newspaper files the I.R.S. found he had about twice as many funerals as he said, with an annual profit closer to $20,000 a year.

A taxpayer doesn't have to get paid in cash to cheat, notes New York's Mr. Rachlin. When paid by check he simply steps into the nearest check-cashing agency or corner luncheonette and converts the check into cash, then records just the portion of the payment on which he feels like paying taxes. And only this portion, instead of the full amount of the check, will appear on his own bank records. The check-cashing technique has reached such proportions in New York, Mr. Rachlin says, that I.R.S. agents now regularly call on places that make a specialty of cashing checks for a fee and note the frequent users of the service. Then they examine those individuals' returns to see if the payments have been reported.

Banks are used less frequently, says Mr. Rachlin, because these institutions get suspicious if an individual regularly requests cash rather than depositing his checks.

T. G. Williams, Portland, Oregon, accountant, reports a variation of this practice. "An account of mine tried to claim a big deduction for medical expenses," he relates. "He had for proof of the expense a stack of canceled checks from a drugstore. I found he was cashing personal checks at the drugstore, then claiming a medical-expense deduction for drugs."

Another evasion stratagem is the country club membership. It works this way: A foursome bets on a golf game and at the final hole the losers fork over, say, $20 to the winner. The latter says, "Fellows, we'll just drink this up." The party has $20 of drinks, but instead of paying cash for the refreshments, the winner keeps the money and signs a check. When it comes time to figure his income tax, he has the club bill, which he claims as a business entertainment deduction; meanwhile, he's had the benefit of $20 of unreported income.

"This is small if done only once," says a Jacksonville tax lawyer, "but it mounts up over the period of a year." The same system is used at luncheon clubs by "check grabbers," who sign the check, then collect cash from each diner in the party.

Harry Graham Balter, Los Angeles tax attorney who is author of *Fraud under Federal Tax Law,* a legal tome he calls a "practitioner's book," cites a growing "off-the-main-course pattern of evasion—credit cards."

"Taxpayers are running hog-wild with credit cards," claims Mr. Balter, "figuring they don't have to differentiate between legitimate business expenses that they charge and personal expenses. Credit cards invite tax frauds by making it easy to do it, and they're going to make a crook out of every taxpayer." Mr. Balter predicts that "failure to segregate credit card charges that are deductible from those that aren't" will be "the next big area of tax evasion prosecution by government men."

Although individuals' tax cheating is a constant problem, I.R.S. officials say an even greater source of trouble is the shady tax adviser. Tax officials figure the "aider and abetter," as they refer to the unscrupulous tax expert, causes more work because he knows how to hide evasion and, although he does it in relatively small amounts, he does it for hundreds of people.

Washington officials cite this example: A disbarred attorney set himself up as a tax consultant and quickly established a reputation as a man who could assure a big tax refund. Obviously, officials note, it wasn't likely that all of his clients were blameless, because his distortions of income and expense data submitted to him should have been clear in many cases. In fact, he was tripped up when one client got a refund so large that it surprised him. Suspecting an error, he turned the check over to the consultant to adjust with the I.R.S.—but the consultant appropriated the check. The taxpayer brought suit for embezzlement, and the I.R.S. moved in on the consultant. It had to ferret out hundreds of tax returns, and in nearly every case found sizable amounts in additional taxes due the Government. The additional taxes and penalties ran to more than $1 million.

Certain tax advisers in the Southwest are doing a growing business as the result of a practice of which I.R.S. personnel take a dim view. Called "income tax buyers," by their customers, these operators fill out the tax forms, then write the client a check on the spot for his refund—less a fee, usually 10 per cent of the refund. The tax adviser gets a power of attorney so the refund check can be mailed directly to him, allowing him to cash it and pocket the profit.

"It's bad," comments I.R.S. District Commissioner White, "because sometimes the guy who is running this sort of scheme gets a little illegal in this enthusiasm for customers." The bigger the refund the client gets, of course, the bigger the fee for the tax consultant.

Why do people cheat on their taxes?

Most of the people who admit they don't pay all the taxes they owe try to wrap their actions in a cloak of moral righteousness, claiming they are opposed to government spending programs, disgusted at corruption and waste in Government, or simply object to taxes "on principle." Only a handful say the reason they don't pay is that when it comes time to file their returns they just don't have the money.

An attractive blond secretary sunning herself at Manhattan Beach, California, admits she didn't report income from a two-week job she held "because it would have put me in a higher income bracket," and adds casually, "I've never paid state taxes, because I object to them." Snaps a Boston securities salesman: "I think you should beat the Government out of every nickel you can. I'm convinced one fourth of all tax money is swindled, wasted or unnecessary." And he adds, "Of course, if I was convinced the money would be used well, I'd pay every cent, but I don't believe in the way the Government is being run."

Some individuals in the middle- and upper-income brackets cheerfully admit they play a little game with the tax collector. They know that their tax returns are likely to be checked, and that the tax collector well may question some of the deductions they've claimed. So they purposely overstate their deductions. If the Revenue Service calls them in for an interview, they figure they'll be able to "compromise," settling on a figure that will be close to the correct total.

I.R.S. officials won't say specifically what their plans are for auditing 1958 income tax returns, but claim that one sixth of the expected 60 million individual returns will be closely examined, and in some brackets and some categories nine tenths of the returns will get a full check.

Commissioner Latham recently told Congress, "We propose, within the limits of our budget, to step up the number of returns that are audited each year. The public should realize that we have no set pattern on the returns we do audit. We are seeking better techniques to audit the returns which would yield the most revenue. We have a trial-and-error method and change each year. But we want to make in a reasonable cycle a complete audit of everybody's return who would appear to even possibly have any substantial revenue so that no taxpayer can ever feel he is secure from an audit."

Here is a general picture of the way the audit machinery works:

Returns selected for investigation may be identified by type of return, type of business or occupation, or by size of income. Certain types of returns get special attention; these may be personal or business returns reporting adjusted gross income above certain designated levels. Further selection may be made on the basis of such factors as substantial income reported from sources not subject to withholding, or businesses which deal largely in cash, or returns presenting unusual dependency exemption claims or very large deductions. In addition, the audit staff may branch out from this in a varying pattern, giving special attention to doctors this year, and to lawyers next year.

But in general, a tax sleuth says, "We go where the money is." Even though a taxpayer might have elaborate means for hiding evasion, "money leaves tracks," adds another.

Another source of information: The I.R.S., although it doesn't advertise it, has a fund for tipsters. If a person tips off the service to an evader, he can collect, upon application, up to 10 per cent of the additional tax money collected by the Government. (The tipster's windfall is taxable, incidentally.) The service's appropriation for this fund for the fiscal year ending June 30 is $600,000, up from $493,000 last fiscal year. But the I.R.S. doesn't boast about the fund; it doesn't want to appear to be courting stool pigeons.

April 9, 1959

A Plague on 'Em Anyway

A Joint Congressional Economic Subcommittee hearing opened in Washington the other day to study ways and means of reducing some government spending so missile spending could be increased without burdening the taxpayers any further, and some economics professors were called as witnesses.

The one from Harvard said it was hard to separate defense from nondefense spending because, actually, aid to education, health programs, housing projects and highway building were all a necessary part of the defense effort. He said the Government ought to spend more money, not less, and tax the people more, not less.

The one from Yale echoed this sentiment. Americans, he said, "need to get over their traditional feeling that taxes are a plague."

Well, we've heard arguments like the Harvard professor's before. It's become almost a tradition to testify that the more money the Government takes away from people the happier the people will be.

But we'd like to straighten out the Yale professor for his imprecise comparison of taxes to a plague. If he had said that Americans think of taxes as a necessary evil, yes; as an abomination, yes; but a plague? No.

Most Americans, whatever their economics or traditional view of taxes, would never commit such a metaphorical blunder. For other traditions have taught them even the Biblical plagues finally came to an end.

November 20, 1957

EDITORIAL

GROWING PAINS

The Quiet Force in Arkansas

LITTLE ROCK—The course Arkansas follows in resolving its school integration crisis may be determined in the end not so much by Orval Faubus, whose name rings round the world, as by a lot of people whose names you have never heard.

With one exception—U.S. Representative Brooks Hays—none is a politician of national stature; most are not politicians at all. Yet they can be exceedingly effective in politics, as events have already demonstrated.

At the end of last week the Governor of Arkansas seemed to be hurrying into violent activity. He was planning to call legislators into immediate emergency session; he was talking up the idea of shutting down Central High; he was welcoming to his mansion a crowd of emotional mothers who seek to wipe out the state's public-school system. So far this week he has been doing none of these things.

What his eventual strategy will be there is perhaps no predicting, particularly in view of the latest crossed signals between here and Washington. But certainly something happened to make Mr. Faubus pause to re-evaluate his maneuvers.

The thing that slowed down Orval Faubus was not outright opposition but the delicate and deliberate application of brakes, in a manner polite but purposeful.

Opposition did come from two political voices, shrill enough to be heard across the nation but pitched too high to gain respectful attention within the state. Little Rock Mayor Woodrow Wilson Mann proved to have little influence even in his own city. Ex-Governor Sid McMath, his old following shrunken mostly to a bloc of union and Negro voters, was almost equally ineffectual. Mr. Faubus wheeled on both and demolished them with scorn.

In the first few days of near-hysteria which followed the Governor's use of guardsmen to bar Negro youngsters from Central High—the time of the riot and the invasion by Federal troops—it appeared that Orval Faubus spoke for all Arkansas, and that none could restrain him. Two major political figures, Arkansas Senators

McClellan and Fulbright, stayed clear of the state. Lesser men appeared afraid to speak out.

But very quietly—at first entirely behind the scenes, and then more and more openly—many men were organizing to apply the brakes. Their tactic: Do not attack the Governor. Do not force him into a position where he will be suddenly deflated and discredited. Instead, surround him with evidence that segregationist sentiment will in the long run pack less political punch, in much of Arkansas, than devotion to law and order, preservation of the public-school system, and restoration of the state's good name in the nation.

Participating in this courteous campaign were a small army of underpaid state legislators (their pay for two years of service: $1,200), businessmen, professional people and clergymen. This was no plot; many worked without knowing what others were doing. And yet, as it turned out, they timed their efforts carefully, almost as if they had all been synchronized. The Governor suddenly found himself surrounded by mobilized moderates. Then, even though the extreme segregationists of the Eastern delta area of Arkansas were still baying for quick and radical action, he stopped to survey the scene.

Admittedly, this is rather strange politics, and to understand it one must know something of Arkansas.

In the first place, Republicans just do not get elected to state office here. So there is no perpetual automatic opposition of the type familiar in the two-party states of the North.

Secondly, Arkansas has no state-wide political machine, such as the Byrd organization in Virginia, capable of direct restraint on a headstrong chief executive.

And finally, it possesses no political personalities of sufficient stature to challenge the Governor now in intrastate combat. During two terms he has had astonishingly uniform success in pushing his programs through the legislature; indeed, many of the moderates who now seek to restrain him on the racial issue have been his most enthusiastic supporters in previous efforts aimed at attracting industry and otherwise boosting Arkansas out of its backward status. So they figure they can most effectively influence him as friends, not foes.

For a glimpse at the undramatic manner in which such influence was exerted, apply the microscope to one man in the multitude.

He is Joshua K. Shepherd, a silver-haired Little Rock gentleman who sits in front of an oaken roll-top desk in a big old house where he conducts an insurance business. He has never so much as run for public office; he finds himself deep in subtle politics now largely because of his long-held belief that good public schools are a cornerstone of American civilization.

So active was his interest that when President Eisenhower called a national conference on education, Governor Faubus included him among 17 delegates. Many state delegations disbanded upon their return home, but Mr. Shepherd and his friends decided to form a permanent group to erase the educational disgrace of Arkansas. (The state ranked 48th in expenditures per pupil; its teachers were the lowest-paid in the nation.)

The Governor, enthusiastic, gave them official advisory status, invited them to draw up an improvement program—which they did, late last year, and it proved expensive. Undaunted, Orval Faubus battled at their side to shove through the legislature a 50 per cent boost in the sales tax, a stiff hike in personal income taxes, over stiff opposition. Teachers' salaries, running about $2,400 yearly, were increased by an average of $800. The integration-segregation issue was not raised. "At this point," says Joshua Shepherd, "Mr. Faubus had done more for education than any Arkansas governor of this century."

Suddenly came the Governor's abortive effort to bar Negroes from Central High, soon followed by the threat that the legislature would be asked to tamper with the public-school system. "I was shocked," says Joshua Shepherd.

So were others he met on the street, he found. "It was the old game; we said to each other, 'Somebody should do something,' and at first we didn't realize we were somebody." Then, quite informally, things began to happen. Mr. Shepherd is a president emeritus of the Little Rock Chamber of Commerce; so are a score of other businessmen. Twice last week they all huddled, without publicity; this Monday they met again and without a single objection issued to the press a mild-sounding statement that it would be "unwise" for the Governor to call a special session of the legislature "while emotions are aroused and the situation is yet tense."

There is one other factor in this political equation, and to a reporter who arrives here from a big city it can be somewhat surprising. That is Christianity. In Arkansas it is taken seriously. Time and again people trying to explain why they feel as they do end up speaking in terms of religion.

So political reporting must in this case take into account what is said from the pulpit—and the ministers were the first group in Little Rock to begin speaking up plainly for moderation. Like others, the pastors are not unanimous; the Reverend M. L. Moser, Sr., told his congregation last Sunday that sending Federal troops into Arkansas violated the Constitution. Most, though, have emphasized such themes as the "brotherhood of man."

If there is any one man who has helped link all of these groups it is that religious politician, Representative Brooks Hays, an earnest, weary man who has been working here ceaselessly and quietly. But the application of the brakes—whether or not they hold—is the patient work of many men.

HENRY GEMMILL AND JOSEPH GUILFOYLE

October 3, 1957

Northern Desegregation

NEW YORK—Every weekday morning several school buses pull up in front of Public School 93 in the Bronx and some 200 Negro children scamper off to class.

Until last September these seven- and eight-year-old tots could walk to their own neighborhood schools. Today the City of New York takes them in buses the 20 city blocks or more to P.S. 93.

Their daily journey is part of an enforced mass migration of school children being launched by New York's Board of Education. It's a matter of racial integration. Until the Negro children were transferred to P.S. 93, that school was attended almost entirely by white pupils living in the neighborhood. Now, like many of the 790 other New York public schools, it is "mixed."

"Mixed" is a big word in New York City these days. Without fanfare—but by no means without objections—city officials have begun a program of racial integration that involves more than a policy of nondiscrimination. As at P.S. 93, many school youngsters are already being transported from one school district to another so that the Board of Education can achieve what it feels is a proper balance.

The aim of all this activity is to eliminate the school segregation that occurs in the North as an outgrowth of local housing patterns. To banish it the officials must also banish the traditional concept of the "neighborhood school."

Elsewhere in the North this campaign to abolish alleged "de facto" school segregation is also picking up in intensity—notably in cities like Chicago, Philadelphia and Detroit. But the most impressive efforts are being made here in New York.

Even here the size of the school migration can't be fully measured. One difficulty is that its operation is decentralized; school officials say they've made no attempt to add up the number of pupils transferred. Another is that the best-informed officials hesitate to give a guess; they shy away from public comment because they think it is an explosive subject.

Nevertheless, all concede that hundreds of New York students are already crisscrossing the city by bus and subway to schools far from home. In the slum-ridden Bedford-Stuyvesant area of Brooklyn, full-scale transfers of children from zone to zone have brought about integration in at least 20 schools since the opening of the school year.

Not only are children from Negro sections like Harlem traveling to hitherto all-white schools; in some instances, white pupils are crossing regular school zones to enter all-Negro schools.

"One junior high school in my three Brooklyn districts was almost entirely Negro last year, and it's now fifty-fifty in racial composition," says Samuel M. Levenson, an assistant superintendent of schools. He adds: "In another junior high school white students were brought in from a mile or so away to prevent it from becoming one hundred per cent Negro."

"We've got busloads of Negro children coming in from big distances," the principal of a formerly all-white school in Manhattan relates. "I hate to think what it's costing the city."

In some cases, integration is being achieved by means of minor gerrymandering of school zones without much transfer of pupils. This is particularly true of schools in so-called fringe areas where white and Negro neighborhoods converge.

School authorities tend to discount the protests they hear. "We had some white parents who threatened violent action if their children were transferred to Negro schools," confides a Brooklyn principal, "but in the end some of them just gave up and moved away." Agrees the Reverend Dr. David M. Cory, executive secretary of the Brooklyn Division, Protestant Council: "You hear a lot of talk about violent opposition to school integration, but I have yet to find any actual manifestation of it."

Nonetheless, some open opposition exists. The scheme to rotate experienced teachers from good to problem schools has already drawn sharp objections from the powerful High School Teachers Association. Its president, Mrs. Concetta T. Roy, warns: "It will only create more dissatisfied high-school teachers."

And the Reverend W. Sterling Cary of Brooklyn says: "I just don't think the schools are the answer. The real problem lies in the housing ghettos themselves which are the cause of Northern school segregation. And I think all this rezoning could be a hardship on children who may have to travel great distances to school every day."

"I believe we're being stampeded into a dubious program," contends the principal of a recently integrated Brooklyn school. "We have incontrovertible evidence of large numbers of white children withdrawing from schools when Negroes are brought in from outside. Many New York schools will be one hundred per cent colored within two years after Negro children are introduced. The hard truth is that we can't have full-scale integration until both Negroes and whites are really ready for it."

But such voices seem unlikely to halt the rush. As one highly placed New York school official puts it: "Any racial issue is political dynamite in a city like this. If anyone suggests that the integration program be slowed down while we find out where we're going he's immediately branded a racist."

PETER B. BART

January 29, 1957

Industry Integration

WINSTON-SALEM, N.C.—Visit the Western Electric plant here during the 10 A.M. coffee break and you come upon four young ladies, clerks in the personnel department, playing cards together around a desk. One of them is a Negro.

Travel on south to Charlotte and you find Negro engineers, draftsmen and lab technicians harmoniously eating lunch among multitudes of white co-workers in the cafeteria at the Douglas Aircraft Co. plant.

And in Greensboro, North Carolina, Burlington Industries, a power in the Southern textile industry, has just hired a Negro chemist—without any fuss whatsoever.

These instances point up facets of Southern race relations often overlooked amid the furor over school integration:

Negroes and whites continue to work peacefully side by side in many Southern plants—though integrated factories still are in the minority in Dixie. Furthermore, in racially tense Dixie, Negroes are continuing to make progress, although at a slower rate, toward greater integration in industry.

This progress follows definite patterns, and some major barriers still remain.

Negroes, for example, find far more skilled jobs in such states as North Carolina and Tennessee than they do in the Deep South, where racial feeling runs strongest. And industries relatively new to the South, such as electronics and aircraft, have opened up more skilled jobs to Negroes than longer-established Southern industries such as textiles and steel.

As for barriers, lack of training and experience still bar many Negroes from skilled jobs, even in cases where employers are willing to hire them. And, with few exceptions, Southern employers continue to shy from placing Negroes in supervisory posts where they would boss white workers.

There's no question the school integration fight has led to increased tension in integrated plants. And Negro leaders say the fight has had its impact on industrial hiring.

According to Herbert Hill, national labor secretary for the National Association for the Advancement of Colored People: "It has become more difficult to win gains for the Negro worker in the South during the past year," because of "the general atmosphere" since Little Rock.

Mr. Hill blames both labor and management: "Invariably industry anticipates, not always with justification, a negative reaction from the white rank and file" toward nondiscrimination. He accuses union leaders of "capitulating to the racists" and "abrogating their responsibility to press for Negro economic opportunity." The A.F.L.-C.I.O. credos on nondiscrimination in employment "have become a ritual without much meaning," he charges.

Although he exhibits much of the impatience characteristic of most Negro antisegregation leaders, Mr. Hill does admit gains have been made this year in the South's oil refinery and chemical industries with some help from the union involved, the Oil, Chemical and Atomic Workers Union.

Working more quietly, and relying entirely on the powers of persuasion, the American Friends Service Committee has been helping Southern Negroes obtain employment on the basis of merit.

"We've had a good reception from top management," notes Tartt Bell, executive secretary of the Friends' Southeastern office in High Point, North Carolina. "They do recognize discrimination in employment as a problem. They realize they don't have the freedom to exercise their right to choose the most qualified person for a job in some cases," he says.

A slight, alert-looking individual, Mr. Bell argues: "No one in these Southeastern communities can do as much to change race patterns as the businessman. He can do far more than the do-good-ers or the unions."

And some businessmen are making changes, "quietly upgrading a Negro to a job formerly reserved for whites," he notes. Statistics are hard to come by, however. "Many times businessmen don't want anybody to know about it," Mr. Bell observes.

The A.F.S.C. did make a survey last month of 402 firms in Greens-boro. Of these firms, 53 said they intend to employ solely on merit without regard to race or religion; 114 firms said they will employ on merit alone for some job categories other than the conventional jobs in which Negroes regularly work; and 43 other firms said they would employ solely on merit in the future "as conditions change." Several in the latter group said they didn't want to lead the way in their industries or neighborhoods, but would follow other firms.

Looking out his office door toward a room full of clerks, the presi-dent of a medium-sized Southern textile firm says: "I'd like to get a Negro receptionist out there. Some day we'll call all the girls in and ask them what they think about it. But we won't do it right now. With all the fuss over schools, it would be like sticking your thumb in their eyes."

Officials of integrated Southern plants say they're watching care-fully for racial friction. "This thing is right in our front yard, you know," says the personnel manager of one plant. "They've inte-grated a school just a few blocks from the plant. There's been a lot of discussion in the plant, but no serious repercussions."

Where friction is threatened, plant supervisors are quick to try to head it off. The president of one North Carolina firm several months ago hired a Negro to work alongside a white production worker. The two got into a bitter argument one day, and the presi-dent came along just in time to hear the Negro say: "You ever do that again and I'll kill you." The president fired the Negro im-mediately.

But it isn't always the Negro who's fired. Consider what happened in Greensboro to Bob Ford, who runs a small machine shop turning out high-precision products—orthopedic surgical implants such as bone screws and bone nails.

When Mr. Ford considered hiring a Negro machinist a couple of years ago his foreman threatened to quit. "I talked it over with my parish priest," recalls Mr. Ford, "and he told me the only Christian thing to do was to hire the Negro." Mr. Ford did, and the foreman quit. "I also lost my secretary and a part-time man," he says.

But now Mr. Ford has a Negro foreman, "a natural-born machinist," who supervises both white and Negro machinists in complete harmony, Mr. Ford says. And to the casual visitor, the shop crew, indeed, appears skilled, hard-working and congenial.

ED CONY

September 29, 1958

A Criterion for Colleges

When the war ended in 1945, thousands of young Americans took advantage of G.I. benefits and flooded the nation's colleges. Classrooms, lecture halls and dormitories suddenly were jammed. Universities set about erecting temporary housing units and lecterns were installed in gymnasiums. Within months the nation's institutions of higher learning were straining their beams and faculty personnel were in short supply.

Today, 13 years later, the cry for Federal aid for college construction continues to be heard. Russia's scientific achievements last fall succeeded in amplifying that cry. Yet just last week two education authorities told a Columbia University workshop for high-school counselors that there is college classroom space aplenty in the United States.

Dr. Hans Rosenhaupt, director of the Woodrow Wilson Fellowship Foundation at Princeton, New Jersey, said parents and counselors should learn more about the hundreds of schools not ordinarily classed among the so-called prestige institutions. Many of these, he indicated, are hungry for students.

Bernard P. Ireland, Columbia College director of admissions, urged the counselors to point out to students the merits of schools in the Midwest and the South—schools which are anxious to increase their rolls.

Both emphasized that the true picture of America's college facilities is thrown out of focus by the lopsided number of candidates who apply to what are known in the campus world as the "top thirty" schools. A college's reputation as a good school, points out Dr. Rosenhaupt, is often nothing more than its name being well known to the public.

Here, it seems to us, is a chief point of confusion in the world of education—or rather the world of the college applicant. A mystic aura has developed about certain Gothic towers and a kind of

"Holy smoke—look what the Russians have done to us!"

chauvinism has emerged which is working against a healthy rise of higher education standards across the land.

There was a time a generation or two ago when it was far less difficult to be admitted to Princeton, Harvard or Yale. Today, with tens of thousands of young people applying to Ivy League schools, even exceptional students are frequently turned away. And because less famous schools are usually low on the applicant's list, they must fill their rolls as best they can. Thus, the prestige of the former swells while the name of the smaller college is often hailed only by its sons.

But a student gets out of school just about what he puts into it, whether he studies at an enshrined citadel or an extension night school.

A student imbued with a desire not only to learn but to wonder can find in an unsung school the way to understanding and fulfillment. He can take advantage of smaller lecture halls and more intimate recitation classes to ask the questions that in large groups are unanswered because they are unasked.

And he need take no less pride in his alma mater than does the alumnus of the Ivy League. He will have placed his faith in himself and his devotion to learning ahead of other considerations, and by his very presence he will have helped a smaller school mold itself while it molded him.

179

There is a unique satisfaction in that. And for all the honor duly attending prestige schools, it is the one satisfaction their alumni can never know.

August 25, 1958

EDITORIAL

Mr. Robeson Takes a Trip

Mr. Paul Robeson, whose great gift as a singer is matched by a talent for bitter criticism of his country, is off for a European concert tour after waiting eight years for a passport.

The baritone is on his way because the Supreme Court decided recently that the State Department didn't have the right to deny a man a passport just because the Government didn't like a man's views about this country or about Communism.

We thought the Supreme Court right then, and we think the President is wrong now to ask Congress to pass a law returning that power to the State Department.

Such a law, we think, would be wrong for several reasons. For one thing, we can see no reason why a man free to travel in any of the 48 states should be barred from traveling overseas. If a man is a danger to the country, then the man should be tried and if convicted he should be put in jail. A great many have. But if a man is not a danger within the country, we can't see how he can suddenly endanger the country once outside its borders.

Paul Robeson is a man with whose opinions about this country we completely disagree. But can a radical baritone's voice drown out Mr. Dulles? Can his views threaten NATO, or nullify all the billions of dollars we've spent on foreign aid to make friends and influence other nations? If so, we have built a foreign policy that is insecure indeed; and we might be the better off for knowing about it.

The fact is that Paul Robeson can't possibly do those things. He will be acclaimed in London, perhaps, for his artistry and acclaimed in Moscow for his political views. But what off-key remarks can Robeson make overseas that he hasn't said right here at home? And what has he said here that hasn't got overseas?

Our Government and private agencies have spent millions upon millions of dollars to strengthen the image of America as the land of the free. But will other people in other places not think of us as the land of the fearful if we deny the right to travel to our own critics? Surely, this is an unbecoming posture for the nation, at best.

And at worst, it could become a dangerous procedure. If the Government is empowered to deny Paul Robeson and others like him a passport because they are disgruntled or critical of our system, what is to stop the Government from broadening that power to include those who disapprove not of the whole system but only of part of it? Is the next step to label critics of, say, foreign aid as too "dangerous" to let abroad and to deny them passports also?

So far as Robeson, the individual, is concerned, it wouldn't matter very much to us if he found life elsewhere so enchanting he decided never to come back here. But so far as all of us are concerned, it should matter very much that even Robeson and his kind shall have the right to go.

July 14, 1958

EDITORIAL

Meet Jimmy Hoffa

MIAMI BEACH—Meet Jimmy Hoffa. This short, tough official of the giant Teamsters Union has emerged even more clearly as a dominant force on the labor scene as a result of the power struggle between the A.F.L.-C.I.O. executive council and the rebellious truck union here.

Mr. Hoffa's rise to power has been swift and with few, if any, major setbacks. He started more than 20 years ago as a Detroit grocery clerk. He then joined the A.F.L. organizing staff, later became business agent for a truck drivers' local union. Before long, he was at the top of the Teamster heap in Detroit. In 1952 he backed Mr. Beck for the Teamster presidency, was named a vice-president and chairman of the Central States Conference of Teamsters. He holds a long list of other union titles, including president of Local 299 and trustee of Teamster welfare funds.

But the way up has not been free of troubles from Congressional investigators or the law.

Hoffa freely admits to a string of arrests, which he says were connected with organizing drives. The record shows 17 run-ins with the law, involving such things as picket line violence, molesting workers

"I'd like to help you up, Mac, but you know what a strong union we have."

and assault and battery. There are three convictions on record, with fines ranging from $10 to $1,000.

In one case he was indicted for extortion but the charge was reduced to a lesser one of violating a state labor law; Hoffa paid a small fine and $500 in costs.

As a result of a 1954 investigation of racketeering in the Detroit area, a House subcommittee said he had been described as the "brains" of an alleged shakedown.

"Hoffa is a dominant figure in the Teamsters Union and virtually a dictator in certain areas, despite the fact that he has been found guilty and convicted of violation of the Michigan State labor law and the Federal antitrust laws," the committee report declared. The report called him "contemptuous" in refusing to answer questions about whether his wife was carried on the union payroll, what his complete business interests were, and whether he had an interest in an auto haulaway trucking firm in the Detroit area. The investigation later was dropped.

Sit and talk with Mr. Hoffa and you're soon calling him "Jimmy." He's a rapid talker and leaves the definite impression that he knows exactly what he has said and is going to say. He has a disarming directness which seems frank. His blue eyes are seldom averted from the listeners. He is seldom without an answer.

Mr. Hoffa's speech is sometimes sprinkled with short, hard, unprintable words. He uses these most freely in reference to certain C.I.O. union leaders. He has a terrific drive, dashing from one meeting to another, talking intensely with a succession of other union men here. An incident he tells illustrates his attention to union business:

A Miami cab driver picked him up, recognized him, told Mr. Hoffa that he and other cabmen in his company were represented by an independent union but wanted to get into an A.F.L.-C.I.O. union. Before he climbed out of the taxi, Mr. Hoffa had arranged to meet with the drivers the next night.

Asked how he extends his authority over such a wide area, Mr. Hoffa replies that as ninth vice-president he is an international officer and entitled to do so.

The Teamster boss is a careful student of legal technicalities affecting union operations. He has at least two personal lawyers in addition to the union's legal men.

"Every important case that comes out, I get my lawyers to give me a brief on it that I can understand," he says.

JOHN A. GRIMES

February 7, 1957

Exurban Lampoon

Recent literary explorations—serious and quasi-serious—into the mores and folkways of exurban life have converted Westchester and Fairfield counties into veritable sociological laboratories.

P.T.A. activities, lawn care, Little League baseball and other problems confronting these burgeoning communities have been examined and catalogued by diverse writers. Though the locales covered have been restricted to smallish areas of New York and Connecticut, the findings can be readily applied to life in Beverly Hills, Shaker Heights or Evanston.

For the reader who prefers his sociology leavened with liberal doses of humor, a new study is now at hand: Max Shulman's *Rally Round the Flag, Boys!* If you have ever been distressed by DeVoto or rankled by Reisman, Shulman's rousing lampoon on life in a

commuting village is your dish. Mr. Shulman, easily one of the
funniest writers of the day, chooses Putnam's Landing, Connecticut,
as the not so mythical town for the scene of his novel.

Like other towns in this area, Mr. Shulman explains, Putnam's
Landing shows "three distinct social categories, vertically divided.
First, there are the Yankees, descendants of the original settlers and
still the wielders of power. Second, there are the Italians—who
initially came into Fairfield County as track layers for the New
Haven Railroad and remained to become storekeepers, artisans,
mechanics, etc. Third there are the New York commuters, also
called the lambs, or the pigeons or the patsies."

Adroitness at spotting his subject's vulnerability is essential for
the satirist; if the subject has history and respectability, so much the
better. The New England town meeting—certainly one of our more
sacrosanct institutions—is handily treated in one of Shulman's best
chapters.

Among those representing the vertical strata of Putnam's Landing
at the town meeting to discuss the controversial garbage disposal
problem was Vittorio di Maggio, who once reflected, "Town Meeting, itsa lika opera. First one fella singsa aria, then another fella
sticksa knife in his back!" Also present was George Melvin, the real-
estate dealer whose talents at fancy nomenclature enabled him to
unload difficult sites to commuters.

Thus "Powderhorn Hill" was formerly a swamp, "Flintlock
Ridge" was 40 acres of salt meadow. His boldest stroke was "Upper
Meadow"—formerly a gravel pit. All of these developments sold
with dispatch after their rechristenings.

Spokesman for the commuters' group was Betty O'Sheel, "a
stolid, modest matron of 34, who had never expected to reach such
heights in politics . . . For weeks her husband and two infant
daughters lived on Spam and made their own beds while Betty had
pored over United States Public Health Service bulletins on the
disposal of putrescible and nonputrescible wastes."

The Moderator of the meeting was a sort of hybrid—"a Yankee
who commuted." You will discover that Mr. Shulman has not overlooked many of the personalities who contribute to this laboratory
of democracy. As an intelligent humorist, the author does not dep-
recate our activities; he simply suggests that we begin to look a
little silly when we take ourselves too seriously.

The townspeople's reaction to a U.S. Army decision establishing
a guided-missile base in Putnam's Landing provides the novel with
what there is in the way of a basic plot. Startled by the news of the
impending Army invasion, the town leaders shelve their current

dispute over the garbage issue and unite in a resistance campaign against the Nike base.

Mr. Shulman's talent for character analysis provides his book with some of its best moments. Here he is introducing Grady Metcalf, the town's leading juvenile delinquent:

> "Grady was not the lean, hard Sal Mineo type. He was more on the well-fed, spongy side. The tenement that spawned him was a $40,000 ranch house on two well-kept acres, and the sight of a switchblade would have put him in shock. . . . A boy was no longer excluded from the glamorous ranks of the delinquents simply because he had the rotten luck not to be born in a slum; all he had to do was *look* as though he had."

As he unravels his story in episodic bursts, Mr. Shulman is immensely engaging; despite the sharp caricatures and slapstick comedy that characterize his work, there is also evident a warmth and affection for the people who come under his scalpel. And it is this quality of sympathy and understanding that distinguishes *Rally Round the Flag, Boys!*

CHARLES PRESTON

August 30, 1957

Underworld Invades Legitimate Business

Frank Costello, sensationalized by Senate crime investigators as a king of the underworld, yesterday gave the nation a quick glimpse of his intrusion into the upperworld of legitimate business.

The racketeer put $40,000 into Tele-King Co., a sizable TV set manufacturer, he told the Kefauver crime hearing in New York—and took it out again. He has bought into another television company (name undisclosed) in the name of his wife—and is still in.

More than $41,000 of his money has gone into the King Oil Co., which has leases in Oklahoma and Texas, he testified. The probers pressed questioning whether he has an interest in Whiteley distillery, of Scotland, which makes House of Lords and King's Ransom Scotch whisky, or in Alliance Distributors, which markets it in this country; Costello insisted not. Earlier in the hearing he had mentioned miscellaneous other investments—he said until last year he had owned 79 Wall Street Corp., which operates an office building and "two or three other taxpayers" (rental properties) in the heart of New York's financial district.

Racketeer Costello began tying the underworld to the upperworld a long time ago. Back in the twenties, he recalled yesterday, he was in partnership with a Horowitz manufacturing concern which was in an innocent business indeed: making kewpie dolls. (They were prizes for the punchboard trade.) He built houses in the Bronx; bought an apartment house in Manhattan. He put $15,000 to $20,000 in Dinky's Products Co., which sold ice-cream sticks.

Costello the businessman has an eye to the future and its technological advances. His favorite investment at the moment, he says, is Jet Broiler Co., which makes contraptions that will cook a chicken by what he calls "infra rays."

It is a portable contrivance (though it does not move by jet propulsion, as the name might imply) and Costello says, "I have confidence in it; you can lay it on a table regardless of apartment size."

This sort of testimony, which would sometimes be humorous if it weren't so ominous, has been pouring into the Kefauver committee ears for months now. Anyone who has thumbed through the mountainous transcripts can reach only this conclusion: The world of business is faced with another serious problem. It will have to keep on worrying about taxes and price controls and labor relations; it had better start worrying also about the gamblers and muscle men and murder suspects who are encroaching on legitimate commerce.

The mobsters have been getting plenty of money ($20 billion gross a year, it is suggested) and they have to put the profits somewhere. Testimony is that they've been putting chunks of it into steelmaking, hotels, liquor, auto enterprises, dressmaking, food companies, breweries, laundries, trucking.

Who is your competitor down the street? Are you sure he is an old-fashioned businessman, competing in the traditional ways?

In Chicago testimony was that a "policy operator" named Peter Tremont has been operating a Chrysler-Plymouth agency on the southeast side of town. In sun-drenched Miami Beach Isadore Blumenfield, alias Kid Cann, described as Minneapolis' "outstanding racketeer," was reported by a witness to have a substantial interest in the swank ocean-front Martinique Hotel.

Not all racketeers prosper when they invade legitimate business. Louis Crusco, a Philadelphia "numbers operator" who, according to testimony, wanted to get into "something legitimate," will testify to that. Shortly after he paid $25,000 cash to buy out a principal stockholder of the Strunk Steel Co. of Royersford, Pa., the firm went on the rocks. Now he's suing to get his money back.

JOSEPH M. GUILFOYLE

March 22, 1951

You Never Can Tell

We got to thinking about multiple-choice tests—you know, the kind where the teacher offers a statement and then a list of answers to choose, such as: Thomas Jefferson is a historic figure. He wrote, (1) the Declaration of Independence, (2) *Lolita,* (3) the Communist Manifesto.

We got to thinking about just such a test when we read of the National Education Association's study of the problem of juvenile delinquency. The N.E.A. has come up with some suggestions how principals and teachers can recognize incipient delinquency. Any youngster with the following among his characteristics should be watched carefully, the N.E.A. suggests. Here's the list:

1. Those who dress sharply, affect "offbeat haircuts."
2. Those with male kin who are tattooed.
3. Those who do poorly in school, miss classes often.
4. Those who use such expressions as "ain't."
5. Those with parents who do not belong to organized groups such as parent-teacher associations, women's clubs, the Elks, Lions, Redmen or other lodges.

Well, we'd like to run off a little multiple-choice quiz on these five characteristics, but we'll keep it easy. In fact, we won't even put our readers—or the N.E.A.—to the bother of matching our examples to the educationists' statements.

We'll do it right off, and the answers we'd suggest are these:

1. Mark Twain.
2. Admiral Halsey.
3. Winston Churchill.
4. William Shakespeare.
5. All children whose parents are nonconforming individuals. And, of course, all children unfortunate enough to be orphans.

February 16, 1959

EDITORIAL

FRUSTRATIONS, ANTIC
AND FRANTIC

Back in 1914 . . .

Howard Elliott, chairman of the New Haven board of directors, stated Saturday night that a wholesale curtailment of passenger service on the New Haven, cutting passenger mileage by 5,000 miles a week, and operating expenses by $5,000 and more a week, would be made by January 31. About 60 runs, local train service chiefly, are involved. The cut in service is necessitated by reduced earnings and increased cost of service, particularly the cost of labor.

Notices have been posted in the car shops at New Haven and Readville, Massachusetts, announcing effective January 3 a reduction of 10 per cent in the wages of several hundred mechanics, boilermakers, steam fitters and car workers.

Howard Elliott will be in Washington Tuesday for further conference with Attorney General McReynolds in relation to the plan of the separation of the Boston & Maine from the New Haven. J. P. Morgan, although no longer a member of the board of directors of the New Haven and the Boston & Maine, had a long conference in Boston Saturday with Howard Elliott.

January 6, 1914

. . . and in 1958

NEW YORK—This morning in the suburban towns outside Chicago, New York, Boston, Cleveland, San Francisco and other major cities, 500,000 commuters boarded trains to go to work. Discounting a few stragglers, approximately the same number will return home the same way tonight.

These people in many ways are a unique breed. Generally above average in income, they often are leaders in their two communities

*"I told you what would happen when you changed to 3½-
minute eggs this morning!"*

—at the office and at home. Some would have you believe that they are tougher and more resourceful than the average citizen, due, no doubt, to the split-second schedules that rule their lives and the harsh discomforts to which they frequently are subjected.

As a group they represent but a small slice of the nation's population, not much larger, indeed, than the number of American Indians still surviving. In fact, many of these daily riders on the railroads believe that the carriers would like nothing better than to consign them to the most distant reservation possible and forget all about them. For, like the Indian, the commuter has become a problem.

The commuter problem, of course, is no overnight development, but it now is growing increasingly acute—and pressure is mounting, particularly in the East, to shove some of the unwelcome burden of taking him to and from work onto the shoulders of the taxpayer.

The reason the commuter is a problem is simple: Hauling commuters, according to the railroads, is one of the quickest possible ways to go broke. Last year, railroad deficits from passenger operations amounted to $723 million, the largest in history; in 1958, according to present estimates, a new record loss, some $14 million higher, is in prospect. How much of the deficit is due to commuter riding is unknown. But the short-haul rider is accounting for a steadily increasing share of railroad traffic. Last year commuters accounted for 59 per cent of all railroad passengers and this share seems likely to increase to two thirds in a few more years, as more long-distance train services are discontinued.

Comments Interstate Commerce Commissioner Kenneth H. Tuggle, "It is well established that the deepest and most troublesome portion of the railroad passenger deficit occurs in commuter services."

This year two developments occurred which added a crisis complexion to the commuter problem in many cities. First, the railroads' freight traffic, which had provided a cushion for commuter losses, shrank sharply as a result of the recession. Freight traffic now is climbing again, but the railroads still stress their recession experience in detailing their commuter service plight.

Then, earlier this year, Congress passed the Transportation Act of 1958. In effect, this gave the Interstate Commerce Commission an overriding authority over state regulatory commissions to discontinue unprofitable intrastate commuter service if it could be proved that continuance of such services put an undue burden on the railroads' interstate business. Since the state regulatory bodies usually are reluctant to discontinue rail services within their states, the new law was hailed by the railroads. Within two days after it was signed by President Eisenhower, the New York Central and the Erie filed petitions with the I.C.C. to end service on some of their commuter routes.

Now, particularly in the East, there is increasing talk—and some action toward—making the commuter, like the Indian, a ward of the Government.

"If you're going to have mass rail transportation, I think subsidy is as sure in the future as anything you can think of," says George Alpert, the peppery, gray-haired president of the New York, New Haven & Hartford.

DAVID R. JONES

November 24, 1958

You Rang, Sir?

Mrs. Roy B. Unger, wife of the sales manager of Sealy Mattress Co., is casting about for a woman to help with the daily chores of bringing up four young Ungers and tidying up the Unger home in suburban Cleveland Heights, Ohio.

"No laundry or heavy cleaning," reads her newspaper appeal. "Bonus. Paid Vacation." Pay is $6 to $7 a day (Thursdays and Sundays off, of course). Added lures: Private room, with private bath and TV.

"I have to offer these things even to get an answer to my ad," Mrs. Unger tells an inquiring reporter. "And I have to assure any applicants this is a pleasant home and promise them the job will be easy."

Mrs. Unger's predicament is far from unusual today. Harassed mothers, working wives, bridge-playing matrons and members of the *haut monde* from coast to coast complain that the hunt for competent house helpers is frustrating and often futile. "The situation," sums up a servant-seeking lady in Newton, Massachusetts, "is simply impossible."

This plight, perhaps of some interest to businessmen who crave domestic tranquillity, has ramifications even beyond the home front. It's boosting the fortunes of a small band of entrepreneurs who specialize in providing household service, and of other outfits that import domestics from abroad. It's also a matter of some concern to Uncle Sam, who now collects Social Security taxes from household employees and their employers.

Today, about 2.5 million persons are employed as butlers, maids, gardeners, chauffeurs, cooks and other household helpers, the Census Bureau estimates. Some other employees who come under the Government's definition of domestics: laundresses, nursemaids, furnace men, valets, footmen, grooms and housekeepers. (Exception: A dog sitter, hired each Wednesday night by a theatergoing New York couple for $1.65 an hour.) The Census Bureau figure represents a better than 31 per cent gain in just over five years.

The Bureau attributes the increase to two main influences: the fact that more women are employed outside their own homes and therefore are hiring others for housework; and the end of the Korean War, which eased industry's demand on the available labor supply. Between 1940 and 1950, the number of employed household workers declined from about 2.5 million to 2 million, and then it climbed again.

But as big as the servant corps is, the number of available jobs is even bigger. Larger families, new hard-to-keep-clean homes in the suburbs, and folks more bent on leisure than labor in their spare time all have spurred the demand for household workers.

The dearth of domestics has not developed suddenly, to be sure. Since 1940, most kinds of household employee have been scarce. The reasons are partly sociological, partly economic. Historically, new immigrant groups provided the main supply of domestics, but this source has almost disappeared in recent years. Since the war, too, new job opportunities in labor-short industry have opened up for many former domestics.

In the American culture, a job as servant or domestic carries a certain connotation of inferiority in social status which is not true in many other countries where butlers, governesses and maids have some professional standing. But even here, a domestic can be—and often is—mighty independent nowadays, partly because she is selling her services in a seller's market.

"It's not like the old days when servants were part of the family," muses a lady in Burlingame, California, who refers to domestics today as "the wanderers." "At one time," she recalls, "I had a maid for twelve years. Today you're lucky to keep one for twelve months."

July 18, 1957

Ennui Unlimited

DETROIT—When a reporter recently objected to the rule of secrecy imposed on contract negotiations between the United Auto Workers and the "Big Three" auto makers, an official of General Motors Corp. had a ready answer:

"It would serve you right if we put you right in the bargaining room. Within a couple of days, you'd be screaming to get out—that's how dull it is."

His remark was an exaggeration, but it is unquestionably true that the sessions are composed of something like six weeks of tedium and a few hours of drama.

Nothing in the business world carries more excitement and drama than the eleventh-hour intrigue and debate of labor contract negotiations. But the long days of haggling over petty details, important only to the handful of workers or supervisors actually involved, are almost as superlatively boring.

In fact, according to one veteran of such talks, the most physically and mentally wearing aspect of collective bargaining is not the all-night meetings and the violent arguments—union and management men nowadays are too polite for much of that. The part that is toughest is spending hours in serious consideration of trivia.

Take, for example, the current sessions between representatives of the U.A.W. and G.M. Union and management talent worth at least $2,000 a day is spending its time arguing over "issues" such as these:

Seven union-proposed changes in the method of dues payment through payroll deductions.

Twenty-five proposed alterations in the contract definitions of the duties and status of union shop committeemen.

A requested ban on picture taking by movie or television cameramen in G.M. plants without the permission of workers being shot.

A demand that workers be granted discounts on G.M. products (in a period when auto and appliance dealers are already discounting heavily).

And a proposal that any worker caught working at two or more jobs shall be dropped from the payroll "as an automatic quit."

In other sessions, bargainers will stall and wrangle over such subjects as the time required for washing up and how promptly notices of union activities must be posted on factory bulletin boards.

Each of these demands, picayune as it may sound, is important to somebody at the local level. And the workers to whom they are important have a hand in electing the union representatives. That's why they must be given some attention in the bargaining room.

"We always figure the first few days of negotiations will be spent listening to speeches by local representatives who have to make their big political pitches for the boys back home," one official explains. "We aren't going to do anything, in a lot of these cases, and the union men know we aren't. But at least they can go back and honestly say they tried."

This is not to say, of course, that all such demands get the brush-off. In many cases the companies do grant requests to straighten out a situation which, because it was minor and unimportant, had not been called to the attention of anyone with enough authority to change it.

More often than not, however, the company is likely to turn down these "form" proposals. And, as union men can tell you, the management side can be just as long-winded in its replies as the union in its demands.

Louis G. Seaton, G.M.'s vice-president-personnel, is fond of telling a story about a past bargaining session with the auto workers in which company officials insisted on reading the complete text of a 60-page brief rejecting union suggestions on the subject of promotions.

One labor representative sat fighting drowsiness throughout the long presentation, then roused himself to observe: "Well, we've heard the long no, the short no, the reasoned no, the arbitrary no, the pleasant no, and the aggressive no. But this is the first damn time we've heard a monumental no."

DAN CORDTZ

Ceilings—Spelled F-l-o-o-r-s

Next Friday all used autos sold will be subject to ceilings set by the Office of Price Stabilization. Sounds fine, doesn't it? At last we'll be protected from the handful of sharpshooters who have been selling new-used cars above the list price.

Why anyone has to patronize these premium extorters we wouldn't know. Anyone who really has to buy a car now can either get a new one—149,000 rolled off the lines last week—or find plenty of good recent-model cars.

But we wondered what else might be happening, as a result of this O.P.S. order. So we made some inquiries among used-car dealers and we'll report just one typical conversation. Said the dealer: "If you're going to buy a used car you'd better get it now. All of 'em here are selling 'way under the book (the O.P.S. ceiling). But on March 2 we're marking them up as high as the law allows."

February 27, 1951

EDITORIAL

Unfair Trade

After a nineteen-year trial, the Eastman Kodak Company has given up fair trade on the ground that fixed prices are unworkable and thus "unfair to retailers." While still believing in the "principle" of fair trade, the firm finds the device of fixing prices "impracticable."

We're not surprised. State courts have been steadily whittling away—and properly so—at fair-trade laws by finding some of the price-fixing provisions unenforceable. Particularly distasteful to jurists and laymen alike was fair trade's concept that a contract between one manufacturer and one retailer in a state was as binding on all the other retailers as though they had also signed up. This feature alone was enough to make fair trade rather impracticable for retailers, whose mounting complaints, Eastman says, led the company to junk its fair-trade policy.

Yet it is likely that the retailers were merely reflecting the attitude of the public, for people have a way of shopping around for the best price they can get. A man may want a camera, and he may even want an Eastman camera, but that does not make the man want to pay Dealer Jones a higher price than is asked by Dealer Smith who is willing to take a smaller profit than Eastman and Jones think Smith should realize. And Eastman's withdrawal from fair trade certainly concedes that a man who wants an Eastman camera can usually find someone who will sell it to him at a price acceptable to the man.

Thus another established manufacturer joins a growing list of makers of products from electric trains to television sets in the realization that fair trade was always a bad device because it sought to deny the delicate relationship of price to supply and demand. Thus it violated from the beginning the first principle of the market place.

The violation of that principle, as Eastman has learned, fore-doomed fair trade as surely as the man who forgets his film at home will not bring back any pictures of the picnic in his camera. And the company that forgets that in the end it's the customer who sets the prices is likely to find that it has been not only "unfair to re-tailers" but unfair to itself as well.

January 3, 1957

EDITORIAL

The Forgotten Tuxedo

Breathes there a man in borrowed braid
Who never to himself hath prayed:
Oh, for my own, my fitted tux?

If there is, these comments are not for him. As for most of the rest of us, Democrat or Republican—and even those Socialists who would be willing to be caught in public in such arrant capitalist attire—we can only have the deepest kind of sympathy for Mr. Nixon's recent tuxedo troubles.

Somebody, it seems, did not pack Mr. Nixon's dinner jacket for his London trip, so he had to wear another man's. Now, it might have made some sense for the Vice-President to have borrowed someone else's clothes, say, if he were returning to South America, considering the wear and tear of the enthusiastic crowds he some-times runs across there. But this trip was to polite and dignified old England, so obviously the missing tuxedo was simply forgotten.

Well, as much as most of us would like to forget all about tuxedos, we know there comes a time when we've got to get the rig on; and if anything is worse than your own tuxedo that doesn't fit, it's a bor-rowed one that doesn't fit. Mr. Nixon's, commandeered from a newspaper reporter, was long in the sleeves, baggy at the knees and far too big at the waistline. To top it all, he was host at the Ameri-can Embassy to the Queen of England.

But things, thank goodness, went all right at the Thanksgiving celebration. The Queen wore a full-skirted white satin dress with pale-red roses formed by bright paillettes. Mrs. Nixon wore a pale-green evening gown flecked with gold. The Queen and Mr. Nixon talked about foreign affairs at the dinner. After dinner Mr. and Mrs. Nixon talked, too, but about private affairs.

The whole occasion has increased Mr. Nixon's stature. We can't think of anything since Checkers wagged on TV to make the ordinary voter feel closer to the Vice-President than to know he squirmed in a borrowed tux that didn't fit. Unless it were to know that the answer he got was the same all traveling men, sooner or later, get: Well, why don't you pack your own bag, then?

December 1, 1958

EDITORIAL

All Washed Up

Monsanto Chemical Company, as its name implies, is primarily a manufacturer of basic chemicals for industry. But now it looks as if it's got to make washing powder for housewives, whether it wants to or not. It seems that not making something can also lead to trouble with the law.

A few years ago Monsanto chemists developed what they thought was a particularly good detergent, and because it seemed like a good idea at the time Monsanto started making and marketing it under the "All" trade name. Later the company decided it ought to stick to its last and get out of the soap business. So it sold "All" to Lever Brothers.

But this week the Justice Department said, "Sorry, no can do." It filed a suit in Federal District Court to make Lever Brothers turn "All" back to Monsanto.

The reason given for the suit is that Lever Brothers, by acquiring this washing powder, automatically increased its share of the market for detergents. This seems incontrovertible, although even with "All" Lever Brothers would still have nowhere near all of the market. Four fifths or more of the market would remain in the hands of some pretty fierce competitors for the housewife's trade.

This suit, if successful, is going to leave Monsanto with a puzzler. If they can't sell to Lever Brothers, to whom can they sell it? If Procter and Gamble, or Colgate, or some other detergent company takes it over they will automatically increase their share of the business too. Apparently Monsanto can't even give it away without running the recipient afoul the antitrust laws.

Under this doctrine Monsanto's only choice seems to be to liquidate and write off its losses or to stay in the dishwashing business willy-nilly. The moral, we suppose, is to think twice before making anything. Once you start, the Government may make it hard to stop.

July 14, 1958

EDITORIAL

A Muse Unbound

The Nobel Prize for Literature, the most coveted honor in the world of letters, has been awarded to Boris Pasternak for his epic novel, *Doctor Zhivago*.

Mr. Pasternak is a Soviet citizen and his book deals with the moral disintegration of a physician and poet after the Russian Revolution. Because it illuminates the lies and failures of Communism, it has not been published behind the Iron Curtain, although it has been a best seller in the West. There is some question, in fact, whether the author will be permitted to visit Sweden to accept the prize.

The award has placed the Kremlin in an awkward position. The Red leaders have attempted to defend their ban on the book by stating that a Communist society has no use for a work of art that doesn't help to build a new world." This blatant example of anti-truth does more than underscore the deceit of the Communist mind.

For one thing, it illustrates the terrible insecurity felt by the Soviets—that they cannot accept such criticism but must denounce it bitterly.

It also points up how the Soviet dictatorship has its hands full in "guiding" the creative energy and curiosity of a traditionally artistic people. And it is a reminder to the world that even 41 years of Communism cannot remake a man's mind—that beneath the enforced placidity of the Soviet Union there is a quiet cry for freedom that cannot be stilled.

October 27, 1958

EDITORIAL

Autodom's Rebel

Much has been written about the joys of auto ownership. Of late even more has been written about the joys of foreign-car ownership. More needs to be written about the joys of non-car ownership.

Literature on this subject is sparse. This may be because the non-auto owner isn't the braggart so often encountered in the owner of an auto, a man who must constantly justify his investment of a half year's income in a motorized cart by loudly singing its praises.

So when someone sings of the joys of non-car ownership it must be a solo voice like ours. We are experts on this subject since we don't own an automobile, and don't intend burdening ourselves with one whether it be of Detroit vintage or a foreign-born import.

Just consider what we, as a member of the exclusive autoless clan, may claim as our own: No parking worries. No traffic to battle. No monthly payments. No arguments with the wife over dented fenders. No bills to pay for those fenders. No repair bills.

Is there an auto-encumbered person who has not considered such a glorious situation at least once after a minor traffic accident, a rough day on a four-lane highway when everybody wants to drive six abreast, or after that "payment past due" notice has arrived in the mail?

The carefree relief of being car-free is akin to that feeling one has when distant relatives (who don't remain distant enough) are leaving after a too long visit; or it might be compared to the lift one has on the first day of vacation (before the rain starts).

Not a day goes by but what the autoless man doesn't have some reason for glorying in his freedom. When a gasoline-tax-increase referendum is held, he can serenely vote "yes" with the knowledge that his own pocketbook will not be affected. An increase in auto insurance rates leaves his blood pressure undisturbed.

When the traffic officer rides down the block ticketing automobiles, the auto-free man may nod in righteous indignation at the callous disregard for law exhibited by some auto owners. His own brushes with traffic law, of course, are behind him.

With the automobile gone, the family garage becomes an oasis of space for the entire family. Junior's bicycle acquires a good home. No longer need one search for a place to store that old rocking chair which nobody wants to junk. The place becomes a rich warehouse of family treasures.

When winter comes the carless chap need not worry about the snow in the drive, for Junior can always push his bicycle through the drifts. Junior, of course, won't be around pleading for the family car or for an automobile of his own when he reaches teen age. He will have been so conditioned by the healthy, worry-free life in a car-free family that he probably will still be riding his bicycle when in college.

Not only has the auto-free man freedom from many cares, he may celebrate this state in a manner which only a nitwit auto owner would try to match. When some cheerful friend offers "one for the road" at the end of a party, he can accept with a light heart, knowing he will be staggering home in the back seat of a taxi with no drinkometer test hovering as a threat over his shoulder.

Unlike the foreign-car crowd we in the non-auto clan have no secret club sign nor any ritual of membership. But we may be recognized by one trait. At the close of a boisterous evening when the check arrives and the auto owners are fumbling futilely for wallets which seem glued in pockets, the non-auto owner may boldly reach for his own pocketbook. We know we have something there besides unpaid bills.

A friend of ours, who also doesn't have a car, confesses he gleans sadistic pleasure from those radio commercials which begin: "Friends. Do you need money?" Since he no longer "owns" a car, he doesn't need money any more, at least not that badly.

If you wonder how one gets along without an automobile, then consider how well many folks are doing without an even more utilitarian object—the kitchen range. Despite all the automatic cooking gadgets which finish dinner while wives play bridge, many a chef prefers cooking steaks over a bonfire in the backyard, while the wife still plays bridge.

If you must have an automobile for some types of trips, there are car rental agencies with their easily acknowledged credit cards. When the rental bill comes in the mail, it is almost certain to be less than those insidious and steady charges which the car owner bears as his burden.

But thumbing through a magazine last night we couldn't help but notice that piece about the new automobiles which are coming out. Those new 1959 models do look pretty nifty, don't they?

RAY VICKER

September 23, 1958

Committeemanship

If America ever does succumb to the Soviet, historians may record this contributing cause: The U. S. tried to defend itself with massed committees.

Intellectual committees, loaded with professors.

Gold-braid committees, banked with admirals and generals.

Bureaucrat committees, businessmen committees and layers of Congressional committees.

They dominate this nation's defense effort, and depress it, and delay it. The testimony, from men in and out of uniform, is all but unanimous:

"Too many committees," declares Navy Secretary Thomas Gates, ". . . . too many groups with veto power, without responsibility."

"I'm overcommitteed," says the Army's ballistic-missile boss, General John Medaris.

"The trouble is committees," says Air Force General Clarence Irvine, Deputy Chief of Staff for matériel. "They sort of grow like weeds on the side of the road. So if you have twenty people . . . who have discovered how to do this . . . you can sometimes have forty committees."

"Do away with the situation that has grown up over the last four, five or six years, where apparently a defense in depth against making decisions has been established with these committees and levels of committees," advises Thomas Laphier, Jr., vice-president of Convair, which is building the Atlas ICBM.

"Maybe I am a little too bitter about it, but it just seems every time I try to do something, I trip over a committee," muses J. H. Kindelberger, chairman of North American Aviation, which is designing the intercontinental chemical bomber. He notes that as the Air Force and its sister services grew, "they got more hooks to hang another committee on until any general or anybody with any real rank has to have a committee. Now the President has to have a committee, and I don't know who is the boss committee. I think there is a committee or committees, but they all take up a subject and they kick it around and half the time it dies, but in the meantime we wait and wait and wait and wait."

The committee malady has been diagnosed, and perhaps the Defense Department reorganization promised by President Eisenhower can help cure it, but what are the germs that have caused it?

One is the fact that the arms race has become a science race, and military officers and officials no longer approach their problems with assurance—even when they have hired able scientists to develop the weapons of the future. Grasping for certainty, they enlist batteries of Ph.D. outsiders to give advice.

Just how this works out in practice was related a few days ago in Congressional testimony by Dr. Wernher von Braun, the rocket expert who in concert with General Medaris is building the Jupiter missile for the Army at Huntsville, Alabama. Here are extracts:

COUNSEL: Did you go to the Pentagon and ask for decisions?
DR. VON BRAUN: General Medaris did once a week.
COUNSEL: How often did you go?
DR. VON BRAUN: Twice a month.
COUNSEL: Why was it necessary to go from Alabama to Washington?
DR. VON BRAUN: I had to go quite frequently because there were committee hearings here in Washington . . . technical and scientific committee hearings, and I had very often to justify why we were doing things this way and not that way, and why the Air Force does it another way, and why we think this way is better, and so forth, and this of course cost much of my time.
COUNSEL: Were these committee hearings constructive for you?
DR. VON BRAUN: Sir, I think we have too many committees in this area. There is a difference between a committee that evaluates something and a committee that continuously interferes with executive operations. The mechanism in the Pentagon is something like this: On practically every level there is an advisory committee advising a particular assistant secretary as to what is right and what is wrong, and since that man wouldn't make a decision without advice from his committee, you can't bypass the committees.
COUNSEL: Was this system impeding you in your work?
DR. VON BRAUN: Yes, definitely. We were very often confronted with the problem that a decision on this or that question wouldn't be made before a certain committee had a chance to talk to you.
COUNSEL: Was that committee consisting of experts in the missile field?
DR. VON BRAUN: Well, sir, put it this way: Most people that have real practical experience with missiles are busy building missiles these days, and such men are not eligible to serve on these committees, because they have missile projects of their own. I would say the great majority of gentlemen serving with these committees are brilliant experts in their particular fields, but the missile business, once you have got a project going, involves many questions which are of a non-scientific nature; they have something to do with project management or time schedules. For example, a physics professor may know a lot about the upper atmosphere, but when it comes to making an appraisal of what missile schedule is sound and how you can phase research and development effort into industrial production, he is pretty much at a loss.
COUNSEL: Some committees came to Huntsville to monitor you, did they not?

DR. VON BRAUN: Yes. How many do we have? Five, maybe. Sometimes the committee does not come together, but members come visiting, to get "a little background information for my work for the committee." I think our visitors' record would show there has not been a week in the last two years that some members of a committee have not been visiting our installation.

COUNSEL: Did they help you in your work?

DR. VON BRAUN: I would say sometimes these discussions are very interesting.

COUNSEL: I'm not talking about whether they are interesting. That impeded you in your work, did it not?

DR. VON BRAUN: Yes, sir, and I would say it impedes probably other missile projects also. My personal feeling, to be frank about this, is the following: that the prestige factor plays a very important part in these things. When there is a decision involving several hundred million dollars, then people want to protect themselves. And if a man can say, "I have on my advisory committee some Nobel Prize winners, or some very famous people that everybody knows," and then these sign the final recommendation, then he feels, "Now, if something goes wrong, nobody can blame me for not having asked the smartest men in the country."

COUNSEL: Who sent these scientists down there to Huntsville? Did you ask for them?

DR. VON BRAUN: No, sir. The way it goes, we get a piece of paper saying, "A new committee has been established . . ."

January 31, 1958

"I'd like a word with you, Fermage."

TEMPER OF THE TIMES

Farmer Yankus, Controls Fighter

DOWAGIAC, Mich.—"The only thing necessary for the triumph of evil is that good men do nothing."

Stanley Yankus, Jr., a surprisingly eloquent 39-year-old poultry farmer, quoted these Edmund Burke lines recently in a letter to United States District Attorney Wendell A. Miles at Grand Rapids. Mr. Miles is employing legal action against Mr. Yankus to collect some Federal fines. For what offense against the United States? For planting too much wheat on his farm.

The evil that Mr. Yankus sees is the surrendering of individual freedom to the Federal Government in exchange for economic security. Sitting before a large framed copy of the Declaration of Independence in his living room, farmer Yankus declares his own independence and his willingness to continue to make personal sacrifices for that principle as he sees it.

"I feel there is nothing to be gained in losing the right to control one's own destiny," he says. "Some people feel that it is possible to get something for nothing, but I know that it is impossible."

Ever since wheat farmers voted for penalties in 1954, Mr. Yankus has refused to recognize restriction on the wheat acreage he plants to raise chicken feed. He doesn't sell wheat, so efforts to support the market are no concern of his, he insists. The law decrees otherwise, but offers farmers who feel unfairly restricted the right of appeal. Mr. Yankus, like some other farmers, has refused all such remedies and his overplanting fines have mounted to $3,848. After two years of trying gentle persuasion, Mr. Miles, who was handed the case by Department of Agriculture attorneys, this spring brought force to bear.

In April, an F.B.I. agent visited egg buyer Sam Daken in Benton Harbor and quickly determined the income Mr. Yankus derives from his eggs. Mr. Daken, who regards Mr. Yankus as one of his most conscientious suppliers, was reluctant but opened his books to the agent. "I was impressed by the badge," he says. "I'd seen it on TV." A request that he not tell Mr. Yankus about the visit "sounded like an ultimatum," Mr. Daken said.

Another visit, to executive-vice-president Max Pugsley of the Dowagiac National Bank, apprised the Government of Mr. Yankus' checking account. "I don't like that sort of thing, but if you tried to stop them you'd be in a mess all of the time," says Mr. Pugsley.

The Washington operative also paid a call on a reporter for the Dowagiac *Daily News* and asked a few cryptic questions about Mr. Yankus' past.

On April 24, Mr. Yankus' checking account was frozen by a Federal court order. Several weeks ago, a court judgment gave the Government Mr. Yankus' half of the joint account, or $1,701. Advised by an attorney that he probably could not get a jury trial or win his case, Mr. Yankus did not contest the government action.

He has since been forced to sell 1,100 of his flock of 6,000 chickens to get working capital, reducing his egg income by about 20 per cent. Plans for a new feed room and repairs to the barn and chicken coops have been abandoned.

That this could happen to "Stanley," who is friendly, open and well liked, perplexes his neighbors in this southwest Michigan farming area. "People tell me on the street that 'they can't do that to you,' even though they've already done it," he says.

He has told his story to the Dowagiac Rotary Club and the township supervisors, received handshakes and sympathy. About $80 has come to him from well-wishers, $50 from a farmer-schoolteacher in another town.

Robert A. Wilson, a printer and one of Dowagiac's two justices of the peace, reprinted newspaper stories of the case and has been mailing them to newspapers, Congressmen and Senators at his own expense.

An impassioned local businessman, veteran of World War II's D-Day, declares: "Stanley has a right to live. He's not waxing rich. His wife and kids have to work gathering, sorting and candling eggs. Why does the Government do this to him?"

Mr. Yankus has joined the Independent Farmers of Michigan, about 15 to 20 men who are resisting controls. Last year was the first that Michigan farmers voted in favor of penalties (4,000 out of an eligible 22,000 voted) but only 30-odd cases still are in litigation, most from the first year. There are other "independent" groups in Ohio, Indiana, North Dakota and Montana, one Ohio group headed by Dr. P. S. Whiteleather, whose car was confiscated by Federal agents because of his fines. A Texas farmer, Evetts Haley, Jr., is fighting wheat penalties in the courts and plans to go to the Supreme Court if necessary. Mr. Yankus keeps track of these doings in the *Wheat Police News,* put out by the Montana group.

Sitting at a wooden desk in his sparsely furnished living room, Mr. Yankus writes 10 to 20 letters a night to other rebels, newspapers, magazines and political organizations. Having dived into an ideological maelstrom, he is being thrown a variety of ideological rescue lines.

Charles Lockwood, a Detroit attorney who is a Democrat and a local board member of the American Civil Liberties Union, objects strongly to the use of the F.B.I. in a Federal civil action against Mr. Yankus.

From the political right, Dan Smoot, a former F.B.I. man himself and champion of right-wing causes through the Dallas-based "Facts Forum" movement, hopes to make use of the Yankus story.

Support of a more moderate type comes from farm publications. Senator Potter (R., Mich.) arranged a meeting between Mr. Yankus and Mr. Miles two years ago, trying for a settlement. It failed after a sometimes heated two-hour discussion.

Through all this welter of conflicting ideologies, Mr. Yankus clings to his belief that the Federal Constitution guarantees him the right to mind his own business without interference.

"I'm not going to give up," he declares with characteristic stubbornness. "I'm not going to pay any fines or make any deals." Nodding toward two young lads nearby and only seemingly engrossed in books, he adds: "I don't want my kids to grow up in a world where they are going to be shipped around like pigs."

GEORGE MELLOAN

July 14, 1958

Don Quixote of Dowagiac

We commend to our readers the story of Stanley Yankus, a man who is making a great deal of trouble for himself when trouble might be easily avoided.

Mr. Yankus is a small farmer in Dowagiac, Michigan, and the Government of the United States has decided how much wheat he should grow on his farm, just as it decides how much every other wheat farmer may grow.

"Maybe I'd better explain how the soil bank works, Mr. Lindly."

Most of the other wheat farmers simply accept the Government-established quotas, whether they like them or not, and in return for their co-operation are financially rewarded by the Government. Mr. Yankus has decided to grow what wheat he wants to, a nonconformist attitude that has already cost him a thousand dollars, very likely will soon cost him more and—if he persists in being unreasonable—may even land him in jail.

There's small doubt that Mr. Yankus is a lawbreaker. At least he is violating a law now on the statue books and not yet overturned as an infringement upon liberty. The country, so far as one may judge, seems to have accepted the philosophy that a citizen may sow only as Washington will let him reap. So surely he has no reason to be surprised to find government agents inquiring among his neighbors and government prosecutors hauling him into courts. It is a formidable windmill at which Mr. Yankus tilts.

Of course, if he'd just be reasonable all his troubles would go away. Even his embarrassed prosecutors would likely forgive the transgression if they could just forget the whole business. That certainly is what we advise him to do for his own sake. He is bound to break his lance in so unequal a contest.

And yet . . . what more formidable a foe can there be for the little tyrannies of distant government than a few Quixotic men who dump tea into a harbor or stubbornly plant a few unlawful bushels of wheat?

July 14, 1958

EDITORIAL

Alcoholic Workers—Problem for Industry

A Texas oil refinery worker came to work with a hangover one morning and turned the wrong valve, wasting a large quantity of oil. The mistake, which wasn't noticed immediately, cost the company about $50,000.

The supervisor of a large utility's motor fleet, who was considered highly competent by his employer, began disappearing on drinking binges and frequently was incapable of doing his job properly. Resulting foul-ups cost the utility an estimated $4,000 per binge.

A large Midwestern manufacturer at first was highly pleased at the pickup in business and earnings after hiring a new chief executive. Then, for no apparent reason, business began slacking off until finally losses began piling up. Investigation by directors showed their new executive had taken to heavy drinking, impairing his judgment and damaging the company's standing with its customers.

These men were alcoholics—persons who leaned on liquor to meet the ordinary demands of living and whose excessive use of alcohol caused them serious problems on the job as well as at home. They were not typical, perhaps, because they were "discovered" and because their dollars-and-cents cost to their employers was measurable to a degree. But their cases illustrate why there is a growing concern over alcoholism in industry.

"Whether management likes it or not—and there is much to tempt us to shun the subject—we must take a position on alcoholism" and "combat its increasing menace," says James F. Oates, Jr., chairman and president of Equitable Life Assurance Society. A big reason: Alcoholism's direct cost to industry "must be in excess of $1 billion annually," Mr. Oates recently told a meeting of the National Council on Alcoholism. The N.C.A. is an independent health group that fights alcoholism as other agencies combat cancer and heart diseases.

Nearly all companies used to treat excessive drinking among workers as a moral problem that was better left alone. If an employee's drinking got too far out of hand he usually was fired, not helped. But as companies have become aware of the high cost of alcoholism in their plants and offices, more of them have started tackling the rehabilitation problem head on.

Several companies have set up their own programs for detecting and rehabilitating alcoholic employees. They include Eastman Kodak Co., Western Electric Co., Allis-Chalmers Manufacturing Co., Du Pont, International Harvester Co., Chicago's Commonwealth Edison Co. and New York's Consolidated Edison Co. Countless other concerns are working closely with such community alcoholism groups as Chicago's Portal House and the Houston Committee on Alcoholism.

Industry's problem centers on an estimated two million alcoholic workers out of a total U.S. alcoholic population of five million, up one million in the past five years, according to the N.C.A. Absenteeism of these workers due to alcoholism will cost employers more than 36 million man-days this year, more than double the time lost by U.S. workers because of strikes in 1957.

Alcoholism's impact on an individual company and its workers often is much greater than many management men would guess. For example, take the case of Norton Co., a Worcester, Massachusetts, abrasives manufacturer employing more than 5,000 workers.

In 1956 Norton made a survey of 33 employees with known drinking problems, recalls Andrew B. Holstrom, vice-president. "The thirty-three employees represented 536 years of service, or an average of sixteen years each. They average forty-six years of age and were skilled workers, every one of them," he reported.

Eleven of these workers were in an acute stage of alcoholism, had been given several warnings and were on the verge of being discharged. They each had, reported Mr. Holstrom, "forty-five days of lost time per year at an average rate of $2.44½ an hour . . . and they lost, each one of them, in excess of $700 a year." The survey's findings spurred Norton to help the workers in co-operation with Alcoholics Anonymous, a group of about 200,000 alcoholics who banded together to help themselves and anyone else with a serious drinking problem. This rehabilitation effort "has decreased lost time, improved morale, and we know we have helped out many a home," Mr. Holstrom says.

The corporate cost of excessive drinking includes many unmeasurable but sizable items such as increased accidents, the expense of replacing trained workers and the reduced output and higher work spoilage from a disturbed drinker.

"Our biggest problem traceable to excessive drinking is the so-called half man—the alcoholic worker whose sense of responsibility keeps him from staying home, but whose effectiveness is off fifty per cent or more from normal," says one company personnel chief. "His mistakes often aren't spectacular, but he doesn't get much done."

Companies often are shocked to learn that as many as 3 per cent of their workers are alcoholics, say researchers in the field. That's because many management men still stereotype an alcoholic as a red-nosed skid row bum. Actually, says a staff member at Yale University's Center of Alcohol Studies, "probably not more than ten per cent of the drinkers on skid row are alcoholics."

Industry's chief problem is the "hidden" alcoholic, say Yale researchers, writing in the university's *Journal on Alcoholism*. "They are not believed to be alcoholics because they do not exhibit the personal and social disorganization held to be typical of alcoholics. They are hidden by their ability to present a fairly normal appearance of personal and social integration."

Discovery of these hidden alcoholics is a major part of most company alcoholism programs. Personnel officers have found that seldom will workers tip off the company about a colleague whose excessive drinking is interfering with his work. And usually the inroads of alcoholism on a worker's efficiency are made at such a slow pace that supervisors will overlook the signs that, doctors believe, frequently flag a serious drinking problem. Alcoholism researchers say most alcoholic workers have a history of 10 to 15 years of heavy drinking before their illness is serious enough to interfere with their vocational life.

Unions, too, have been stepping up their efforts to help detect and rehabilitate workers with drinking problems. The A.F.L.-C.I.O. has a "singular responsibility to help all its members by helping its alcoholic members," says Leo Perlis, director of A.F.L.-C.I.O. Community Service Activities.

"Thousands of union counselors across the country are trained to recognize alcoholics and refer them to proper agencies," says Mr. Perlis. In Birmingham, Alabama, seven companies and 17 unions have joined their efforts to help alcoholic workers. Few unions will argue if a company fires a man when his drinking interferes with his job. But most unions argue that alcoholism should be considered as an illness subject to the same benefits and consideration as more commonly recognized illnesses.

Some scientists regard alcoholism as a disease resulting from some kind of physiological disorder—a vitamin deficiency, perhaps. Others are partial to a psychological explanation, blaming compulsive drinking on the drinker's efforts to combat some neurosis, such as a guilt complex or inferiority feeling. Still others think alcoholism is a combination of many things. But most researchers agree that rehabilitation efforts seem to get further when alcoholism is treated as an illness rather than a disgrace.

Alcoholics can "recover" but so far can't be "cured," say most researchers. That is, they cannot resume normal drinking without courting a relapse. Scientists say they have been handicapped by lack of research funds in their search for better ways to combat alcoholism. Many alcoholism agencies claim that alcoholism ranks as the nation's fourth most serious health problem (after heart disease, cancer and mental diseases) and believe that the problem should get a larger share of health contributions.

March 28, 1958

Employee Thefts

"We've told most of our security officers to stop watching for shoplifters and start watching the clerks," the personnel manager of one of New York's largest department stores commented privately this week.

The reason: soaring inventory shortages, which can be explained only by systematic stealing "from the inside."

Such thefts, estimated at a hefty $500 million for U.S. retailers last year, are increasing at the very time that many storekeepers find their sales and profits sliding downhill. New clerks dipping into the till, veteran employees stealing merchandise by the truckload, book-keepers inventing new and intricate systems to conceal their pecula-tions, route salesmen selling wares and pocketing the proceeds, and buyers taking hefty kickbacks from vendors—all these offenses against mercantile morality have been increasing lately, say retailers, protection services and insurance companies.

"Two years ago a clerk's husband was working and getting a lot of overtime. A year ago, he was working but the overtime was cut off. This year he's laid off. If she was stealing before, she's stealing more now; if she wasn't stealing, she's likely to start," says M. E. Hament, president of Merit Protective Service, a retailing protective outfit.

A hard-bitten New York store detective agrees. "The reasons for employee thefts usually boil down to one or more of the three R's—rum, the races or redheads. Now, I guess, you can add a fourth—recession," he says.

"Losses are on the rise, no question about it," says James M. Henderson, vice-president of Fidelity & Deposit Co. of Maryland, one of the country's largest fidelity firms.

Such losses aren't limited to retailers, of course. Banks, savings-and-loan associations, insurance companies, wholesalers and manu-facturers also face the problem of the light-fingered employee. Nor-man Jaspan, president of the New York City business consultant firm bearing his name, predicts total employee theft this year will top last year's figure of over $1 billion. But there's no doubt that the theft-minded employee finds the most—and the most varied—oppor-tunities in the retailing field.

The virus has infected veteran employees and newcomers alike. Three days before the head shipping clerk of a Chicago department store was to receive a "quarter-century pin" this year for faithful service, he was caught taking a $250 evening dress home from the store. His explanation: He wanted something nice for his wife to wear to the award dinner.

The manager of a Portland, Oregon, hardware store was due to retire after 31 years. A month or so before retirement he started out-fitting his home workshop. Using the company's truck after hours, he carted away 43 major pieces of woodworking equipment, includ-ing lathes, sanders, bandsaws and jigsaws.

A New Jersey food store clerk siphoned off 17,000 trading stamps, cashing them in for merchandise, with the aid of an accomplice, at nearby redemption centers.

The dollar take in some cases is sizable. Until a few weeks ago, seven cash registers were busily ringing up sales at the Evanston, Illinois, branch of a big Midwestern supermarket chain. Every night the register stubs checked out, usually to the penny. There was only one thing wrong; the chain had equipped the store with but six registers. The seventh was the idea and personal property of the store manager and his assistant, who had set up their own private checkout counter. This share-the-wealth scheme defied detection for 27 months. Meanwhile, more than $70,000 jingled through the extra register into the two conspirators' pockets.

At the other extreme, you have the $135-a-week manager of a Seattle variety store who admitted taking $2 a week from the charity canisters in his store.

How much do the depredations of light-fingered employees cost retailers? None has a precise answer. Like a sheepish bumpkin who has just been hornswoggled by a fast-talking stranger in a phony uranium stock deal, storekeepers don't like to talk about their losses. Unless the theft is very large, employers seldom prosecute, and one insurance company estimates that less than 10 per cent of all store thieves are jailed. Furthermore, many stores believe that giving publicity to this kind of larceny only encourages more of it.

Private studies, however, indicate the loss is large.

Joseph B. Hall, president of Kroger Co., this year estimated that inventory shrinkage is costing his company between $4 million and $5 million a year and that at least half of this is due to the take-home habits of employees.

Inventory losses on a national basis average about 1.1 per cent of total retail sales, according to the National Retail Merchants Association, trade group for 10,300 department and specialty stores. This loss figure is more than half as large as the retailers' average profit performance, only 2.1 per cent of sales in 1957.

FREDERICK TAYLOR

March 29, 1958

Tracking Deadbeats

A collection agency in Edmonton, Canada, had been trying for years to locate an individual who bought a $75 diamond ring on credit from a local jeweler and then disappeared without making a payment.

Letters to the customer's address were returned unopened, marked addressee unknown. Phone calls to his credit references, neighbors and others elicited no further information as to his whereabouts. He was almost forgotten until one day when an agency employee came across a newspaper death notice involving his family name.

She looked up his file and learned the item was about his father. On the chance the son might make an appearance at the funeral, the agency sent a man there. The son was recognized, followed to the cemetery and back home again, where he was finally presented with a bill for his debt. It was paid in full, by check, on the spot.

This story, not necessarily typical of collection agency decorum, nevertheless points up a problem of increasing concern these days to all kinds of entrepreneurs and a great many professional men as well. With consumer credit at last report totaling $43 billion, 3 per cent above a year earlier, and Americans on the move as never before (an estimated 40 million changed their addresses in 1957 compared with just over 30 million as recently as 1953), those who trust others for payment for their goods and services often find a special premium placed on their sleuthing talents.

Listen to a top executive of the National Retail Credit Association, a large trade association of credit men based in St. Louis: "The job of locating the delinquent debtor has never been bigger—or tougher—than it is today." Among credit men, the delinquent debtor who cannot be badgered by collectors because he hasn't told them where he's moved is known as a "skip."

"I don't think we had more than ten or twelve skips out of the ten thousand to twelve thousand accounts we had when I first joined the company just before World War II," asserts Earle A. Nirmaier, budget director of W. Wilder-Otter & Co., purveyor of furniture, appliances and soft goods from five outlets in and around Newark, New Jersey. "Now," says he, "that ratio is about four hundred to five hundred in a total of fifteen thousand to twenty thousand accounts, largely because our clientele is considerably more mobile than it was before."

Eugene B. Greer, vice-president of Business Service, Inc., which operates 12 collection offices in Alabama, Georgia, South Carolina and Tennessee from headquarters in Sylacauga, Alabama, notes: "Eight years ago we had only four full-time skip tracers (people who do nothing but hunt down skips). A few months ago we hired our eighth. Part of that is due to our own expansion, but the rise in consumer credit had something to do with the increase, too."

Practically every store, financial institution and doctor's office does a certain amount of its own skip tracing. Generally, such tracing centers on the telephone and the mails. References are checked and neighbors called through the help of a somewhat costly "crisscross" directory that lists phones by streets and house numbers. Letters are sent to the skip's last known address with notations such as "Form 3547 requested," so the post office will provide his forwarding address for a few cents if any has been left. Registered mail marked "Deliver to addressee only" sometimes helps establish the fact the skip really hasn't moved at all but only has been ignoring his mail.

In most cases, say credit men, routine skip-tracing procedures prove sufficient. It's only when the going gets tough that the task is tossed to professionals. These professionals usually are employees of a collection agency. Such agencies generally take on collecting assignments with the understanding they'll keep half of what they collect.

Hard work, persistency and imagination are the main tools of the professional skip tracer. "We don't do anything the merchant himself couldn't do if he had the time," maintains Sherman Harris, proprietor of the Creditors Service Bureau of Houston. However, Mr. Harris and his colleagues believe they can do the job more efficiently simply because experience has armed them with some useful secrets.

What are some of these secrets?

The most important of all, perhaps, is the emphasis the skip tracer places on the credit application itself. "It's the best thing we have to go on," declares William F. Fluegel, manager of the Iowa Adjustment & Credit Bureau of Cedar Rapids. Mindful of this fact, says he, merchants attempting to keep their crop of difficult skips down will get not only the name and address of the credit applicant but also those of his employer, others who've granted him credit, and a few references who might later know where he or she has gone. Above all, he'll verify this information before he grants credit.

Among references prized by one veteran skip tracer: mothers-in-law. "They're more likely to tell the dirt than 'most anyone else," says he.

Next to the application, there's perhaps nothing more important to the professional skip tracer than his imagination. Some exercise it to a very considerable degree.

One individual who's been skip tracing for over 30 years now but, for reasons which will become obvious, prefers to remain anonymous, volunteers this information: "Quite frankly," says he, "I believe in subterfuge. After all, we're here to get people to pay their bills and there's nothing evil in that."

While collection agencies publicly deplore the use of subterfuge in their business, there's apparently enough of it going on to nourish more than one enterprise catering to it. A number of little outfits specialize in providing collection agencies with forms which look as though they might have come from a Federal agency; the aim, of course, is to scare skips into atoning for their financial sins. The collection agency itself fills them out, puts them in addressed envelopes and bundles them up for mailing to Washington where the form firm can post them individually to give an appearance of authenticity.

Among those in recent circulation was one carrying the letterhead of "The U.S. Division of Settlements Control Bureau."

Uncle Sam regards such tactics as an improper use of the mails and has banned the forms of some such companies. However, the offender occasionally reorganizes his establishment under another name—and sometimes under ostensibly new ownership as well—and snaps right back into business.

Skip tracers have developed other postal tactics, too. The use of fake "opinion" surveys to trap the recipient into parting with just one morsel of information that might be useful for tracing him or his assets is a technique that has its devotees.

Hard work, persistence—and just plain luck—as well as a thorough exercise of the imagination, bring their rewards to skip tracers, too.

Skip tracers contend the average skip is basically honest and means to pay his bills and that at least 50 per cent of them, when confronted with their obligations, will willingly do so if some easy-payment system is worked out. One who says he's convinced of this illustrates his belief with a story about an old man who walked into his store in 1950 with a sales slip and statement dated 1923. He'd come to pay his bill. "The fact that he had that slip twenty-seven years indicates he at least had some conscience about it," this storekeeper maintains.

If there is any one category of debtors more apt to skip out on their obligations than others, say the sleuths, it's those who owe on a medical or dental bill. "You can repossess a car but you can't repossess a baby," says Joseph Davis, general manager of the Doctors Service Bureau, Inc., of Chicago. Mr. Davis also says time tends to cause a rapid diminution in the patient's appreciation of the doctor's services.

MITCHELL GORDON

July 30, 1958

Fat under Fire

Recessions have unpleasant consequences for many and unpleasant overtones for most. But as a report in this newspaper noted the other day, they are not without some benefits.

For example, what seems like a necessity in boom times suddenly can become "fat" when times are less prosperous. And when times improve, the over-all operation of a business likely will be more efficient than it was before the recession set in. "During a recession," said one company president, "we find there are some very normal and natural cost-cutting things you can do and, in fact, should have been doing."

It is perhaps unfortunate in some ways that this is true, but the fact of the matter is that it is true. Public-relations consultants probably would prefer such words as "corrections of imbalances" to "recessions" even as "recession" was a euphemism to overcome the use of the word "depression"—which in its time was considered more diplomatic than use of the earlier term, "panic."

But whatever the label, it is all part of a viable economy, and the economy has yet to be devised that does not undergo "corrections" of some kind from time to time.

Too, the economy has yet to be devised that during resumption of a boom fails to put on new layers of the "fat" it has just pared off. But some individuals—businessmen, or consumers—may succeed. And they, invariably, are the ones who will suffer the least in the next downturn.

September 23, 1958

EDITORIAL

The Right to Tour

A number of decisions of the United States Supreme Court during recent years have excited severe and not unjustified criticism. Such a respected and erudite figure in the world of law as Judge Learned Hand has used expressions like "third legislative chamber" and "Pla-

"Now starts the 'pay later.'"

tonic guardians" in oblique criticism of the Court's trend in the direction of making law rather than interpreting law.

But individual Supreme Court decisions, like everything else, should be appraised on their merits. The recent decision of the Court, denying the right of the State Department to withhold passports from American citizens because of doubt as to their political sympathies or affiliations, is pointed in the right direction of diminishing the arbitrary control of government over the individual citizen.

It only seems regrettable that the ruling should have been by the narrow 5–4 margin. There might be a more decisive majority if the broad issue of the right of an American citizen, not under indictment for any crime, to travel freely in countries of his choice when the country is not at war should come up for adjudication. The recent 5–4 decision was on narrower grounds.

While there is no specific affirmation of the right to travel abroad in the Constitution, the whole spirit of the Bill of Rights is strongly against its denial or abridgment. In contrast to employment by the government, which is a privilege, not a right, freedom of movement outside as well as inside the country is a right, not a privilege.

It is the totalitarian countries that make their frontiers prison walls for their subjects. We should not imitate them in this, even in minor degree. There could be no better affirmation of the reality of American liberty than observance of the principle that an American citizen, however distasteful his views might be to the Government and to the majority of his fellow citizens, may go anywhere in the world, that every application for a passport is granted immediately and automatically.

There is a very real danger to individual liberty in a bill which Congressman Francis E. Walter, of Pennsylvania, has introduced as a retort to the Supreme Court ruling. This provides that the Secretary of State may deny a passport if convinced that the applicant's activities would violate the laws, be prejudicial to the orderly conduct of foreign affairs or otherwise be prejudicial to the interests of the United States.

This last provision seems especially sweeping. It could conceivably apply to someone against whom the Secretary of State had some kind of personal prejudice. And under our system, and that of other free countries, penalties are imposed after there has been due process of law and conviction of violating the law, not on suspicion that someone might violate the law.

Much of the sentiment in favor of denying or restricting the right of freedom of travel for Americans is linked up with the belief that this is a valuable weapon in the struggle against Communism. But concrete proof of this proposition is conspicuously lacking. Take an extreme case, a well-known fellow traveler going abroad to take part in some Communist-inspired "peace" congress.

Suppose he is allowed to go, to speak his piece, to vote for the stock made-in-Moscow resolutions. Does this shake the foundations of the American Republic? Such a person is actually probably more useful for Communist propaganda purposes if he can be played up as a martyr who is not allowed to leave his country.

This country was founded on the proposition that the best antidote to wild and foolish talk is to tolerate it, so long as there is no incitement to sedition or violence. Part of the price of free speech for all of us is that some of us will express ideas and opinions that are foolish and ignorant and irresponsible.

Recently a man compared Mr. Dulles with the German ex-Kaiser and the F.B.I. with the Gestapo. To most Americans this sounds like pretty silly talk. But very few Americans (and those have forgotten the ideals of the Founding Fathers) would suggest that this man and the minority who share his ideas should be forcibly curbed in the exercise of their Constitutional right of free expression. And does it make much difference whether such views are expressed in New York and Chicago or in London, or Paris, or Moscow?

Conservatives who approve writing into law sweeping travel restrictions which, as they think, would apply only to Communist sympathizers may be preparing an unpleasant surprise for themselves in the future. Suppose at some future time we should have a radical administration in Washington. Might not this proposed broad power to bar foreign travel to anyone as prejudicial to the interests of the United States then be used against a conservative economist or political scientist who wished to attend a meeting of like-minded persons in some foreign country?

There is no proved or visible advantage in dealing with Communist conspiracy that warrants giving bureaucrats more power to regulate the coming and going of ordinary citizens or justifies the denial to Americans of their historic traditional right to leave their country, temporarily or permanently, for travel or residence abroad. After all, as is sometimes said, this is a free country, isn't it?

WILLIAM HENRY CHAMBERLIN

June 30, 1958

Business Spy

The police squad car rolled to a stop in front of a Midwestern glass-making factory. A uniformed policeman and a companion in civilian clothes hopped out and went directly to the office of the plant's personnel manager.

"We have information that a man wanted for questioning is working here," the officer informed the official. He added they didn't know their quarry's name, but he had a pretty good description so they would recognize him if they saw him. The personnel man, eager to assist, directed the pair to the department in which they thought their man was working. Returning some time later they explained to the personnel manager that it was a case of mistaken identity. Back in the car the officer's companion whipped out a notebook and sketched a machine he'd just seen.

Strange behavior? For a policeman it would have been. But the gentleman in civilian attire was not a law enforcement officer. He was Ulmont O. Cumming, professional business spy who had enlisted the aid of a co-operative police officer to get into the plant of his client's competitor. His client wanted to know what sort of equipment the competitor was using that enabled him to turn out a better and cheaper product.

Professional business espionage is not new. For years, business spies have found ways to garner secret processes, formulas or production techniques without the consent of their owners. And they've been able to delve into companies' plans for future expansion, production, sales or other operations. Yet, because business espionage is shrouded in secrecy, it is only on rare occasions that the general public becomes aware of its existence.

One such occasion came during a New York legislative investigation of wire tapping a few years back. At the time a representative of Hazel Bishop, a cosmetics firm, told the probers that the company believed its phone lines had been tapped for some 18 months in an effort to obtain its business secrets. In another instance, a witness in a wire-tapping case testified that he had tapped the phone lines of E. R. Squibb & Sons and Bristol-Myers Co. because a client suspected "some chemical formulas were leaking out to competitors." Mr. Cumming was not involved in these cases.

Today, although little is heard of their activities, the men who engage in this unusual vocation say more and more businessmen are using their services to ferret out competitors' secrets.

"I'm getting more and more assignments for this kind of work," reports the candid Mr. Cumming.

"We get more requests than you think from businessmen who want us to find out what process or material a competitor is using," declares the vice-president of a national detective agency. "But we turn them down because we're not in that kind of business," he adds.

Comments a third sleuth: "There's no doubt that some businessmen are showing increased interest in this sort of thing."

Why? Here's one explanation by Mr. Cumming:

"It's the pressure of competition. When a manufacturer sees a competitor pulling ahead because of a better or cheaper product he naturally wants to know how come. So he hires somebody to find the answers. Assignments of this kind always mount when competition is as rough as it is now."

Many businessmen have devised ingenious schemes to prevent their secrets from falling into enemy hands. Drug-maker Upjohn Co. sought to thwart would-be spies by filing patents on a new cortisone process in South Africa, with which the U.S. has a patent reciprocity pact. The automobile industry—always a prime target for spies—spends millions of dollars each year on security measures to protect new model secrets.

But even precautions such as these won't guarantee your secrets are safe, warns Mr. Cumming, who operates from an unpretentious three-room office in a midtown Manhattan building. Seated behind a desk cluttered with papers, a couple of pill bottles and a tape recorder, he tells his visitor matter-of-factly: "There isn't a plant in the United States that I can't get into."

Monty Cumming has not always been a business spy, although he has been a private investigator for more than half his 62 years. Starting as a patent investigator—collecting evidence in infringement cases—he moved into the espionage field at the behest of clients who wanted information about their competitors. The move was an easy one, he explains, because the techniques in both types of investigations are similar. The main difference is the end use of the information obtained.

Today, Mr. Cumming's business is pretty evenly divided between patent cases and business espionage work.

Five feet, seven inches tall, balding and of medium build, Mr. Cumming looks more like a successful businessman than an investigator—the word he uses when describing his work.

"Appearances are a big help in this business," he notes with a chuckle. "You've got to be able to convince people you're what you say you are. In other words, you've got to be a good salesman."

One time, for example, he assumed the role of a kindly stockholder. "My client—a papermaker—wanted to know what kind of a process a competitor was using to apply a special coating to its paper," he recalls with obvious relish.

Selecting a branch plant "because they had no immediate way of checking their stockholder list," he explained to the manager that although he was a long-time shareholder he had never seen the company's products being made. "The manager was most courteous and offered to personally escort me through the plant. Before the tour had been completed I had the answers for my client," he relates, a big grin wreathing his face.

Neither an engineer nor a chemist, Mr. Cumming attributes much of his success to the advance preparation he puts into each assignment. "Only a small fraction of my time is spent gathering data," he states. "Many times I'll spend a couple of days studying every aspect of my client's product and manufacturing process so I'll know what to look for and understand what I'll see."

All answers and data about the size and shape of equipment, amount of ingredients used and other pertinent facts are memorized by Mr. Cumming while he's on forbidden territory. As soon as he leaves the premises he scribbles the information in a notebook so he won't forget any of the details.

Each assignment represents a new challenge, avers Mr. Cumming, requiring an entirely new plan of attack. Consider, for instance, this request from a consumer goods manufacturer: "One of our competitors does practically no advertising and yet we lose about twenty per cent of our business to him. We want to know by what process they make their product, and why they are able to make a better product than we do."

Sleuth Cumming decided against the direct approach in this case. Instead, he approached the company which made the equipment used by the competitor and explained that he was considering installing some of the machines in his plant but first would like to see them in action. Were any manufacturers using them in his area, he asked, naming a community not far from that of his client's competitor. Armed with letters of introduction to several firms, including his quarry, Mr. Cumming proceeded to the scene of action.

"I presented the letter to the production manager," recounts Mr. Cumming, "who, obviously proud of the plant's accomplishments, showed me the machine himself. I soon discovered that it wasn't the machine that made this firm's product superior; they had added a special heat-treating step not used by my client."

Not long ago an inventor dumped this one in Mr. Cumming's lap: A device he had developed unexpectedly turned up in the cars of one of the Big Three auto makers. When did the auto maker conceive and test the device, the inventor wanted to know.

This time, assuming the role of a doting parent of a teen-age hot-rod enthusiast, the investigator walked into the engineering headquarters of the auto company. Chatting with an engineer while waiting for his man, he mentioned why he was there and explained that he wanted the information for his son who was writing an article for an auto hobby magazine telling how a big development takes place.

The trusting technician pointed to a set of engineering drawings on his desk, exclaiming: "You're lucky. I'm not in charge of this work but I just happen to have the first sketches of our system here." A few minutes' perusal told the visitor all he wanted to know—including the date which was neatly printed in the margin.

On those occasions when his ruses fail, Mr. Cumming enlists the aid of his wife. Engaged to find out how the operator of an Oklahoma zinc mine was handling fumes from its diesel trucks, Mr. Cumming could find no pretext to get down into the mine. So he sent his wife (she'd been coached on what to look for), who posed as a magazine writer preparing an article on mining from a woman's viewpoint.

Foremen and officials eagerly explained all their secrets to her, gleefully recounts Mr. Cumming, and even gave her, as a souvenir, a sample of the rock material used in the device that absorbed the diesel fumes.

"She ruined a beautiful Christian Dior suit and an expensive pair of shoes on that assignment," recalls the investigator, "but it was well worth it."

So confident is Mr. Cumming of his ability to penetrate even the most elaborate security guard that he frequently tells groups of patent attorneys (they're potential customers) some of the things their companies could do to better protect their secrets.

"Take a chemical process as an example," he says. "One way to keep it secret is to separate each stage of the process. Have different identification cards and tags for workers in each room. Then apply code names to the raw materials used, and make sure that workers know neither what the code names mean nor what happens to the thing they work on before it comes to them or after it leaves."

But he cautions that even measures such as these are not foolproof. As proof he cites the time he was employed to discover the ingredients used by a New York chemical firm in a particular product. He arranged with the building superintendent to let him have, for a price, the contents of the firm's wastebaskets for inspection. Weeks of scanning telephone doodles, routine correspondence and invoices paid off when he found the information he was after.

Actually, no secret is safe unless a way can be found to prevent employees from talking, contends Mr. Cumming. Engaged by a food processor in Pennsylvania to find out what ingredient a rival was using as a flavoring and coloring agent in a certain product, he spent several days interviewing the competitor's workers in bars and lunchrooms, until he finally found one who agreed for a price to bring him a sample of the elements involved.

Posing as an executive recruiter, he has on occasion approached middle-management personnel of companies whose secrets he covets, offering them attractive jobs in rival firms. While dangling high salaries and big posts before them, he adroitly pumps them for the information he's after.

Even if the dupes should discover, after their "rejection" for the job, that they've been taken, there usually is no kickback to Mr. Cumming. The talkers are afraid to admit to their superiors that they had been blabbing.

Despite his many forays into enemy territory, Mr. Cumming has been caught only once. "It was one of those things you couldn't foresee," he explains, wincing slightly at the memory of it. "I proposed to a fire inspector acquaintance that he take me along as his assistant on an inspection of a plant I wanted to get into. He gave me some excuse why he couldn't do it, so I arranged with another inspector to take me through. What I didn't know at the time was that the first inspector was a friend of the firm's president and had tipped him off to my mission. When I arrived at the plant they were waiting for me. They tried to make me tell who I was working for, even threatening jail, but I kept mum. Finally, they let me go."

JOSEPH M. GUILFOYLE

March 3, 1959

Parkinson's Return

How many people should there be on a committee? How long should a meeting last? These questions are among some serious proposals for study by social and political scientists.

They are the suggestions of a man who holds the unlikely title of Raffles Professor of History at the University of Malaya in Singapore. He is C. Northcote Parkinson, a man many Americans know by now as the author of *Parkinson's Law,* a thin satirical volume which deftly illuminates the absurdities inherent in the administration of people. The "law" can be stated: In any public administrative organization, the number of new subordinates increases at a predictable rate, "irrespective of any variation in the amount of work (if any) to be done."

Professor Parkinson emerged as a flesh-and-blood individual recently in a lecture at the Harvard Business School, where he expounded on some other subjects. On the matter of committees, for example, he declared that if it were known for sure the optimum number of people for a committee, a lot of needless effort could be avoided. He also treated this subject, if lightly, in his satirical book and concludes that the "Golden Number" lies somewhere between three ("when a quorum is impossible to collect") and about 20 ("when the whole organism begins to perish").

He further believes that if a clear scientific rule could also be developed as to the proper length of time a meeting should last, the concept would likely pay for itself in the first week of operation.

Professor Parkinson was pleased to discover that some such research on committees has actually been carried on in this country. About four years ago, the *Harvard Business Review* carried an article, "In Conference," written by Robert F. Bales, then a research associate in Harvard's Laboratory of Social Relations, which concluded that five to seven members make up an ideal committee.

The Harvard response to his lecture gratified Professor Parkinson because, as other satirists such as Mark Twain have discovered, he sometimes has difficulty when he wants to be taken seriously. There are many people who still think both the Parkinson name and his chair as Raffles Professor are some kind of humor; his chair exists in fact, named after Sir Stamford Raffles, founder of the colony of Singapore.

But the bald and tubby Professor expresses some hurt at the success of *Parkinson's Law*. He believes it tends to obscure the fact that he's written some 18 other weightier volumes on naval, military and economic history, as well as political thought.

As a matter of fact, his suggestions on the study of committees arise from a recent treatise he wrote on types of political organization, soon to be published in this country. The book's argument is that political groupings appear to proceed, rather inevitably, from absolute monarchy through aristocracy and democracy to chaos, from there to dictatorship and, as may now be happening in Spain, back to monarchy.

The chief Parkinson point, however, was that present-day political organizations are based on comparatively old bodies of thought. Especially compared to natural science, such as physics and chemistry, political science seems hardly to be developing at all. Much of the world today is politically based on the thinking of Karl Marx, who began writing in 1845. U.S. political theorists still hark back to Thomas Jefferson. Modern times have produced no seminal political thinker, save possibly Mahatma Gandhi, according to Mr. Parkinson.

The Professor therefore proposes that the social scientists get busy on mankind's political institutions where, many people will admit, progress is needed. Researchers should resist the temptation to start with big problems—such as whether democracy or totalitarianism is better—because such a study is bound to be unscientific; breakthroughs in natural scientific understanding usually come only after a series of small advances. Political researchers should adopt this technique and look first at the little, seemingly unimportant "political" problems—the matter of committees, for instance.

If the social scientists eventually want a slightly larger topic, Mr. Parkinson proposes they study such things as "What size of community is most effective?" The study could be directed to villages, towns and cities, some of which are obviously too small and some obviously too large to best serve mankind, and also to nations and economic market areas, to which the same observations may apply. A scientific study of these matters might result in clear indications as to the optimum size of human communities, the Professor believes.

Good points all—even if fraught with many of the same difficulties of administering people that the Parkinson pen caught so well in his satirical book.

DAVID O. IVES

July 31, 1958

Round and Round

The hula hoop, that latest development of American culture, is fascinating people all around. At first strictly a toy for children, mothers discovered it might supplement the 21-day diet and fathers were convinced it might help the golf score. Even football players took to it to shake off the summertime's indolence.

Now the hula hoop has brought England into orbit. Newspapers there are devoting whole pages on how to swing the thing, and TV stations are giving visual instructions. The editor of England's *Family Doctor* says "hooping tones up the muscles" and beauticians are convinced it puts a better bloom in the cheek than a cold London fog.

"These are just the trading stamps—the groceries are out in the car."

Psychologists say there is another reason for its popularity. The hula hoop, they say, is symbolic of the times that put the world not only out of joint but into circles.

Could be. Some Wall Streeters can see in it a symbol of the Federal Reserve's well-rounded policies. Voters who think about it may conclude it represents the average office seeker's promises, having no beginning, no end and no middle. When the hula hoop reaches Formosa, as it doubtless will, who can blame the Nationalists for suspecting the thing arrived in a State Department attaché case?

Still, we're not sure. We have a suspicion that some things are here to stay and some are not, no matter what we do. When the hula hoop has gone the way of Nineveh, Tyre and the sack dress, our worrisome but not altogether displeasing old world will still be going round and round in the same old aimless way.

October 9, 1958

EDITORIAL

Mikoyan and Macy's

There seems to be a deal of difference of opinion about the visit to this country of Mr. Anastas Mikoyan, who—as of this writing—is a top-ranking leader in the Russian hierarchy.

Some people think he should not be allowed to set foot in the United States, let alone Macy's, because, as everyone knows, the Russians are a dictator nation and operate a slave state. Others are afraid that Mr. Mikoyan may sell a soft bill of goods to bankers, manufacturers and shippers, as well as to Mr. Dulles and Mr. Eisenhower.

Well, we think these fears and objections are about as silly as the enthusiasm some people have shown over his visit. We would be a simple people, indeed, if a folksy manner and a hearty smile could make us all forget the kind of country Russia is, what the Communist doctrine proposes for the world, and the cold war that has existed between the two most powerful nations since before the time we sent them all-out aid to help defeat Hitlerism.

But we would be a foolish people, too, to reject visitors to this country just because we do not agree with them or like them or approve of them. The Russians live in the same world with us, and it can't do any harm for us to get a look at Mr. Mikoyan and for him to get a look at us.

In fact, since Mr. Khrushchev and all the rest believe that nobody but nobody has a better system than the Russians, it might do them all some good to come here and learn the truth. And if Mr. Mikoyan is serious about competing peacefully with the U.S., he could hardly have gone to a better place to learn about competition than Macy's. Or maybe Gimbel's.

EDITORIAL

January 16, 1959

Recession Lesson

WASHINGTON—The Eisenhower Administration has relearned a new set of economic lessons from the recession they believe hit bottom back in the spring.

The biggest, or at least the most specific, lesson is that taxes don't necessarily have to be cut every time business suffers a setback. The second lesson is that the economy has the basic strength to absorb a severe jolt without sliding into a depression, and right itself without the need for large-scale government tinkering at the controls.

Administration officials now date the low point of the recession as coming as early as April, and see no present probability of a relapse. Indeed, the bottom was reached—if in fact it was—somewhat earlier than had generally been expected. And the pace of the comeback up to now, while not dramatic, has been a pleasant surprise.

This is not to say the Government sat back and let the business slump burn itself out. The Administration, pushed by Congress, poured money into housing and made the terms to home buyers easier. It stepped up the placement of defense contracts and speeded up Federal buying of supplies and services. The Federal Reserve Board, in comparison with past actions, eased off rapidly on credit.

But despite the so-called antirecession steps it did take, the Government did not move nearly as far in this direction as many lawmakers and others wanted it to. Just a short time ago, Democratic lawmakers were drawing up schemes to pump billions into a massive public-works program. Some frankly labeled it a W.P.A.-type approach, covering everything from town sewers to huge dams. Faster spending by the Administration was urged on military and civilian programs already under way. Lawmakers and others kept up a running fire on the Federal Reserve for not freeing more billions in credit. Tax cuts ranging from $5 billion to $10 billion were demanded.

The Administration's firm and successful stand against a general tax reduction seemed to be in defiance of established economy theory that taxes should be lowered in the face of a business decline.

Strangely, the Eisenhower Administration itself embraced and helped perpetuate this tax cut theory. In 1955, the President's economic report credited the tax reductions of 1954 with helping to end the 1953–54 recession. When the 1957–58 business slide got seriously under way, the theory that taxes should be cut in a period of falling business activity was presented as a necessary step if the recession was to be halted short of a possible depression.

This view came from all sides, both in and out of Government. Government economists at the working level were almost unanimous in favor of a reduction. Former President Truman and Dr. Arthur Burns, former chief of President Eisenhower's Council of Economic Advisers, both urged a sizable tax reduction before it was "too late." The issue finally split the President's official family, with such high officials as Vice-President Nixon, Labor Secretary Mitchell and others lining up in favor of the cuts.

Even those who had their doubts about how much good a tax cut would do were saying privately that the "next big step" the Administration took would be to push for tax reduction. But this step was headed off by Treasury Secretary Anderson, who, more than any other official, influenced the President against it on the grounds it would deepen the Federal deficits and add to inflationary problems in later years.

Mr. Anderson's master stroke in opposition to the tax cut pressure was a unique alliance with Speaker Sam Rayburn and Senate Majority Leader Lyndon Johnson which, in effect, put the lid on the move.

"Had we cut taxes this winter or spring," one top official now asserts, "there's no doubt that step would have gotten full credit for ending the recession."

Instead, Administration policy makers are citing the lack of a tax cut as "proof" that taxes don't need to be cut for the economy to work its way out of a recession.

"If there's one thing this recession has taught us," flatly asserts one high official who was inclined toward a tax cut, "it's that you can hold back on a tax cut and not wind up looking like an irresponsible boob."

Officials don't contend that the antirecession steps that were taken turned the recession around. But they do claim that what the Administration did not do during the business setback was perhaps more important than what it did do. These policy makers cite the record of the recession as evidence that the basic strength of the economy was the main factor in bringing the slump to a halt.

"Looking back," claims one White House adviser, "it was largely a matter of some of the downward forces just fizzling out." Another gives credit to the fact that consumers kept up a relatively heavy rate of spending all through the decline. In short, policy makers now contend that what turned the recession around was not what the Government did. Instead, they argue, the recovery has resulted from the private decisions of millions of businessmen and consumers.

Old theories—particularly those relating to tax cuts and public works—die hard. But the lessons from the 1957–58 recession have provided some fresh ammunition for those who, like Mr. Anderson, believe the Government should refrain from rushing off in all directions.

JOHN A. GRIMES

August 6, 1958

————————❀————————

THE YEARS OF THE BEAR

1893 Panic and a Clear Diagnosis

It was difficult to find the clear and specific cause that started the panic yesterday. Banks did not call loans to any very large extent, and certainly not as a general thing. It may have been done in particular instances, and probably was done, but the remarkable ease in money suggests individual embarrassments as to the real state of the case, rather than general circumstances affecting everyone.

The utter absence of support, except from shorts, was a feature in the final smash. When Chicago Gas was at 78 a trader tried to sell 100 shares, with the result that his stock did not find a buyer until it was offered at 76. The same thing held good in an even greater degree as regards Cordage and Sugar once the resistance offered by the covering of shorts around 93 was overcome.

Another feature was the break in good railroad stocks, such as Northwest. The number of good stocks for sale undoubtedly pointed to realization of stocks held as margin on loans. It is fair to attribute this rather to the calling for extra margin than to the calling of loans.

The wildest rumors were current last night after business. They chiefly referred to banks, National, State and foreign. As far as could be accurately learned, there was no foundation in fact for these beyond the fact that one small bank is believed to be somewhat embarrassed. But the suspension of this bank is not looked for by those who are most likely to be accurately informed. At the same time, it is feared that if further failures on the Board occur, there may be a further contraction of the present facilities given by the banks to the Street, which would result in an aggravation of the present sensitive state of feeling.

May 4, 1893

A Clear Diagnosis

In sizing up the situation as it exists for the moment, and in assigning the principal causes which have brought about the recent heavy declines in the market, one of the most active and prominent brokers in the Street said last evening that, as a matter of course, the primary reason for the weakness in the market was to be found in the increasing want of confidence in the financial situation. This uncertainty as to the stability of our finances has been growing for some time, but the pronounced weakness displayed yesterday was the direct outcome of greater discrimination on the part of the banks, trust companies and other institutions having money to loan, against many of the collaterals. They have insisted since the beginning of this week upon the substitution of more desirable collaterals in the place of many of those held, and an increase in the amount of the security in hand. Where the parties have been unable to respond to the demands of the money lenders, they have been forced to liquidate at least a part of their holdings, and it goes without saying that the bears were not slow in comprehending the situation, and seeing to it that the sellers obtained as low a price as possible for their securities.

The situation is anomalous in another respect. The demand from the West for funds is exceptionally heavy, partly on account of the requirements incident to the World's Fair and in part because that section of the country is carrying an unusually large amount of grain and other products. Furthermore, the West has bought heavily of Eastern and imported goods in recent months which have to be paid for. As a rule, the Western banks discount local paper and send a portion of it to New York to be rediscounted here with the endorsement of the Western banks. Owing to the present unsettled state of financial affairs the New York banks have either hesitated or entirely refused to furnish the usual accommodations to their Western correspondents. The outcome of it all has been that where a year ago paper of the kind described was discounted in New York at 3½ to 4¢ it has been sold here this week at 8¢. This rate represents the price which the Western banks have been compelled to pay for gilt-edge double name paper, while single name paper has gone begging at 12¢ even with the Western banks endorsing it. In closing his diagnosis of the situation, the gentleman quoted remarked that it was extremely fortunate that the downward movement had been gradual, the public growing step by step to an appreciation of the situation, instead of coming as a cyclone, as might have been the case under other circumstances.

May 4, 1893

Interviews with Mr. Sage and Mr. White

Mr. Russell Sage expressed confidence last evening that the worst had been seen. This was certainly the case, unless weakness should be developed in some unexpected quarter. He said he probably loaned more money yesterday than any other person in the Street, and he had done what he could to check the decline in the Industrials, which were at the bottom of the trouble. He thought the Government would have to make a bond issue with which to obtain gold to replenish its supply pending action on the silver question by Congress.

May 6, 1893

Mr. S. V. White was seen this morning and in reply to inquiries as to how he was getting on says: "I am not badly bad off at all. If a man is struck by a runaway team he may have an arm broken or his back broken. In my case it is not in my judgment going to be anything worse than a bad bruise. Any man connected with the business will appreciate that borrowing as I was millions of dollars with a drop of $23 per share in 23 minutes on some of the securities I was carrying, it was perfectly evident that calls would be made for margins greater than I could respond to on the instant and it was my duty under the laws of the Stock Exchange to promptly notify them of the fact. I did it and did not then know how bad the storm was going to be. As it appears this morning things are looking not at all serious for permanent results."

May 6, 1893

T.R. on "The Good and the Bad"

In reading his McKinley oration at Canton, President Roosevelt came to the passage:

"It would be a cruel disaster to this country to permit ourselves to adopt an attitude of hatred and envy toward success worthily won, toward wealth honestly acquired."

This sentence was received in dead silence.

Then the President went on to speak of the dishonest business-men and of "the chicanery and wrong-doing which are peculiarly repulsive when exhibited by men who have no excuse of want, of poverty, or ignorance, for their crimes."

The crowd listening to the President cheered this denunciation.

Then the President raised his hand and stopped the applause and said that he would not permit them to cheer that statement unless they also applauded the one that had gone before, and he went back and reread the sentence in regard to success worthily won and wealth honestly acquired. Thus admonished, the crowd applauded this statement.

This incident illustrates vividly the fact that the multitude are eager to applaud denunciations of wrong-doing and wrong-doers, but have no particular enthusiasm over praise of the good and the right. It is this trait of human nature that is responsible for the fact that our general newspapers make such parade of the crime, the cor-ruption, the villainy of men, and put into comparatively small space, or ignore altogether, the honest achievements.

Thus it is that we get a distorted view of actual conditions. It is important to note this fact at this time when we are having a series of disclosures of wrong-doing in high finance. There is a great parade of the evidence and a great outcry from the people, all of which is proper enough, but as there is comparatively little said regarding the honest and beneficent achievements of high finance, there is no true sense of proportion, only a distorted view of facts.

The fact is that the good greatly outweighs the bad. This is as true in the region of high finance as it is in every other field of endeavor. We hear of the thousands of divorces, but we hear nothing of the millions of contented marriages. We hear of the defalcations, but nothing of the magnificent accounting to the penny for billions of dollars by thousands of honest men. We hear of the betrayals of trust, but nothing is said of the absolute fidelity to contracts and to oral promises by the great body of businessmen. We hear of the crooked management of corporations, but nothing is said of the fact that the vast multitude of our corporations are faithfully, economically and honestly administered in the interest of their stock-holders and without detriment to the public.

The Public Service Commission is performing a good work in the investigation of the New York traction situation. The facts should be made known and those responsible for the misdeeds should be made to feel the weight of public odium and receive the punishment which the law provides for their offenses. But let us not fall into the error of believing that such misdeeds characterize the entire business of the country, and, in applauding the exposure of wrong, let us not forget to think of and commend the splendid fidelity to truth and beauty which is characteristic of American business as a whole.

October 12, 1907

Another Panicky Day

Wall Street passed through another panicky day yesterday as a result of a continuation of the chain of disturbing developments, and prices for securities broke to an even lower level than reached on the preceding day. It was agreed after the close of business, that conditions were being rapidly readjusted. Westinghouse Electric shares, which broke violently on Tuesday, suffered another sensational slump to $35 a share. It developed shortly after the opening of the Stock Exchange that the Westinghouse Company was in serious trouble and that as a result of its inability to meet maturing obligations, a receivership would be necessary.

As a precautionary measure the Pittsburgh Stock Exchange was closed, and this served to aggravate local financial conditions.

A run was started in the Trust Company of America and its Colonial branch as soon as the doors opened, and continued up to the close of business. All depositors requesting their money were paid in full, and even after closing hours, the bank continued its payments to about three hundred depositors in line who were fortunate enough to be in the building when the doors were closed at the regular hour. This was regarded as one bright spot in the day's developments.

Call money rates again reached an exorbitant level, touching 96

"There's this to be said. We don't have to worry about the recession coming."

per cent. Secretary Cortelyou was at the Sub-Treasury all day and rendered valuable monetary assistance. He remarked that the situation was much clearer, and was highly satisfied with the day's developments. The Knickerbocker Trust Company did not open its doors yesterday and the institution is now in charge of the State Banking Examiner.

From a banking standpoint, the situation seems much clearer, and opinions expressed by prominent bankers was that the worst was over.

The run upon the Trust Company of America at the main office in Wall Street, and its Colonial branch at Broadway and Ann Street, began at 10 o'clock, at which time long files of anxious depositors had formed in readiness to present their checks.

Additional paying tellers had been provided, and the disbursements to depositors continued without interruption throughout the day.

Ten million dollars in small notes were sent from the Treasury in Washington to the Sub-Treasury at New York for use in paying depositors.

Secretary Cortelyou arrived at the Sub-Treasury at 9:30 A.M. and remained there until after the close of business, keeping close watch upon the progress of affairs and conferring with a number of bankers who visited him in the room of Assistant Treasurer Fish.

At noon Secretary Cortelyou said that the situation was much clearer. A large amount of United States deposits was placed in banks during the day and Secretary Cortelyou has promised to remain in New York to do all in his power to strengthen public confidence.

October 24, 1907

1907 Panic—and the Day After

October 23 will pass into the history of Wall Street as one of its memorable days. Not since the panic of 1884 has Wall Street witnessed such a picturesque spectacle as that which it presented yesterday. The panic of 1893 was much more severe than that of 1884, but it was devoid of the intense excitement and the big crowds which gathered during the earlier crisis.

Even more impressive than the immense throng which filled Wall and Broad streets was the spectacle of the Secretary of the Treasury —a man of few words, but large executive ability—sitting calmly all day in the office of Assistant Treasurer Fish, at the Sub-Treasury, assuring all his callers of his determination to do everything which his powers as Secretary permitted him to do for the protection of the financial situation.

He was impressive because he represented the great authority and strength of the United States Government. His presence there during the scenes of excitement which were enacted outside recalled the memorable words of James A. Garfield, uttered from the Custom House steps on the day following the assassination of President Lincoln:

"God reigns and the Government at Washington still lives."

Scarcely less impressive than this was the spectacle of J. Pierpont Morgan in his office directly opposite from the Sub-Treasury representing the power of private capital directed for the relief of the financial situation. Mr. Morgan represented confidence. It is significant how in this time of strain Wall Street has turned to Mr. Morgan as to the only individual in private life who seemed to have the prestige and the ability to lead it out of danger, and in this connection it is noteworthy that Mr. Morgan has come out of the stress and storm of the past two years without any cloud upon his fame as a financial leader.

The day was one of intense strain with money, in spite of the efforts of the banks to break the rate, mounting up to 97½ per cent on call, and with every interest watching with solicitude the run upon the Trust Co. of America. The fact that this company met the run upon it with prompt payment of every demand made the situation at the close of the day seem much more composed notwithstanding the fact that owing to the embarrassment of the Westinghouse companies the Pittsburgh Stock Exchange had closed its doors, thus inflicting a new blow to confidence.

The price averages again declined to new low points, the average for twenty railroads' stocks touching $6.69, a decline of 2.04 in twenty-four hours.

With the Secretary of the Treasury depositing millions in the banks, with the big bankers coming together for relief, and with all demands upon the banks and trust companies being met during the day it may be said that the situation at the close was much improved.

October 24, 1907

The situation was better yesterday than it was the day before, just as the day before it was better than on Tuesday. Each day's successful combat with the panic of depositors reduces the excitement and fear and brings the financial district closer to sound and composed conditions.

That the situation has been saved thus far is, as everyone knows, due first to the support of the United States Treasury, and second to the heroic leadership of Mr. Morgan. Mr. Morgan has shown his old-time courage and aggressiveness. He has not hesitated to call the other members of the financial group to order, he has sternly repressed their animosities and differences and compelled them to come together for mutual protection.

When the members of the Stock Exchange yesterday afternoon were confronted with the situation in which there appeared to be no money in sight for their necessities to carry them over the night, Mr. Morgan was made acquainted with the situation and told that $25,000,000 was needed at once, and he gave immediate orders that it should be supplied.

There has been much renewed talk of Clearing House certificates being issued. There are some important bankers who are in favor of this move. It may be said, however, that the controlling elements in the Clearing House were up to the close of business yesterday strongly opposed to any such measure as being a cure worse than a disease.

October 25, 1907

. . . And the Wall Came Tumbling Down

Black Tuesday, October 29, 1929, has become the history-book date for the devastating 1929 crash. A scrutiny of market movements in the autumn of 1929, however, reveals the market did not collapse on any single day. Rather, the crash can be likened to the crumbling of a huge wall. The first cracks appeared toward the end of August 1929. Quick patch-up jobs in the form of bullish rallies went on through all September. By the middle of the month the cracks became larger and multiplied; no amount of repair work could keep it together, and when this realization swept across the country the panic was on. During September stocks were falling five and ten points a day. On October 10, stocks began dropping 15, 20 and 30 points. By November 1, 1929, there was little left on the corner of Broad and Wall but a pile of debris. Yet, even then, it was hard for the nation to realize what had happened.

This is the way the end of an era was chronicled in The Wall Street Journal:

The first pages of the Friday morning and Saturday morning newspapers brimmed over with the bear market. The first pages of the Saturday afternoon and Sunday morning papers brimmed over with the bull market.

After the break Friday and the recovery Saturday, experienced traders expressed the opinion that the market is still "all right." If conditions had not been sound fundamentally the market would not have acted the way it did.

August 13, 1929

Bulls Hold Sway

Stocks derived further powerful impetus on the up side yesterday from the establishment of simultaneous new highs in the Dow-Jones industrial and railroad averages at Monday's close. According to the Dow theory, this development re-established the major upward trend.

Reassurance on this score gave fresh stimulus to bullish enthusiasm, and a long list of representative stocks surged upward to new highs. In view of the general list's ability to climb into record territory so speedily after the stunning blow received from the advance in the local bank rate, it was taken for granted that the buying power underlying the market was too strong to be destroyed by any developments which might reasonably be foreseen.

Even the economists who predicted an autumn recession in business, following the swift pace set during the summer months, have swung around to the view that the momentum recently attained appears to assure a high rate of trade activity over the balance of the year. The outlook for the fall months seems brighter than at any time in recent years.

August 21, 1929

Reaction Develops

Substantial recessions took place in the principal trading stocks yesterday representing the first technical correction of importance. Many commission house observers had been expecting such a development, and advices to take profits gave impetus to the selling movement throughout the morning.

September 5, 1929

New Lows on Reaction

Price movements in the main body of stocks yesterday continued to display the characteristics of a major advance temporarily halted for technical readjustment. Trading was marked by intermittent selling waves, demonstrating that the process of correction was still uncompleted.

September 11, 1929

Renewed Decline

Stocks broke badly under a heavy selling movement in yesterday's late trading on the Stock Exchange. Signs of a temporarily oversold condition were shown in the early dealings, and rallying tendencies developed in the principal trading issues.

Special weakness cropped out in General Motors, which broke to new low ground on the reaction. Aviation shares also were weak, United Aircraft selling below 100. Selling spread to the principal industrials during the last hour, and the whole market was under severe pressure in the final dealings.

September 25, 1929

Dullness Appears

Reports of industrial activity over the weekend showed that slight recessions were occurring in various branches of trade. However,

these largely represented a falling off from the unprecedented activity of the summer months. Arthur W. Cutten, an outstanding bull leader throughout the Coolidge-Hoover market, denied reports recently current that he had been liquidating long lines, and declared emphatically that he had not sold a share of stock. Mr. Cutten said no relaxation of national prosperity was in sight, and expressed the opinion that the market structure could support brokers' loans of $10,000,000,000 to $12,000,000,000.
October 1, 1929

Heavy Liquidation

Trading yesterday was largely devoted to the adjustment of marginal accounts impaired by the recent convulsive declines in the main body of stocks. Commission houses sent out the biggest number of margin calls after Thursday's close that had been found necessary this year, and forced liquidation came into the market in huge volume during the morning.
October 5, 1929

Spirited Rally

Stocks turned sharply for the better in the weekend session. Confidence regarding the immediate position of the market was greatly strengthened by the vigorous recoveries which took place in Steel, American Can, Westinghouse and other leaders in the last few minutes of Friday's session.
October 7, 1929

Optimism Prevails

In the way of news developments, bulls have had much the best of it over the last week or so, and this, perhaps, is the main reason why the market has been able to score such a quick comeback.

A week ago you heard all over the Street pessimistic forecasts as to the future of the market. You read in a number of newspapers comments to the effect that we were in a major bear market.

Stocks are now 10, 20 and 30 points above where they were a week or so ago and optimism again prevails.
October 12, 1929

With Steel off approximately 50 points from its high of the year, Allied Chemical 44, Can 20, Brooklyn Union Gas 40, Canadian Pacific 50, Consolidated Gas 41, Chrysler 70, New York Central 36, and General Electric 54 points, no one can say that we have been in a bull market.
October 18, 1929

Heavy Selling Wave

A heavy selling wave caught the market off balance shortly after the first hour of Saturday's abbreviated session and prices melted away with startling rapidity. . . . Accompanying the decline, reports were circulated of financial difficulties encountered by one of the country's large bull operators. These reports were branded as "ridiculous" by sources close to his operations, and commission houses who usually act for him have been heavy buyers of those stocks with which he is identified.

October 21, 1929

The market has had a very bad break, the most severe in a number of years. There may be some stocks that are still selling too high on a basis of selling price times earnings, but on the other hand there are a number of stocks that are now selling at attractive levels. Many fair to good common stocks are selling to yield 5% to 7%.

From the viewpoint of yield, the copper stocks look more attractive than any other group. As an example Anaconda is selling to yield over 6%, Calumet & Arizona over 8%, Kennecott Copper over 6½%, and Magma over 7½%. Texas Gulf Sulphur is selling to yield over 6%. There are scores of stocks selling on an attractive basis on the times earnings a share theory, but net the investor comparatively little in the way of dividends.

Whether the market is destined for lower levels no one can say, but it would be strange indeed if it failed to recover some of its loss which, based on the high and low prices of the year, shows a maximum decline of over 90 points for Westinghouse, approximately 58 points for Steel, 33 General Motors, 55 Allied Chemical, 68 General Electric, 54 Consolidated Gas, 30 Kennecott Copper, about 50 for Montgomery Ward, taking rights into consideration, and so on down the list.

There is a vast amount of money awaiting investment. Thousands of traders and investors have been waiting for an opportunity to buy stocks on just such a break as has occurred over the last several weeks, and this buying, in time, will change the trend of the market.

October 22, 1929

. . . There are people trading in Wall Street and many all over the country who have never seen a real bear market, as, for instance, that which began in October 1919 and lasted for two years, or that from 1912 to 1914 which predicted the Great War if the world had then been able to interpret the signs. . . . Some time ago it was said in a *Wall Street Journal* editorial that if the stock market was compelled to deflate, as politicians seemed so earnestly to wish, they would shortly after experience a deflation elsewhere which would be much less to their liking. . . .

October 25, 1929

To say, as leading bankers have said, that the severe break in the stock market is "technical" is not illuminating, perhaps because it was not intended to illuminate. . . . So far as the barometer of the Dow-Jones average is concerned it has been clear since last Wednesday that the major movement of the market has turned downwards. The market will find itself, for Wall Street does its own liquidation.

October 26, 1929

Something New

It was a panic, a purely stock-market panic, of a new brand.

Everyone seems to agree that it was due to the fact that prices of some stocks were selling beyond respective intrinsic values and a correction was necessary. This correction has taken place in a number of stocks that show declines ranging from 50 to more than 100 points.

Some stocks may be still selling too high, but many are worth more than they are selling for on a basis of current earnings and future.

Panics of the past were brought about by something fundamentally wrong with finance or business, crop failures, earthquakes, strained international relations, prohibitive rates for money, inflated inventories and the like.

The recent break was due to the position of the market itself. It came when money was 5%, with a plethora of funds available for lending purposes, normal inventories, corporations flush with surplus money, sound industrial conditions and so on.

It is because of the fact that the slump was due to the market itself that the storm has left no wreckage except marginal traders forced to sell at a loss.

Mr. Baker, Mr. Morgan, Mr. Mellon, Mr. Rockefeller and others who hold stocks outright, stand just where they were before the break. Their income is the same. They have lost a few tail feathers but in time they will grow in again, longer and more luxurious than the old ones that were lost in what financial writers like to call the debacle.

October 28, 1929

Stock Trading Hits Record Volume

With the sale of 16,410,000 shares, the stock market passed through its record day of business on Tuesday as the general level of prices reached new lows. The drastic declines carried industrials used in the Dow-Jones averages to new low ground for the year at 260.64, a decline of 120 points from the record high established September 3.

October 30, 1929

The Sun Is Shining Again

The sun is shining again, and we will go on record as saying some good stocks are cheap. We say good stocks are cheap because John D. Rockefeller said it first. Only the foolish will combat John D.'s judgment.

Having had 70 years' experience in business, and having accumulated the greatest fortune of any individual in the world, the elder Rockefeller should have an opinion worth something, particularly when he backs what he says with millions of dollars.

But bear in mind that the statement from John D., Sr., published by Dow, Jones & Co. in advance of all other news services, said he was purchasing "sound common stocks." So if you do buy, know what you are buying.

Mr. Rockefeller says things are fundamentally sound. There has been no inflation in commodity prices, inventories or business in general. There was inflation in stocks and money. That has been removed, so that everything is now resting on a firm foundation, which means that industry can go on expanding.

No one can deny that thousands of people have lost money in the market through forced selling, but we repeat that every stock has an owner just as it had an owner when selling at peak.

But bear in mind that all security holders did not "actually" lose money although most of them were a little bent after the "debacle."

Ninety-five per cent of the people of the United States still hold what they had, which, intrinsically, is worth just as much today as it was before the smash.

In the matter of yield it may be worth more before the end of the year as scores of corporations are expected to increase dividends. Others are planning split-ups and stock dividends.

Many small marginal traders who were worrying a few weeks ago over the heavy taxes they would have to pay as a result of profits on the long side are now worrying because they won't have any taxes to pay.

November 1, 1929

Worst Break Since 1929

Stocks broke on a wave of savage selling yesterday. President Eisenhower's heart attack—and its political implications—set off the sharpest wave of liquidation in over a quarter century's trading on the New York Stock Exchange. The Dow-Jones industrial average closed down 31.89, the widest decline in points since it dropped 38.33 on October 28, 1929, in the great crash of that year. The railroad average was off 11.15, more than it had ever lost in a single session before. The most this compilation had ever fallen previously was 10.91 on October 28, 1929.

Percentagewise, however, yesterday's break in the industrial average has been equaled or exceeded a few times in the last 25 years. Yesterday's decline in that calculation amounted to a little more than 6.5 per cent. The one of October 28, 1929, however, amounted to 12.8 per cent, and the very next day, October 29, 1929, when trading volume amounted to 16 million shares, the largest in Exchange history, the decline in the industrials was 11.6 per cent. Two other big percentage declines in the same average came in May 1940, during the fall of France. On May 14 there was a break of 6.7 per cent and on May 21 of 6.8 per cent. Both, however, were of less than ten points; the average that month fluctuated between 148 and 114.

Another pair of sharp one-day declines took place in July 1933. They came at the end of a steep rise which followed the 1933 "bank holiday," when banks all over the country had been closed to stop depositors from trying to withdraw their funds in fear of a spreading wave of bank failures. The industrial average then broke from 103.58 to 88.71 on two successive declines of 7.1 per cent and 7.6 per cent.

Volume of trading on the Big Board yesterday also broke recent records. At 7,720,000 shares, it was the largest since July 21, 1933.

Excited conditions in the biggest stock market of the country were naturally repeated on other stock exchanges, including the American Stock Exchange in New York, where similarly wide declines took place.

Other kinds of markets responded, too. Among commodities, grains rose sharply during the day, although they lost a big part of their advance near the close. The influence behind their rise was the thought that if the President's illness improved Democratic chances in the 1956 election, the probability of a return to high and rigid farm price supports would be heightened.

High-grade bonds, led by U.S. Government obligations, rose on the theory that the Democrats might return to bond-price-pegging policies, although these were halted in 1951, while Truman was still in office. This market also was influenced by the idea that any decline in business activity would free for investment in bonds large amounts of funds now invested in loans to business.

Brokers reported the selling was of country-wide proportions. However, they added most of their orders were in relatively small lots, the preponderance being 100 to 300 shares. A number of leading houses said the bulk of the selling came from individual holders rather than from institutions such as pension funds. Indeed, some brokers noted that there was some institutional buying throughout the day. Orders previously placed at prices under the market were filled, and in addition further buying orders at prices under those recorded yesterday were placed.

The heavy selling gave the governors of the New York Stock Exchange an extremely busy day. The selling orders so greatly overmatched buying orders that many stocks could not be "opened" until the governors had collected enough buying orders to meet the sales. They sought such orders from all kinds of sources, including institutions and officials of corporations. By 11 o'clock, when the Dow-Jones averages are usually calculated for the first time in each trading session, only 11 of the 30 stocks in the industrial compilation and only four of the 20 rails had sold. As a result, no average was figured out until noon—the first time this has happened as far as anyone can remember since hourly averages were first calculated.

The result of these delays was that the ticker tape early in the session gave an appearance of extreme dullness, with few stocks being traded and practically no popular favorites showing up. Finally big blocks began to appear one at a time as the governors solved each problem in turn. There were many blocks of 10,000 to 30,000 shares at 55, off 7½, the largest.

Individual stocks kept being "opened" in this painstaking fashion throughout the session, the final opening being that of Sutherland Paper, which was not recorded on the ticker tape until after the closing of the session at 3:30 P.M.

OLIVER GINGOLD

September 27, 1955

THE YEARS OF THE BULL

5,110,000-Share Day

A tremendous wave of profit taking hit the stock market in the last half hour yesterday. It brought volume of trading for the day up to 5,110,000 shares, largest in three years, and forced the stock ticker to fall 13 minutes late in reporting transactions from the floor of the New York Stock Exchange.

Trading was the heaviest since the 5,500,000 shares of September 27, 1955, which followed a day of more than 7,000,000 shares on the news of President Eisenhower's heart attack.

Yesterday's declines in prices, however, were relatively small for most stocks. At the close, the Dow-Jones industrial average was off 4.23 points, or 1.54 per cent, and the utilities 0.14, or 0.17 per cent. Only three of yesterday's ten most active stocks ended the day with declines.

First hints of yesterday's decline had been given, according to brokers, late in Monday's session when, after being strong all day, the stock market weakened suddenly, causing earlier price gains to be sharply reduced. Yesterday, price movements were restricted most of the day, although trading was heavy from the opening gong. A few stocks weakened from time to time, but then an upsurge would come in some special group, seemingly pulling the rest of the market back up with it. One such group was the leading oil shares, a number of which closed the day with gains. These included Standard Oil (New Jersey) and Texas Co., on the New York Stock Exchange, and Humble Oil on the American Exchange.

The consensus among partners in several large brokerage houses was that the selling had come from the general public, rather than from any special sources, and represented profit taking by people who had become uneasy over the sharp rise of prices during the past three months. These brokers noted most of yesterday's transactions, as reported on the ticker tape, were in relatively small amounts of 100 or 200 shares, rather than in big blocks. This, they believed, seemed to reflect the activity of small investors, rather than big ones. On the other hand, one or two men reported that they had executed buying orders for large portfolios, such as those of pension funds.

Another fact stressed more than once was the strength of demand evidenced by the smallness of most price declines. This meant, they said, that orders to buy stocks yesterday were from people willing to pay recent advanced prices, rather than from buyers seeking wide price concessions. Many standing orders on the books of these firms, placed by customers wishing to purchase stocks at specified prices several points under recent markets, remained unfilled, they stressed, because prices yesterday did not fall to preset buying points.

John J. Smith, partner of Fahnestock & Co., said he "never saw anything so bullish in my life" as the way prices held. He pointed to the predominance of 100-share and 200-share trades to indicate that the small trader was getting out.

An oil analyst with Carl Pforzheimer & Co. said the strength in the oil stocks was caused by the news Ohio Oil had drilled a successful discovery well in Libya. This, plus what he termed the restraint in price rises of oil stocks in recent markets, yesterday kept them firm in the face of general market easiness.

Richard Leahy of J. W. Sparks & Co. said the market "acted like a million bucks," but he had little idea who was buying or selling.

At Merrill Lynch, Pierce, Fenner & Smith's office at 70 Pine Street, in the Wall Street area, 60 people were crowded into the board room, which seats 28, watching the tape flash across the board in its closing minutes. The group was quiet; it included a large number of elderly men. One was using a pair of binoculars to read the board some 20 feet away.

"When the market is off, this place always gets a big crowd," commented one man. Added another, a man of about 60, who said he had been there since 2 P.M.: "This has been a busy place all day."

Several offered comments on the day's activity in the market, but nobody seemed very excited. "The boys must be taking profits, that's the way I figure it," commented one. "Today is nothing," added another. "It'll be back up tomorrow."

In the large tenth-floor customers' room at Bache & Co. head-quarters at 40 Wall Street, customers' men and women seemed relatively unimpressed.

"There was nothing unusual round here as far as I could see," one Bache employee said. "Oh, there was a rush of sell orders during the last few minutes and the tape has been behind, but I imagine things will recover and we'll have still higher prices."

Robert C. Cease, a gray-haired customers' man in tweeds, confided: "Most of my customers are not influenced by a tradeoff like this. Of course, day-to-day traders are perturbed, but the man who buys for the dividends says, 'So what?' "

October 15, 1958

Puzzle at Broad and Wall

When the stock market this week pushed through its all-time, boom-time high there were many more puzzled people at the corner of Broad and Wall streets than along the sidewalks of Main Street.

One of the interesting things about the surge of the stock market since last winter is that most of the so-called experts were wrong. Every cave in the canyon of Wall Street has its own sad tale of the experienced investor who missed the boat, or who at least caught it rather late. Take it by and large, and with all the usual exceptions, this has been a people's market.

Now it would be a mistake to think the experts were showing unreasonable caution. If you look at the usual statistics—the relationship of earnings to stock prices, for example—the booming market makes little sense. At present prices stock buyers are not only discounting the improved corporate earnings just ahead, which the market would normally do, but all the foreseeable gains for some time to come. It has been pretty hard to justify this market boom by sound economic judgment.

Yet it would also be a mistake to think that the public was acting without any judgment at all. For one thing, the public has been able to anticipate the business statistics. The local businessman in Syracuse or Seattle was in a position to note a change for the better in his own business long before it showed up in lagging national statistics. So to some extent this recovery in the market from the winter lows stemmed from an accurate assessment of improving business.

But that still doesn't explain an all-time high. It is hardly any secret that the additional impetus for all this buying is the fear—or expectation—of inflation. The reason why people are willing to pay more dollars for an equity than they would by any traditional standard is a widespread feeling that the dollars used to pay for it will not for very long be worth what they are today.

This forecast is at the bottom of a number of other actions of people with their money. The bond market is weak because people are reluctant to lend present dollars for tomorrow's dollars where existing rates of interest don't seem to make enough allowance for dollar depreciation. The same effect, though for more complicated reasons, can be noticed in the outflow of gold from the United States. The dollar may still be a hard currency but it doesn't seem as durable as it once did.

"Well, who has a better right to look smug and self-satisfied?"

Now it is quite possible that this inflation fear has overrun itself. That is, that people are anticipating big effects of new inflation sooner than they can be felt. Indeed, this is likely; overcompensation is an all too human tendency in economic as well as other affairs. At Broad and Wall this could mean that the stock market may over-reach itself and, in the parlance of that corner, have a "corrective reaction." That reaction could be big or small depending on how greatly enthusiasm smothers restraint.

But it is hard to argue that the basic inflation fear is unfounded. Conceivably the Government could reverse course, bring its budget into balance and thus give monetary policies a chance to halt the progress of inflation. We prefer to hope this is not wholly out of the question. Yet when you look at the course of events for the past several years and at the present political climate in Washington it is not easy to stretch that hope into an expectation.

So the puzzle of the stock market is not inexplicable after all. The present stock market is not so much a reflection of feverish speculation as it is of quiet desperation. If a man has a little money but little confidence that its buying power will remain the same, what is he to do with it?

And so it seems to us that if the Government is uneasy about a too rapid rise in the stock market—as well it might be—the problem is not what new curbs on credit or on speculation to apply at the corner of Broad and Wall.

What needs to be curbed are the things in Washington that have left the impression on so many people along Main Street that the Government of the United States cannot be trusted to safeguard the value of their money.

September 18, 1958

EDITORIAL

Boiler Room Boom

A Utah grocer recently got an unexpected telephone call from New York City, which, in part, went something like this:

"Listen, this company is stupendous! This stock is selling at $9 a share now, but it'll double and is sure to triple within a few months. The company will earn $12 a share within a year, and in the next fifteen months will pay a $12 dividend."

The caller—a highly persuasive securities salesman—found the grocer eager to get in on a "good thing." The Utah merchant sent the salesman $4,500 plus a commission for 500 shares of the stock. But he soon discovered his "gilt-edged" investment was somewhat tarnished. For one thing, the grocer claims, the salesman forgot to tell him there is no public market for the shares he bought. And he's worried about another oversight that clouds the salesman's glowing profit "guarantee": The caller didn't mention that the company hadn't even started operating.

The grocer is a victim of a "boiler room" operation, according to the Securities and Exchange Commission, the Federal agency which, among other duties, polices securities transactions. In the S.E.C.'s own words, the term "boiler room" refers to "an organization engaged in the sale of securities primarily over the telephone, particularly the long-distance telephone, by high-pressure methods ordinarily accompanied by misrepresentation, deception and fraud."

Boiler rooms have been growing a great deal busier lately, due largely to increased public interest in stocks. Despite periodic setbacks, generally increasing stock prices over the past year have encouraged a growing number of Americans to purchase securities in hopes of making a profit.

Stock prices, as measured by the Dow-Jones average of 30 industrial stocks, have soared from a 1958 low of 436.89 last February

25 to a historic high of 597.66 on January 21 and until yesterday hovered between 590 and 600. Yesterday the average closed at 588.53, down 6.13 points from the previous day. The average daily volume of trading on the New York Stock Exchange last year was up 33 per cent from the previous year and at the highest level since 1929. And the number of individuals entering the market has continued to climb.

This increased interest in stocks has unfortunately boomed the business of a "fringe element of confidence men" as well as that of bona fide securities brokers, says the S.E.C. "The operations of these confidence men," explains the agency, "have been encouraged by the expectations of a substantial segment of the public that it is possible for the unsophisticated investor to reap large and quick profits in the securities markets."

Boiler room operations are not new, of course. The illegal enterprises, which got the tag "boiler rooms" from the high-pressure sales spiels and the noise made by the telephone salesmen working in close quarters, sprang up amid the speculative fever of the 1920s. They dropped out of sight following the 1929 market crash but mushroomed again in the post-World War II boom. In mid-1957, as stock prices sagged, the S.E.C. reported a downtrend in boiler room activities. Since then, however, both stock prices and the boiler room business have headed upward again.

Illegal tactics used by boiler room operators frequently include interstate selling of unregistered securities; omission of facts such as the bankruptcy of the company whose stock is being touted; and various misrepresentations about profit prospects, the market for the stock and about the securities' concern itself.

It's not known how much money boiler rooms take from investors yearly, but it's perhaps significant that about 10 boiler room stock deals in 1956 caused an actual loss to the public of over $100 million, according to S.E.C. officials. By contrast, the S.E.C. will operate its 900-man staff in the coming fiscal year on an expected appropriation of about $7 million.

Bona fide broker-dealers are aware that boiler room operators give their business a black eye. "Boiler shops breed discontent with markets and securities in general with the public," says a New York broker. "It's only the fringe area of the securities business that causes trouble but we all suffer." The securities industry helps police itself through the 3,820-member National Association of Securities Dealers, Inc., which, during the year ended last June 30, considered 116 formal complaints that members had violated rules of fair practice.

Although Federal, state and private securities-policing agencies are stepping up their battle against boiler room operations, there are signs that the problem is growing. The S.E.C. in the last half of 1958 started legal actions against 57 securities brokers and dealers, about one fifth of whom were involved in boiler room operations. That's the same number of total proceedings started in all of 1957. Last month the S.E.C. went to court in New York to get an injunction against 46 defendants accused of using boiler room methods in selling a stock issue. This is the largest group of defendants in a single civil case since the agency was formed in 1934. And S.E.C. officials privately hint that even bigger cases may be in the offing.

Federal and state agencies are convinced their efforts are fast putting an end to the larger, old-fashioned boiler rooms that historically have clustered in the large financial centers such as New York.

The boiler room that the S.E.C. claims bilked the Utah grocer fits the classic pattern. Inside a lower-Manhattan office which was locked "so people wouldn't wander in," says an S.E.C. investigator, a dozen or so salesmen worked their phones and prospect lists. Unpainted wooden packing cases piled atop shabby desks provided each salesman with a tiny cubicle in which the chatter of his colleagues was muffled enough to keep a prospect from getting wary.

An S.E.C. official describes his first visit to a boiler room this way: "A bunch of the toughest-looking guys you ever saw was sitting around a table making phone calls. Most were stripped to the waist —it was August—and many were tattooed. You wouldn't have believed it; they looked like thugs straight out of a Hollywood movie."

But a "new look" in so-called boiler rooms is plainly giving securities policemen plenty of headaches. For one thing, today's confidence men aren't staying put. "In the place of the old-fashioned boiler room has appeared a group of small firms which spring up suddenly, sell one or two spurious issues quickly and then disperse," laments the S.E.C.'s recently issued annual report. "Salesmen and organizers go out and form new boiler shops almost as fast as we can close down the old big ones," says Paul Windels, Jr., the S.E.C.'s New York regional administrator.

Also plaguing the S.E.C. is a "noticeable increase" in "migratory operators moving from state to state, particularly in the Western part of the country." And today's boiler room salesmen frequently work from hotel rooms and apartments as well as from alleged business offices. To conceal the nature of illegal transactions and the identity of operators, today's boiler rooms make extensive use of intermediaries, often in foreign countries such as Canada and Liechtenstein, reports the commission. And payments often are made in cash rather than by check.

State law enforcement officials confirm the increase in boiler room operations. The Illinois Securities Department, for example, reports "an appreciable increase in the number of complaints against out-of-state securities dealers soliciting business within Illinois." In the past the state agency received many complaints about high-pressure stock peddlers phoning from Canada.

In New York, State Attorney General Louis J. Lefkowitz within the past year has obtained about 240 court injunctions against stock dealers and brokers using procedures he charged were illegal. This is an 80 per cent increase over as recent a year as 1956, reports an associate.

Boiler room salesmen in action sound much alike. "It's just as if they used the same script in every deal with just the names and figures changed," observes one securities policeman. Most salesmen claim to represent an "old, reliable Wall Street investment banking house"; the stock they're selling is described as a "sure thing"; it will triple or at least double within a few months, the salesmen promise, and the stock will be listed shortly on either the Big Board or the American Stock Exchange. In most cases, none of these boasts is true.

By using long-distance telephone calls—some boiler rooms run up phone bills as high as $50,000 a month—the high-pressure salesmen feel free to say almost anything about the stock without fear of being called back for omitted details. Boiler room salesmen seldom put their claims in writing, and it's difficult for enforcement officers to check their oral sales spiels. The shops often trade their "sucker lists" —which usually are heavily loaded with names of doctors, teachers and small businessmen.

Boiler room salesmen seldom allot more than three minutes to a sales call. If the prospect hasn't taken the bait within the time limit the salesman just hangs up. If the prospect is hesitant the salesman may resort to a tactic known as a "wooden sales." He will send a confirmation of the stock purchase to the undecided prospect. If the latter complains that he didn't order the stock, the salesman may, ironically, threaten to make trouble for him with the S.E.C.

Some boiler room salesmen may make as much as $5,000 during a particularly good week when they have a "hot" deal going. The shop takes a liberal markup on securities it pushes and the salesmen usually get a commission on each sale plus a generous weekly bonus.

Boiler rooms like to push stocks of dramatically named companies in glamorous fields although during a "rapidly rising stock market, it's easy for them to sell anything that looks like a stock certificate," says the S.E.C.'s Mr. Windels.

"Now any stock with electronics in its name seems to have great appeal to investors," says a spokesman for the N.A.S.D. "Before that it was uranium and before that oil. In other times I guess it was gold and copper."

RICHARD L. MADDEN

January 29, 1959

A "Sure Thing" Goes Wrong

NEW YORK—2⅝s, Feb., 1965 95.16 95.22 95.30 3.38.

Those cryptic numbers are a progress report on a beating—probably the roughest beating ever absorbed by investors on a single new securities issue.

The symbols represent Friday's closing quotation on the U.S. Treasury's 2⅝ per cent bonds which mature in February 1965. They indicate, among other things, that buyers last Friday were willing to pay only $951 for a $1,000 bond issued by the Treasury barely two months ago. The fall of the 2⅝s already has cost purchasers real or paper losses totaling well over $300 million.

Thousands of Americans got the bonds originally by putting up 5 per cent or less of the purchase price and borrowing the rest. They counted on a quick price rise, after which they would be able to sell out and take their profit. As the price fell, they've had to scramble around to put up more and more money.

"All the amateurs in the world were caught—dentists, doctors, newspaper store dealers, nearly everyone with an extra $1,000 of itchy money," says a New York City banker, contemplating the carnage.

Why did the amateurs get in? Because the professionals told them they couldn't lose. So sure were the professionals of their own advice that they backed it with their own money. One New York stockbroker was so certain he had a sure thing that he invested $2 million of his mother's money in the 2⅝s. But he was more fortunate than most have been up to now; he sold out early, losing only $20,000.

A prosperous New York doctor, who leaves his investments in the hands of his broker, returned from vacation a few weeks ago to find he owned $3 million of the 2⅝ per cent bonds. His paper loss so far is $150,000. "He's sore as hell at me," says the broker.

In another New York brokerage house, a $70-a-week stenographer, with the aid and encouragement of her employer, bought $200,000 of the bonds. At the moment, she's out $10,000 and both she and her boss are praying for a price rise.

Others in the strange assortment of losers include a senior vice-president of a major New York City bank, a television singing star, an editor of a financial magazine, an American Army officer's widow living in Japan and a Florida brewery owner.

The story of the sure thing that went wrong had its beginning in late May. The Treasury, anxious to retire some older securities, offered their holders the chance to trade them in on new 2⅝ per cent bonds, and agreed to take all the old securities offered in exchange. The announcement was greeted with enthusiasm—an enthusiasm that far surpassed anything the Treasury had expected. When the Treasury had counted up all its exchanges, it found it had to issue $7,250,000,000 of the new 2⅝s—nearly double the amount it had anticipated.

To understand the overwhelming response, it's necessary to look briefly at recent money market history. When the business recession began in late 1957, the Federal Reserve System began to see to it that banks were supplied with ample funds for lending.

At the same time, of course, the recession cut into the demand for credit. The combination of ample supply and slim demand pushed down the price of money—interest rates. As interest rates fell, yields on government securities tumbled right along with them; prices, of course, rose.

In late May, most of the professional bond traders were convinced the end of the recession was not in sight. They confidently expected the Federal Reserve to continue its easy-money moves; such moves, they were sure, would push government bond prices higher and higher. With such convictions, they felt the 2⅝ per cent yield on the Treasury's new bonds was high and would start falling as soon as the bonds reached the market. As yields fell, of course, prices would rise.

For anyone who wished to speculate on this basis, the step was simple: He merely bought some of the old Treasury securities which were to be exchanged for the 2⅝s. He could borrow almost all the money through his broker or his bank; the Federal Reserve's margin requirements do not apply to government securities. In some cases, where the speculator was an old and valued customer, he was able to borrow the full amount of the purchase price.

The first hint that all might not be quite well came on June 10, when the Treasury announced the surprising size of the issue. The huge supply of the bonds made a sharp price rise less likely.

Some professional traders saw the significance of the issue's size; several were able to sell out at a slight profit. But most of the purchasers still held on.

Their debt was heavy. Federal Reserve figures show that loans by reporting New York member banks to brokers and dealers for purchasing or carrying U.S. Government securities skyrocketed from $349 million on May 28 to $1.4 billion on June 18. Brokers and dealers, in turn, were lending much of this money to their customers. The June 18 figure was the highest since December, 1945.

But much of the money does not show up in Federal Reserve figures—it came from banks outside New York. Since the government securities market is centered on New York, the Reserve System never has felt it was worth while to keep detailed statistics on government securities loans made by banks outside the city.

Though the speculators were disappointed at once by the failure of the 2⅝s to jump sharply in price, real disillusionment did not set in until June 19, when for the first time the bonds dropped below the issue price of 100.

The basic reason for the decline was simple: The economic outlook had begun to improve. The Federal Reserve took no steps to further ease money; Administration officials made it clear they were more concerned with heading off future inflation than with taking new steps to pull the country out of a recession. Inflation fighting and easier money, to put it mildly, are incompatible.

The decline began to feed on itself. Speculators in growing numbers rushed in to sell to minimize their losses. But, with prices falling, buyers were far from eager—except at lower and lower prices. The decline has not been limited to the 2⅝s, of course; it has spread through the entire bond market, because all bonds, to some extent at least, are competing products.

Apparently embarrassed by the decline, the Treasury between June 19 and July 9 bought back $589.5 million of the 2⅝s. But its action was not enough to halt the decline.

Bond traders are quick to point out that the two-month fall of the 2⅝s has hurt only the speculators, those who thought they saw a chance for a sure—and quick—profit. The long-term investor will continue to draw his 2⅝ per cent interest regularly and, come February 1965, Uncle Sam will pay him $1,000 for each $1,000 bond.

PATRICK CARBERRY AND LEE SILBERMAN

August 11, 1958

"In short, we highly recommend this company's stock—they pay a steady quarterly dividend, have excellent growth prospects, and serve a really delicious box lunch at their annual meetings."

Social Speculators

The Allegheny Almshouse Association, the Jack Daniels Memorial Foundation Investment Club, and the Willy K. Sutton Relief Society this year have staggered out of a financial upheaval that's left them gasping—but still very much alive.

These outfits are amateur investment clubs dedicated, for the most part, to stock market speculation. And like the roughly 12,000 other such clubs that have sprung up around the U.S. since 1953, they emerged earlier this year from the first big stock market break in most of their histories.

The 1957–58 recession—severest slump since World War II—clipped billions of dollars off security values, and prompted some clubs to give up the ghost. But most weathered their first serious stock market setback, and the investment club movement, with the market booming again, now is expanding once more.

"Very few investment clubs are more than five years old, and their experience had all been in an upward market. But the recession did an excellent job of weeding out a few of the more frivolous clubs and we're going to go places now," says Thomas E. O'Hara, chairman of the National Association of Investment Clubs, headquartered in Detroit.

Mr. O'Hara says the membership of his association—which represents about one quarter of all the investment clubs in the nation—has grown from 112 groups in 1953 to 3,224 clubs with some 45,000 members today. "Within the next few years," predicts Mr. O'Hara, "I would not be surprised to see one million people enrolled in investment clubs."

Investment clubs to a large extent are a phenomenon of stock market boom. Booms always attract flocks of little investors—more of them out for a quick, speculative killing than for dividends or long-term gains. The soaring stock market of the late 1920s attracted thousands of such investors, most of whom saw their investments largely wiped out by the 1929 crash. During most of the 1930s, such Americans for the most part had neither the money nor the inclination to buy stocks. Since World War II, climbing personal incomes and generally rising stock prices have lured the small-scale speculator again—often through an investment club.

The return of such little investors is reflected in the rise in the total number of stockholders. Results of the first New York Stock Exchange stockholder survey in 1952 showed there were 6.5 million stockholders. The latest such survey in 1956 lifted this figure to 8.6 million. There seems no question the figure is higher now.

Through a club, an investor may gain a certain sense of security or, at the least, shared misery. Unlike his counterpart of the 1920s, the investment club member may make a thorough study of the market and his club's investments. And many clubs offer social activities which may be of some solace to the unsuccessful investors.

Among the more enthusiastic backers of investment clubs are securities dealers—not entirely for selfless reasons.

"These clubs are a growing factor in the stock market, and doing a great deal to improve investor education," says a Bache & Co. official. This big securities house, like other brokers such as Merrill Lynch, Pierce, Fenner & Smith; Goodbody & Co.; Paine, Webber, Jackson & Curtis; and Thompson & McKinnon, supplies information and speakers to investment clubs.

Talks with dozens of investment groups across the country indicate that the stock market decline had a sobering effect on most clubs and significantly changed the investing policies of many of them. "The recession made us defensive-minded," says Don Robinson, program director of radio station KIXL in Dallas and head of Daltex

Investors, Inc., which had the paper value of its security holdings trimmed 15 per cent by the stock market drop. Daltex now is concentrating on blue-chip stocks listed on the New York Stock Exchange.

"Prior to the recession stock market trouble, we seldom attempted to compare our performance with the Dow-Jones industrial average," says John Pillsbury, an executive with the American Trust Co. in San Francisco and member of the Gopher (for Go-For-Broke) investment club. "But we were pretty disappointed with our lack of progress and decided to start making comparisons."

Mr. Pillsbury says that in 1957, when the market began its decline, the value of the Gopher club's stock holdings fell faster than the 30 stocks making up the Dow-Jones average. Since the beginning of this year, he adds, the club has been employing a new investment plan that stresses speculative stocks, and he claims the club's security holdings have risen faster than the D-J average. "We're now buying heavily in electronics stocks," Mr. Pillsbury says, "and have had unusually good luck with one particular issue. We bought this stock at an average price of $33.50 a share, and its market value is now close to $90 a share."

While many clubs conduct their affairs with dedicated seriousness, the majority of them continue to consider fun and investment education just as important as financial gain, and the stock market drop has not altered this sentiment one jot. Take the case of the Jack Daniels Memorial Foundation Investment Club of San Francisco, for example.

This investment club was formed in April 1956, by a doctor, lawyer, radio advertising salesman, two chemists, the president of an electronics firm, an insurance broker, a Woolworth Co. executive and a stock broker.

The night these gentlemen decided to start their club, they were sipping Jack Daniels bourbon, and everybody soon felt so optimistic about the stock market outlook that they decided to memorialize the whisky maker. Club members chip in $15 a month, have invested $3,964 to date, and their security holdings have grown by about 34 per cent to a value of $5,332 on paper, despite a few substantial losses.

"We took a real beating on Kaiser Aluminum stock," says club member Dick Schutte, the radio adman. "We bought nine shares at an average price of $45, and we were so upset when we decided to unload at $24 a share earlier this year, that we felt obliged to consume two bottles of Jack Daniels Green Label."

Many investment club members seem to enjoy a good belly laugh at their own expense, and because their selection of securities frequently results in disaster, they get plenty of opportunity for merriment.

"Nothing is eligible for consideration by the Flask & Swig Investment Club unless it's at an all-time high," chuckles Dick Smith, treasurer of this Pittsburgh investment group primarily composed of young Jones & Laughlin Steel Corp. executives. This club has invested $3,109 since its formation in October 1956, and has a paper profit of only $31.36—or less than it would have earned by putting its funds in a savings bank.

Flask & Swig owns small odd lots of Hagan Chemicals & Controls Corp. (on which it has a loss), International Business Machines (gain), Jones & Laughlin (gain), Loew's, Inc. (loss), Socony Mobil (loss) and Westinghouse Electric (gain). The club's most profitable investment was 13 shares of Polaroid purchased at $50.875 a share in February and sold at $59.75 in May. "It's the only one on which we made a cash profit, not a paper profit," notes Mr. Smith.

The club's worst venture was the purchase of three shares of Koppers Co. at $64.75 each in December 1956. "We bought this one on the idea that the stock market was going to re-evaluate it as a chemical company, and we thought it could go to the eighties," says Mr. Smith. "Then Koppers started to drop and when it hit $55 we figured it was a terrific buy but we just didn't have the guts to buy any more. When it sank to $45 we thought it was a whale of a buy, but we still didn't get any. This policy of not buying Koppers paid off handsomely," says Mr. Smith, whose club watched its Koppers stock sink to the thirties before getting out.

The average investment club's tongue-in-cheek approach to the hazards of attempting to outguess the stock market is often reflected in its name. Sobriquets include such titles as Defunct Investors, Golden Fleece, Sewickley Sharecroppers, Duffers, Motherlode Club, and WIG (a ladies group whose initials optimistically stand for Watch Investments Grow).

The women's clubs frequently outperform the men's groups—a fact which irritates the men no end, because they're convinced the ladies have no head for financial matters. One distressed male tells the story of how he advised his wife not to recommend a certain company to her club because it "was controlled by hoods. But the little lady went ahead and told her club to buy the stock because 'gangsters always make money.' The girls bought the stock and they've got a profit in it," admits this perplexed gentleman.

For a peek at just how the ladies do it, join an 11 A.M. meeting of the Ace Investment Group of Jacksonville. First the girls drop their $25-a-month investment checks on the chairman's table, and the meeting begins with a stern lecture on getting the cash in on time.

"And now who's done their homework?" asks Mrs. Robert Milam, a chic white-haired widow who heads the club. Mrs. James Patton, a blonde whose husband is in the dog-racing business, stands up and says she'd like the club to consider Dresser Industries. "Assets and liabilities are three to one, and it pays a $2 dividend," she notes. Then Mrs. Patton reads a list of the company's products that include various oil well drilling equipment and says "all these things are foreign to me, but it still sounds awfully good."

The discussion soon moves on to ABC Vending, and several ladies tell the club how they have seen these vending machines in all kinds of strange places. One woman says she has even seen a machine that changes one dollar bills into coins. "Could we have a show of hands on ABC Vending," says Mrs. Milam, and the ladies vote to buy 16 shares of the stock. "Now," says Mrs. Milam, "I want everybody to run around and put money into these vending machines." Ace Investment holds Columbia Gas, National Distillers, W. T. Grant, Carter Products and Sonotone—and has at least a paper profit on every purchase.

"Women's investment clubs will always beat a men's club because the girls pay more attention to the club," says George Nicholson, Jr., head of the investment counseling department at Smith, Hague & Co., a securities firm in Detroit. He's also chairman of the board of advisers of the National Association of Investment Clubs, and a member of the Mutual Investment Club of Detroit with holdings of $103,344, making it one of the richest clubs in the nation.

Gentlemen investors like to have a little fun and sometimes are tempted to put their money into all sorts of dubious ventures. One club bought a race horse and reportedly invested in a young actress it figured might be another Ingrid Bergman. A St. Louis club bought an Irish Sweepstakes ticket as an investment and lost. And Dick Schutte, member of the Jack Daniels Memorial Foundation Investment Club, confesses, "A couple of times I've suggested to the group that we take some of the money and give my bookie a call, but much to my dismay, I've been soundly voted down every time."

August 19, 1958

Stock Trader

NEW YORK—In a cacophonic stock-trading room high in a skyscraper overlooking Wall Street's serene Trinity Church, a slim girl surrounded by Western Union teleprinters puts a red megaphone to her lips and bellows, "San Jacinto for Lundborg" at a shirt-sleeved, Napoleon-sized man seated a scant eight feet away.

"Thirty-one ah half two ah half," he yells back. He then swivels around, plugs a phone jack into a wildly buzzing switchboard and says, "You sold a hundred Food Mart at eleven three quarters." Seconds later, a lad tending two teletypes hollers, "Mick, Polaroid for Worchester." "Tell 'em thirty-eight-nine," the man fires back before gulping down a sip of lunchtime coffee and a mouthful of chicken soup.

The man in the midst of this madhouse is Milton "Mickey" Pauley, 51, a professional stock trader for Troster, Singer & Co., Wall Street specialists in buying and selling the thousands of stock issues traded outside America's 18 securities exchanges. His operations mirror the most varied, least known and zaniest securities bazaar in America—the over-the-counter stock market.

Mickey singlehandedly trades more shares in a week than most investors do in a lifetime, knows which over-the-counter stocks the biggest brokers, banks and investment trusts are buying, and frequently picks up rumors of corporate developments—many right, some wrong—days before any news is released to the general public.

Mickey Pauley earns his living buying and selling unlisted stocks in competition with some of the smartest securities men in Wall Street—who often are better informed about market conditions than he is. Brokers, banks, dealers and other potential customers will do business with him only if his selling or buying price is as good or better than his competitors', whose quotations they also check.

Brokers buy and sell securities as agents for customers, charging a commission for the service. Dealers such as Troster Singer buy securities, maintain an inventory and try to sell their securities at a profit.

"During the past few weeks," says Mickey, "this over-the-counter market has been in an absolute turmoil. I've had to give up my usual custom of going out for an hour lunch with friends once or twice a week, and even canceled a trip to Canada. When the market is falling on its face, a stock trader like me has got to be in there trading stocks."

An estimated 50,000 to 60,000 different stocks are traded over the counter, compared with the roughly 3,000 listed on the New York Stock Exchange, American Stock Exchange, and the other formal trading arenas. The market is such a potpourri that $60,000 or so will get you one share of stock in the Los Angeles Turf Club, Inc., or some 3,500,000 shares in a penny stock such as Beehive Uranium Corp. If you like safe situations, the o.t.c. market offers shares in the Bank of New York and First National Bank of Boston, both of which have paid dividends continuously for 173 years. But if you're a bit of a gambler, you can buy shares of Tucker (Motor Car) Corp., which never paid a dividend, never sold a car, and went out of business in 1949.

The o.t.c. market deals in thousands of tightly held and rarely traded stocks such as Upjohn Co. that may go for a decade without more than a few dozen shares changing hands. But it also boasts stocks such as Tennessee Gas Transmission Co., Kaiser Steel Corp., Collins Radio Co., Anheuser-Busch, Inc., and Vitro Corp. of America, that are as actively traded as many stocks listed on the exchanges. This market, much to the chagrin of the New York Stock Exchange, also makes regular—if modest—markets in American Telephone & Telegraph Co., Standard Oil Co. (New Jersey), General Motors Corp. and many other Big Board darlings.

O.t.c. market trading primarily is conducted by nearly 4,000 dealers in cities and hamlets across the country who are members of the National Association of Securities Dealers, Inc. They range in size from small brokers who stand ready to buy or sell shares in a locally prominent firm, to Wall Street giants such as Merrill Lynch, Pierce, Fenner & Smith, Inc., Blyth & Co. Inc., Carl M. Loeb, Rhoades & Co., and Kidder, Peabody & Co. that deal in the shares of many of America's most famous firms. The latter four firms not only trade over the counter but, as members, deal in securities on most of the nation's major exchanges.

Troster Singer, which limits itself to the o.t.c. market, makes markets in some 535 stocks, handles 800 to 900 trades daily, and sometimes loses well over $10,000 a day, which puts it in the same league with the giants. But unlike most of them, it does business exclusively with brokers, banks, insurance firms, investment trusts and other dealers. It does not deal with the general public. The company occupies three large rooms. These consist of the partners' office, which is festooned with autographed pictures of Harry S. Truman and Al Smith, three dozen photos of Colonel Oliver J. Troster's Army friends, and shelves of Moody's and Poor's stock manuals; a middle chamber where stock certificates are received and dispatched; and the all-important back room where Mickey Pauley and 15 other experienced traders buy and sell shares worth millions.

The trading room is divided by a worn wooden table, topped with telephone switchboards leading to some 150 Wall Street brokers and dealers. Along both walls there's a battery of teleprinters and teletype machines linking the room with a nation-wide network of other firms that trade with Troster Singer. Across the far end of the room, there's a green blackboard where a man wearing a telephone head-

set continuously chalks up the changing quotations on the most
active stocks the company buys and sells.

Mickey Pauley occupies the first trading chair and makes markets
in some 50 stocks including Polaroid Corp., San Jacinto Petroleum
Corp., M. A. Hanna Co., Weyerhaeuser Timber Co., Great Western
Financial Corp., Food Mart, Inc., and Standard Register Co.
Mickey's trading tools are packed into an area no bigger than a card
table top. To his left is a long sheaf of white sheets where an assistant jots down his completed trades. In front of his switchboard
there's a fat pad containing customers' orders which are too big to be
transacted quickly or which must be traded at a figure other than
the going market price. To his right sits a slim tablet covered with a
running total of every stock he owns or owes. Within easy reach of
either hand is Mickey's trading bible, a half-inch-thick book of pink
sheets published daily by the National Quotation Bureau, Inc.,
which lists the previous day's wholesale bids and offers on about
2,600 of the most actively traded over-the-counter stocks.

Troster Singer has entrusted Mickey with a trading portfolio of
stocks worth some $250,000, and from this base he battles to make a
buck. In the course of a seven-hour working day, Mickey usually
answers several hundred phone calls from customers asking him to
quote his bid or offer on any stock he trades, but without disclosing
whether they want to buy or sell. Mickey averages about one trade
on every ten quotes he gives out, and considers a gross profit of one
eighth of a point or 12½ cents on every share swapped to be a trading victory.

To understand why this is so, it's necessary to illustrate the over-
the-counter market's stiff competition. This morning, for example,
the "pink sheets" show 10 houses trading Weyerhaeuser Timber at
between $30.50 and $31 a share. Brokers with orders to buy Weyerhaeuser probably will ask several traders to name their price—
Merrill Lynch insists its order clerks check at least three houses—and
if Mickey is to grab the business his quote must equal or fractionally
better that of his rivals.

Mickey's knack of making profitable trades puts him in the van-
guard of the 1,500 to 3,000 professional over-the-counter stock
traders. His trading techniques are best described by himself. The
tale may ramble a trifle because it was unfolded in a darkened bar
near the American Stock Exchange, at a Park Avenue supper club,
in Troster Singer's trading room, and while strolling along Wall
Street behind a gentleman wearing a sign reading "Amazing, Mys-
terious, Mexican Jumping Beans on Sale at the Latin American

Shop." But it will give you some idea how a stock market pro operates.

"Eighty per cent of what makes a good trader is his ability to tell which way the market is going," says Mickey. "I try to do this by watching the preponderance of bids to buy stocks over offers to sell them, and vice versa; by keeping an eye on our New York Stock Exchange ticker that indicates how things are going there (the Big Board can influence the trend of the over-the-counter market but we rarely affect it), and even noting what's happening on the Canadian and London markets.

"Now, if an investor knew exactly which way the market was going," Mickey says, "he'd attempt to buy when it had struck bottom and sell when it hit the top. But for a trader it's not good to sell into strength and buy on weakness. When the market is dropping, my normal strategy is to sell stock knowing my latest sale is at the market while all prior sales were above that point. If I suddenly come up against a wall of strength, however, I'll probably stop selling and start buying. On a rising market," Mickey says, "I'll keep buying because the stock I just bought at the market will have been purchased at a price below what the market will be when the stock makes its next move upward. It doesn't pay to buck a trend," says Mickey.

While Mickey often trades stocks only as numbers, he also buys and sells them as shares in corporations whose history and outlook he studies intimately. "Many traders trade stocks as numbers and nothing else," says Mickey, "and this often proves profitable. They watch the stock's short swings and bid them up or down on purely technical considerations without particularly caring whether the company itself is in the entertainment business, like Cinerama, Inc., or part of the drug industry, like Eli Lilly. These fellows will probably catch more of the stock's day-to-day swings and win the battles," says Mickey, "but I'll usually get the trends that are a little longer term and win my share of the war."

CARTER HENDERSON

October 31, 1957

Nicely Nicely's Broker's Tip

Damon Runyon's Nicely Nicely sits in Mindy's the other rainy day looking at the daily paper's racing form sheet for a good dry tracker in the seventh at Saratoga. The reason he looks for a good dry tracker is that Nicely Nicely understands it does not rain that day at Saratoga though the water is running scared under Mindy's front door making Mindy's cheesecake even soggier than Mindy makes it.

Nicely Nicely is thinking of this and that and even of something nice in the sixth at Saratoga when in comes a wet character who sits down next to Nicely Nicely and orders a coffee and salami in a mad voice.

Nicely Nicely does not like this wet character from the first for the reason that the character splashes wet water all over Nicely Nicely's daily paper's racing form and even if the character does not splash wet water Nicely Nicely does not like him as only a drip eats salami that early in the morning to begin with.

But Nicely Nicely does not do anything about the drip because before he can do anything the drip starts to speak as follows:

"Can you ascertain for me," the drip says to Nicely Nicely, "the whereabouts of a trustworthy turf accountant? I wish some advice on the horses as I wish to make a small investment for I cannot get any advice very much on the kind of investments I make which is in the stock market."

What Nicely Nicely gets out of all this is that the drip wishes to meet a bookie and so he mentions Harry the Horse who always has a good thing in the morning though the guy Harry the Horse gives the good thing to in the morning often does not think so much of it in the afternoon.

But the drip says this is just what he wants as he is sick and tired to death of brokers' tips telling him things go wishy this way and washy that way in the investment field he is in which is the stock market in Wall Street New York New York.

And the drip pulls from his pocket some stock market commentaries that are even wetter than the drip thinks they are on account of all the water and he reads to Nicely Nicely as follows:

"It is interesting to note that the sharp increase in the number of investors in recent years has been mostly during a period of favorable market action."

"It is probable that the market will have to form more of a base before it can initiate another sustained upward trend."

"The equity market is currently reflecting the public's opinion."

"Thus, analysts do not feel that they will be far wrong in not predicting that the selling will pick up momentum this fall and cause the market to go into a real tailspin."

Nicely Nicely thinks for a moment and then speaks to the drip as follows: "Why, these Wall Street characters do not only not tell you what is a good thing they do not even tell you the distance or the

'Hello, Acme Investment? Buy ten shares of Modern Motors for me.'

jockeys. In fact," Nicely Nicely says, "they do not tell you where the track is. All they tell you is that all the horses run slow this summer."

The drip says to Nicely Nicely that is exactly his beef too and when Harry the Horse comes into Mindy's the drip goes off with Harry the Horse to a bookie joint or maybe even to Saratoga to make an investment on a parlay Harry the Horse gives the drip by the name of You Guess and Double Talk.

But Nicely Nicely thinks he does better not to go to a bookie joint or even to Saratoga. Nicely Nicely thinks he does better to go down to Wall Street New York New York where all the customers stand around and about on one foot and another and wait for more information than they get from such brokers' tips as Nicely Nicely sees which give information about like horses eat oats.

So Nicely Nicely makes himself a proposition and he does not for the life of him see why it does not occur to the brokers who make up the tip sheets for Wall Street New York New York since it occurs to sensible horse players one and all and maybe even to Harry the Horse.

And what occurs to Nicely Nicely is that even in a summer like this one when all the horses run slow some horses just naturally run slower than other horses.

—With apologies to some market letters and all Runyon fanciers.

W. H. Fitzpatrick

September 3, 1957

Reprise: Three Veterans of 1929 Again Ride High

BOSTON—"I made more than a million dollars before I was forty. Between '29 and '33, I lost not only all of that but wound up owing $250,000 to $300,000 more. So I still feel that anything can happen."

Were it not for this chilling memory of the Great Depression, investment banker Arthur X could hardly restrain his enthusiasm for the booming present and the rosy future of the U.S. economy.

"The business and investment climate right now is excellent," says Mr. X in his clipped Boston tones. "My theory is that this country will stay strong for a long time to come. Of course, if history means anything, it means that no nation can stay on top indefinitely. But I can't see any signs of weakness yet."

Mr. X is about 60 and, in his proper Bostonian phrase, "well to do." In 1955, his income was over $200,000. Each of his several children will inherit roughly a half million from him and his wife. His greatest satisfaction is the success he has had in helping to bring his firm back to its present sleek and prosperous condition.

A remarkably similar optimism toward the future, tempered with prudence learned from the depression of 20 years ago, characterizes the present attitudes of two other Boston businessmen who have wealth and position comparable to Mr. X's—Bertram Y, a millionaire manufacturer, and Christopher Z, a wealthy engineer who owns his own business.

What sort of men are these? What accounts for the confidence they show in the future? How do they view the trends of our times? How are they managing their personal affairs these days?

As supersuccessful members of the senior generation in active business life, their views may be noteworthy. Like other people of their generation they experienced the boom of the 1920s, the debacle of 1929 and the depression which followed, along with three wars. No one knows how typical their views may be. The men themselves are pretty untypical. For one thing, they exercise considerably more economic power than most. For another, their views may be more carefully thought out than those of most people of their generation or any other.

Like Banker X, Manufacturer Y thinks business conditions right now are "very healthy." As for the future, he says, "the U.S. is the great hope of the modern world. The most important thing is that the rights of human beings to freedom and property have gone farther here than in any country in history."

But always in the back of Mr. Y's mind is a tiny doubt: "Every one of us who lived through the depression can never be quite sure again. Looking back, I can't understand how we didn't know it was coming—but we didn't."

Mr. Y makes a special point of the need for keeping an eye on the past as well as on the milk-and-honey future he sees ahead. He's a man with long experience as a "business trouble shooter," and he says, "I wouldn't give much for a man in a responsible business position who hadn't been through some very tough times." He worries a little because of the increasing number of business executives who have known only prosperity. "It's one of the dangers of the times ahead," he warns.

Mr. Y himself has been through the wringer. He was almost broke in the early '20s, rode through the depression fairly well, but, just after World War II, suffered a collapse from overwork that nearly finished his career. He's now a hale and contented 71. His income last year was about $150,000 and his estate is "well over a million." He's stopped trying to accumulate money and gives it away freely— over $40,000 in cash and securities in 1955.

Engineer Christopher Z, 56, wishes he were 29 again so that he could take the fullest advantage of the years ahead. "Business is healthier than I've ever seen it," he says. "But one thing that bothers me," he adds, "is that my children have never had to fight for anything." In an effort to give his youngish son some understanding of heavy business responsibilities, Mr. Z not long ago made him head of a subsidiary company to see what he could do with it. "Because of the boom times the thing prospered so easily that I don't know as he learned much," the father says.

Mr. Z's business (he's been running it for 30 years) was late to feel the 1929 crash, but when it did, "It was a long, hard struggle." His personal income in 1928 ran around $60,000, all from the company, but by mid-1933 the firm had only $2,900 in the bank and "was over six figures in debt." Mr. Z refused to go through bankruptcy and paid off 100 cents on the dollar by 1940. Since 1950, his annual income from the firm has fluctuated according to the volatile fortunes of his industry. Last year, his earnings were about $45,000; and in some recent years they have gone as high as $100,000.

In other ways besides their unusual financial success, the three men are plainly untypical of their generation.

Banker X was born with a silver spoon in his mouth. Like so many blue-blooded Bostonians of his age, he went to Harvard, then into a brokerage house. He is unmistakably a product of his city in accent, appearance and attitude. He thinks quickly and gives his views with crisp certainty. One of his favorite expressions is "perfect damn nonsense." He doesn't mind spending money, but he doesn't like to have it show.

Engineer Z, too, was born into a family with money. Also a Harvard graduate, he is rugged and forthright and goes straight to the point. Though he generally approves of the younger generations, he has little patience with "their seemingly constant" preoccupation with the gadgets and appliances of this mechanical age. "Talk like that bores me to death," he grumbles.

Manufacturer Y was helped through Dartmouth by his father but has been entirely on his own ever since. His business career started with a day laborer's job that paid $7 a week. "I wouldn't swap that year for any other in my life," he said. He is small in stature, mild-mannered, and at peace with himself and the world. His idea of pleasure is solving complicated financial problems. But the most important problem of our time, he believes, is getting rid of racial and religious prejudices.

All three men are lifelong Republicans and contributed substantially to President Eisenhower's campaign. None has ever voted for a Democrat for President or, except on rare occasions, for any other office. Interestingly enough, however, all appear to have accepted as the normal order many of the things their party stanchly opposed during the Roosevelt era.

Engineer Z thinks it would be a "material psychological blow" to business if a Democrat were elected. But he describes himself as "all for" the basic aims of both the New and Fair Deals. He says he disapproves of the means used by the Democrats in reaching their ends. Over the long term, however, he doesn't think a return to the Democrats would slow down the advance of the economy—"Stevenson wouldn't do much of anything the Republicans aren't already doing," he guesses. Furthermore, his interest in politics is waning. "I'm getting more and more lethargic about it," he says. "My blood pressure doesn't rise the way it used to."

Manufacturer Y isn't going to change a lifetime habit of voting Republican. "I'm aware of all the faults of the old Republican party," he says. "I never liked Roosevelt, but I must admit that some of the things he set in motion have proved to be very important."

Banker X, who considers himself "on the left wing" of the G.O.P., had a brief flirtation with socialist ideas when he joined the La Follette Club at Harvard. "I do not think the average American is basically a leftist," he says. He also thinks the day is past when, as in Roosevelt's times, the public can be "set against" business. He sums up his attitude: "I try to change with the times; there's no sense in fighting the inevitable."

Being men of considerable wealth, these successful executives spend freely. But they don't spend what they could. Manufacturer Y is getting a brand-new Chrysler shortly but not from choice; some stockholders in his company are so pleased with his management that they're giving it to him. He's a little sheepish because the car is so luxurious—the price tag is $6,800 and the car is air-conditioned.

In his Boston apartment, Mr. Y and his wife have a "six- or seven-year-old TV," and he thinks he'll probably buy a color set "when they've been improved a little more." He has about ten suits that he bought for $200 apiece and the other day he gave away a suit that was 20 years old. The manufacturer's wife gets $1,500 a month to run the apartment (they also have a summer place in New Hampshire) "and she keeps anything she has left over—she usually has something, too."

Banker X doesn't spend very much on himself, but a good deal of money flows out to his family. He buys two or three suits a year from an English tailor, paying about $150 apiece for them. In the best frugal tradition of his generation each of these suits "has a waistcoat and two pair of pants." He's a good customer of Boston bookstores for books that will help him pursue his hobby of archaeology—a fascinating study for him, but a bore to his family.

In cash and goods, he estimates he and his wife give perhaps $20,000 a year to their children and grandchildren. He has a family house in suburban Milton and another in South Carolina, both "with every gadget you can think of—washers, dryers, freezers, eye-level ovens and so forth." He has "no notion" what these things cost him. He's a "little ashamed to say" that he never pays any attention to a budget. He has a Lincoln, his wife a Chevrolet, but he honestly can't recall what year they are. "Don't care a damn about a car," he says characteristically. "Just a thing to go places in."

Engineer Z sold his suburban house when his children grew up, keeps an apartment in town and a "real home" in western Massachusetts. His company buys a Cadillac for him "every 60,000 miles, whether that's one year or three," and his wife has a one-year-old Plymouth. The country place is well equipped, spacious, and Mr. Z thinks nothing of having 20 people there for a weekend. He doesn't know how much such a party costs him and he really doesn't care.

Mr. Z never buys anything on time. "I bought a car on installment once, in 1936," he says, "and I'll never do it again." Installments, even mortgages, are "outside my way of living," he believes. But he adds with emphasis, "I consider this kind of buying one of the important means for making the good life available to more people."

He believes that "the important thing" about the economy of

present-day America is "the basic demand that has been unleashed for more gadgets and appliances and for an easier way of living. Who scrubs shirts on a board nowadays?" he asks. "Who hasn't got a television set or a toaster? Do you ever see a car without a radio? The young people just can't get along without these things."

Although there's often too much concern with goods rather than ideas these days, Mr. Z believes, this demand for material things has had a "terrific impact" on our system. Looking at the steadily increasing population that presumably will swell this buying urge, Mr. Z "can't see anything but health in the business situation."

Manufacturer Y concurs in these views even though he also has personal prejudices against installment buying and mortgages. Brought up in the old tradition to believe that debt was evil, he rented a home until he had enough money to buy and never bought anything by the down-payment method. He has come to believe, however, that mortgages and installment purchases are essential in carrying out "redistribution of the wealth."

No admirer of Franklin D. Roosevelt, Mr. Y nevertheless credits his administration for switching the emphasis in the U.S. economy to boosting buying power for low-income people. "That is going to stand out as the biggest turning point in the nation's history," he says. The main cause of depressions, to his mind, was the old system that permitted too much money to be concentrated in too few hands.

Banker X has taken out a couple of mortgages in his time and holds one now, but only to make more salable a small property he owns. He finds nothing alarming in the low-down-payment, long-term mortgage arrangement under which so many houses are bought today. Modern mortgages, he points out, require pay-off of principal as well as interest. "They have nothing in common with the old mortgage loan," he says.

For example, in the '20s Mr. X once borrowed $40,000 to fix up a house he had bought and all the bank demanded was regular payment of interest. "The bank didn't care if I paid my taxes or anything else, so long as they got their interest," he explains. "As a matter of fact, mortgages in the '20s were practically never paid off until the house was sold. They were just renewed from time to time. And very frequently the bank would discover when they tried to get their money back that taxes hadn't been paid on the house for years. I know. I lost a lot of money in a mortgage company once."

This story is one of many Mr. X likes to tell to demonstrate what he calls the "enormous improvement" in business ethics, attitudes and, therefore, health between 1926 and 1956. He recalls a case when a company he was involved with filed an earnings statement at the Massachusetts State House in connection with the issuance of some preferred stock. "Like so many businessmen of that time," he says, "the people who ran the company were scared to death to let the public know anything about what they were doing." So all the statement said, as he remembers it, was "Earnings in the past few years have been satisfactory and have amounted to several times the preferred dividend requirements." Nowadays, Mr. X claims, "securities aren't sold on emotion any more. The Securities and Exchange Act requiring full disclosure of investment facts was one of the greatest things that ever happened."

Mr. Y, the manufacturer, also remembers ruefully some of the shenanigans that many engaged in during the '20s. "It was extremely common," he says, "for a man who borrowed from the bank to slip the bank a little piece of the pie if the loan produced the hoped-for profits." He also remembers a big Boston savings bank which, in the old days, would turn down a mortgage customer they didn't know with the excuse that they were "all loaned up," but would refer the applicant upstairs to "a broker who sometimes makes loans." This broker would agree to lend the money at 6 per cent or 7 per cent, "then run down to the bank and borrow the money for it at 2 per cent or 3 per cent."

In addition to better business ethics, the executives cite many other reasons for thinking that a depression is far less likely to occur now than 30 years ago. Engineer Z, for example, thinks that the still-haunting memory of the Crash is itself a factor in preventing another one. "People like me have been educated to look for trouble and they are looking for it. It's the best guard against trouble," he says.

Mr. Z, however, isn't so sanguine about the so-called "built-in anti-depression factors" often mentioned by economists as props against collapse. Such things as Social Security payments, unemployment compensation benefits, minimum wage levels and others may have some psychological value, he believes. They are also important, he agrees, as indicators of increased awareness of the problems of lower-paid people. "But economically, I'm not impressed with them," he says. "A good old-fashioned depression would knock out those props in a very short time."

Banker X thinks that the major reason why there won't be a depression soon is the cold war. "It's the desire of the nation to stay militarily strong in the face of the Soviet threat. May be a ridiculous economic reason, but there it is." Personal fear of atomic warfare, however, plays no part in Mr. X's calculations nor in those of the other businessmen. They all agree that such a war would mean the end of civilization as they have known it and that there's no sense in planning for something that can't even be guessed at. Mr. X, typically, is impatient with most Civil Defense activities. "If a hydrogen bomb drops here, there's no point being in the basement of this building," he snorts.

Investments of the three men reflect their confidence in the future. None of them is worried about the level of the stock market, and common stocks predominate in their holdings. Engineer Z has relatively few investments of his own, but he makes the decisions for a substantial family trust and for other family holdings. These investments are at the moment 85 per cent in equities and Mr. Z says he "goes the whole distance" in approving common stocks as the most sensible investment these days. Manufacturer Y's capital is 60 per cent in common shares and 40 per cent in corporate and government bonds. Last year, he received between $40,000 and $50,000 on his investments and, in order to reduce taxes a little, converted some corporate debentures to tax-exempt municipal bonds.

Roughly one third of Banker X's money is in common shares, the rest being in his firm, which underwrites, buys and sells all sorts of securities. Mr. X believes firmly in the value of common stocks as a hedge against the seemingly inexorable decline in the value of the dollar. "We seem to have a built-in, compounded 3 per cent annual inflation," he says. "Our money is steadily worth less. This doesn't worry me so much now, but it does seem as though it has to go out of order sometime."

While all three men like common stocks, they also stress the importance of insurance in their financial planning. The banker and the manufacturer have about $300,000 worth of life insurance apiece, with large parts of it paid up. The engineer carries "better than six figures' worth" of insurance and he considers it "the basic protection that should be coupled with investment as a hedge against inflation."

All of these big earners are also big taxpayers and they have strong views on this subject. The only levies that don't bother them much are the inheritance taxes and this is because each of them has blunted the effect of these through the device of family trust funds. As Manufacturer Y puts it, "anyone with my kind of money is a fool if he hasn't taken advantage of the laws for passing on as much money as possible."

Engineer Z particularly dislikes very high income tax rates because, he says, they encourage seeking tax shelters instead of creating new capital. He's contemptuous of a tax system that produces "all these phony foundations—most of them nothing but tax dodges." Banker X says, "Don't get me started on taxes." The thing that annoys him most is the "vicious" 25 per cent capital gains rate. "I'm convinced the Government would take in more revenue if this rate were lowered," he declares.

Banker X has one major gripe about what rich men do with their money. "The average well-to-do man, generally speaking, contributes a paltry sum to charity. It's beyond my understanding, but it's true." He himself gave away about $35,000 last year, roughly 15 per cent of his income. His argument for bigger charitable giving is that, if wealthy people don't do it, somebody's got to and that somebody is going to be the Government. Mr. X deplores Federal aid to hospitals, research, schools and so forth, not because he thinks these are unworthy aims, but because he thinks private capital, not Federal bureaucracy, should support them.

Engineer Z thinks it's too late to do anything in this area. "The day when a few rich people supported most of the charities is past," he says. Furthermore, he believes, many of the charitable institutions of the past, settlement houses for example, have become "sociologically obsolete." People now pay much more in taxes than they ever did for charity, he notes, while government support of social programs has become so well established that there's no point complaining about it. He gives to charity about $3,000 a year.

Despite their near-certainty that the economy and the nation are on a firmer footing now than ever before, the three Bostonians every so often force themselves to remember that they had much the same thoughts during the '20s. They believe that the problems of that period may have been licked. But what, they wonder, of the entirely different problems and conditions that may lie ahead?

Banker X has a story to illustrate this point. He cites the case of a well-known present-day financier who has startled the business world in recent years with his unorthodox manipulation of manufacturing companies. Not long ago, the story has it, this financier was boasting to a friend about the cleverness of his innovations and about his success in avoiding old mistakes. His friend waited for him to finish, then said, "Friend, you're the type of man who'll think up new ways of going bust."

DAVID O. IVES

May 7, 1956

High Altitudes

Mountain climbers, balloonists and jet pilots like to tell about the exhilaration of high altitudes. But they are also wont to warn that there are perils amid the pleasures. For the same rare air that brings cheerfulness can also addle judgment and make the heights look safer than they are.

That effect is not unknown in everyday affairs. There's always a tremendous exhilaration when business is booming and the stock market is soaring, especially when a few months earlier everyone's mood was deep in a recession trough. Then it becomes very easy to forget that enthusiasm, as well as discouragement, can sometimes overreach itself.

We are not suggesting that there aren't some good reasons for the present business optimism. In the past twelve months the American economy has again proven its tremendous resilience. The 1957–58 recession was sharp, and in some places deep, and yet the worst forebodings were never realized. There's no question that business is once more pointed upward.

Nor would it be wise to suggest that the stock market, high as it is, is necessarily "too high" in relation to the business outlook. We must keep in mind that such traditional measurements as the ratio of stock prices to stock earnings, now so high as to puzzle many people, can be brought down either by a decline in stock prices or by an increase in earnings. A continued increase in earnings is certainly a possibility; this newspaper's recent survey of third-quarter earnings shows them still rising from the recession's low point.

And we would be the last to suggest that the prospect of inflation, which can knock all traditional measurements cockeyed, is not a very real one. When you read the wild spending plans of the dominant wing of the now dominant Democrats, you realize that the man who buys "things" to beat inflation is not acting without some reason.

Nevertheless, it is when the heights look most lovely and the path most sure that it's time to watch for that risky overoptimism that overcomes a mountain climber just before his foot slips.

It's always impossible to name the moment when that will happen. But when you see the stock market soaring day after day without interruption, when prices discount not only next quarter's earnings but the most glowing prophecies of future prospects, when the market jumps nervously at the most insubstantial of rumors, when every Tom, Dick and Harry decides to pile his savings on this bandwagon—well, you begin to wonder.

It's one thing to have confidence that the American economy will climb higher; or to recognize a long-term inflation trend that may make dollars worth less and prices higher. It's another thing to think this new inflation is going to be here the day after tomorrow or that next quarter it's going to be transferred into double profits for business.

The danger doesn't lie so much in what has happened as in what can happen. Although nobody can say when the market is too high, anybody can be sure that it will soar too high when the public gets caught by the idea that the thing to do is to buy stocks no matter what, to pay any kind of prices today because tomorrow inflation or prosperity or whatever is going to make bad purchases good.

November 12, 1958

EDITORIAL

THE WORLD AROUND US

❁

NORTH

Canada's "Consciousness"

OTTAWA—What makes a "national consciousness"? In the United States it includes hundreds of things. Plymouth Rock, Harvard University, the Ford car, Gettysburg, and the Bill of Rights all play a part.

There are things which are distinctively "American," and which added together help make the American what he is. In the great land across the border, Canadians share some of the same traditions but they also have some distinctive institutions of their own. They and their impact are not easily understood by the non-Canadian, or even by all Canadians. But their existence and some measure of their influence are necessary in understanding the "Canadian national consciousness," which is bursting forth in new and powerful directions.

There are very many influences which go into the making of Canadians. There is the national tradition of "anti-Americanism," which is perhaps better described as 175 years of trying to maintain separateness from the larger nation to the south. There is also a Queen, and a beautiful Parliament building in Ottawa with the famous "Mounties" on guard. Then there is a federal constitution which reverses the U.S. system and reserves to the federal government all powers not expressly delegated to the provinces.

Too, one finds such diverse expressions of a separate Canadianism as a distinctive Canadian whisky, a series of TV programs on "Canadiana," and a school of painters who revel in the wild land-

"Now we have to start worrying about states' rights!"

scape, picturing a quality that is recognized abroad as definitely "Canadian."

Other things strike the visitor. He notes the many divisive forces in Canadian life and the reaction of Canadians to them in their own way. He notes the same thing about the very strong forces for unity.

As a sample of the divisions, take the matter of the national anthem—or anthems, for there are four.

"God Save the Queen" is strongly favored by the more British elements but is regarded as "foreign" by many French-speaking Canadians. "The Maple Leaf Forever" is the favorite of the most nationalist Canadian citizens of British extraction but is positively abhorred by the French element (long in conflict with these other Canadians). Finally there is "O Canada." But it comes in both French and English versions, and the translations differ. "O Canada" is dearly loved by the French, but has never won such acclaim from the rest of the population.

Such factionalism is not noted as any indication that the great Dominion to the north is about to fly apart, or is even as fundamentally divided as the U.S. may be with its race issue. But it is necessary to understand the existence of such factionalism in order to understand two important things about the Canadian national character—its cautiousness and its pragmatism.

"The need to compromise has always been with us—and will be for all foreseeable time," says the editor of a leading Canadian newspaper. "It has made us a careful, cautious people—conservative and apt to make changes slowly."

"Sometimes I wonder what holds this country together," says a Halifax businessman who travels it constantly. He notes the Canadian factionalism and, rather characteristically, professes to see it as something of a virtue.

The same remark is heard over and over.

"There is some question," says a young schoolteacher from New Brunswick, "that we are really a nation at all." A Montrealer makes the same comment, and so does a native of Edmonton.

This feeling perhaps reaches its ultimate in the extreme French-speaking "nationalists" of Quebec who advocate separation of their province from the Dominion and establishment of the "State of Laurentia."

Factionalism is fostered by Canada's difficult topography. But its roots doubtless are historical. When, in the French and Indian War, the British General Wolfe defeated New France's Montcalm, the pattern was set.

Thenceforward the French would live in Canada but as an island in an ever growing Anglo-Saxon sea. By law they would maintain their own language, religion, courts and schools, and, having these, their distinctive culture. There would be little integration with *les Anglais*—and some of this spirit seemed to spread among the various branches of *les Anglais* themselves.

One also hears Canadians cite the fact that there are relatively few "big" companies and industries, as compared with the United States. As a result, personal acquaintanceship among industrial top brass and political top brass is quite common.

"When we want to do something here, we can just get together and do it," says a businessman. "We don't have to form a lot of interlocking committees in and out of government." A banker illustrates the point with this statement: "The most effective instrument of monetary policy in this country is having lunch."

Canadians are consciously proud of their parliamentary system of government, too. They believe it is more efficient and more democratic to have it headed by a Prime Minister who is both legislative and administrative head of the country. "We don't have all that bickering you Americans have between Congress and President," says a man who reports on the doings of Parliament for a large Canadian newspaper.

These are just a few of the factors which contribute to the Canadian national consciousness. There are others—for example, the nearness to the average citizen of the Canadian frontiers. Concentrated in a 200-mile broad ribbon coast to coast, the population is constantly subject to the influences of both the wilderness to the north and the United States to the south.

But however many facets have gone into the Canadian "national consciousness," there is no doubt that it is becoming more intense.

JOHN F. BRIDGE

November 14, 1957

War of the Fishes

Two of our North Atlantic Treaty Organization allies are having their troubles about some fish. The troubles arise because they disagree over what are fishing rights and where are international waters.

British fishermen have trawled for years off the coast of Iceland, catching the fish which provide Iceland with its main export industry. Iceland would rather have the British buy the fish the Icelanders catch, so the Icelandic Parliament passed a decree extending

Iceland's territorial waters from the three-mile limit recognized by Britain to a twelve-mile limit. This takes in most of the good fishing waters.

Britain, though, told the Icelanders they were going fishing anyway and when the trawlers arrived they brought along their own license in half a dozen British armed frigates. Just the other day an Iceland Coast Guard vessel captured a British trawler, whereupon a British frigate captured the Iceland Coast Guard vessel. Fortunately, nobody yet has fired a shot in the war of the fishes.

And we hope nobody will, because we don't like to see our allies quarreling with one another over who's going to fry the fish. Both Britain and Iceland are members of the North Atlantic Treaty Organization, both have guns aboard their ships and both have their tempers up.

How much of a threat to NATO this disagreement actually may come to be nobody knows, but history does show that little quarrels have a way of becoming bigger. There was the time a kingdom was said to be lost for want of a nail for a shoe for a horse, and the present dispute might have an equal influence on history, especially if the U.S. gets mixed up in the quarrel. That would be a fine kettle of fish, indeed.

So we suggest that Iceland and Britain sit right down and cut bait on this matter and reach a compromise between the three-mile-limit and the twelve-mile-limit claims.

Let Iceland fish from her shores to four miles out. Let Britain fish from eight to twelve miles out. That would leave a *cordon sanitaire,* we think people who settle such matters call it, of four miles between the disputants where neither side would fish. A settlement giving four miles to all parties, it seems to us, would serve the interests of all concerned—including the fish.

September 3, 1958

EDITORIAL

SOUTH

Awakening Africa

CONAKRY, Guinea—Guinea's Premier Sekou Toure is a broad-shouldered, 36-year-old strong man, who won this Oregon-sized African nation's freedom from France less than a fortnight ago by persuading 98 per cent of its 2.5 million black citizens to vote *"non"* to General de Gaulle's new French constitution.

French Guinea thus became the world's newest nation since nearby Ghana gained its freedom from Britain early last year.

Guinea's plunge into self-government heralds a quickening of an independence movement that could add well over a dozen new nations to the Dark Continent in the near future. "Within the next five years, eighty million people in Africa will gain their independence," predicts one veteran African diplomat.

U.S. diplomats here and in Washington are already pondering the probable impact of Africa's rush for freedom on America's foreign policy. Almost all agree that Africa's growing desire for freedom poses new problems for the U.S.

Each new nation to emerge in Africa represents a pristine pawn in the unending East-West struggle to win the allegiance of the world's uncommitted countries. And if less than two weeks' experience here in Guinea is any criterion, the U.S. and other Free World nations face a bitter and costly battle.

Pudgy Soviet boss Nikita Khrushchev gained a march on the West by promptly recognizing Guinea and reportedly offering it aid. But Marxist-trained Premier Toure says he may await French recognition before answering Moscow so as to avoid being accused of international "blackmail." But if France and the other major Western countries, including the U.S., do not give him what he wants, then it's a safe bet Guinea will look to the Communists. So far, neither France nor the U.S. has formally extended diplomatic recognition to Guinea.

Ghana's semiofficial Accra *Evening News,* founded by Prime Minister Kwame Nkrumah, already has urged Guinea to join Ghana in seeking economic aid from Russia to speed industrialization and agricultural mechanization. So the U.S. is confronted with pressure to pour still more millions into the dollar-ruble cold war. "We are going to have to help these new countries in Africa," says one of President Eisenhower's foreign-affairs advisors, "because there's nothing else we can do."

The new nations of Africa will also bolster the Arab-Asian-African bloc in the United Nations, threatening to enlarge the vote against the U.S. on many important issues, including the admission of Red China to the U.N. And their shortage of capital, low literacy rates, and lack of trained public servants and technicians augur for economic and political instability that could speed a drift toward Communism. It could even endanger private American investments already in Africa, such as Olin Mathieson Chemical Corp.'s 53.5 per cent interest in a $135 million bauxite and alumina project now under way here in Guinea.

A Communist beachhead in any one of the emerging nations of black Africa might break out into the vast body of this restless continent that's four times bigger than the U.S. and is home to more than 220 million people. Africa is also a treasure house of gold, diamonds, copper, uranium, cocoa, lead, chrome, cobalt, antimony, tin and even some oil. Its loss to the West would represent a staggering political and economic defeat.

Africa is desperately dependent on the political traditions, technological know-how and investment capital that such historic colonizers as France, Britain, Belgium, Portugal and Spain have been supplying for decades. Yet its desire for freedom is so fierce that it's willing to trade these advantages for the right of being master in its own house.

"We prefer poverty in liberty to riches in slavery," Premier Sekou Toure shouted from a platform here in Guinea's capital city several weeks before the Guinease turned their backs on France. Yet nobody knows better than Premier Toure that his fledgling nation's economy is so closely tied to France that a complete break with the French could result in chaos.

Guinea's exports, which once consisted largely of gold and slaves, now center on more prosaic items such as bananas, coffee and bauxite—the raw material for aluminum. With the exception of some 300,000 tons of bauxite sold to Canada each year, almost all of Guinea's wares go to France. Guinea's stores are loaded with French goods. French technicians fill key posts on the country's French-built railroad, at the seaport currently being expanded with French francs, and in business establishments throughout this sausage-shaped land. The French also hold nearly three quarters of Guinea's government posts despite a massive program to teach these jobs to the natives.

Guinea's handful of college-educated citizens are concentrated in the medical, legal and educational professions because, in common with most Africans, they look down on engineering and technical training. If the French left this country in force, it would leave Guinea without leadership in these and other vital areas.

Guinea's biggest single potential loss from a French evacuation is the giant Konkoure Dam, a $275 million project which would create a reservoir as large as Lake Geneva in Europe, and produce a power potential of 3 billion kilowatt hours of electricity annually. Further construction would have given birth to an aluminum industry that would use the current, plus locally mined bauxite, to turn out 150,-000 tons of the lightweight metal a year.

When Guinea voted against De Gaulle, France announced its intention to substantially withdraw French officials and financial aid from Guinea within the next two months or so. But there are indications that the French are as loath to completely divorce themselves from their former territory as Premier Sekou Toure is to see them go.

"There will be negotiations to determine Guinea's relations with France," says Roger Chambard, diplomatic adviser to the High Commissioner for French West Africa, as he sits in his air-conditioned office overlooking the cosmopolitan skyline of Dakar. "Perhaps," adds M. Chambard, "agreements may be drawn permitting the Guinea government to rehire French officials now due to be withdrawn from the country."

But the French have maneuvered themselves into a tight corner in Africa and seem destined to lose whichever way they jump. In the recent election, General de Gaulle courted France's eight West African territories with glowing promises of development aid in a new French community where member states could handle their internal political affairs but retain all the advantages of partnership with the French, who, among other things, would look after their foreign affairs.

Although nationalism is rising throughout French West Africa, the states of Senegal, Dahomey, Niger, Mauritania, French Sudan, the Ivory Coast and the Upper Volta, voted to stick by France. Only Guinea said *"non"* to General de Gaulle, and if the French bend too far in helping the Guinease, the seven states that voted *"oui"* may figure there's nothing to be lost by deserting De Gaulle and choosing complete independence, a move the French say they would not resist.

Developments in French West Africa are also being watched by the states of Gabon, Ubangi-Shari, Chad and the Middle Congo, in French Equatorial Africa, as well as on the island of Madagascar. These states also voted to remain within the new French community, and if France starts offering favors to Guinea, despite its "no" vote, the whole French African empire could collapse. Should France ignore Guinea, however, Premier Toure may ask Uncle Sam to shoulder the Frenchmen's burden—or he may cozy up to Russia.

There are decidedly conflicting opinions here in West Africa concerning just how far to the left Premier Toure may swing his infant nation.

"The man is a Communist," says one high French official, who emphasizes that M. Toure rose to power as a radical trade union leader, after being educated in various Communist countries. "Nonsense," counters Liberia's conservative President William V. S. Tubman in his pleasantly cool office in Monrovia. "I know Sekou Toure very well," says Mr. Tubman as he puffs on a cigar stuck in a yellow holder. "He believes in democracy and is trying to bring it to his country."

Many diplomats here rate Premier Toure as naïve economically, but extremely shrewd politically. "He is a Marxist, all right, but not one who takes orders from Moscow," says one French official. "He is too much the dictator to take orders from anyone, and if Guinea is any sample some of these new African nations are going to trade colonialism for black dictatorship."

Guinea's newly won independence, and its fiery, leftward-leaning Premier, have thrown this nation into the world news spotlight. But to the diplomats charged with keeping watch over African affairs, it's merely one of many lands here that are caught up in a massive move toward freedom. Outside the French area of influence, the nearness of this independence is strongly affected by the identity of each territory's mother country and the number and influence of its local white settlers.

Britain's possessions in West Africa, where the white population is small, are advancing steadily toward freedom. Nigerian political leaders have been meeting with British government officials in London, and Prime Minister Alhaji Abubakar Tafawa Balewa has urged that April 2, 1960, be set as the target date for Nigeria's independence.

Sierra Leone is also hopeful of gaining its freedom from Britain at about the same time Nigeria does, even though it may be hard put to exist as an independent nation with its 2 million people crowded into an area smaller than South Carolina. Since Guinea won its freedom, suggestions have been raised in Sierra Leone that it seek a merger with the ex-French colony. And some Liberians would like to see neighboring Sierra Leone join them.

The six million people of British-controlled Uganda, located in east-central Africa on the headwaters of the Nile, are expected to achieve their independence soon after 1960—provided the current wave of nationalism doesn't bring it about sooner. Uganda is already running its own affairs at the local level, and the absence of a hard core of landowning whites there presages a relatively smooth transition to self-government for its black citizens.

Other British territories on the eastern side of Africa, where a relatively few whites dominate many blacks, are another story entirely. White settlers in Kenya and the Rhodesian Federation intend to cling to control of governmental affairs—and retain ties to Britain—as long as they can.

The federation hopes to establish a racial "partnership," with whites remaining as senior partners for the foreseeable future. But the native Africans, particularly in Nyasaland, feel the Rhodesians are much too slow in granting them their political rights. There is a danger that Nyasaland and Northern Rhodesia may break away from the federation, leaving Southern Rhodesia alone. "Should this occur, Southern Rhodesia would probably merge with the Union of South Africa," says one British colonial official in Ghana's capital city of Accra.

White settlers in Kenya have offered the Africans a few seats in their legislative council. But the natives rejected the deal because they felt it did not give them true representation in this land of 50,-000 whites and 5.5 million blacks.

A minority of Kenya's blacks attempted to wrest control from the British through the bloody Mau Mau insurrection. But the British suppressed the rebellion by meeting terror with counterterror, and the Africans are not anxious to give the lion's tail another twist.

RAY VICKER

October 10, 1958

Barefoot Girl

ACCRA, Ghana—The tall, English-educated lawyer's conversation sparkled, whether talk dealt with England's angry young men in the literary field, or with De Gaulle's current experiment in France.

A hot breeze blew through open windows into the living room with its stuffed chairs, its picture of Queen Elizabeth on the plaster wall, its teapot tray on the table and its atmosphere of middle-class English respectability. The lawyer could have passed for a middle-class Englishman, too, were he not a Ghanaian Negro. Despite the heat, he kept both his suit coat and his vest neatly buttoned, as if to admit discomfort would have been ungentlemanly.

As his guests—an English public-relations official and a journalist —rose to leave, a barefoot colored woman entered. Her gaudy cotton dress swept the floor as, eyes downcast, she picked up the tea tray. For a moment the grigri, or native charm, around her neck, fell forward on its leather thong. It swung over a teacup, making a circular swing as if its magical powers might be imparting some bush witchcraft into that cup.

Then, as the woman disappeared into the next room, the sound of childish voices came through the open door in the brief moment before it closed.

Courteously the colored lawyer led his guests to the street where the Austin sedan waited beneath a mango tree. The English public-relations man slid behind the wheel, broad body taking most of the front seat. As the car pulled away from the curb, he said: "There you see an example of one of Africa's biggest problems."

Puzzled, the passenger said: "I'm afraid I must have missed something."

The Englishman swung the car onto Ring Road, heading toward the Ambassador Hotel. A smile wrinkled his features as he asked:

"You noticed that woman, didn't you?"

"You mean the servant girl?"

The Englishman's wry smile deepened. "She was no servant girl. She was his wife." He seemed to enjoy the incredulous pause which followed.

He swung onto Dodowa Road, skirting a bicyclist pedaling down the middle of the street, then added: "She is just a bush girl who can't even read and write, while he is an Oxford man; yet she is his wife.

"There you have one of Africa's most serious problems," the Englishman went on. "You would think that a man like him would seek a girl of his own mental class as a wife. He wouldn't even if such a girl were available. The African man wants his woman to be ignorant and obedient, somebody to do his housework and to mother his children without complaint or questions."

"But is that such a serious problem?" The passenger still tried to reconcile the educated lawyer with the peasant girl who wore a witch doctor's charm for a necklace.

"You heard the children in the back of the house, didn't you? Well, there are four of them, four children who are being reared by a bush woman who can't even speak English." The Englishman cleared his throat, eyes fixed on the road, which had a heavy pedestrian traffic. Then he went on: "It is the mother who has the most effect on a child in Africa. Those children are receiving the culture of the bush, not that of Oxford."

On the street another barefoot woman padded by, toting a pile of faggots on her head, each hand holding straw bags of market produce. A child's head poked from the bundle on her back. A man beside her garbed in a kente cloth robe carried only an umbrella, which he was using to shield himself from the bright sun.

The Englishman nodded toward the couple. "How can you have much progress when each generation must start anew from a bush background because of the mother's ignorance? If education is to lift the African upward, shouldn't it work through the mother as well as the father?"

The questions were left unanswered as the doorman of the Ambassador Hotel stepped forward to open the door of the car. The passenger bade him adieu, then walked thoughtfully up the steps past the bookstore. He remembered the pessimism of so many other Englishmen concerning nationalism in Africa, wondering if perhaps this Englishman's reactions were not based on long-established prejudices rather than on objective conclusions.

But, as he rang for the elevator he also remembered the African woman of the house. Once again he saw the grigri hanging from her neck as she bent to pick up the tea tray, swinging back and forth while childish voices sounded in the next room.

RAY VICKER

January 16, 1959

Mexican Oil

MEXICO CITY—Bullfights, brass bands and a gala ceremony at this capital city's Palace of Fine Arts wound up a festive celebration this past month—the twentieth anniversary of Mexico's seizure of foreign oil properties within its borders.

The official verdict of the oil industry expropriators: Nationalization, despite some "grave," unsolved problems, has been an "outstanding success." Judging by the "viva"-yelling celebrators, most of the owners of the "people's oil industry" seem to agree. But those seeking solid signs of success argue that, at best, the claim of Petroleos Mexicanos, the state agency that administers the national oil industry, is unsubstantiated. And some Pemex critics insist there's evidence that the exercise in expropriation has been a fiasco.

Mexico, these critics note, is not now as large a factor in petroleum production as it was when the industry was in private hands.

"Oh, Clifford!"

This Latin land currently ranks ninth in oil output in the world, down from the No. 2 spot 40 years ago—though it's only fair to note that the decline started before nationalization. Last year Mexico produced only about 1.4 per cent of the free world's oil, compared with about 40 per cent for the U.S. and 16 per cent for Venezuela. And Mexico, long an oil exporter, now must import some types of refined products to meet its own needs.

Problems faced by Pemex in operating Mexico's far-flung oil and gas empire point up the special woes that frequently befall governments when they set their hands to running industries. Also, Mexico's nationalization experience may hold valuable lessons for would-be expropriators everywhere, and especially here, where radical leftists relentlessly agitate for government take-over of the power industry and many mining activities.

The Mexican government took over the country's oil industry March 18, 1938, after a period of growing antagonism toward foreign domination. The expropriation decree of then-President Lazaro Cardenas was precipitated by the refusal of foreign oil companies to grant higher wages and other benefits as ordered by the government. Among the ousted companies were several American concerns. The ejected firms included such international corporate giants as the Standard Oil Companies of New Jersey and California, the Royal Dutch-Shell Group and Sinclair Oil.

From then on, said the expropriators, the oil wells, refineries and pipelines were to be operated "in the interests of the people of Mexico" rather than for the "economic aggrandizement" of "foreign imperialists." The new operators were to indemnify the former owners and, hopefully, step up production and development. Also, the newly formed Pemex was expected to lower the prices of oil products and speed the industrialization of Mexico.

There's no doubt that Pemex is big business. The government monopoly now operates some 1,900 oil wells in eight producing areas strung out along Mexico's east coast. Pemex runs eight refineries, three gas plants, some 4,200 miles of pipelines and a vast marketing system. It claims to be Mexico's largest taxpayer and, as employer of 40,000 Mexicans, its activities have an impact on a large share of the nation's 31 million citizens.

But there is doubt about Pemex's claim that Mexico's oil industry has progressed further in the past 20 years under nationalization than it would have if private enterprise had continued to run the industry. Talks with private businessmen here, both Mexican and foreign, and with oil industry experts and other observers, indicate much questioning of Pemex's judgment on itself.

"You won't find any Mexican admitting it in public," says a veteran foreign oilman here, "but from the economic point of view anyway, expropriation has been nothing but a national disaster. Most Mexicans, unfortunately, don't even suspect this because the facts have been so completely concealed from them—but what they're really celebrating is a fiasco."

It's difficult, to be sure, for anyone to judge accurately Pemex's economic progress. For one thing, as with most nationalized industries, there is no valid yardstick for comparison. Also, Pemex has practiced great economy in the dispensing of meaningful facts and figures, such as year-to-year earnings statements and balance sheets. The latest balance sheet, for example, is for 1947. And the spate of statistics in Pemex's twentieth-anniversary report sheds little light on financial matters. About all the industry's owners are regularly told comes from roadside neon signs that flash: "Pemex in the service of the Nation."

"Pemex's finances are none of the people's business," insists dapper Antonio J. Bermudez, the Pemex chief. This sharp rejoinder to an interviewer's question, made in the oil czar's plush office here, wasn't repeated in his recent 20th anniversary oration. But Senor Bermudez did tell his listeners that "making money" is not the exclusive purpose of the government's oil monopoly. Other purposes cited: eliminating a "colonial" economy and raising the standard of living.

Such reasoning apparently appeals to many Mexicans. Says a banker here: "Pemex is not an economic institution, but a social one. The assistance it has provided to our rapid industrial development through low prices doesn't show up in Pemex accounts. But it's a contribution to our economy, nevertheless. An American cannot be expected to understand this."

Be that as it may, even Pemex Director Bermudez publicly has conceded that the oil monopoly's financial plight is of growing concern. "The problem of Pemex," he recently said, "is the level of its income, which, in proportion to its operations, is the lowest of any company in the world." Thus, Pemex is faced with "a grave financial problem because the limitation of its own resources prevents development in keeping with the rapidly increased domestic needs of the country," he said.

Pemex is in serious need of new capital, concedes the highly cautious Senor Bermudez, to build new pipelines to move oil and gas to market, to expand refineries and to drill exploratory wells to raise reserves. Senor Bermudez, who owns a whisky distillery in addition to running Pemex, indicates Pemex currently is negotiating for a large loan. The oil monopoly already has loans outstanding from U.S. banks of perhaps as much as $100 million. And Pemex is getting substantial credit from some of its U.S. suppliers.

Some Pemex critics are quick to chide the nationalized industry for turning to "foreign interests" in developing Mexico's oil. They note that one of the principal purposes of expropriation, repeatedly expressed here, was to rid the industry of outside interests. But, says Senor Bermudez, speaking of the new loan negotiations: "The deal will be strictly a banking proposition."

Actually, Pemex has long since backed away from its early stand of refusing to permit foreign participation in Mexico's nationalized oil industry—but the foreign participation is invited only on a strictly controlled basis and to provide needed know-how. Back in 1948, for example, it borrowed $10 million from the Cities Service Oil Co. under an arrangement that gave the U.S. concern the right to buy 50 per cent of any oil it finds.

Commercial petroleum production in Mexico began in 1901 and in 20 years soared to the still-unequaled yearly record of 193 million barrels. During this time Mexico became the world's No. 2 oil producer and in 1921 supplied about one fourth of total world production.

After reaching its 1921 peak, output began to fall sharply. The reasons included exhaustion of some old fields and what the companies considered excessive government restrictions and taxes. Some companies withdrew, fearing imposition of still more government controls on their activities. After 1927, several oil companies began to concentrate on the newly discovered oil fields of Venezuela in preference to Mexico. And the depression, of course, sharply cut world demand for oil.

By 1932, Mexico's output had skidded to an annual total of 33 million barrels. Production had inched up only slightly by the time the government seized the industry in 1938.

After 20 years of nationalization, Pemex claims it has boosted daily crude-oil production to 272,000 barrels, up from 106,000 barrels at the time of the take-over. But, note critics, that's a comparison with a depression year. Last year's output was only slightly more than half the peak output reached by the industry when it was in private hands. Production, critics contend, has never kept pace with consumption under nationalization.

MITCHELL GORDON

April 1, 1958

EAST

Living It Up in Laos

VIENTIANE, Laos—A precedent of sorts has been set in this far-away Southeast Asian kingdom—freehanded Uncle Sam has suddenly snapped his wallet shut and won't pay out another cent of foreign aid until the Laotians promise to reform their currency.

Such undisguised interference in the internal affairs of a sovereign nation is uncommon in the annals of U.S. foreign-aiders, who have paid out $60 billion to foreign governments since World War II. But the circumstances that prompted it are even more striking. They add up to a story of flagrant misuse of U.S. aid funds—and profiteering that may give Communist propagandists a weapon offsetting the anti-Communist influence the aid program was designed to have in Laos.

Laos has been ecstatically drowning in American aid ever since 1955, not long after it was carved out of what used to be Indochina. The nation was created as part of the settlement of France's war with Communist guerrilla forces for control of that former French colony.

Often called "The Land of a Million Elephants," the country, for the past two years at least, could just as well have been described as "The Land of a Hundred Million Dollars"—for that is roughly the amount the U.S. has poured into the local economy. For comparison's sake, the Laotian government's own income, mostly from customs duties, is barely $1 million a year.

Most of the U.S. dollars have been turned over directly to the Laotian government, either for various U.S.-sponsored economic projects or to support the 25,000-man Royal Laotian Army. Strangely enough, the Minister of Plans, who administers the whole program, as recently as last fall was battling the Army as leader of a Communist guerrilla force that kept fighting after the main Indochina truce. He joined the government under terms of a cease-fire. The peculiarities surrounding the U.S. aid program here, however, are too widespread and have gone on too long to be attributed solely to this gentleman.

Local traders buy America's aid dollars from the Laotian govern-

297

ment, purchase goods abroad and sell them for kip (the native currency) in Laos. These imported goods—supposedly—are of a nature to raise the Laos standard of living and to provide working tools for industrial expansion.

The principal effect of the U.S. largess, however, has been a wild and rather weird boom, based on nothing more solid than cash on hand and an unquestioned assumption that there is more to come.

Sleek Cadillacs, Buicks and Fords have been imported by the dozen, although the principal highways still are hardly more than jungle trails. Other items on last year's import list make delightfully wacky reading—four and a half tons of feather dusters, 73 tons of sporting goods, fishing tackle and thermos jugs, 180 tons of automobile covers, $13,400 worth of festival decorations, $11,500 worth of musical instruments, and thousands of dollars' worth of costume jewelry.

Retail shops are stocked to their bamboo ceilings with items that the Laotians have hardly ever seen before—American tooth paste, badminton racquets, roller skates, Japanese dolls and French perfume.

A lot of the U.S. money went to buy products from Red China—cherries in syrup from Shantung and Five Goats beer from Canton. Much of this stuff is unsalable, but it doesn't matter; the importers have already made their profits from foreign-exchange manipulations.

To understand this, one must acquaint himself with the magic kip, the highly overvalued Laotian currency unit. The official exchange rate, set by the Laos government, is 35 kip to the American dollar. But in the hardheaded money markets of Hong Kong, Bangkok or even in Vientiane, a Laos trader can buy 100 kip for a dollar. This sets the stage for fantastic profits.

A Laotian trader can buy 100,000 kip in the free money market for $1,000. He then applies for an import license for, say, $1,000 worth of building cement, but puts up only 35,000 kip to get the $1,000 from the government at the official rate. This leaves him 65,-000 kip before he has even moved the goods. Then he can simply sell his import license for more cash, if he wants.

If an importer decides to use his license, he still stands to profit heavily. Suppose he imports inexpensive men's shirts at $1 each. Buying his dollars from the Laotian government at the official rate, each shirt costs him 35 kip. But then the free-market money values come into play. When the shirt goes on the market in Laos, it is priced at about 100 kip. So the importer has nearly tripled his money. Repeating this process under Laos' free and easy import rules, a businessman quickly can amass a considerable fortune.

In neighboring Bangkok, reports of collusion between foreign exporters, particularly in Hong Kong, and Laotian traders are commonplace. One source estimates that only about 20 per cent of the contracts from Hong Kong are free of kickbacks to importers for underweight, underfilled or overpriced shipments, which allow the importer to further build up his foreign-exchange hoard.

Many shipments, it is said, are diverted in Thailand (95 per cent of Laos' imports pass through Bangkok and then are transported to Laos overland), where there is a lively demand for a wide range of goods. Other items arrive in Vientiane only to be shipped out again for greater profits. Thus, industryless Laos has become an exporter of automobiles and outboard motors.

It is estimated, although no one really knows, that well over half of the goods paid for never reach the Laos market. "The country is now straining to absorb $12 million worth of goods, yet $35 million is supposed to be coming in. If all this stuff actually arrived, it would be lying all over the streets," claims Ralph A. Epstein, a management consultant with the American firm of Howell & Co. of Washington, D.C., which has sent a three-man mission here as part of a $2,576,000 U.S. aid project in civil administration.

Since 1955, the United States has provided $15.8 million in assistance that was supposed to go for specific economic-development projects. Another $31 million has been given in the form of salable commodities to generate needed local currency for these projects. And $30 million or so yearly has been to support the army.

Before the aid program can be resumed, the U.S. insists the Laos government must devalue its currency and enact other reforms in handling the aid funds.

Though there have been temporary suspensions of aid to other countries—Yugoslavia and Egypt—in the past, these were ordered because those nations shifted their foreign policies closer to Russia's, not because of dissatisfaction with their domestic economic doings. And in no case was any cut as drastic, in terms of the effect on the country's economy, as the action taken against this tiny jungle kingdom promises to be, if the suspension is not lifted soon.

Laotian officials, right up to the cabinet level, are fighting hard to prevent the proposed exchange revision. Many, like the Minister of Health, who controls the Pharmacie de Laos, the largest drug house in the country, operate flourishing businesses which would be seriously affected by any change in the present rules of the game.

"If Laos ever enacted a conflict-of-interest law," snorts a local

American official, "the country would have to give up either government or commerce. They couldn't do both."

In this new jungle nation, of course, it might be difficult to find people outside the business community qualified to fill government posts. Mr. Epstein, one of whose jobs is to school Laotians in the arts of government, attests to this difficulty: "You can't make ministers of trade out of elementary-school graduates."

No one in Laos seems overly worried that the Americans will stand firm in their demand for currency reform. Both sides expect the deadlock will be broken before June, when Laos' next budget must be drafted.

"What would happen here if American aid were withdrawn permanently?" Prince Souvanna Phouma, Prime Minister and son of aged King Somdet Prachao Sisavang Vong, is asked.

"It seems so unlikely that we have not considered such a possibility," he replies blandly. "Laos is part of the Free World and I can hardly conceive for what reason the United States, the principal supporter of the Free World, would refuse us aid. Laos has done nothing to justify abandoning us."

The Minister of Plans is solicitous Prince Souphanouvong, another son of the King who until a cease-fire last year was leading a Communist guerrilla army against his father. Patiently, the Prince emphasizes that the U.S. will lose favor with the population if it insists on the kip devaluation and continues to suspend aid.

What does he think about his role—administering an aid program designed to strengthen Laos against Communist attack and subversion? "If you offer something better than Communism, the people will take it," the Prince answers smoothly.

"We want internal peace and neutrality in foreign affairs," he says. "Our people shouldn't be left or right. The U.S. aid program was badly administered in the past but we hope you will continue to help us. My ministry is now drafting a long-range program for using American aid."

The talk around Vientiane is that Prince Souphanouvong may be getting ready to claim the credit for straightening out the U.S. aid program in Laos.

Even the local U.S. officials privately will admit doubts that they can ever achieve a complete reform in the aid program, even if the currency exchange reform goes through.

"There is still no assurance that Laos will import the things it really needs to improve the economy, rather than luxury goods," one International Co-operation Administration man admits.

I.C.A. officials, uneasy at the flood of unessential imports financed by the U.S., did win one major concession early this year. They were allowed to place a representative on Laos' National Export-Import Council, with the power to veto any import. The current I.C.A. man, L. G. Daniel, suffers from a major handicap, however, in pursuing his job as watchdog. All the council's deliberations, and the import applications as well, are in French—a tongue Mr. Daniel neither speaks nor reads.

Besides the kip devaluation, the U.S. now wants to institute a monthly release of project funds with strict accounting by the Laos government on its uses. At present, funds for an entire project are released in a lump sum and the I.C.A. loses control of the money completely from that point. As a result, Laos officials, besides granting import licenses for luxury goods, often have siphoned off the funds for their own uses, some of the U.S. representatives claim.

There is a lush building boom going on. Leading traders and government officials (often the same people) are huddling with architects and contractors for lavish new residences or flashy additions to formerly modest homes. Both the Laovieng Bank and the Bank of Indochina are preparing to move into sleek new glass-brick-and-concrete structures. The Finance Ministry is constructing an ultra-modern building right next door to the newly completed Ministry of Plans.

It is generally agreed that some two or three hundred leading families in Laos (population 3,000,000) are getting most of the benefit from the massive import program. One I.C.A. official frankly admits that "certain favors" are granted Laotian political and government leaders to keep them "friendly," but he declines to elaborate further.

Meanwhile, back in the countryside, the rank and file of the Laotians, a handsome dark people, live much as they have always lived, oblivious of the U.S. help. Their flimsy shacks are built on stilts to protect them from snakes and flooding during the rainy season. They farm rice and a few vegetables and raise chickens. In the torrid climate only the scantiest cotton clothing is needed and hardly anyone wears shoes.

The Communists, of course, don't hesitate here or elsewhere to exploit corruption in government or riches flowing to a few favored hands. And Americans here are beginning to wonder how long the United States, in doling out assistance, can afford to ignore this unfortunate part of their program.

Talk to I.C.A. officials and they will admit that, except for a few projects, their whole program to date hasn't gone far in raising the standard of living of the general population.

"One trouble is that in 1955 we started to throw in anything just to impress the Laos government," says one official. "And now we're stuck with a bunch of assorted, unrelated projects but no real program. It would be easier to start all over again than to correct what we have."

However, Daly La Verne, newly named chief of I.C.A.'s mission in Laos, firmly upholds the value of the program. "Maybe not much has seeped down to the little guy," he says, "but I know one thing— without U.S. military aid, this country would be part of Communist North Vietnam, and that certainly wouldn't help the little Laotian."

Husky, crew-cut Colonel Ouan Rathikoun, chief of staff of the Laos Army, proudly insists he would still have an army without U.S. aid, "though it would be a little smaller."

IGOR OGANESOFF

March 9, 1958

Aiding the Afghans

Foreign aid doesn't seem to work for the Russians any better than for us, our Mr. Bonner reports from Afghanistan. Some Afghans are beginning to think that Russian foreign aid, like the bread it produced, is for the birds.

The bread is, literally. Russia built a bakery and the Afghan government bakes a European-type bread the Afghans do not like as well as they like their own flat, crusty bread, called *nan*. There isn't enough flour to go around, so the local bakeshops are being forced out of business. Meanwhile, Afghans with a taste for *nan* eat the crust from the government bread and toss the middle disconsolately to the birds.

The Russians are also coming in for criticism in Afghanistan because the 1,200 trucks they sent along as a gift are as much trouble as so many white elephants, which might have been better at that since elephants don't break down very often. The trucks do; they're under repair more often than they're in use.

So it's no wonder that a U.S. State Department analysis of Russian aid can sum it up this way: "There is evidence to suggest that the Afghans have become somewhat disillusioned" about its effects.

Fortunately for us, the Afghans aren't quite as upset about U.S. foreign aid. For one thing, the biggest portion of our aid is rather remote from Kabul, the capital where the Red trucks break down and the bread gets the bird. What we're doing isn't so apparent to the people.

Our biggest single project, for example, is the Helmand Valley irrigation project in southwest Afghanistan, where we are trying to make over the desert. One trouble, though, is the lack of water thereabouts. Another is that nobody seems able to make the nomads who live in the desert stand still long enough to learn to plow.

Altogether, Mr. T. Y. Johnson, an engineer on the project, reports it is likely to take a generation before we make the desert bloom. This will make the U.S. foreign-aid advocates a bit impatient, but there's one bright spot.

If both countries continue foreign aid to Afghanistan on the same basis, it will be quite a while before the Afghans can learn to dislike U.S. aid as much as they now dislike Russian aid because things don't turn out right. And in the cold war that's a victory of some kind or other, we suppose.

EDITORIAL

September 23, 1958

Mr. Okada's Rise

KOROMO, Japan—Every afternoon at 4 o'clock, smiling Eiji Okada switches off his smoking automatic welding machine here in the Toyota auto plant's thundering body shop. Then he bicycles home, often for a quiet interval with his favorite hobby—formal Japanese flower arranging.

He'll probably also glance at the evening paper to see how his 300 shares of Toyota stock, worth a total of about $240, are doing. And, starting in a week or two, Mr. Okada and his family will spend evenings squatting on straw mats before a new, 14-inch television set, purchased for cash with his year-end bonus.

This busy gentleman illustrates some striking new facts about industrial Japan. First, the Nipponese factory hand today is financially a lot better off than he is commonly pictured abroad, with more leisure to indulge his traditional artistic bent. And second, Japan's automobile industry, which barely existed before the war, now is sprinting ahead to a position of importance—and is invading the U.S. market in the process.

The firm that employs Mr. Okada, Toyota Motor Co., Ltd., is Japan's biggest automotive producer, accounting for half of the some 50,000 passenger cars and 140,000 trucks turned out in this country last year. Though this still is pretty modest by Detroit standards, Japan's auto men are planning to crank up their output this year, perhaps by 15 per cent or more. Exports in 1958 of over 10,000 Japanese-designed vehicles, about a quarter of them passenger autos, are expected to double in 1959, with passenger cars accounting for most of the gain.

Not surprisingly, the biggest overseas push will be in the U.S. market. In 1959 Toyota expects to boost last years' trial exports of 700 Toyopets (compact, sturdy sedans that are about 25 per cent shorter than recent American models and sell for around $2,000 to $4,800). The firm also will double its present chain of 33 U.S. dealers, now only on the U. S. West Coast, to embrace Eastern states.

"It's a big gamble," confesses Shotaro Kamiya, aggressive, 62-year-old president of the auto company's sales subsidiary, Toyota Motor Sales Co., and prewar sales manager for General Motors in Japan. "But we figure that American makers won't produce anything smaller than the prewar models, so there's still a market for a small car."

American-educated Roy T. Sumitani, Toyota deputy export manager, spreads on his desk a new Toyopet advertising layout for U.S. papers. "By 1960, Americans are expected to import five-hundred thousand foreign cars annually. Why shouldn't we get part of this market?" he asks earnestly.

To meet expected new demand at home and abroad, Toyota now is building a new $11 million plant here in Koromo, 170 miles west of Tokyo, to boost its production to 120,000 cars and trucks annually by next year. The World Bank already has lent the firm $2,260,000 for new machinery to lower costs.

Nissan Auto Co., second largest Japanese producer, also has its eye on the American market; 840 of its midget Datsun sedans have reached the U.S. to retail at around $1,800. The firm also turns out under license around 300 British Austins monthly. The other foreign autos produced in Japan are British Hillmans and French Renaults, each at the rate of two or three hundred monthly, partly from imported parts.

Both Toyota and Nissan face big hurdles in their U.S. invasions, of course. Competition for the American market has stiffened greatly in the past year, as a growing number of European auto makers have begun to offer their cars in the U.S. A push for nation-wide distribution can be costly, too; it involves setting up a network of repair facilities and parts warehouses around the U.S.

Japan's auto makers are well aware of these hurdles. But one discovers a keen awareness right through worker ranks that Japan needs to boost its exports of manufactured goods to pay for needed food and raw materials from abroad. "We have made the Toyopet

not only a good car for Japan, but a good car by world standards
so people everywhere will buy it," says Mr. Okada firmly.

Automobiles, however, are on a lengthening list of export products that are facing rising labor costs—a trend that is weakening one
of Japan's traditional advantages in world markets.

Mr. Okada, for instance, receives a basic salary of 40,000 yen (or
$111) monthly for a six-day, 42-hour week. But besides this, he and
5,100 other Toyota employees, including 400 girls doing upholstery
and minor assembly work, get summer and winter bonuses, each
corresponding to nearly two months of regular pay. This brings his
total earnings to the equivalent of $145 monthly, out of which
comes something like $16 in national income tax.

Some Toyota workers make a good deal more. Take stocky Ka-
zumasa Suzuki, also in his thirties, who scurries from machine to
machine, drilling and milling cylinder heads. He makes around
$185 before taxes. Mr. Suzuki owns a gleaming new $8,000 house
in the rice paddies near Koromo, 3,000 shares of assorted stock
worth $1,300, a television set, washing machine, and plans to pur-
chase a used Toyopet this year. He's in the upper stratum of Japanese factory labor, of course; a skilled job in a small company may
pay only half as much.

However, it's not just higher cash wages but also traditional Japanese paternalism that is boosting labor costs at many Japanese
factories and that has made the average Japanese worker far more
prosperous than ever before.

Besides regular pay, Toyota workers get family allowances
amounting to $2.80 monthly if they're married, plus $1.40 for each
child. This firm also has a highly modern productivity-sharing program; if output in a department rises, say, 10 per cent per worker
in a given month, pay automatically is hiked around one per cent.

Finally, though both Mr. Okada and Mr. Suzuki own their own
homes, about one third of Toyota's factory hands live in company
dormitories or houses. Here, a single man pays the equivalent of 80
cents a month for a room; for about $2 a month, a family can rent
a three-room bungalow. Such benefits, plus free medical care, subsidized lunches, and extensive recreation facilities, help explain why
most Japanese companies don't even attempt to estimate how much
their labor really costs them.

To see what's happened to the Japanese consumer visit Toyota's
retail commissary, whose main outlet and eleven branches sell to
8,000 Toyota employees and their dependents. This departmental-
ized emporium sells fish, vegetables, clothing, hi-fi record players,
furniture, cameras and nearly every consumer need at prices 10 to
15 per cent below outside retail levels. The company operates the

commissary on a break-even basis. Diminutive, gold-toothed manager Usaburo Kasai happily relates how Toyota families buy an average of one $165 television set a day and a score of $56 movie cameras monthly. "Three quarters of the homes around here now have television and every house has a washing machine," he says with obvious pride.

Like other Toyota housewives, Mrs. Okada does nearly all her shopping in the company store, which offers time payments of up to 12 months for the more expensive items. This, too, is an entirely new concept for the Japanese, who used to be acutely embarrassed to exhibit any shortage of cash. There's also a large flower shop where devotees such as Mr. Okada can select twigs and blossoms, and a nursery where his wife can park the kids for a few hours.

Probably the most dramatic sign of a changed era is the securities counter in the Toyota store, which provides bustling contrast with the prewar concentration of corporate stock in a few wealthy hands. Several major securities dealers staff the counter daily, trading in all securities listed on Japanese exchanges and totting up $850,000 worth of transactions monthly. Most of the time, actual buying and selling is done by the demure Japanese ladies while their hubbies make autos. One dignified grandmother at the counter sheepishly admits she watches the market every day.

Mr. Okada is one of Toyota's 50,000 stockholders. About 35 banks, stockbrokers, and Toyota-affiliated firms hold nearly half the outstanding stock, the general public most of the rest. Shares currently sell for around 288 yen (81 cents), though they were traded for as little as 77 yen in 1955.

The Toyota commissary also operates the several plant mess halls, each seating 1,000 for lunch. Here Mr. Okada can get a noontime meal of fried fish, rice, meat curry and pickled radishes—washed down with green tea—for a flat 500 yen ($1.40) per month, far under cost. "We have very fine food in our dining room," nods the slightly built welder.

Stroll through the gray concrete buildings that make up Toyota's 82 acres of clanging production lines. Throughout, there's a good sampling of American machinery, such as Gleason gear-cutting equipment, but mostly the factory is outfitted with Japanese machinery, some of it a bit overage.

There's automation, too, here and there. For instance, 34-year-old Toyoji Asada oversees a bank of machines which automatically turn out steering-gear cases. All he has to do is mount the part on a carrier that whizzes around a track through eight automatic processing steps. This young man has been on the job only six months; it's considered an unskilled operation and he makes around $80 monthly.

Mr. Okada's task involves assembling the three parts of sheet steel that make up the upper panel of the cowl, setting them in his automatic welder, and pushing a button that sends power through 150 little welding points. He's been using this machine for only three years; before that, the operation was done by hand welding.

One item that is still pretty much beyond Mr. Okada's financial reach is, ironically, the very product he makes. The six-passenger Toyopet Crown sells in the U.S. for $2,187—about the same as in Japan. The four-passenger Corona retails for about $200 less, still far too expensive for most wage earners, even spread over 12 months of installment payments. A Toyopet cost $4,000 a few years ago; prices have been cut 20 per cent in the last three years alone.

Nevertheless, Mr. Okada is getting a driver's license this month, after a course at the company driving school. Then he can join Toyota's immensely popular Green Motor Club, where, for $1.95 monthly dues, he can take a car out all day once every two months, paying for gas and oil himself.

Though the average Japanese can't afford a new auto, a used-car market is slowly growing. "In our sales company, one year ago only the president owned a car. Now fifty office workers are automobile owners," declares export salesman Mr. Sumitani. To boost private buying, Toyota and other makers may soon bring out small, cheap autos for domestic sale.

But today Toyopets are aimed at a home market still composed 80 per cent of taxi companies and other commercial users and only 20 per cent of private consumers. Currently, 250,000 passenger cars —one for every 370 persons—crowd Japan's narrow streets. Of these, 170,000 are domestic models, nearly 50 per cent more than a year ago. The remainder are overwhelmingly American, including some 22,000 cars operated by American military personnel and Defense Department civilian employees. Unlike American auto makers, Toyota turns out far more trucks than cars; currently, monthly output is around 2,000 cars, 1,000 large trucks and buses and 4,000 small trucks.

To help spur its domestic industry, Japan has clamped down hard on imports. Duties and taxes on an imported U.S. car, for example, total as much as 100 per cent of its price. And the Japanese government refuses to permit any American auto maker to set up a manufacturing subsidiary here; several U.S. companies in the past have expressed an eagerness to build cars in Japan.

Rising labor costs are only one reason for Toyota's surprisingly high prices. Another is low production, which leaves sections of the factory operating inefficiently. Then, too, Japan, which imports much iron and coal, suffers from higher raw-material costs than many other countries. Finally, interest rates are high. Toyota had to offer 9 per cent to float $500,000 worth of bonds recently and borrowed $3 million from the Japan Long-Term Credit Bank at the same interest rate.

Eiji Okada doesn't have to worry much about job security; hardly anyone ever is fired in Japan. "It's very rare that anybody ever quits our firm," declares Mr. Keimei Yamamoto, assistant personnel director, completing the picture of general labor immobility.

This lack of staff turnover has required most firms to keep the compulsory retirement age quite low in order to give new employees a fighting chance for higher positions. In Toyota, a worker is retired at 55. Any employee who leaves the firm for any reason is given a severance allowance, depending on how long he's been around. For example, a man with 35 years' service will get, on retirement, a lump sum representing nearly eight years of full pay at his highest salary; a 15-year man, around two years' pay.

One of the peculiarities of the Japanese wage system is that very little merit is involved in pay raises. If one asks Mr. Yamamoto how much a skilled toolmaker earns as compared with, say, a man who just tightens bolts all day the personnel man will counter with another question: "How old are they?"

If both have been with the company the same time, chances are their wages aren't more than 10 to 15 per cent apart—no matter what duties they have, unless they're foremen or managers. "We don't hire skilled workers," says Mr. Yamamoto. "We train them ourselves from youth."

Pay increases are given automatically every year. Thus, the average manufacturing worker in a big plant who starts at $30 or so per month is almost sure to be making around $100 after 12 years' service, $170 ten years later, and perhaps $220 after 30 years' service. Through this entire period he may have been doing exactly the same job. Nowadays the implications of this system—a constantly rising wage bill for the same work—are beginning to worry Japanese exporters, who fear they'll soon be priced out of overseas markets.

Toyota workers also can pick up extra cash by dropping suggestions for plant or product improvement into a box placed in each shop—another profit-sharing innovation. Mr. Okada gets around $3 each for suggestions that he submits about once a month. One was a new dashboard lock which he devised using the principle of an umbrella spring catch. Other employees have made up to $140 for important patents and ideas.

Family finances are in the hands of Mrs. Okada, who at home kneels quietly on a cushion near the door and slightly behind her husband. She estimates that about 20 per cent of her husband's monthly take-home pay, excluding bonuses, goes for food. This covers breakfasts of thick soybean soup, dried squid or crab, sour pickles and rice; lunches of noodles and vegetables; and dinners of raw sliced tuna dipped in black soy sauce, some grilled fish, and vegetables.

Biggest chunk of the Okada budget—25 per cent—is set aside for what the welder calls "social expenses." This comprises the constant rounds of gift giving that characterize Japanese social relations by which favors received and favors given are kept in rough balance. Such obligations take precedence over family needs.

The rest of Mr. Okada's pay goes for clothing and school expenses, some savings, and contributions to two brothers who are building their own houses.

Mr. Okada, who's now 35, started with Toyota at the age of 15—only five years after the company was formed as an offshoot of Toyota Automatic Loom Works. The first passenger car was produced in 1935. Today, Toyota Motor Co. has 109 dealers throughout Japan and over 300 service stations. Company assets are valued at the equivalent of $72 million and current profits are at the rate of $13 million yearly.

January 9, 1959

The Arab "Antis"

BEIRUT—On the terrace of this city's St. Georges Hotel overlooking the Mediterranean a young Arab newsman with a shock of blond hair and a keen grasp of world affairs cheerfully admits he is carrying the torch for Arab nationalism.

His cheerfulness fades as he leans across the table to say: "If Israel were eliminated there would be no trouble in the Middle East. Look to your history. You will see that Arab nationalism wasn't much of a force until Israel was carved from Arab territory."

In Cairo, where the sun shines intensely on the muddy Nile, another well-educated Arab in a cluttered government office cynically says: "Americans pretend to be champions of democracy. But you are imperialists just like England and France. There will be no

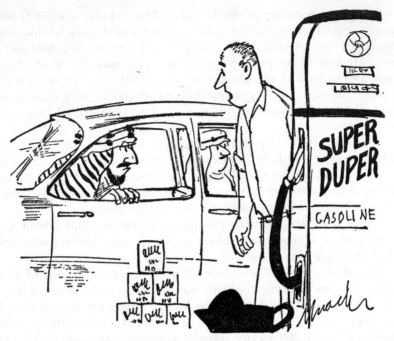

"No, sir, I'm sorry, sir. Our oil comes from Texas."

peace in the Middle East until the last remnants of imperialism are cleansed from this area."

These sentiments reflect two facets of Arab nationalism which are evident to anyone who tours the Middle East. Like the mesons binding the particles of an atom together, Arab nationalism is bound by twin hates—hatred of Israel and hatred of the West. Whatever the rights or wrongs of this hostility, it is a fact—one of the most important facts in the Middle East today.

"Arabs are anti by nature," insists one Western diplomat in a Middle Eastern trouble spot. "They stick together like brothers when they are against something. But they fight like hell among themselves when there is something constructive to be done."

This may be a rather harsh appraisal of Arab nationalism. It may be outdated by constructive co-operation in the future. To date, however, the march of Arab nationalism toward more power in the Middle East has been fired more by negativism than by positivism. If the reasons for Arab hatred were removed, Arab nationalism might be hard put to find a new binding force to hold itself together.

Past history provides many instances of this ability of Arabs to stand together against something. When the spirit of Islam first swept through the Arab world in the seventh century, fanatic Moslems found it easy to join together against the "infidel."

During the medieval crusades it was the jihad or countercrusade of Saladin which did a lot to break the power of the Franks in Jerusalem. Modern Arab nationalism really began as an anti-Turk rather than a pro-Arab movement. It is significant that in the nineteenth century the word "Arab" was used only rarely to describe the Turkish-dominated forefathers of the present Arab population.

The first major revolt against the Turks, that of the Wahhabis of Arabia, was directed more as a protest against infiltration of Western ideas into the Turkish Empire than anything else.

As Arab nationalism sprouted in various anti-Turkish movements before and during World War I, it was nourished by intellectuals. It might have remained only a topic for debating societies, though, if Britain and France had not provided a reason for anti-Western sentiment with their broken promises regarding Arab freedom.

Even today, 40 years after World War I, Arab leaders still talk bitterly of how Arabs aided the West under the impression they were to obtain freedom come peace. Instead France established a mandate over Syria and Lebanon, England moved into Palestine and Egypt, and the entire area became a pawn of European interests.

"The reaction and protest of the Arabs against the ascendancy of the West, against its partition of the Middle East into mandates and zones of influence, found expression more and more violently in the most potent of all new forces generated recently in this part of the world, namely the force of Arab political nationalism," says Professor Zeine N. Zeine, a slender, intense historian at the American University in Beirut.

When the Israel question exploded into open war in 1948, the Arabs took a beating which still rankles. That hurt pride feeds their hate. The realization that defeat stemmed from their own disunity provides a spur toward unity today.

The depth of Arab anti-Israel feeling is difficult for an outsider to comprehend. In the Middle East you find evidences of it on every hand, in the way the Jerusalem shopkeeper in Jordan refers to "the other side" when speaking of Israel on the opposite side of the barbed-wire barricade; in the way the Egyptian consul at Beirut studies every page of the passport to make sure there is no Israel visa in it before granting a United Arab Republic visa; in the way little Kuwait sells its oil to Britain with the proviso that not a drop shall be resold to Israel.

The much discussed problem of the Palestinian Arab refugees contributes to the anti-Israel feeling. Many Westerners seem to think that the longer this problem is swept under the rug the more chance there is of diluting that anti-Israel feeling. The reverse appears to be true. Each day that settlement is delayed increases Israel's danger because of the way this matter unites the Arabs. Each day of delay diminishes Israel's chances of ever developing into a self-supporting nation working in economic co-operation with its neighbors.

The usual picture of the 800,000 Arab refugees from Israel is one of natives living in squalor in camps on bleak deserts. This is only part of the picture. Those Arabs still in camps are those with the poorest educations and the least ambition.

There were thousands of well-educated Arabs among the refugees. These did not remain long in poverty-stricken camps. They fanned out throughout the Arab world. Today, you find them holding office jobs in Kuwait, working in responsible posts with oil companies in Saudi Arabia or Iraq, broadcasting over Nasser's Cairo Radio, working for newspapers in Lebanon or lecturing in Middle Eastern universities.

Included are men like the newspaperman on the terrace of the St. Georges Hotel. His family still has valuable property in Haifa, Israel. Today he works on an influential Beirut publication; one brother is an executive with Chase Manhattan Bank's Beirut branch; another is a lecturer at the American University here.

"We have never been offered one penny of compensation for our property in Haifa," says this newspaperman.

As he describes the hard struggle of his penniless family in making a new start, you begin to see the depth of his hate. There are many like him throughout the Middle East. Now that they are in a position of influence they do their best to spread that anti-Israel spirit, creating more glue for holding Arab nationalism together.

The United States thrust itself into Middle Eastern politics with its unsuccessful attempt to isolate Nasser's Egypt from the rest of the world after it had saved Egypt from total disaster during the Suez crisis. Instead of isolating Nasser, the U.S. merely provided Arab nationalism with another target. "We helped to unite different factions in the Arab world against us," admits one weary-spirited U.S. diplomat. The landings in Lebanon provided more reasons for Arab suspicion and distrust of U.S. policy.

Today as you move through the Middle East you find Arab nationalism to be a live and vital force which is uniting Arabs in a way that they have never been united since the days of the glorious

Omayyad and Abbasid dynasties of the seventh and eighth centuries. But it is a unity being achieved through hate.

RAY VICKER

August 19, 1958

Illusions of Democracy

Pakistan, a democratically conceived nation, is now a military
dictatorship, and in that bald fact are a couple of sobering
reflections.

One of the numerous nations to achieve independence in the
wake of World War II, Pakistan organized itself on the democratic
example of the United States and the Western world. But somehow
democracy does not seem to have been working very well.

The President of the country, in his proclamation of martial law,
put it this way: "For the last two years I have been watching with
deepest anxiety the ruthless struggle for power, corruption, the
shameful exploitation of our simple, honest, patriotic and industrious masses, the lack of decorum and the prostitution of Islam
for political ends." He said the "present action has been taken with
utmost regret" but had become inevitable.

Well, is there, after all, something basically deficient in democracy, as the enemies of democracy constantly contend? We think
the deficiency is not in this particular form of political organization, but in some illusions about it. One of the most prevalent of
these is that a newly independent country need only to desire democracy and, presto, it exists.

Actually the type of free society which "democracy" connotes is
usually very slow in developing. It took Britain centuries to attain
it, and when the United States was created it not only borrowed
much from Britain but was also blessed with leaders and a populace steeped in freedom's principles. That is not often the case with
the new nations of today.

Unfortunately the United States itself has sometimes seemed to
share in this illusion that functioning democracies can always
spring full-blown out of colonialism. Pakistan, for instance, has
become one of this country's important allies and has been considered one of the firmest in the East, being a member of both the
American-sponsored Baghdad Pact and the Southeast Asia Treaty
Organization.

Perhaps the alliance will continue firm, but the Pakistan the United States is allied with this morning is certainly not the Pakistan it has been relying on for the defense of democracy.

October 10, 1958

Mr. Meged Builds a Dream House

LENINGRAD, U.S.S.R.—In the village of Bucha, near Kiev, Grigory Meged is having his own home built. And in Stalingrad, Alexei Dmitrievitch brings carrots—via Volga boat—from his home 19 miles away to sell at free prices in the open-air market.

Private housing and free commodity markets are the outstanding examples of growing nonstate enterprise in the Soviet Union. They are not the only ones. Many a carpenter, electrician and dentist makes extra money doing private work on his own time. Some people rent out a room or a corner of a room. In addition, there is a good deal of illegal enterprise in the form of black markets. And despite Communism, most people show a strongly developed taste for private ownership; a man lucky enough to own a small Pobeda car thinks of the day he may be able to acquire a Zim or even a Zil.

All this does not, of course, prove that the Soviet system is changing in the direction of private enterprise. In some ways state control is, if anything, widening. Collective farms are theoretically co-operative, nonstate undertakings, but they have always been under the thumb of Moscow and still are. Producer artels, which in theory are industrial co-operatives, are rapidly being taken over by the state.

What the existence of nonstate enterprise—particularly private home building and free market farm sales—does show, in the opinion of experts on this country, is that the Soviets are perfectly willing to depart from Communist principles when they feel they have to. Some experts contend that the system wouldn't work at all on a purely Communist basis.

Need, at any rate, is the explanation for the big surge of private home building. The housing shortage is so desperate that the government, besides greatly stepping up public-housing construction, is encouraging people to do it themselves.

From 1951 through 1955, 144.2 million square meters of urban housing were put up, of which 38.8 million, or more than one fourth, were private homes. In this country, where quarters are crowded, that 144.2 million square meters is enough to accommodate an estimated 16 million people, or 4 million families of four. At the end of last year a total of 640 million square meters of urban housing were in use, of which 208 million were private. Moreover, the private trend is on the rise. In 1950, 6.4 million square meters of private homes were built; in 1955, 8.4 million.

Drive around some of the hilly outlying parts of Kiev, like the Pechersky and Stalinka regions, and you see lots of brick houses, some of them two-story, going up. (There are also many old log-and-clay whitewashed structures.) Stop at one of the houses abuilding and you find a modest dwelling that will consist of four rooms plus kitchen, bath and veranda.

How do Soviet citizens go about buying or building, what does it cost, and where do they get the money?

It's not too difficult, as Mr. Meged, who is the manager of one section of the Kiev State Swine Farm in Bucha, will tell you. He and his wife (they have a married daughter in Odessa and a younger daughter studying in Kiev), now live in half of a two-unit house built by the farm administration in 1953.

Their present home consists of a small combination living-dining room (a tiny-screen TV set perches proudly on a table), a small bedroom and a kitchen with stove but no refrigerator. No bathroom; there is a communal bath down near the fodder kitchen. You enter the house through a small outside portico directly into the kitchen.

The house Mr. Meged is having built will be small, too, and in-expensive—only about 10,000 rubles ($2,500). Construction began last spring and Mr. Meged expects it to be finished by the end of this year. Most private homes take longer—18 months to two years.

The 10,000-ruble cost is somewhat deceptive. It doesn't include Mr. Meged's own labor, and down on the state farm they use cheap materials. Also, Mr. Meged doesn't have to pay the workers he hires as much as city folk would; in Leningrad a skilled worker like an electrician will get one and a half to two times his normal pay for outside work on his own time. However, there is a good deal of skill swapping; if you are a carpenter you help a plumber on his house and he helps yours.

For this reason it's hard to estimate the cost of an average private home. In Kiev the figure is said to be about 25,000 rubles ($6,250), but in Rostov-on-Don and Tiflis you hear higher estimates, 40,000 rubles ($10,000) or more; in Moscow 35,000 rubles ($8,750) is said to be tops for an average home.

Mr. Meged is putting up 5,000 rubles of his own savings. The other 5,000 is a loan from the farm administration, to be repaid in seven years through pay deductions (unlike collective farms, state farms pay straight wages as in industry). There is no interest. In the same way a factory worker can get an interest-free loan from the factory administration or trade union or both together. Banks will also provide money to individuals, usually seven-year loans of about 10,000 rubles at 3 per cent interest.

Though all land belongs to the state, a home builder is allotted a small plot of ground. In Kiev no rent is charged, but elsewhere, as in Rostov-on-Don, there is a nominal rent of about 100 rubles a year, paid to the local branch of the Gosbank (State Bank).

The buying and selling market, however, is not exactly brisk; when a family builds, it is likely to stay put. But when a house is sold, the buyer and the seller agree on a price and go to a lawyer to close the deal, much as in other countries.

Sometimes people have to move whether they want to or not. Right after the war in Stalingrad, which was almost wiped out, people put up little whitewashed log houses; they look no bigger than children's playhouses. Now the city wants to tear them down and put the people in apartments that are being built or planned.

"But many don't want to move," says Mrs. Marya Somova, assistant manager of the Stalingrad city government. The people are supposed to get compensation, so they could presumably build elsewhere if they don't care to go into a flat.

Even with all this public and private building, there is no sign of an end to the housing shortage. A Leningrad building engineer figures it will be 10 to 15 years before housing catches up with needs, and that is probably a highly optimistic estimate.

The same reason—need—explains why Alexei Dmitrievitch and his family, and the nearly 20 million other families on some 86,000 collective farms throughout the Soviet Union, can sell their privately grown produce at their own prices.

The U.S.S.R. has just brought in a record grain harvest, now estimated at somewhere around 125 million metric tons, as compared with 100 million to 110 million last year. But there is no certainty that agriculture, which has always been the worst laggard of the Soviet economy, has finally turned the corner.

Many experts doubt, for example, that the new lands in Kazakhstan and Siberia will bring in as good harvests every year as they did this year. So the Soviets need not only the peasant's private production, but perhaps even more the psychological incentive this gives him to work harder.

In the Stalingrad free market you see stall after stall with a profusion of potatoes, pears, onions, carrots, red peppers, radishes, eggs, chickens and mutton—all at higher prices than charged in the state stores, where no such abundance prevails. There is Ivan Valentine-vitch, who has traveled from Saratov 370 miles away because the Stalingrad price is better. Here selling radishes is Matrena Dmie-trievna, who lives only about a mile out of Stalingrad.

In Tiflis, the capital of the Georgian Republic, the market is in a big building, on two floors, and the abundance is even greater. It's a real bazaar atmosphere, with the peasants hawking their wares and the buyers busily bargaining.

To get an idea of how this private agricultural economy works, visit the Red Partisan Collective Farm of the Leningrad District, just outside the city limits. On its 2,200 hectares (nearly 5,500 acres) are 400 farm workers, including members of families 16 and older. The main products are milk, swine, potatoes and vegetables. Some 30 Red Partisan families, incidentally, are currently building their own homes.

Each family has its own allotment of about one fourth of a hectare, on which many grow strawberries, apples, pears and radishes. Strawberries are the most profitable; Pavel Saveliev says he made about 25,000 rubles ($6,250) on strawberries last year. On the other hand, Adam Stern, who has been here only a couple of years, isn't selling much of anything.

Mikhail Petrunin, manager of the Red Partisan, estimates the average income from an allotment at 15,000 to 20,000 rubles a year. Even if this estimate is considerably on the high side, a family wouldn't have to make much to overshadow its share of the collective produce sales: it's less than 6,000 rubles a year on the average, though the peasants also get various amounts of food from the farm.

On his private allotment the farmer is permitted to have one cow and two calves, no horse and an unlimited quantity of poultry and bees.

In theory the collective farm is itself a form of co-operative enterprise, with the farmers banding together to organize it and electing their manager and decided all their problems in pure-democratic fashion. In theory the Red Partisan farmers jointly own everything you see as you trudge through the mud in a pouring rain—the clean, new (1955) swine and cattle barns (electric milkers), the poultry house with its 2,000 White Russian (Leghorn-based) hens and roosters, the 6,000 hogs, the 264 cows (most of them Black Swedish, relatives of Holstein), the 86 horses (the pride of Red Partisan is Pearl, a huge Ardennes) and all the things grown collectively. (This is one of the better collectives; at the end of 1954 only 41 per cent of collectives had electric power.)

Actually, Stalin dragooned the peasants, with considerable trouble, into the collectives in the late twenties and early thirties. They are operated by and for the state and if the farmers "own" them there is little to remind them of the fact. Still, some vestiges of co-operative enterprise do remain.

Thus Mr. Petrunin estimates the farm's gross income this year at 3.5 million rubles ($875,000). Fifteen per cent of that goes for capital investment and repayment of the 10-year 3 per cent loan given by Gosbank when the farm was reorganized (it was first founded in 1930) after being razed during the war. Another 15 per cent goes to the state as taxes. The remaining 70 per cent covers current needs and what is left of it is distributed among the farmers at the end of the year. So there is some attempt to retain the idea of profit sharing.

Also, the farm sells some of its collectively produced commodities —like milk, vegetables and potatoes—in the same free markets where the farmers sell their private produce; the farm can sell in this way only any excess over what it must deliver to the state. The prices are free, set by the manager in accordance with supply and demand. In 1955 the private sales of individuals and collectives accounted for a little over 15 per cent of the total sale of food commodities.

Collectives are sometimes called agricultural artels in this country, but the industrial artel is on the way out, as you can see by calling at No. 6 Promishlenniy Pereulok in Leningrad. Here Mrs. Vera Bespalova presides over the Leningrad Co-operative Textile Artel, or Lenco-optextile for short.

Theoretically, industrial artels, like collective farms, are co-operative ventures in which artisans, often in the handicrafts, band together, pooling their resources and sharing the profits. In the first years of Soviet power, some were in fact organized that way, Mrs. Bespalova says. But year by year they came to be organized more and more by local soviets, or city councils. Now the workers have the same wage scales as in state factories, and there is little if anything of a co-operative nature.

Yet there are some differences. The workers are supposed to elect the management. Artel workers have no trade union and no union dues. When a worker joins the artel he pays a fee of 15 rubles, and thereafter he pays a certain part of his salary—about two and a half months' pay a year on the average—into a special artel fund.

Mrs. Bespalova, who has been with Lenco-optextile 12 years, now has 3,100 rubles ($775) in this fund. But it can hardly be called a profit sharing arrangement. The money is simply her own, and she will get it back when she leaves or the state takes over (the state keeps the initial 15 rubles). The fund's only use seems to be as a contingency reserve in the case of fire or other accident.

In 1954 there were 114,000 industrial artels accounting for less than 6 per cent of the gross national product; 212,000 state industrial enterprises accounted for nearly 92 per cent. Last year between 1.6 million and 1.8 million people worked in artels, out of a total of 17.4 million workers in Soviet industry. Now the state is taking over the artels rapidly. In the third quarter of this year 42 artels of all types in Leningrad alone became state factories, according to Mrs. Bespalova.

Artels normally get the short end of the raw-material and equipment stick. When a state factory gets new equipment it sends the old to an artel. In the case of Mrs. Bespalova's textile artel, it makes blankets, among other things, from cotton waste. In fact, Mrs. Bespalova indicates that this artel's main reason for existence is to use up industry waste.

Lenco-optextile is going the way of the other artels; it will become a state factory in another year or two. Some artels, however, will probably continue to exist, particularly to employ handicapped persons and to serve distant, little-industrialized parts of the country.

Do the workers of Lenco-optextile feel any sentimental regrets at the doom of the artel? Not at all. Mrs. Bespalova speaks of artels rather contemptuously as a rudimentary form of the organization of labor. Besides, she says, when the state takes over there may be better equipment and materials.

And Mrs. Marya Mukinya, who is a helper checking on quality, says she plans to stay on after the state takes over. She has been with the artel 25 years but has only 530 rubles in the fund (the ruble was worth more in the old days). "It's all the same to me," she explains. "I get my money back. And I have to work anyway."

November 30, 1956

JOSEPH E. EVANS

The Hard Buy

STALINGRAD, U.S.S.R.—"Women's Dresses 30 Per Cent Off" proclaims a big sign in the Univermag (department store) on Stalingrad's Square of Dead Warriors. The reduced dresses are on circular racks behind a railing in one corner of the first floor.

In Moscow at the Univermag at No. 11 Novopechanya (New Sand) Street in the suburb of Sokol, Manager Yuri Illitch has a special counter piled with ready-made dresses, also reduced about 30 per cent.

And at the huge GUM (State Universal Store) in Moscow's Red Square, across from the Lenin-Stalin mausoleum and the Kremlin,

Assistant Manager Boris Tolstikov points to a streamer arching over one of the arcades which make up this labyrinthine building. The streamer says: "20 to 60 Per Cent Off," with an arrow indicating where these bargains can be found. "Means a loss for us," remarks Mr. Tolstikov ruefully.

In short, Soviet store managers have headaches not unlike those of their counterparts elsewhere—though naturally there are also some rather basic differences. They have to worry not only about dealing with goods that don't sell well, but also about such highly "capitalistic" problems as profits and competition.

"If we've had a dress twenty months and it hasn't sold, the price is cut," says Anna Mikhailovna, the saleswoman behind the barrier in the Stalingrad Univermag. But can Soviet store executives decide to cut prices on their own?

It isn't quite that simple in the Communist economy. For one thing, the government now orders price cuts on individual goods from time to time, in place of the general annual price reductions that used to prevail. Apart from that, a particular store must go through the Ministry of Trade before it can put a lower price tag on an item.

Thus when Mr. Tolstikov, a pleasant bald gentleman who started working in the retail business in prerevolutionary times at the age of 11, finds a lemon on his hands he tells the Ministry and the Ministry sends a representative around to find out why the article isn't selling. Then the Ministry and GUM come to an agreement on how much to cut the price.

But if the Ministry decides the item is really terrible in quality or appearance, it will confer with the appropriate production ministry, and in due course output will be halted. This happened to one model refrigerator, the predecessor of the current "North 2" made by the Moscow Gas Works. People just didn't buy the original model because it wasn't decorative enough, Mr. Tolstikov says. So the plant put the old machine in a new and prettier box; it's now selling all right.

How does a Communist store get its "profits"? At the moment, for one example, Mr. Tolstikov has 10 "Dneper" model tape recorders in stock in the appliance section. Before he ordered them, he and the factory knew—because the Ministry of Trade sets almost all retail prices—that they would retail at 1,500 rubles ($375 at the artificial official exchange rate) each or 15,000 for the lot. Of this 15,000, GUM keeps 5 per cent, or 750, and the rest goes to the factory. Different items carry different percentages; the average is about 6½ per cent.

"That's our bonus," beams Mr. Tolstikov. Out of it must come wages and maintenance and a percentage for the state as well as operating reserves for the store. Not surprisingly the "bonus" is a matter of keen interest to store managers.

The real incentive, though, is the "norm," which in the case of stores is the sales volume that must be met or exceeded; it differs from store to store, based on the past performance of each. For Mr. Illitch's emporium in Sokol, this year's norm is five million rubles (over $1.2 million) a month; last year, it was over four million a month, the year before 3.5 million. By contrast GUM—which has 5,500 employees and on an average day greets 250,000 visitors and wraps 160,000 parcels—sells 10 million rubles' worth of goods a day.

The steady boosting of norms is naturally calculated to keep a manager on his toes. And despite the fact that the same item sells at the same price everywhere in the Soviet Union except at some far distant points, it means that there is a certain amount of competition; in order to fulfill his own norm, the store manager has to be alert to what others are doing. Store managers usually don't call it competition, or at most call it "peaceful" or "social" competition, but it shows up in such ways as better service in one store or more attentive salespeople in another.

In Mr. Illitch's neighborhood, for instance, is a special TV and radio shop. Yet Mr. Illitch, a short, slight, rather intense man in his forties, says that when he opened his own TV and radio department people began coming to him because he makes a point of very carefully checking the sets first and thereafter of providing very good service.

Or listen to a saleslady at the Shop of Presents, opened less than a year ago on Moscow's Gorki Street. Why, she is asked, does a customer buy a 2,500-ruble ($625) set of china at this store when he can buy the same thing at the same price at GUM and other stores? Her reply is that the Shop of Presents is a particularly beautiful place (it is in fact quite attractive), isn't as crowded as a vast maze like GUM and puts considerable stress on pleasing the customer.

Stores do differ strikingly from each other, which seems to indicate—to some extent, at least—the managers' differing ideas of how to compete for the sales ruble. Naturally, the main Stalingrad Univermag is not as big and handsome as GUM. Stalingrad has only 525,000 people, compared with Moscow's nearly five million, and Moscow is the capital of the country.

But consider Tiflis, capital of Georgia. On one side of Lenin Square in the center of the city is one Univermag. It's dirty, dimly lighted, with sawdust on the floor and goods heaped every which way on counters. It reminds you of a picture of a general store out of the last century.

Right across the square is another store, also called a Univermag but chiefly selling a full line of men's and women's clothes. Here suits, dresses and hats are given special displays, often on dummies, and the whole place is much cleaner and more spacious than the other store.

The competitive spirit induced by norms gets right down to the individual employee. The average GUM worker makes a minimum of 700 rubles ($175) a month, but can get up to 900 or even more by exceeding his norm. In some cases, this works in reverse as well.

For example, Antonina Giorgievna, bookkeeper of a Gastronom (state grocery) in Sokol, explains that an average employee's norm there is 4,700 rubles of sales a month; on this basis his salary is 462 rubles (about $115) a month. But if he fails to meet the norm he gets only 90 per cent of that sum. So it behooves him to "compete" with the other clerks.

All the same, a visitor is not struck by the aggressiveness of the salesmanship in the Soviet Union. Since there is too little of almost everything, it is more often the customers who seem aggressive.

If the Soviet store manager shares some of the problems of his retailers elsewhere, he is nonetheless free—if that is the word—of other worries. Most obviously, perhaps, no executive here is an owner, and so the manager has no money of his own at stake in the enterprise.

Then, too, the Russian retailer doesn't have to bother his head much about advertising. When the Shop of Presents opened, the state radio announced the fact, describing what kind of store it was and where, and that was pretty much that. Occasionally an ad for a store will appear in the *Evening Moscow* newspaper, and sometimes a store will get the radio to announce some special offering. But most advertising is by word of mouth.

In fact, the store manager doesn't even have to supply a distinctive name for his establishment. The name of a dress shop is "Store for Women's Clothing." A barbershop is "Barbershop No. 9" or whatever. Mr. Illitch's store is just one of a flock of Moscow Univermags—there are seven others in Sokol alone—but people know it is the one on Novopechanya Street. A Gastronom is a Gastronom, often in neon lights.

In a store such as GUM and in other big stores in big cities like Leningrad and Kiev, considerable attention is paid to attractive display, though there is no evidence of any attempt to promote one product against another. But the average store manager doesn't seem to worry much about appearances, or sometimes even whether the goods he wants to sell are clearly visible at all.

What's it like shopping in these places? If an American had to do it as a regular thing, it would probably drive him crazy in short order.

First of all, prices are steep, even though they are not as high as they were several years ago. Goods are expensive when translated into dollars, but more significantly they are expensive when translated into Soviet incomes. Some non-Soviet sources reckon the national average income at 600 to 650 rubles ($150.00–$162.50) a month. Since most wives work, the average family income might be somewhere in the neighborhood of 1,000 rubles ($250) a month.

With that in mind, consider these random prices: The cheapest TV set in Mr. Illitch's establishment, equipped with a microscopic screen, is 850 rubles. The best, with only a slightly larger screen, costs 2,000—two months' income. An ordinary bike will run 650–750.

In the window of a Moscow men's store is a typical Russian-style suit—bell-bottom trousers and fingertip jacket sleeves—selling for 1,660, or over six weeks' income. In the Stalingrad store, salesgirl Valentina Grigorievna will show you suits from 400 rubles to 1,755. In the Tiflis clothing store there is one for 1,805, but in the junkier department store across from it the range is from 440 to 879.

The reduced price on a crepe-de-Chine dress in the Stalingrad store is 375 rubles ($93.75). In Tiflis there are ready-made dresses from 336 to 709 and black dress shoes at 446 ($111.50). One pair of men's brown oxfords in Stalingrad sells for 292, another for 346.

At GUM a vacuum cleaner with seven attachments resembling the original Lewyt model costs 650 rubles. The smallest refrigerator costs 680. You can buy an unappealing, three-piece living room suite in Tiflis for 1,879 and in Stalingrad a bedroom suite for 9,930 ($2,482.50). The latter consists of twin beds, two night tables, a dresser, two chairs and a hassock.

There's no installment buying; everything is for cash. According to Soviet Minister of Trade D. V. Pavlov, however, installment buying will be introduced "soon," perhaps next year, on big items like furniture.

Meantime, people do buy, despite high prices and low average incomes. Raisa Marochkova, a salesgirl in the main Stalingrad Univermag, says the store sold 13 dining-room suites in the last month and a half—at 7,439 rubles each.

Soviet figures on total turnover aren't too helpful because they include co-operatives and restaurants, but for what they are worth they show that the country's retail commodity turnover rose from 359.6 billion rubles (almost $90 billion) in 1950 to 501.5 billion rubles (over $125 billion) in 1955. Also, the number of retail establishments (again including public dining) increased in the same period from 298,000 stores and 117,000 tents to 352,400 stores and 135,100 tents.

Besides price, what might also annoy an American suddenly transformed into a Russian is the question of quality. Some fabrics seem excellent, but most things don't. The best men's suit in the Stalingrad store (1,755 rubles) was described as of Polish tricot, but it is a little hard and gritty to the touch. Also on display is an old-fashioned metal bed for 413 rubles and old-fashioned lamp shades at 98 to 199 rubles. Most appliances have, at best, a faintly tinny look.

In addition, the selection of brands of appliances available to the customer is modest. The Russian's choice of refrigerators is limited to four sizes, though there are a number of different names, depending on where the refrigerator is produced.

Of course, you may very well not be able to buy what you want at all. In the Tiflis department store there is only one medium-sized refrigerator on display. The appliance section in this store contains mostly washtubs and pails.

Then there is the inconvenience of shopping. You will find one Gastronom for preserves, another for milk and milk products. If they do happen to be under one roof, they will be compartmentalized so that you have to go out on the street to get from one part to another. There is nothing resembling a supermarket in this country, though some self-service stores have been started.

Or take a look at a "Store for Women's Clothing" on Moscow's Gorki Street. Inside, it's a long rectangle with a barrier running the width of the store. The ready-made dresses, on circular racks and on tables, are on one side of the barrier, the customers on the other. Women crowd up against the barrier two or three deep in this narrow space.

The customer points to one of the dresses she likes, and then is admitted behind the barrier so she can try it on in one of the tiny booths along the wall. If she is going to take the dress, she leaves it behind the barrier, gets a chit which she presents to the cashier outside the barrier, pays, gets her receipt, returns to the barrier and collects her dress. If she likes a dress but it isn't the right size, she can't order the right size.

However, this clumsy system may be slowly on the wane. At least Mr. Tolstikov says GUM is getting rid of the barriers as fast as it can—as a result, interestingly enough, of criticism by Americans visiting the store. In place of the barrier system, the customer in a number of GUM departments can now inspect the goods right on the counter or floor and pay for what he takes right there.

And Soviet customers can get delivery service, at least on big items and at a big store like GUM, which uses trucks from stations maintained by the Ministry of Trade and charges a small extra fee. Also, Mr. Tolstikov says, they can exchange defective items or get their money back, usually during a period of five days but up to six months on durables like refrigerators.

JOSEPH E. EVANS

November 19, 1956

Nyet Drunkski Russkies

As is well known, Soviet Premier Khrushchev is not averse to a potation now and then. In fact there have even been a few counter-revolutionary reports that the Kremlin boss believes that one good drink deserves another. So it is somewhat surprising to read that Soviet citizens are now forbidden to lift more than one glass in restaurants and other public places.

The one-drink-to-a-customer law was adopted because the Red hierarchy felt too many comrades were seeking utopia in an entirely revisionist manner. Mr. Khrushchev, however, has softened the restriction somewhat by permitting particularly sociable socialists to move from bar to bar, on the theory that with but one drink at each stop even the driest proletarian will find the interim trudge in the brisk Russian air conducive to sobriety.

Particularly noteworthy in this new dictum is the fact that the penalty for consuming more than one glass at one place was not made clear. What would happen, we wonder, if a daring deviationist finished his ration and then quietly slipped down to the other end of the bar and ordered a second? A firing squad? Siberia? Probably nothing so drastic. Most likely two secret policemen would step up and throw him out in the snow, leaving his vodka and bar money behind.

And in the absence of stiff punishment we doubt the one-drink law will work. Sooner or later an outraged comrade, seeing his friend deposited in the street, will exhort his fellows to rebel against such tyranny.

"Fellow workers, arise," he will cry. "Step up and order a second —you have nothing to lose but your change!"

October 23, 1958

EDITORIAL

The Passing On of Power

It was March when Caesar died and brought the years of anarchy to the Roman Empire.

Caesar himself had once been one of three, in triumvirate with old Crassus and young Pompey; Crassus was slain on the fields of Mesopotamia and in Egypt they brought Pompey's head on a silver shield, leaving great Caesar master of Rome and Rome master of an empire.

Caesar dead, there was again the rule of three. But Lepidus died in prison and Mark Antony died at Actium and soon there was only Octavian known as Caesar Augustus. Then it was that Rome, under the banner of Caesar and the leadership of Augustus, came briefly to its greatest power: after Augustus there was proscription and a slaying of men for power and slowly the crumbling of empire.

Caesar's was not the first empire built by strong and ruthless men to be destroyed within itself. Alexander the Great dead, the world that he conquered flew apart and few can even remember the names of Craterus and Perdiccas, regents to the heir of this empire that was to have been in perpetuity.

Nor was Caesar's last. Once there was a great Mongol empire that ruled all of Asia and swept westward into a Europe which lay defenseless before it. Then one day the Great Khan died; his armies swept back from Europe as strong men struggled for the succession. And it was seven hundred years before they returned.

General Bonaparte, too, was once one of three. But who now speaks of Cambraceres and Lebrun? And in the chaos after Waterloo even Napoleon's conquerors could not solve the succession of power with the little king they brought for France in their baggage.

After the Czar of All the Russians passed, and after him the futile men who thought anarchy could be resolved with good will, power came to a rule of three, who were to wield it as co-consuls. But the dictatorship of the proletariat became the dictatorship of Lenin. Leon Trotsky never could understand why despotism could not be a co-operative affair. Joseph Stalin did, and he was content to watch patiently while it rested for a time in Lenin's hands.

Stalin had to be patient long, for after Lenin came again the years of anarchy. Yet in due time Trotsky, who could never understand, died in exile with a hatchet in his head. Soon the triumvirate of Stalin, Kamenev and Zinoviev was the rule of one; and one by one the ambitious Bukharins and the disgruntled nameless passed not only from power but from Soviet history.

Stalin understood. When despots pass, the vaunted strength of despotism passes; the vaunted strength of despotism is a fragile thing. Loosed, it can only fly into anarchy, until it forms new shapes of power or until it can be seized. The power of despotism cannot be quietly inherited or peacefully shared.   ·

It was March when Joseph Stalin died. They say his power passes without disarray or panic to a man named Malenkov. Yet in the dark of despotism what man can see what this ending is the beginning of?

EDITORIAL

March 9, 1953

WEST

Return of German Cartels

DÜSSELDORF—Chalk up as a failure the attempt to sell American-style capitalism to German big business.

West Germany today has a private enterprise economy; that is, it's not run by the state. But it can hardly be called a free-enterprise economy in the American competitive sense, and it's probably going to become less so. Quietly and methodically trade and industry are returning to their traditional prewar patterns of cartel and trust.

This "reconcentration" comes after eight years of efforts by the U.S. and its allies to dismantle the whole West German business setup as replete with "dangerous concentrations of economic power." On paper, the Allied High Commissioner or their predecessors broke up the Ruhr coal and steel trusts, the film and chemical cartels and the big banks. But take a look at what's actually happening to some of these groups.

Prior to the end of World War II, the Deutsche, Dresdner and Commerz Banks dominated the German financial and industrial world. These "big three" were taken apart by the Allies and nine regional banks were formed out of the wreckage—each independent and each with separate managements.

Recently the three successor units of the Deutsche Bank, located in Hamburg, Düsseldorf and Frankfurt, issued their separate annual reports. They were identical word for word, except for the respective financial statements. On Düsseldorf's Breitsstrasse, the "Wall Street" of Germany, it is taken for granted that the big three will soon be reassembled under their old corporate identities.

"Deconcentrated" coal and steel are now under the control of the Schuman Plan High Authority. Before the Schuman Plan went into operation, the Allied High Commissioners in Bonn protested that the Ruhr iron and steel producers were fixing prices in violation of occupation decrees. After the Schuman Plan became effective, its chairman, Jean Monnet, accused German, French and Belgian steel producers of price fixing.

Many Allied and German officials privately consider the High

Authority simply a logical continuation of the prewar International Steel Cartel, founded in 1926 by German, French, Belgian and Luxembourg steelmakers. Today the High Authority has the power to fix prices and regulate production—as did the International Steel Cartel—to bring order into the European steel and coal community and to prevent international trade warfare.

Observers here also detect signs of cartel practices in other fields, including radios, chemicals, soap, household goods, food retailing, paper and photographic supplies. The signs: price-fixing production and sales quotas assigned within an industry.

Such practices are usually handled by the trade associations—and a trade association in Germany is far more dictatorial toward its members than a similar body in America. The embryonic West German aircraft industry both illustrates this authoritarianism and shows how a cartel gets going.

West Germany is still forbidden to produce civil or military airplanes. But the five surviving aircraft producers—Heinkel, Messerschmitt, Dornier, Focke-Wulf and Daimler-Benz—are busy preparing for the day when they can again compete on the world market; they've formed the "Aero Union."

Dr. Claudius Dornier, head of the firm bearing his name, explains the Aero Union as follows: "Five producers who once competed with each other are now joined together, together with our resources and know-how, to make good use of the means of production still available. We will avoid fighting with each other economically in striving to put Germany's war-crippled air industry back on its feet."

The Aero Union will finance necessary research in various fields, drum up required capital investments, allocate contracts among the five members and organize production in the interest of all instead of that of any single firm. Not surprisingly, the Allies see an aviation cartel shaping up.

Since few people in Germany—including Bonn's private-enterprise-minded Minister of Economics, Ludwig Erhard, and the Socialists—oppose cartels as such, the Bonn Parliament has done little to prevent their revival, even though the Allies obtained a pledge from the government that it would pass laws against "excessive concentrations of economic power."

For the past 18 months the Bundestag (lower house) has avoided taking any action, and political experts in Bonn doubt whether any anticartel law will ever be passed. Meanwhile a draft of a bill has come out of a Bundestag committee; it would permit, not forbid, creation of cartels—in time of depression or to boost Germany's exports, or to secure cheaper production and prices, in effect, this bill would okay any cartel beneficial to Germany's economy and punish cartels acting against the national interest.

And Parliament just recently voted almost unanimously to restore the guild controls invalidated by then Military Governor General Lucius Clay in 1948. These controls restrict the free entry of Germans into given trades, professions or industries. Prior to the Clay decree, for example, no German could open a bakery unless he had the approval of the bakers' guild.

The law restoring such controls—a far cry from the U.S. concepts of free enterprise—can be vetoed by the U.S. High Commissioner. But such action would be so politically unpopular it is considered unlikely.

Why the aversion to American-style capitalism? Explanations abound. For example, it's argued that in a capital-short country like this it was natural and inevitable that the "big three" banks again emerge—only by pooling their resources can banks furnish the necessary funds for an expanding economy.

In the case of aviation, the Germans say it's "rationalization," not cartelization. Faced with foreign competition far in advance of what an individual German plane manufacturer could produce for years to come, all manufacturers must pool their physical and technological resources even to get started, it's contended.

This line of reasoning is summed up by a Düsseldorf steel exporter: "Sure we are building cartels in Germany. We Germans can't afford the luxury of a free and uncontrollable market as you rich Americans do."

Another reason for the failure of American capitalism to catch on here is indicated in the case of the I. G. Farben chemical empire. The original Allied intention was to dismember completely this "state within a state," the largest single industrial combine in Europe and a party to over 150 domestic and international cartel agreements.

But on second glance even the most ardent American trust buster began to have doubts whether complete dismemberment could be accomplished; the cure might be worse than the disease. It was found, for one thing, that the "Leverkusen group" of Farben, comprising five large plants and 17 subsidiary firms, couldn't be broken up because the individual units were interdependent, in some cases sharing the same factory site, power plants and other facilities.

So the original plan to form 80 separate units out of Farben was revised downward to 40, and later to 12 basic firms. The final Allied reorganization plan provided for five new successor companies.

But underlying these justifications are more basic considerations.

There is a strong strain of nationalism in German trade and industry today. A German manufacturer will accept dictation on production and sales quotas from the trade association in the firm belief that his industry as a whole, and his nation, will benefit in domestic and foreign trade. His German worker, who may be a Socialist, will also accept it because he thinks that his job will be more secure.

Finally there is a fundamental difference in attitude. To a German, as to most Europeans, a cartel is not antisocial or iniquitous, as it is to most Americans. Germany is the home of the cartel, and the Germans are if anything proud of the institution; they say the pre-World War I coal and steel cartels helped to make the Ruhr the dominant industrial power of all Europe. It is this attitude perhaps more than anything else that the U.S. has failed to change.

EDWIN HARTRICH

August 27, 1953

Socialized Law

LONDON—Britain's scheme of socialized medicine has a little brother you should know—socialized law. He's four and a half years old, and growing like crazy.

Instead of offering free false teeth, Legal Aid puts the public purse behind those who have the urge to litigate but not enough money to pay the lawyers. For instance, there's Herbert Loader, of Westwood Hill, Streatham, who was irked when his brother-in-law's will left him only $200 of a $40,000 estate. He applied for and got a Legal Aid certificate, then had a go at breaking the will—but the judge ruled it valid.

Amy Edith Gwendoline Greenwood was taken to divorce court by her husband, Herbert, who had the socialized suing system backing his claim that she refused to let him bathe more than once a week. But the judge granted the decree to the wife instead, noting that Mr. Greenwood had once written her: "The best Christmas present you could give me would be to jump in the river."

Mrs. Doris Sudell, 35, of Ansdell Road, Blackpool, entered a suit for negligence against her hairdresser, Mary Evelyn Eckersall, claiming the ends of her hair fell off after a permanent wave. The judge rejected her evidence and muttered that "this legal aid is really becoming scandalous."

But socialized suing pays off for most of its beneficiaries, statistics indicate. The Law Society, which administers the scheme, claims that in the first four years only 5,304 cases it backed were lost, against 59,959 cases won or settled out of court. Sample win: The widow and two daughters of Thomas Richard Hollis, killed by a fall of stone at Gresford Colliery, sued the National Coal Board—itself a socialized institution—and were awarded £2,500, or $7,500.

The government, while financing the legal victory of a private litigant, often discovers that it is inflicting a defeat upon one of its own nationalized industries. Thus the celebrated case of Starkey vs. Railway Executive concerned a lady who won damages from the socialized transport system for injuries suffered when a train moved as she alighted.

Often the Law Society makes quite sure it can't lose a case—by backing the litigants on both sides. It supported, all the way into the Court of Appeals, both Miss Diana Grace Rains-Bath, a young lady who claimed she suffered damages during a stage show at the Brighton Hippodrome, and also the defendant who was charged with negligence, Ralph Slater, the hypnotist. Miss Rains-Bath, wending her way along this legal lane, was awarded £1,132, or more than $3,000.

On occasion the taxpayers' funds are thrown behind as many as three sides to a lawsuit. These triangles tend, naturally, to involve marital matters. For example, Legal Aid successfully supported the case of the Reverend Kenneth Caesar Davis, vicar of Hawley, near Blackwater, Surrey, who sought a decree of judicial separation from his wife. But it simultaneously backed the separate cases of the wife, Mrs. Winifred Eileen Davis, and of a person named as corespondent —and succeeded in convincing the judge that neither had misbehaved. The court found that the estrangement of the vicar of Hawley and his spouse was due largely to theological differences; the wife was more "High Church" than her husband.

American jurisprudence is rooted deeply in English law, and, though their paths have long since parted, an American cannot help but be fascinated by the British switch to socialism in the courtroom, and at its general acceptance. It is almost universally lauded. Except for a few vigorous dissenters, who have never organized in opposition, the island's lawyers approve of the scheme and have signed up to accept fees from it. It was conceived during the Churchill coalition government, enacted under Attlee, and now is about to be vastly expanded with bipartisan support. The British press approves. Scores of crusty judges have criticized its operation from the bench, but they are rated old and conservative, soon to be heard no more.

Actually it was a judge, T. M. Backhouse, who summed up the

favorable British attitude early this year. Mrs. Hannah Sutton, of New Balderston, Newark, came before him at Nottingham Divorce Court. The judge noted that she had had grounds for divorce nine years ago, but could not afford to hire a lawyer. When socialized law came into force in 1950, she was too proud to accept such aid, but kept saving money until she could finance the action herself. Said Judge Backhouse:

"She should not go away thinking she has done anything clever. She has merely been very stupid." Legal aid is paid for by Mrs. Sutton herself, and by others through taxation, he observed, and it "is not charity."

Like socialized medicine, it springs from the deep British desire for "fair shares for all." But its development has followed a rather different course.

Socialized medicine is thoroughly government-run, through the Ministry of Health. In the matter of law, on the contrary, the government has for the first time in history handed over a major function to a private organization, the Law Society, Britain's equivalent of the American Bar Association, financing it with governmental grants-in-aid.

The Law Society now has about 1,000 full-time employees at work on the scheme, including 24 divorce solicitors traveling all over the country to mass-produce the dissolution of marriages. But most of the work is done part-time by attorneys in regular practice, who are paid two and a half guineas apiece—$7.34—whenever they meet in local committees to decide to accept or reject petitions for Legal Aid certificates. A session lasts about three hours, and about nine minutes are allotted to consideration of the average application. About three out of four are granted.

Once an applicant has obtained his certificate he can, except in certain divorce actions, choose his own attorney from an approved panel; the lawyer handles the case from there on, but is pledged to take a 15 per cent reduction from his normal "profit" on such a case.

The aided client may pay nothing at all toward these legal fees, or he may be required to make a "contribution." This depends on the prior findings of the National Assistance Board, the same government agency which hands out the dole to jobless folk. Indeed, unless the body certifies that the applicant's "disposable income" and "disposable capital" are small, he cannot get a certificate for Legal Aid at all.

Such contributions, usually on the easy installment plan, had provided the equivalent of about $5.9 million to finance the Law Society's program from the start of operations through January of this year. The government had chipped in with about $7 million, a figure which does not include work of the National Assistance Board. A third source of revenue, over $3.3 million, was court costs recovered from unsuccessful opponents of those granted legal aid.

The total is but the faintest fraction of the cost of socialized medicine, and *The Law Times* comments that "the price does not by modern standards seem high." Retorts A. A. Martineau, a distinguished lawyer who has criticized some phases of the scheme: "That's what they said about the illegitimate baby—'It's only a little one.' "

The baby is growing. So far Legal Aid has been largely confined to civil actions in what is called the High Court of Justice, which is really a body of courts handling the larger claims and divorce actions. Legal Aid has almost taken over its Divorce Division. Now the system will, within a few months, be extended to the County Court, handling smaller civil suits, and the expectation is that a rash of landlord-tenant cases will result.

The Law Society would also like to see Legal Aid extended to the criminal courts, and it has constantly urged the establishment of informal legal-advice centers all around the country.

When socialized law enters a courtroom, it replaces not a complete vacuum but an older form of assistance to poor litigants, quite similar to that employed in the U.S. Under this older scheme an impoverished person might have a lawyer assigned to him, without choice and without legal fee. The only lawyer likely to volunteer for this profitless service has been the young fellow, short of clients and eager for experience.

It is generally agreed that government-supported Legal Aid has helped many who would not otherwise have obtained justice. The London *Economist* has cited approvingly the case of an old lady badly injured by a careless errand boy on a cycle; with Legal Aid she sued the small uninsured shopkeeper who employed him, and won £1,000. The defendant didn't have that kind of money, but said: "I'll pay her thirty bob a week while I can."

Criticisms, when voiced, have taken myriad forms—one of them being that Britain's socialized law, like socialized medicine, extends its benefits to foreigners.

Mr. Justice Hilbery was surprised when two subjects of Iraq appeared before him, both of them granted Legal Aid. "Do you and I subscribe for people who are not English to litigate?" he inquired. "And do we pay for their litigation in English courts?" The barrister before him said such was the law, and the case would be heard in London instead of Baghdad unless his Lordship could provide a magic carpet. Sighed the judge: "I only wish I could."

Roman Kloss, a Pole, was injured at work in England and was

granted a Legal Aid certificate after emigrating to America. He booked round-trip passage from the States to press his suit. Asked Mr. Justice Ormerod: "Why is he still an assisted person if he is able to travel to America and back?" Replied counsel Roger Willis: "The situation does seem a little strange."

The case of Ammar vs. Ammar last year established that a husband on Cyprus, sued for divorce in England, could apply for Legal Aid to pay his travel expenses from the one island to the other so that he could defend the case.

Judges have taken an unkindly view of cases in which Legal Aid has backed both contestants though it was apparent neither could extract any money from the other.

Mrs. Jubilee Bennett, 64, of London, sued for damages when, she claimed, an Alsatian dog named Prince butted her in the pit of the stomach, sending her wrong end to. The defendant, Albert Wilson, maintained instead that Mrs. Bennett was dragged off her feet by her own spaniel, Rex, during a dogfight. Both cases had the full backing of Legal Aid, to which they contributed nothing because neither had any ready cash. Ruling in favor of Prince and his owner, his Lordship inquired:

"Suppose this action had been successful, what damages could have been recovered?" Attorney H. Lester, Mrs. Bennett's attorney, replied: "None. It might be, however, that the defendant's future financial position, possibly by winning a football pool, might have been improved. It is always a contingency to be taken into account."

Even within the Law Society there is much sympathy for people who are sued under Legal Aid and found to be in the right. Unless they themselves can qualify for support from the taxpayer, they must foot their own lawyers' bills through the High Court and sometimes even into the Court of Appeals. Ordinarily they can recover little or none of their costs from the subsidized plaintiff.

Frederick W. C. Woodham, of Graylandsroad, Peckham, got a job sorting out animal skins at Long-lane, Southwark, for Britz Bros., Ltd. He stayed just long enough to collect a week's wages; later he filed suit claiming he had contracted dermatitis. He lost. Said Justice Stable:

"This man is legally aided, and his contribution for his own cost is assessed as nil. It is no good making any order for costs against him. I shall go on protesting against this system under which the state subsidizes litigants and then does not pay the costs of the other side when the assisted person loses. I have protested before but nobody listens and nobody, I suppose, ever will."

HENRY GEMMILL

April 6, 1955

Life in Berlin

BERLIN—Most Berliners today, caught between two irreconcilable economic systems, are living a day-to-day, hand-to-mouth existence. Their chief interest lies in a fight for survival.

On one side is the "normal" economic system through which goods are bought and sold at fairly reasonable prices; on the other flourishes the black market. It is possible for the Berliner to avoid the latter and still exist; he can buy the rationed minimum essentials at controlled prices more or less in keeping with his wages. For this reason, the money situation here, violently abnormal as it is, does not represent inflation of the kind Germany knew 23 years ago.

But for anything on the luxury side—butter, a piece of candy, a new suit of clothes or, of course, an American cigarette—he must turn to the black market and pay prices fantastically out of range of his income.

For food he is best off if he is a heavy worker, for then he gets Lebensmittel card No. 1 authorizing 2,473 calories a day. This, along with other ration categories, is almost certain to be reduced in Berlin, as it has already been in the American zone of Germany.

Hans Pielmeier, for example, is employed by the Reichsbahn as a railway laborer in Berlin. A 49-year-old ex-soldier, he lives with his wife in a two-room apartment in the Russian section. Released from a prisoner-of-war camp last September, he had been in the Wehrmacht six years. Before the war he was an independent grocer.

A couple of days after his return to Berlin he registered with the German labor office in his district and was given a job as slater. This lasted about two months, and then collapsed because of lack of material. Soon after, he got his present job with the railway. He works 10 hours a day starting at seven in the morning and five hours on Saturday. The work is common labor—repairing tracks, carrying equipment from one place to another, unloading trains.

Hans is paid 55 reichsmarks a week, minus 10 reichsmarks for social security. At the current exchange rate, this translates into $4.50 a week net, but the actual buying power of the mark is closer to about 35 cents so that in effect he receives about $15.75 a week.

With his food ration card, Hans can buy enough food to provide him with a breakfast of groats (coarse cracked wheat or oats), two or three pieces of bread and ersatz coffee; lunch of soup, potatoes, sometimes a small piece of meat; afternoon snack of bread and ersatz coffee; and supper of soup with bread and potatoes. Although enough to eat, this diet is monotonously unvarying and it is seriously deficient in vitamins provided by fruits and vegetables. Vitamin deficiency is a universal complaint in Berlin; it is causing tooth decay, gum diseases and skin disturbances. There is an unhealthy sallowness in the complexions of most of the Berliners one sees.

Because his diet is so dull and because it rarely affords him as much as he would really like to eat, food is a major preoccupation with Hans, as with almost all Berliners.

The ration category in which Hans belongs is determined by the district nutrition office, on the basis of the evidence which Hans produces. This includes an authorization stamped by the labor office, a job certificate from the employer testifying to the type of work and the number of hours devoted to it during the past month, and the control-receipt from last month's ration card (a new card is issued each month). This involves not only a good deal of running around from one place to another, but also endless standing in line.

Hans must spend about four reichsmarks a day for food, which takes a sizable portion of his 45 reichsmarks a week. He pays 60 reichsmarks a month for his little apartment. He has little left for clothing, household articles and recreation. It doesn't matter too much because clothing at least is simply not available through normal channels. He can get certificates for such things as cloth, shoes, shirts, gloves, but the articles themselves are not to be had except on the black market. On the black market where it is plentiful cloth for a suit would cost him between 2,000 and 5,000 reichsmarks.

If Hans had the money, he would buy it, for there is no more moral compunction about the black market among Berliners than there is among the occupying forces who help sustain it. But Hans doesn't have the money; the only way he could get it would be by selling valuable personal possessions—diamonds especially—which he either never had or has long since disposed of. His story is that the Russians stole everything; true or not, it is one of the most common refrains in Berlin.

There are, however, many things in Berlin which Hans can buy without recourse to the black market. Dishes, kitchen utensils, household articles of many types are available in the hundreds of small shops which are springing up in ever increasing numbers amid the ruins. Prices, although relatively reasonable compared with the black market, are far higher than in prewar times, because of the general shortage of material and the fact that so many things which were formerly machine-made are now hand-made.

For Hans, his income mostly exhausted by the cost of food and rent, they are too expensive.

It is the same with recreation. Every day Berlin offers a wide variety of operas, symphonic concerts, ballets and chamber-music concerts, as well as plays and movies. But it is costly—six to eight reichsmarks for a mediocre seat at a concert or opera, and two reichsmarks for the same at a movie.

Hans is not, however, too much concerned about this; his work is hard, and he is sufficiently content to go to bed early. Besides, he has a piano at home, and he plays relatively well, accompanying his wife as she sings Schubert and Schuman. An hour or so of this is enough relaxation after 10 hours of hard, dull work.

What Hans thinks about during those hours is not difficult to reconstruct. An intelligent man used to better things, he has a pervading sense of self-pity. He cannot and will not adjust to the idea that he personally is guilty for the war and the fruits of war, although he is willing enough to place that guilt on the Nazi leaders. He feels himself, rather, a victim of forces he could neither prevent nor control—a line of thinking which would probably bring him into the Communist fold were it not for the fact that for him Communism is indistinguishable from Russians, for whom he has no love, although he is by no means as bitter against them as many of his fellow Berliners.

Whether or not he ever had Nazi sympathies, Hans is violently nationalistic. Like almost all Germans, he cannot think beyond Germany and her present sorrows. He is aware that all Europe is suffering, but it is an awareness that does not really impinge upon his consciousness. As to his own future, he can only be hopeless— it is simply a question of going on from day to day. As far as accomplishing anything is concerned, his life is finished and he knows it. But he is reasonable enough to evaluate his own situation and see that it could be far worse. He survived the war, he has a place to live and his ration card in fact puts him in a kind of aristocracy.

It is somewhat misleading to regard Hans as an average Berliner. In the utter confusion of the lives and activities of the three million inhabitants of this smashed, sprawling city there is no such thing as an average man. Hans is typical only of his class—the holders of ration card No. 1. As such he is far better off than most people in Berlin.

At the other end of the scale is the person who has no job and no money to buy food on the black market. Hilga, for example, is a pretty 25-year-old girl, a waitress by profession. Like thousands of other waitresses and waiters she is jobless. She sold her rings and whatever else she could and for a while was able to buy black-market food. But now the money is mostly gone and she is totally dependent on the food provided by her ration card, No. 5, the lowest issued.

She is not starving precisely, but there is a lot more to hunger than simply collapsing on the street. There is gradual weakening; there are physical disorders, emotional unbalance and above all an obsession about food that is unbelievable. With nothing to do except look for work she knows does not exist, she is rapidly becoming a psychopathic case. She sleeps as much as she can and then she goes for walks, very often past American messes simply to smell the food cooking.

Hilga's one and admitted desire now is to become the consort of an American officer and share in his wealth of food and cigarettes; this would be as near to paradise as she can currently contemplate. But it is not so easy; those positions, too, are already mostly taken. It is doubtful if she will turn to professional prostitution; it is not, in Berlin, an especially lucrative profession.

Multiplied by thousands of unemployed men and women in Berlin also subsisting on ration card No. 5, Hilga's psychology, by virtue of its abnormality alone, is ominous. There is a fog of utter depression in this city so deep as to be impenetrable. The suicide rate is high, and will go higher as the food rations are cut further. If Berlin is a criterion, Germany is well on the way to being the slum of Europe.

Joseph E. Evans

Berlin Portrait—13 Years Later

BERLIN—Otto Klinke, a skilled machine tool operator who owns his peaked-roof house near West Berlin's city limits, has never had it so good. The same goes for most other West Berliners, including Bruno Wawrzyniak, an electrical plant worker, and Hans Thimann, a city government interpreter.

But because their city lies 100 miles behind the Iron Curtain, they know their new prosperity wouldn't last long if Nikita Khrushchev triggered another blockade of West Berlin to try to enforce his demand that the Western Allies end their occupation of the city. Even temporary interruptions and harassment of traffic to Berlin —a more likely Red move because it would involve less risk of war —could tarnish the West Berliners' new and glowing prosperity.

There's danger such action could make Western buyers uncertain of deliveries, leading to a drop-off in orders and an economic slow-down here.

Visit the homes and apartments of the Wawrzyniaks, the Klinkes and the Thimanns in this isolated city and you readily see how im-measurably better off they are now than a decade ago—and how much more difficult it would be to prevent a drastic drop in their living standards if the Reds again interfered with traffic to Berlin.

Bruno Wawrzyniak, a slim, 33-year-old machinist employed lo-cally by Germany's giant Siemens electrical company, recalls that be-fore the last blockade he and his family, like other West Berliners, lived in an economy still numbed by defeat in World War II. They were ill-housed in bombed buildings, what little clothing they had was of poor quality and often threadbare, and there were no such things as modern conveniences or luxuries. The blockade could not worsen this. The blockade's main impact was a reduction in food, fuel and electricity.

During the last blockade Bruno and his dark-haired wife Christa, and their young child shared a crowded bomb-damaged apartment in the Spandau district of Berlin. Gas was rationed and home elec-tricity was cut off for all but two hours daily. "You had to do all your day's cooking in that period," relates Christa, a slightly plump woman in a beige dress and red "party" apron.

Today, Bruno, Christa, their baby Michael and 12-year-old Peter, who wants to become a "rocket expert," live in a small but sunny apartment in a three-year-old housing project. It's situated in a nearly self-contained community of modern factories and workers' apartments roughly in the center of West Berlin.

In 1948, the Siemens' factory, unlike some, managed to keep its workers busy, but, as Bruno recalls, "everything had been impro-vised after the war damage and the dismantlement of machinery by the Russians. We made electric irons, hot plates, anything we could, from whatever materials were available." Because power was rationed, the factory was shut down 20 per cent of the time.

There were few goods on which Bruno could spend his meager pay in the controlled market and "three pounds of bread cost the better part of a week's wages" on the prospering black market.

Today, Bruno can afford to live well, though not unusually so, for a skilled German worker his age. For working 44 hours weekly, he grosses $139 a month, some $39 more than the average gross monthly wage for male workers in West Germany, including unskilled.

Out of his take-home pay of $120, Bruno, who believes in eating well, gives $72 to Christa, most of it going for food. His solidly built apartment costs him $24 monthly, including heat and electricity. Another $12 is spent on a monthly life insurance premium, books, a tax for owning a radio, movies and pocket money for Bruno, who doesn't need much since Siemens serves a subsidized lunch that costs him only 15 cents and the plant is only eight minutes away on foot. The remaining $12 is saved for larger purchases, such as clothing and furniture.

Once a year, under Siemens' profit-sharing scheme for employees, Bruno gets a bonus. His share received this year was $240, which he immediately spent on clothing for the whole family, including a fur coat for Christa, an extra loudspeaker in the kitchen hooked up to his living-room radio, a fancy five-lamp brass chandelier for the parlor and new wallpaper for the kitchen and bathroom. Past bonuses have gone into his solid, upholstered living-room furniture.

Bruno is proudest, though, of his appliances, a striking symbol of how far he has come in the past decade. If another crippling Berlin blockade or some other mishap doesn't prevent it, he'd like to add a vacuum cleaner and a washing machine—currently the rage in West Germany—to his six-cubic-foot refrigerator, electric range and 20-gallon hot water boiler over his bathtub.

"If people can talk about rockets to the moon," reasons Bruno, "I figure I should at least be able to have a completely mechanized household."

He is somewhat bewildered by all the current proposals for easing tension over Berlin. But he nods agreement when his wife declares: "They should leave things just the way they are."

Maintenance of the improved living standards of the Wawrzyniaks and other West Berlin families requires more than a steady flow of food, clothing and consumer goods from West Germany; it also requires a flow of raw materials to the factories that provide these families with their livelihood, and the delivery of these factories' products to markets in the West. The city's economic growth makes this transportation chore a bigger one today than at the time of the last blockade.

Despite today's bigger cargo planes, military men here believe it would be practically impossible for a new airlift to haul the 19,000 tons of shipped-in fresh meat and fruits, coal and gasoline, steel, bricks and industrial raw materials consumed here daily.

There are many indexes that show how living standards in West Berlin vastly surpass pre-blockade standards of 1948 and even exceed pre-World War II standards by a considerable degree. For example, this encircled city, about the same area as New York's boroughs of Queens and the Bronx together, today has 130,000 private passenger cars, compared with practically none in 1948. Its 133,500 television sets are more than double the total only two years ago. More significant, only 74,000 West Berliners were unemployed in March, compared with about 300,000 idle in 1950, when the city already had made remarkable progress along the road to comparative prosperity after the blockade.

The average West Berliner now consumes 2,900 calories daily, compared with only 1,880 during the airlift. Not only does he eat more, but he eats a lot of things not available in the spring of 1949, such as fresh meat, fruits, vegetables, milk and eggs. His diet even before the last blockade was exceedingly drab, and during the Red stoppage consisted largely of dehydrated and canned foods to save space and weight on planes.

"We had too much to starve on but not enough to ever get fat," recalls Hans Thimann, the West Berlin city government employee.

Mr. Thimann, like Bruno Wawrzyniak, also insists the Berlin crisis hasn't affected his plans or spurred him to find work at a safer distance from the Russians. "We've made no plans to leave," insists the debonair, dark-haired Mr. Thimann as he sips straight Scotch whisky German-style, as an after-dinner cordial, in his spacious, well-furnished apartment. "The people of Berlin could stand another blockade," adds the 35-year-old interpreter. But a visit with Hans and his wife Marietta in their middle-class apartment near Tempelhof Airport soon reveals that Hans has much more at stake now than in 1948 should the Reds again tighten the screws in Berlin.

Hans arrived in West Berlin in 1948, equipped only with foreign language training and a knack for surviving. A native of Goerlitz, which is located in the Russian-occupied Eastern Zone, Hans in World War II had "fought the Americans in Italy until they took me prisoner." When he was refused admission to his home-town university because he was the son of a businessman, he went to Leipzig and studied English, which he now speaks fluently.

After coming to West Berlin, Hans managed to land two jobs that in 1948 gave him a total monthly income equivalent to about $60. Although this was more than most Berlin workers made, "still I never had any money," he recalls. A single man then, he found a small furnished room only about 10 feet square in the bomb-ravaged city and spent a good deal of his time trying to keep warm.

"Each family got only 50 pounds of coal for the whole winter, so you can imagine how cold it was. I had the lowest category ration book. And for food we had only corned beef hash and other canned meats and those infernal dehydrated potatoes." He recalls how families went into the Tiergarten and other parks to chop down trees for fuel.

"Only the Berliners could have gotten through it. The spirit in those days was terrific," declares Hans.

Today, Hans and Marietta, whom he married in 1953, live comfortably and perhaps even luxuriously in some respects—on a combined after-tax income of $240 a month. "We don't pinch pennies," says Hans, whose thick horn-rimmed glasses and receding black hair give him the air of a German junior executive. A glance around his well-furnished 12-foot by 24-foot living room—very large for Germany—and a look at the Thimann's spending habits confirm his statement.

The Thimanns, who have no children, figure they spend $75 a month for food, including liquor and snacks for occasional parties they give. That doesn't include dining out at expensive restaurants such as that of the famous Kempinski Hotel on West Berlin's neon-glittering Kurfuerstendamm. "We like to eat out or go to the theater four or five times a month," says Marietta, who figures this adds up to about $25 a month.

The Thimanns' apartment costs $40 monthly, including heat, gas and electricity. They also enjoy the convenience of a telephone ($5 monthly) and a five-year-old Volkswagen, bought secondhand, which Hans estimates costs $25 a month to operate. If the Berlin crisis doesn't erupt, the couple will motor to Finland this summer.

Hans, who didn't have money or much opportunity to spend what he had 10 years ago, today manages to salt away $70 a month in savings—a lot by German standards. Hans explains he likes to pay cash for everything, but more important, "I want to save for a rainy day." So far he and Marietta, a secretary at a foreign consulate here, have saved about $1,200. Hans has been following West Germany's skyrocketing stock market, but so far hasn't bought any shares.

EDMUND K. FALTERMAYER

May 20, 1959

Saga of a Salesman

MADRID—This is a trivial tale about a middle-aged American salesman named Ed Kreisler, who is surprised to find himself working in a strange country. Or maybe it is a rather important story that will give you some idea of what the high-tension variety of U.S. super-merchandising could—and can—accomplish in the more leisurely lands of Europe.

Ed represents some of the things many Europeans dislike about

Americans. He talks fast and he talks bluntly; he has an eye for the quick buck. Having started at three colleges and lacked patience to finish any of them, he doesn't pretend to be a highly cultured gentleman; probably the American Government would never pick him to head a diplomatic mission.

Yet in less than a year this heavy-set, balding businessman has become one of the most popular Americans in Spain. His friends and fans include a number of high officials of the Spanish government and a much greater number of impoverished but equally haughty artisans scattered all around this dusty country.

At age 41, Ed Kreisler is a confirmed job-hopper who started on the West Coast and kept moving east until he finally hopped the Atlantic. In Los Angeles he learned the fundamentals of merchandising as an employee of a department store. Next stop was Akron's M. O'Neil Co., a May Co. store, where he was a buyer of men's furnishings.

Then he drifted into a quite different selling medium, acting in such radio soap operas as *Life Can Be Beautiful* and such cereal serials as *Superman;* he appeared also on the stage and TV. By 1949 Ed was back at straight selling, vending ladies' hats in a New York specialty shop. A year later he left and with his brother formed the Kreisler Corp., importing foreign movies, French fashions and food. Early last year he decided to take off for Europe, just for a vacation.

Soon after arriving here in Madrid, Ed wandered into a side-street bazaar which was flying a tattered flag bearing the faded words, "Official Handicraft Exhibition of Spain." He intended to buy a souvenir or two, but as he looked over the wooden castanets, black lace mantillas, carvings of Don Quixote and white porcelain whisky bottles that played "The Toreador Song" when tilted, all he could think of was the abominable salesmanship. "They were doing business like we did two hundred years ago," he says.

Ed Kreisler had to tell somebody it was all wrong. He soon confronted a tall and austere gentleman, Señor Jacinto Alcantara, whose sense of dignity is so profound that he serves as General Franco's chief of protocol. In addition he heads the government's Organización Sindical de Artesanía, which sells the work of 900,000 Spanish craftsmen through the Madrid handicraft exhibition and 15 smaller shops throughout the nation.

When Ed talked, the *señor* was sold. He offered to make Mr. Kreisler director of the Madrid store—on a gambler's terms. Ed wouldn't be paid a penny, except on sales brought in over and above those rung up the year before. So the salesman went to work last May, and several weeks ago Señor Alcantara totted up the results:

"During 1953," he says, "our store's sales were 1.3 million pesetas (about $32,000), and that was the highest they had ever been. But last year, with Mr. Kreisler on the job for just seven months, they rose to 3.7 million pesetas (around $92,000), and this year they should be considerably higher. Mr. Kreisler is just what we've needed," confides Señor Alcantara. "You see, we're artists—but Mr. Kreisler, he's a practical businessman."

When he walked back into the store as boss, Ed recalls, "the Spanish salesgirls resented me terribly at first, because I was disturbing their tranquillity. Most of them didn't care if they sold one peseta's worth of stuff a day, or a thousand." After a few days he decided to try the old soap opera approach. He called them together, and through an interpreter—for he spoke nary a word of Spanish—he made a speech, brief but impassioned.

"Do you girls realize," he asked them, "that thousands of talented workmen and their families all over Spain are going to live in poverty unless you get busy and start selling their work to tourists who are anxious to buy?" The señoritas, though ruffled, began putting more oomph in their selling, he says. "Soon some of 'em were coming to me and bragging a bit about an unusually big sale they had just made."

The next step was to hire some salespeople who could speak English. Although Americans and Britons were by far the exhibition's best customers, and although there was a brightly colored Union Jack with the claim "We Speak English" pasted on the front window, Ed found that the only employees who had an inkling of the language were a Madrid University student who worked from four to five in the afternoon and a Spanish girl who could say "Hello."

Today English-speaking souvenir seekers are welcomed by five Spanish salespeople who can speak their language fluently; one of these can also manage French and German; Mr. Kreisler's assistant, petite and pretty Señora Araceli Pujol, is at home in all these plus Portuguese.

Mr. Kreisler shifted his attention to publicity. "The shop was here," he says, "but it was a secret." Ed has printed thousands of brightly colored postcard-sized advertisements which read: "Two places you must visit in Madrid: 1. Del Prado Museum. 2. Official Handicraft Exhibition of Spain." Ed saw that these cards were strategically placed in all Madrid's leading hotels—which co-operated willingly, perhaps partly because they knew the exhibition is a personal pet of several top officials in Dictator Franco's regime.

Whenever any celebrity hits town he's invited around to the exhibition, and somehow a newspaper reporter and photographer usually show up, too. Greer Garson, Gloria Swanson, Senator Sparkman, cartoonist Al Capp and leading Spanish film stars have co-operated in such publicity—and to prove it their photos now hang on the shop's walls, amidst signs proclaiming such sentiments as "We Package and Ship All Over the World."

More important than his merchandising methods, Mr. Kreisler figures, is the advice he's giving Spanish craftsmen on how to redesign their work to match the tastes of tourists—especially big-spending Americans.

His suggestions are passed on every day to the artisans who come to the shop with paper bags filled with sterling-silver jewelry, pockets full of castanets, or battered cardboard suitcases bulging with handbags.

A maker of hand-tooled leather bags, for example, will be urged to replace the customary cheesecloth lining with silk, rayon or soft leather. "A finer lining only costs the artisan about thirty-five cents more, and it can change a 'no sale' into a cash transaction," says Ed. "Ladies attracted to these beautiful bags are repelled if they see cheap linings they know would wear out in no time."

Tablecloth makers are warned against using too many different colored threads and extremely fancy lace edging. American wives hesitate at buying such stuff, for fear it would be ruined in the washing machine. This would never occur to a Spanish craftsman; chances are he's never seen a washing machine.

To carry the gospel, Ed Kreisler is willing to travel many miles— the rocky miles to Toledo, for instance. There he and Señora Pujol talked with one of the famed craftsmen who create some of the world's loveliest jewelry by delicately scratching antique Arabian designs into hard Toledo steel and then pounding slender strands of gold wire into the metal with tiny hammers.

This particular workman had been supplying the store with cuff links—ones no bigger than a dime, the kind preferred by Spanish gentlemen. Ed suggested he try making some the size of half dollars, the kind preferred by many Americans—well, anyway, Americans on the loose in Europe. "When I translated Mr. Kreisler's suggestion into Spanish," says Señora Pujol, "this artisan turned to me in amazement and exclaimed, 'Este Americano esta loco completamente.' "

But he followed the crazy American's advice and made two dozen of the outsized cuff links. "The first day we put them in the case we sold eight pair at $4.25 a set," reports Ed. "And before the week was out we had sold them all."

Another reluctant convert to the Kreisler philosophy of handicrafts is 43-year-old Juan Manuel Arroyo Ruiz de Luna, of Madrid, who, like his father and grandfather before him, is a maker of tiles.

He bakes them in his wife's kitchen oven. Up until a few months ago he decorated them with ornate landscapes painted in anemic greens, yellows and reds, and with dull reproductions of Goya masterpieces which hang in the Prado.

Mr. Kreisler sat down with Señor de Luna one afternoon and suggested he try making some more simple tiles—each perhaps bearing a single flower, fish or animal. He suggested, too, that the craftsman switch from Goya's somber shadings to the more vibrant colors of El Greco—one thing he might do would be a six-tile reproduction of El Greco's "Burial of the Count of Orgaz," which tourists flock to see in Toledo's Church of Santo Tomé.

Señor de Luna still insists that "we Spaniards don't like bright colors, and I don't like to work with them." But he's following Mr. Kreisler's advice, "and I'm selling more than twice as many tiles. My girls Palama and Mercedes had only one pair of shoes apiece before Mr. Kreisler came; now they each have three. My son Manuel is attending a better school. For my wife there is now a little candy and some flowers. And sometimes on Sundays we all go for a ride in a taxi."

When he first began talking to the craftsmen, Ed was forced to rely for interpreting on the store's English-speaking university student, and the results were often disastrous. "This lad translated what I said word for word," recalls Mr. Kreisler, "and because I was pretty blunt, my advice didn't go down too well." Nowadays any translation is handled by Señora Pujol, and it runs about like this:

MR. KREISLER: "The colors you're using on these wine jugs may be all right for Spanish customers, but they're 'way too dull for American tastes."

SEÑORA PUJOL: "Señor Kreisler thinks your earthenware jugs are beautiful and real works of art."

MR. KREISLER: "What's more, these jugs are too ornate. They've got to be made simpler, or the American tourists won't buy 'em."

SEÑORA PUJOL: "Señor Kreisler says the American tourists admire your jugs very much. He wonders if you would be willing to make some special jugs using simple designs and bright colors that are popular in the United States."

Ed must still keep a sharp eye on his sales staff to make sure they're not leaning on the counters gossiping in mile-a-minute Spanish when they should be waiting on customers. Some of his merchandising ideas—such as putting a bright spotlight on an apparently unsalable $440 slab of dreary leather sculpture—have flopped. His advice to artisans sometimes backfires; one jewelry maker learned how to redesign his product and then promptly sold all his wares to rival souvenir shops.

Some Spanish art lovers say Ed is corrupting handicraft traditions. He denies it. "Spanish craft has been bastardized by generations of artisans who each added their own elaborations; they've overdecorated something that was originally very simple and beautiful. I'm trying to get them to return to their old ways."

CARTER HENDERSON

March 23, 1955

Roots of French Travail

PARIS—What has brought France to the edge of chaos and civil war and now to at least a temporary semi-dictatorship?

The usual answer is parliamentary paralysis. But that cause is itself an effect. The root causes go deeper than Parliament; they are to be found in the postwar experiences of the French armed forces, and still further in the political psychology and recent history of the French people. And in these roots are some curious and possibly tragic ironies.

To be sure, parliamentary paralysis was what immediately precipitated the situation in which the strong-man government of General Charles de Gaulle, installed yesterday, seemed the only solution.

In any case few Frenchmen in or out of the National Assembly really believed, when they thought about it at all, that the unwieldy parliamentary machinery could keep creaking along indefinitely. It worked after a fashion—but it worked very badly indeed. Based on a weak Constitution, it made important decisions almost impossible except by crisis.

This way of doing government business was not so serious as long as "crisis" meant merely the fall of successive cabinets. But it was not edifying either; the people's disgust and cynicism toward the politicians in Paris became, over the postwar years, intense and total. Subconsciously at least the people, including the politicians, were ready for a drastic change if only something gave the parliamentary system a shove.

The shove came with the rebellion of the French generals in Algeria, who formed a military-civilian "Committee of Public Safety" there and clamored for the return of General de Gaulle after his twelve years of retirement from the government. Apparently

"Comprenez-vous charge account?"

this coup in Algeria was long and carefully planned with the co-operation of the armed forces in France. Thus it faced the French Government not just with a couple of dissident generals but with the united strength of the French armed forces on both sides of the Mediterranean. The army had entered politics in a very big way indeed.

Plainly confronted with a force against which the government was powerless, many deputies in the National Assembly understandably felt that De Gaulle was inevitable. Except among the Communists and a number of Socialists, a kind of bandwagon atmosphere developed, with deputies declaring for De Gaulle even though they would not have dreamed of doing any such thing just a few weeks ago.

In short, the bulk of the parliamentarians decided to commit political suicide because they were already fed up with their rickety machinery, because in their hearts they felt it had to go sooner or later anyway and, by far the most important, because the threat of an army coup gave them no real alternative.

But why did the military men finally arrive at a point of no return? Partly the answer is cumulative. Morale has inched downward year after year with defeat after defeat—World War II, Indochina, Suez. A tremendous emotional resentment against the restrictions of the politicians built up among the military officers. "Half-way operations," one man contemptuously comments. To understand this, one has only to visit the Pentagon in Washington and find the same kind of resentment, even now, against the political hamstringing of the military operations of the Korean War.

The military demanded an authoritarian De Gaulle government as the only way of saving France from anarchy or worse. But this does not mean that all French officers, any more than the parliamentarians who finally lined up for De Gaulle, are devoted to the man himself. The Gaullist movement among the military is more protest than positive program. Says one French officer: "For nearly twenty years we have been killing and being killed because the politicians would not let us win anything. They have made a complete mess. Surely De Gaulle can't do worse."

In other words, if at any time since World War II the Paris government could have made a clear-cut decision either to fight its colonial wars to the finish or else get out gracefully as did the British, last week's collapse might have been staved off. But Parliament could do neither; it let the Indochina war drag on for eight years, to end in ignominy, and it has been letting the Algerian war drift for nearly four years.

But the boiling hatreds are not confined to the officers alone. They are shared by most other Frenchmen. You would not believe this to walk around springtime Paris these past few days as the Republic tottered and civil war seemed hourly more imminent. The people seemed as busy and vital—and normal—as ever. "It's as though they were living in a dream world," says one foreign expert, "and this thing were happening in some other country."

The apathy was evident at the monster demonstration against De Gaulle the other day. It was dominated by Socialists and Communists, and there were a lot of placards proclaiming "Vive la Republique" and "No to Fascism." Yet the affair was tepid, seeming to arouse little enthusiasm among either the demonstrators or the bystanders at the Place de la Republique, where the parade wound up.

The apathy, however, is only apparent. What it masks is an almost unbelievable popular contempt for the politicians, and a longing to be touched again with greatness of France's past. In newsreel theatres people sit on their hands when politicians appear on the screen: they applaud when the Army is shown doing anything the least bit impressive. Again, it is not because the people love the

Army; they tend rather to be distrustful of it. It is simply that they want something, almost anything, to be proud of.

For the civilians too have seen the humiliating decline of France since the inglorious, and for Frenchmen unforgettable, defeat of World War II. And it is not only the military defeats. After the liberation had given them new hope of a new future at home, they saw instead the dismal political patterns of the prewar Third Republic repeating themselves—weak governments, falling cabinets, indecision and hopeless confusion. Politically, obviously, things were no better than before the war; in fact, they were constantly deteriorating.

Other circumstances intensify the angry disillusionment. The French can see that the U.S. is all over their country—"Like a skeleton across the land," one man puts it—with its troops and military installations, and this hardly helps make the French feel free and independent. Nor do the billions of dollars of American aid help, with the inherently patronizing implications of that aid. Many an ordinary Frenchman in self-defense turns the aid against the U.S. "Don't tell me the Americans are doing it for nothing," a cab driver will opine; "they're getting plenty out of it."

Thus anti-Americanism is to a considerable extent a lashing out that subconsciously springs from the Frenchman's own frustrations. This appears vividly in widespread criticism of the U.S. attitude toward the Anglo-French invasion of Suez in 1956. If the U.S. had kept hands off [instead of demanding, in the U.N., that the invasion be halted] a French officer insists, "we wouldn't be in this mess now." He reasons that the French would have been victorious in Egypt and gone on to clean up Algeria as well. The logic has some rather large defects, but you hear it all over; a French doctor vitriolically denounces Secretary of State Dulles for his "ruinous" Suez policy.

French frustration and its converse—the yearning to regain national greatness—also shows up in the tremendous sums of money France is pouring into the development of its own atomic bomb. It doesn't matter that the bomb will be primitive compared to those of the U.S. and Britain, or whether it will contribute anything at all to western defense; the all-important thing is that it is a French bomb.

All this helps explain why many French people—not just the military—are turning to De Gaulle as a symbol of hope. The hope is of stable government, and even more of a new French independence and a comeback on the world stage.

The feeling was palpable here in Paris the other night. At about 7:30 P.M. De Gaulle's car, with a huge siren-screaming police escort, raced into the back gate of the Elysee Palace where the General was to confer with President Rene Coty about taking over the government. There were scattered shouts of welcome from the people on the Champs Elysees; some started running to catch a glimpse. For blocks the people looked really happy.

But it was later that night that Paris responded in a big way. About midnight, after it was announced De Gaulle had agreed to form a government, streams of cars in many parts of the capital suddenly started tooting their horns (horn-blowing is forbidden, but no cop interfered), beep-beeping the V-signal, and this went on for hours. How much opinion it reflected can't be measured, but it didn't seem organized, and you got the inescapable impression that many people felt as though a great weight had been lifted.

That may prove ironic, because the new weight could be more oppressive; an authoritarian regime is coming in, and whether it will end with just a year or so of De Gaulle is far from certain.

Yet it is these same French people, after all, who created that condition—who voted for the weak Constitution in 1946, and who ever since have been voting into office the politicians they despise. The reasons they have done this lie in historical contradictions and conflicts in the French character.

On the one hand is the strong tradition, born of experience with authoritarians, of opposition to executive power—a deep suspicion of government coupled with a powerful jealousy of individual liberty. On the other hand is the enormous sense of national pride combined with an almost childlike national sensitivity.

In recent years the pride has been badly bruised, the sensitivity deeply hurt. The French have felt increasingly put upon by parliamentary whims, increasingly abused and misunderstood from abroad, until finally it no longer seemed possible to revive the reasons for pride without drastic political change. The armed forces rebellion in Algeria was the catalyst for an explosion long brewing in the whole armed forces, in parliamentary institutions, and in French psychology.

So it is that, while the French have been fighting a nationalist rebellion of the Algerian natives, there has paradoxically sprung from Algeria the spearhead of a new French nationalism. And so it is that the liberty-loving French have finally seen no other course but to turn to authoritarianism.

These are ironies that run deep in France. It remains to be seen whether they are also tragic ironies.

JOSEPH E. EVANS

June 2, 1958

TIME OUT FOR LEISURE

THE STRENUOUS LIFE

Home Plate

From the moment this week when blue-suited umpires in eight major-league and countless minor-league parks called "Play Ball" to the crisp October day which sees the last out in the World's Series, baseball dominates the American sports scene. And with good reason.

For baseball is more than America's recognized national game, which almost every American boy has tried to play. It is not only an American institution. It is the American national character in action.

Politics stops at the baseball diamond's edge. Ex-President Hoover, whom a sports writer called the truest fan who ever sat in the White House, is a familiar figure in photographs of World's Series spectators. Ex-President Truman watched a game in the unusually exciting 1949 championship series between the New York Yankees and the Brooklyn Dodgers, only to miss the decisive blow when his attention was distracted by some unwelcome affair of state.

Adlai Stevenson, on the other hand, proved himself unversed in the lore of the national pastime. Meeting Allie Reynolds, a part-Indian who acquired fame by pitching for the Yankees, Stevenson committed the grave *faux pas* of saying: "I wish I could *hit* like you." And the baseball fan vote went aglimmering.

What makes baseball such an authentic expression of the American national spirit? First, it is intensely dynamic, fast in execution, charged with the elements of suspense, uncertainty and crisis. Nothing can ever be taken for granted. The worst team in the league, on occasion, can rise up and beat the best team in the league. The rules make for frequent situations of intense drama, when everything seems to hinge on what will happen to the next pitch.

There could hardly be a better key to understanding the differences of American and British temperament than to watch in quick succession a baseball game and a cricket match. The action in the first is fierce and concentrated, in the second leisurely and diffused.

Tempers seldom rise above normal pitch among players and spectators during cricket matches, however keen the rivalry. In baseball, it's different. One of the Napoleonic figures of baseball was the renowned "Muggsy" McGraw, manager of the New York Giants, one of whose snarling axioms, which he frequently put into practice, was: "Good losers are easy losers."

Second, there is a "shirt sleeves to shirt sleeves" quality in baseball. Baseball stars rise and set. In a game that places a tremendous strain on the arm and leg muscles a player is a veteran at 30, an aging relic at 35 and an almost unheard-of phenomenon at 40. This makes for the quick turnover of personnel which has always been more characteristic of America than of Europe.

Indeed, the same player in the same game may be transferred from hero into scapegoat, and back again, as rapidly as a distinguished politician behind the Iron Curtain. The man whose costly muff or wild throw let the enemy score in the early innings may redeem himself with a resounding home run later in the day. This process can also be reversed. For the baseball fan, although passionate, is fickle in his loyalties.

Third, baseball, like the American Constitution, has qualities both of stability and of elasticity. A Rip Van Winkle waking up after a sleep of 50 years would find the essential rules of the game little changed. A proposal to change the number of Justices of the Supreme Court would probably excite less embittered rejection than a suggestion that a batter should be called out on two or four strikes, or go to first base on three or five balls.

The authority of the umpire, as absolute as that of the traffic cop, has remained undiminished for half a century. From his ruling there is no appeal. When the umpire, after viewing at close range one of the hairline plays in which baseball abounds, jerks up his thumb in the signal "Out" the player is out, even if half a dozen enraged teammates and 50,000 screaming fans in the stands voice long and loud dissatisfaction.

The methods of baseball competition have also remained much the same. At the top of the pyramid are two eight-club leagues, the American and the National. Each team plays each other team 22 games. At the end of the season the two winners meet in a best-of-seven-games series, somewhat chauvinistically called the World's Series. No team outside the United States ever competes, although baseball has long been popular in Canada and has also caught on in Mexico, Venezuela, Cuba and other Latin lands. Some excellent Latin-American players have made their way into the big leagues.

For almost half a century the roster of cities maintaining National and American League clubs remained unchanged. But changes in population and the magnetism of television, which has created some stay-at-home fans, have brought about shifts. The former Boston Braves are now the Milwaukee Braves. Both the quality of their playing and the income of their owners improved noticeably after the migration from Boston, where they had been playing to empty stands, to Milwaukee, where the eager populace has been packing the new stadium to see big-league baseball.

The St. Louis Browns are now the Baltimore Orioles, and moved up one modest notch, from last place to seventh, in the first year of the transfer. The Philadelphia Athletics, a once-great team long in the doldrums, have started a new career in Kansas City. The baseball empire now includes Los Angeles and San Francisco.

Baseball, a rock of stability in many aspects, has succumbed to one modern change. A livelier ball and shorter fences have led to an inflation in baseball scores, comparable with the inflation of the dollar. Home run records have gone up; stolen-base records have gone down. The preferred strategy today is not to risk being put out trying to steal a base when a Willie Mays, a Ted Williams or some other mighty man with the bat may be coming up to drive you in without risk with a home run.

WILLIAM HENRY CHAMBERLIN

April 20, 1956

Wheeling and Dealing

HAVANA—Professor Vernon Stone, late of Las Vegas, runs a most extraordinary school here—his scholars do nothing but play cards and roulette.

Play is perhaps not the precise word; the students work at their gambling a minimum of two hours a day, seven days a week. Among the pupils, an earnest lot, are a Cuban secret-service agent, a weight-lifting champion, a precocious 17-year-old, an accountant and a policeman. They're vying for some of the most lucrative jobs in this hustling city of riffle and roll—card dealers and wheel operators in the fancy new gambling casinos opening here.

Dealing "21" or spinning a roulette wheel in the gaming rooms is no job for amateurs—at least from the point of view of the house. Subtleties of an operator's manner and movement (mostly unnoticed by the casual player) largely determine how a game goes—and how the house fares. This is not to suggest that all is not aboveboard; it's merely that the casino keeper, like the retailer, operates on the principle that the greater the volume of business, the greater his profits are likely to be.

"The faster the money moves across the table—no matter what direction—the better the chances the house will end up winning in the long run," instructs bland, talkative Professor Stone, 45, a 24-year veteran in the business.

To educate Cubans in the arts of wheeling and dealing, Hilton Hotels International imported Mr. Stone two months ago from Las Vegas. His specific job: Train 25 to 30 native operators to handle the seven blackjack games and five roulette tables in the casino of the new Havana Hilton. (There will be two dice games, too, but they will be run by Americans.)

Mr. Stone started his card college six weeks ago in two rooms of an office building hard by the rising Havana Hilton, a structure that somewhat resembles a stack of light-blue dominoes. Donor Hilton pays the rent ($150 a month) and supplies $2,000 worth of equipment (four roulette tables, four blackjack stands). There's no tuition; the pupils merely contribute their time and whatever talent they may have.

Not just anybody can get into the school, and many of those who do make it flunk out after a few sessions. Most of the aspiring wheel-and-deal men were recommended by such influential folk as the chief of police, Havana lawmakers, or operators of top night spots. Of a total of about 150 original candidates, only about 45 are still in the running (though Mr. Stone says he hasn't yet told the luckless students for fear of alienating their patrons).

Competition for the 25 or so jobs at the Hilton is sharp, the rewards substantial. "A dealer here can make more money than a doctor, once he gets into the union," advises Mr. Stone, letting a pile of chips rattle through his well-manicured fingers. That's a bit of exaggeration perhaps, but not without some foundation. A union dealer earns $91 a week for a seven-hour, 20-minute working day and, if he's lucky, almost as much as that in tips. In contrast, take Armando Riva, 31, a Stone student studying to be a "21" dealer who makes just $300 a month now as a working accountant. Or consider Justo De Latorre, a stocky fellow with thick-lensed glasses who tells you he has two kids to support and earns only $200 a month (plus one meal a day) as a secret-service agent.

WILLIAM E. GILES

February 7, 1958

Out of the Mouths of Children

Q. Daddy, what is a sport?

A. A sport is a game, played indoors or outdoors, sometimes in teams, sometimes man to man.

Q. Like prize fighting, Daddy?

A. Well, no.

Q. Like professional football, Daddy?

A. Well, no.

Q. Well, what is a sport, Daddy?

A. Professional baseball.

Q. Is that the only one, Daddy?

A. Yes.

Q. That's funny, Daddy. Baseball is a sport, but football and prize fighting aren't. How is that?

A. The Supreme Court says so.

Yep, the Supreme Court said so just the other day, Son. Professional baseball is a sport, and not a business, so professional baseball does not come under the Sherman antitrust law. But professional football and boxing are not sports because they are business and so come under the Sherman law.

The reason for this strange discrimination, Mr. Justice Clark tried to explain in the majority decision which ruled pro football a business, comes about because 30-odd years ago baseball was ruled a sport by the Supreme Court. It was ruled not a business, because it was judged not to be engaged in interstate commerce to a great enough extent to come under the Sherman law. As late as 1953 in *Toolson v. New York Yankees,* the High Court upheld this ruling.

The ruling, of course, may have been meritorious all along.

But in 1955, in *U.S. v. International Boxing Club,* the High Court ruled that what applied to baseball did not apply to boxing.

And now, in *Radovich v. the National Football League,* the Supreme Court ruled that what applied to pro baseball did not apply to pro football.

"We continued to hold the umbrella over baseball because it was concluded that more harm would be done in overruling than in upholding" the original decision, Justice Clark explained—if that is quite the word. The reason was that "enormous capital had been invested in reliance on its permanence. Such reasons, of course, have not prevented the Supreme Court from overturning other previous decisions.

Thus what the Court has said is that baseball, with its vast farm systems and playing schedules reaching from Los Angeles to New York, is not in interstate commerce as much as boxing and pro football are, and thus that all other sports are businesses while baseball alone is a sport.

Q. I don't understand the differences, Daddy.

A. Don't worry, Son. Three of the justices are still shaking their heads about the decision. They can't see any differences between baseball and football and boxing, either.

Q. Well, Daddy, aren't you glad the other six are just judges and not umpires?

February 27, 1957

EDITORIAL

Up from Buffoonery

The rubric at the top of this column is "Reading for Pleasure." It has certainly been a pleasure to read Frank Graham, Jr.'s, *Casey Stengel: His Half Century in Baseball,* but if the make-up man had happened to pull a Stengelesque boner of his own and placed this review under the heading of "Reading for Business" it would still have made excellent sense.

Mr. Graham has probably never read Peter Drucker's book on the "practice of management," but with the famous skipper of the New York Yankees as his model and illustration he does better than most serious writers on the subject. Great as he has been as a clown, Casey Stengel has been still greater as a businessman in his profession.

As befits any book on Stengel, this one is studded with mad witticisms, laced with anecdote, and salted with a bubbling joy in the ups and downs of life. Casey's clowning, his mumbled orations (spoken in the oblique language known as Stengelese), his mimicry, and his habit of spinning (like the earth itself) on a tilted axis, make for some of the best fun since the disappearance of vaudeville. But all of this is mere byplay; the real value of Mr. Graham's work is that it offers a handbook on how to be crazy like a fox.

Casey first hit his stride as a purposeful madman when he was a rookie outfielder for Maysville, Kentucky, in the Blue Grass League. A bandy-legged recruit from the sandlots and pool halls of Kansas City, Casey was primarily concerned in those days with the problem of getting enough practice to develop his still highly clumsy skills. Since his manager couldn't be bothered with rookies, Casey resolved to combine base-running practice with his ordinary work in the outfield. Accordingly he would catch a fly ball, hurl it back to the infield and, almost simultaneously, toss his glove in the opposite direction. Taking out after the soaring glove, Casey would end his antics by sliding into it as it settled on the turf. As he explained to reporters: "I'm getting a jump on guys who waste time sitting around. I'm practicing catching, throwing, running and sliding all at once."

Casey soon realized that foolishness could have a double purpose: It could be used to mask an intention and it could also be made to pay off commercially as pure spectacle. Spectacle was uppermost in his mind on the occasion when he caught a fly ball with one hand while holding aloft a manhole cover with the other. However, when he doffed his cap to jeering fans in the Brooklyn baseball park and let a sparrow fly out of it, his purpose was not buffoonery. He was tired of being ridden by the bleacherites, and he used the sparrow to get a hostile crowd off his neck.

As manager of the Brooklyn Dodgers and the Boston Braves (then officially called the Bees) back in the thirties and early forties, Stengel had such poor material that he was forced to use his clowning to perk up the gate receipts. He did a wonderful job in those years, keeping his incredibly inept teams out of eighth place. Meanwhile he was cannily investing his money in Texas oil wells.

Since he never got a winner with Brooklyn or Boston, Casey, the seemingly inveterate clown, inevitably lost caste with the undiscerning. But George Weiss, the astute general manager of the New York Yankees, carefully watched Casey's work in the high minor leagues throughout the late 1940s, when the "clown" had winners at Milwaukee and at Oakland, California. Eventually Weiss brought Casey back to the big time as his field manager at Yankee Stadium. The rest, as hardly needs to be said, is a gorgeous history of almost unbroken success: eight pennants and six world's championships.

The Yankees are, of course, both rich and exceedingly well organized. But the Yankee teams which Casey Stengel has managed have never been so deep in talent that they could win without intelligent direction. Mr. Graham's recital of Casey's stratagems—the mixture of power baseball with tricks taken out of the "dead ball" era of the old Baltimore Orioles and the New York Giants of John McGraw

—shows how a system can be manufactured out of a seeming lack of system.

Casey's "practice of management" has been to combine planning with opportunism in whatever proportion seems needed to do the job at hand. He runs his own superior rookie schools in order to provide himself with a continual flow of talent, but if the talent seems to be running thin he "makes do" with castoffs from the National League. He has been easygoing one year and a slave driver the next. A kindly man ordinarily, he can be cruel to a player for his own good.

The payoff? It has come in many ways. At the age of sixty-eight Casey is still the winningest manager in the game. But he has those oil wells for a cushion, and he has recently become a director of a bank. Not bad for the man they called a "clown."

JOHN CHAMBERLAIN

May 1, 1958

Golf and Freedom

The Singapore City Council, led by its left-wing mayor, has voted to terminate its ground-lease arrangements with the Singapore Royal Island Club for golfers on the ground that golf is not a constructive pursuit. The Council says the game doesn't fit in with the thinking of New Asia.

All golfers will sympathize with their Singapore brethren, but smart golfers will see an opportunity here. For the Council's view about golf isn't anything new. We'd guess that it wasn't very long after the first Scot banged a ball across the pasture that he found himself in the rough at home, and golf widows have been asking ever since what good is golf.

But thanks to the mayor of Singapore we're ready now for the lady at our house. And the next time she suggests we forget the fairways next Saturday and do something constructive, we intend to point out that her backswing's just like that left-wing mayor's. And that unless she wants to caddy for Communism she would do well to lay off golf and stop undermining the ancient and honorable institution of free enterprise and to cease her attacks on the U.S. Constitution and the Bill of Rights.

August 26, 1958

EDITORIAL

"You've just made us the first country to have a golf ball in orbit."

A Diplomatic Dilemma

It is no secret that one of the more difficult problems facing the State Department is a certain divergence between the American and British minds. But lest our diplomats be unfairly disparaged, the public should be fully acquainted with the complexities.

Consider, for instance, that on the day when the British chargé d'affaires in Peiping, Mr. Humphrey Trevelyan, was presenting the protest of Her Majesty's Government over the shooting down of the Cathay airliner, the front-page lead dispatch of the London *Sunday Times* was headlined, "Pakistanis Collapse in Third Test." The grave situation confronting the former Indian subjects of Britain was then reported as follows:

> In the third test at Old Trafford today England, having declared at 359 for 8, bowled Pakistan out for 90 in their first innings. Following on Pakistan lost four wickets for 25 runs.
> The hour before lunch brought England 66 runs on a pitch that was too deeply soaked to be responsive.
> Evans left almost immediately, but Wardle resumed in the same confident vein of Thursday evening, hitting his third six

beautifully straight over the screen. He was eventually caught at cover off Fazal Mahmood. Bedser then asserted himself by some powerful driving, including a six to long, only McConnon was hit on the thumb, a matter of concern to a spinner with a wet wicket in prospect. At lunch it was announced that the innings had been declared.

From the first over bowled by Statham from the Stretford end it was apparent that neither the roller nor the interval had done much to enliven the pitch. When Hanif Mohammed had hooked him for four and Imtiaz Ahmed had shown no sign of disquiet Statham retired. Bedser taking his end and Wardle coming on at the other. This soon had results. Wardle got the ball to turn sharply and Imtiaz pushed at a leg break, but, giving it room to turn, was well caught by McConnon in the gully.

Waqar Hassan and Hanif went quietly along and it seemed the pitch had lost its momentary life and reverted to apathy. Wardle was then dispatched to the farther end to displace Bedser and McConnon made his bow as a test match bowler.

With the score at 58 Imtiaz drove McConnon hard and low to his right hand and was out to a sharp catch. Five runs later Hanif, who had been the mainstay of the batting, tried to swing a sprightly short pitched off-break to square leg but miscued it gently to short fine leg. The unfortunate Chazali was then called upon to face an exceedingly unpleasant last over before tea from Wardle.

The only American we know who talks like this, and so might be able to shed some light on what the Pakistani situation was after tea, is Mr. Charles Stengel, known in some circles as Casey. But this points up not the least part of the State Department's dilemma. It is barred from using the services of our one acknowledged peer in the English languages because he has built his reputation as a Yankee Imperialist.

August 4, 1954

EDITORIAL

A Crutch to Happiness

NEW YORK—"Healthy, wealthy and wise." Ben Franklin ranked the objectives of American life in that order, and so have most who've lived since. A few have sought wisdom; many have sought wealth; but the desire for health has been universal. National spending on good health is now running at the rate of $20 billion annually.

We wish to utter a qualified dissent. We have discovered, after a week and a day on crutches, that a carefully controlled measure of ill health, clearly visible though imposing little real discomfort, is a joyous thing.

Try it. You will find that the world, normally so harsh, softens into agreeable sentimentality. So mellow is this new mood that one would perhaps be lacking in graciousness, certainly in astuteness, if he failed to exploit it.

The idea that you should whitewash the cellar walls, which your wife has been expounding sporadically and with increasing urgency for 13 months, can now be effortlessly sidetracked.

The children, inspired by no more than a mild moan, will drop the discussion of their financial requirements and deliver a quieting newspaper to your chairside.

This favorite chair, normally occupied by the cat, whose rights have been held paramount to your own, will now be instantly available.

Not only will breakfast be delivered to your bed, as if you were Louis XVI, but a subtle exhibition of helplessness will procure lunch at your office desk, as if you were J. P. Morgan.

The boss, noting how easily you tire, will urge you to go home early.

Hurried young men, and even crusty old ladies, will gallantly pause to hold doors open for you.

Instead of plunging into the subway, you can, with every appearance of a clear economic conscience, hail a taxi. And the cab driver, who customarily protests a trip across Brooklyn Bridge as if it were an expedition to the Sahara, glides off—if not in silence, at least leading an amiable political discussion.

Now the remarkable thing about all this is that—with the possible exception of the cat, whose emotions are unfathomable—everyone appears to enjoy the rituals of courtesy and kindness. The boss is pleased to realize he is a prince of a fellow; the old ladies leap at the chance to hold a door for someone else; the cabbie congratulates himself upon his unaccustomed calm. And we are happy to make them happy.

This raises questions of national policy which are very broad indeed. The Government has been pouring millions into the National Institutes of Health. Great volunteer organizations have sprung up, dedicated to wiping out whole categories of human ailment. The citizenry invest billions in everything from vitamins to vibrators, with the sole aim of keeping hale.

It would be a hasty man who would suggest that all this be abandoned. For one thing, such a blow would be like sudden destruction of the protective tariff: it would dislodge too many vested interests —very likely unsettle the economy.

Nevertheless, it may well be that certain constructive steps could be devised to capitalize upon the truth disclosed here. Perhaps the Department of Health, Education and Welfare, concentrating upon the last word of its title rather than the third one, might devise some scheme for encouraging the accident-prone.

It might be that some new volunteer organization could be formed around the idea of Happiness Through Hypochondria. Possibly we, as individuals, could contribute our bit by leaving the ice on the sidewalk and permitting the youngsters' skates to rest at the turn of the staircase.

HENRY GEMMILL

November 7, 1958

"What won't be too well done before my husband finds a parking space?"

OUT FOR THE EVENING

Shall We Dance?

NEW YORK—Miss Cathy Olsson, a pert, hazel-eyed brunette, stood stiffly erect, took four marchlike steps to the right, then whirled about to the lively rhythms of the clacking castenets.

"This," instructed Miss Olsson as the curls of her Italian-bob hairdo bobbed prettily, "is the Paso Doble, a bullfighting dance. The man represents the matador, the woman is his cape.

"Try it," she suggested to a young businessman taking his first dancing lessons in the mirrored Manhattan studios of Fred Astaire. "Chest out, chin in," she counseled. "You must have the matador's arch, and," she added with feeling, "you must have a great feeling."

To the recorded strains of "El Relicario," the new student shuffled through the basic Paso Doble step, essayed the walklike "Three Little Words" step, and thus joined the growing legions of other Americans, young and old alike, who are going to dancing schools to learn how to put their best foot forward.

The dance business today is big business. No precise figures are available, but dance folk estimate Americans spend a cool $150 million a year—much of it on the installment plan—on dancing lessons for themselves and for their offspring. That's more than the $132 million they spend in eyeglass stores, and about the same amount they lay down in bookstores.

Putting a solid bounce in the swing-sway-and-sashay business is the soaring popularity of some relatively recent foreign imports: the Cuban mambo, the cha-cha-cha from Haiti, the merengue from the Dominican Republic. Also livening up the dance trade are new versions of old flings: the frenetic Charleston of the 1920s, Western square and round dances, and the teen-agers' adaptation of the ancient jitterbug step, the Lindy, to the rock 'n' roll beat.

"There's been a tremendous swing to ballroom dancing in the past few years," notes William "Skip" Randall, lithe, boyish-looking president of the Dance Educators of America, a national association of more than 800 teachers. "Rumba and fox trot are perennial favorites," he reports, "but the new Latin dances have caught on, too.

"Take the merengue, for instance," suggests Mr. Randall as he springs from his chair to demonstrate. "It's been around a long time, but only in the past year or so has it really been danced widely. You do it with a gimpy leg," he went on, sagging at one knee, then the other, as he merengued across the floor with an imaginary partner. "See?"

All manner of folks take dancing lessons nowadays, teachers confide. A well-known general is very privately brushing up on his tango in a Manhattan studio. In another studio, a short, balding businessman marches doggedly through the Paso Doble. Not so long ago, a leading oilman mastered the youthful Lindy. A New York lawyer recently gave up trying to learn the simple rumba step, told his teacher he dealt so much in abstractions that he just couldn't visualize the step.

"People are a lot less shy these days about coming in for dancing lessons," asserts Arthur Murray, head of a 400-unit chain of franchised studios that includes three in Australia, three in South Africa and one in London. "There was a time when men were ashamed to admit they were taking lessons. We used to have a private entrance here for them in our studio. But they don't feel sheepish any more."

Sitting in a small, paneled office in his midtown studio, Mr. Murray, deeply tanned and wearing a pink shirt, dark-brown tie and light jacket, rattled off some sales statistics: "Last year, we grossed close to $50 million. So far this year, we're running twenty to twenty-five per cent ahead of 1955." Mr. Murray's gross with 250 studios in 1951: $22 million.

One small but growing part of the dance instruction business is company-sponsored classes for employees. Such large concerns as Pan-American Airlines, Metropolitan Life Insurance Co., American Telephone & Telegraph Co., National City Bank and Ford Motor Co. have at one time or another joined with various chains to arrange employee dance sessions. In some cases, the company merely provides the facilities for the lessons; in others, the company chips in to pay for the lessons as part of its employee relations program.

"Businessmen are becoming increasingly aware that dancing and the poise and confidence it develops helps men get ahead," maintains Charles L. Casanave, president and part owner with Mr. Astaire of the 130-unit Fred Astaire Dance Studio chain. "You know," he adds, "ninety-five per cent of American males really don't know how to dance anyway. They sort of just push their partners around the floor."

WILLIAM E. GILES

September 5, 1956

Of All Ages

The Circus is back resplendent and redundant in the modern manner. Again the stentorian voice of the amplified announcer proclaims Ringling Bros. and Barnum & Bailey as the greatest show on earth, for children of all ages.

But while the older children, say from 20 years and upward, may be asking themselves where are the trained seals playing "My Country 'Tis of Thee," or what has become of the black panthers, or why isn't there an opening grand march this year, more curious questions engender in the minds of the other children. For a mind of seven or eight sees something more than a pageant and an exhibition of skill and daring, the Circus of Life.

This department had secured the services of an unbiased observer, aged seven and one half, in an effort to see to it that children of all ages had their say on Mr. John Ringling North's big, lavish 1953 show which is ready to invade the country.

First there were the lions. An intrepid man, named Oscar Konyot, equipped with a whip, two pistols, a pith helmet and red riding breeches, had surrounded himself with snarling pussies of giant size.

"He thinks he's tough," observed my companion. "But they ought to shoot that one (a particularly nasty lioness)—that really mean one."

This train of thought soon gave way to the practicalities: "Are there real bullets in that pistol? How many shots does it take to kill a lion?"

But this was a mask for a growing anxiety: "They (the lions) really don't like that man."

A pause, as Mr. Konyot sparred against fang and claw, then: "I'll be glad when this act is over. I like the bears better, anyway."

The nearby bears, under the prodding of Albert Rix, were behaving much more angelically than the lions, although they may have been twice as dangerous.

Then the clowns came on, laden with new gags and more outrageously clad than ever. The purveyors of refreshment passed among the patrons. The young observer was soon busy trying to laugh, with his mouth full, at Emmett Kelly, greatest clown of them all, and his foolish friends. The eating and the laughing were performed simultaneously, with not inconsiderable skill.

Mr. North's parade of talent continued, and soon there was an elephant act. This display, entitled by someone who probably is the world's greatest master of alliteration "Peerless Proboscidian Presentation," stimulated my companion. "But where do circus elephants go to die?" he asked gravely, turning over in his mind the old myth of the jungle graveyard where the great beasts sleep their last sleep.

Performers on the high and low wires engaged his attention, which took a personal turn.

"How could I get a pair of shoes like those (the slippers which the artists shed before embarking upon their superhuman feats)?" he inquired.

It was mostly animals and clowns which kept him pleased during the long evening. The huge parades of befeathered damsels left him cool, but there was an occasional tribute when some familiar figure such as Popeye the Sailor passed by. Cries of "Oh, boy!" greeted the appearance of monkeys clad in human costume, and he was amused by a solemnly humorous trained dog.

When Mr. Mistin, Jr., a child xylophone prodigy, appeared in a Lord Fauntleroy suit and flaxen curls he kept referring to him as a girl. He expressed no desire to learn to play the xylophone.

But I may have been deceived by his lack of enthusiasm over some of the more crowded displays. The evening was very long indeed, stretched out by the appearance of the Cerebral Palsy fund drive. For at 12:30 A.M., after four hours of it, he was still as fresh as when he had bought his first bag of popcorn. It was his older companion, mentally paying tribute to the great pageant of beauty and brawn, who became restive under the surfeit of good things.

But that, of course, is a mark of differences which exist within the family of children of all ages.

RICHARD P. COOKE

April 3, 1953

"Serious" Music

Americans, who gave birth to such forms of music as be-bop, jazz and jive, are now becoming the world's most avid consumers of symphonies.

They're also becoming devotees of such other related types of art as opera and ballet in ever growing numbers. This year more than 30 million folks have paid money to attend performances of "serious" music—about 30 per cent more than five years ago and nearly double the number in 1941.

Columbia Concerts, Inc., big musical booking concern, estimates three times as many concerts will be given in the U.S. this year as in the rest of the world combined. O. O. Bottorff, president of National Concert & Artists Corp., another big booking company, notes U.S.-born singers and instrumentalists outnumber their foreign-born counterparts here by more than two to one. "Twenty years ago," he adds, "the figure was the other way around."

This boom in demand for what one man who manages and stages the events calls his "product of cultural maturity" will push box office receipts to the $45 million mark this year.

That figure is, of course, relatively small potatoes as U.S. industries go. A comparable business, for example, is the sale of popcorn in movie theaters, which also runs about $45 million annually. But it's more than the $40 million spent by the public at stadiums to see professional baseball games this year.

Impresarios (managers of musical events) take particular joy in the way their business has been growing in the smaller U.S. towns and cities. This year, for example, more than 2,100 towns have featured the "long-haired" musicians, compared with only about 1,000 in 1940. Big Spring, Nebraska (population 600) and Clarksdale, Mississippi (population around 13,000) are among those which have taken to serious music in recent years.

"A few years back," recalls David Libidins, manager of the Ballet Russe de Monte Carlo dancers, "some Clarksdale people asked me before performance time what language ballet was spoken in. Today, people there are just as enthusiastic about ballet as the so-called sophisticated audiences in New York or Chicago."

Further evidence of the way serious music is spreading geographically may be seen in the growth of the number of symphony orchestras identified with a specific town. Some, like the New York Philharmonic and the Boston, St. Louis, Chicago and Cincinnati symphonies, have been in business since the nineteenth century. But in the last decade orchestras have sprung up, too, in such smaller places as Phoenix, Arizona; San Jose, California; Bridgeport, Connecticut; Jackson, Mississippi; Great Falls, Montana; Casper, Wyoming; and the atomic town of Oak Ridge, Tennessee.

Several reasons are given for the making of America into a land of lovers of great music.

Julian Olney, spokesman for the National Association of Concert Managers—sort of a trade association for impresarios—is partial to the theory that the U.S. is reaching "cultural maturity."

John Woolford, manager of the Baltimore Symphony Orchestra, thinks concerts for schoolchildren, such as those given by his orchestra over the past ten years, have helped develop a taste for symphony. Increased music education in the public schools has probably helped too.

"Don't forget movies, the radio and recordings," say such bookers of talent as Elmer Wilson of Pasadena, Cecelia Schultz of Seattle, and Marvin McDonald of Atlanta. But one cynical European impresario, who arrived here a decade ago to find himself surrounded by "savages," puts it this way: "Americans are still savages. Only now they've hit on supporting fine music as the most ostentatious way of displaying their wealth and playing they aren't savages."

Perhaps the most important reason for the increased popularity of serious music is the relatively recent revolution in programs. Time was, when an impresario would aim an artist's program at a relatively small group of people educated to understand the technical fine points of music. The average man was about as much at home in a concert hall as in a convention of atomic scientists. He might like music, or be interested in the atom, but was in the wrong place to get the satisfaction he wanted.

Says Mr. Bottorff of National Concert & Artists: "The mass musical audience wants 'music for enjoyment'; it wants to be entertained. Topflight artists can meet that demand as well as hillbilly singers. And that's what many are doing."

Sol Hurok, independent impresario who books through Mr. Bottorff's concern, agrees program reform has been in part responsible for the serious music spree. Donald Nugent of Columbia Concerts adds that only a few artists today would dare to present, for instance, a series of piano sonatas arranged in the order they were composed, as once was a general custom. Few people are able, or interested enough, to enjoy listening to the development of a composer's technique through the years as is supposedly revealed in such an arrangement.

"They'd just as soon read the Koran, whose chapters are arranged in order of length," comments one music lover.

Bringing the new-type programs to audiences throughout the country has been done primarily by two groups which have their roots in the 1920s—Community Concerts, a Columbia Concerts affiliate, and N.C.A.C.'s Civic Concerts. These two organizations work almost entirely in towns with populations of less than 500,000. Together they presented last year more than 8,000 concerts, with the two groups dividing the field about fifty-fifty.

These organizations operate on what is known as the "organized-audience plan." Memberships are sold in a city on a season basis for $5 and include four or five concerts. With all tickets sold before any artists are booked or the season opens, there's little gamble, by either impresario or artist. And some local music lover isn't forced to make up deficits, as used to be the case in smaller cities before the organized-audience plan began.

Biggest city under the organized-audience plan is St. Louis; the smallest: Big Spring, Nebraska. In between are roughly 2,000 other cities including such smaller places as LaPorte, Indiana; Glen Burnie, Maryland; Magnolia, Arkansas; Chester, California; Olney, Illinois; and Goodland, Kansas. Among larger cities participating are Seattle, Oakland, California, and Worcester, Massachusetts.

While the organized-audience concert continues to thrive, the men who book attractions on an independent basis in the larger cities are one part of the industry who find their business in something of a slump. Typical of these is James A. Davidson, New York impresario and manager of Miss Margaret Truman. He attributes the current dip to the same decline which has hit movies, baseball and other entertainments in the past year.

How is Miss Truman doing? Pretty well. "She's an exception, of course," Mr. Davidson asserts. This impresario, formerly with the

New York brokerage firm of Hayden, Stone & Co., got into the business of handling musicians through a connection with the motion picture industry.

Miss Truman gets about $1,500 per concert—very good for a relatively new artist. Performers starting out in the business usually get $50 to $100 a performance. Many beginners work for nothing too, in the hope they'll be "discovered."

Outstanding artists, like Artur Rubenstein, the pianist, earn as much as $100,000 a year—an amount comparable to the salary of Ted Williams, ace Boston Red Sox baseball player, or that of Ralph H. Tapscott, chairman of Consolidated Edison Co. of New York, Inc., the nation's largest gas and electric utility company.

Jascha Heifetz, one of the premier violinists, ordinarily receives $3,500 a concert, plus a percentage of the gate. Near the top financially is Ezio Pinza, Metropolitan Opera bass-baritone, who gained even greater fame as the romantic lead in the Broadway hit musical *South Pacific*. Mr. Pinza gets $5,000 to $8,000 a concert.

The huge increase in the number of symphony orchestras in the nation has come despite the fact that few of them make money. Today there are close to 200 professional ones in the U.S., about 80 per cent more than in 1940 and 900 per cent more than in 1920. However, they earn only about 50 per cent of their aggregate $16 million-plus-a-year expenses through sales of tickets and radio and recording incomes.

The rest comes from contributions from music-minded citizens— such gifts are deductible on the Federal income tax—and symphony experts think one reason for the continued growth is local pride.

Says Hans Heinsheimer of G. Schirmer, Inc., New York City music publishers: "Orchestras add glamour in any community." Arthur See, manager of the Rochester (New York) Philharmonic Orchestra, a particularly successful one, adds: "Radio, recordings and motion pictures have let Americans everywhere—not only in the larger cities —know what a wonderful thing is symphonic music. They hear it on radio or records; they want it in the form of a 'live' orchestra at home."

In Rochester, an average of 2,500 people show up at each concert in the huge auditorium built by the late George Eastman, founder of Eastman Kodak Co. In Oklahoma City it's almost impossible to buy a single ticket at a performance of the Oklahoma State Symphony. Each year the Utah Symphony Orchestra, located in Salt Lake City, visits Logan, a Rocky Mountain community of 12,000. Some 4,000 children show up at the afternoon concert; some 4,000 adults at night.

The growth of ballet and opera—while less spectacular—is impressive.

The Sadler's Wells Ballet is perhaps the most successful of the ballet companies. In its 1950–1951 tour of 32 U.S. and Canadian cities it gave 153 performances and grossed $2,500,000. At a recent week's run of three days in Seattle and four days in Portland, Oregon, the troupe's sister company—the Sadler's Wells Theatre Ballet —grossed $74,000. During the same seven days in New York such top Broadway musical shows as *South Pacific* and *Top Banana* pulled in only $50,000 each.

Ten years ago the nation had only two major opera companies— New York's Metropolitan and the San Francisco Opera. Today there's a third major company—the New York City Center Opera Company. In addition there are about 12 minor companies including the New Orleans Opera, the La Scala in Philadelphia and such touring troupes as the Charles Wagner Touring Opera Company.

STANLEY KLIGFELD

December 18, 1951

Tough and Tender

West Side Story, a musical presented at the Winter Garden by Robert E. Griffith and Harold S. Prince. Book by Arthur Laurents, music by Leonard Bernstein, lyrics by Stephen Sondheim. Jerome Robbins directed and did the choreography. Irene Sharaff did the costumes and Oliver Smith the settings. Carol Lawrence, Larry Kert, Chita Rivera, Art Smith, Mickey Calin and Ken Le Roy have leading roles.

The American "musical" stage, with its *South Pacific*, its *Guys and Dolls* and its *Porgy and Bess,* proved that it has still another dimension when *West Side Story* opened at the Winter Garden.

Musicals of the past have usually been dominated by the composers and lyricists, but here is one dominated by a choreographer, Jerome Robbins, whose idea it was that the story of Romeo and Juliet could be set in modern juvenile gangland.

Although Leonard Bernstein has composed a supercharged score, Arthur Laurents has written an excellent book and Stephen Sondheim added quite appropriate lyrics, it is the tremendous pace and vigor of the dancing and the movement of the young people about the stage which makes *West Side Story* such a tough, tender and wonderful evening.

Instead of Montagues and Capulets, the warring clans are the Puerto Rican gang known as the Sharks and the "native" gang called the Jets. Maria, a Puerto Rican girl, is *West Side Story*'s Juliet. She is beautifully played, sung and danced by Carol Lawrence, who under Mr. Robbins' direction gives us an immensely moving portrait of a fine individual caught in one of life's uglier whirlpools. As her lover, the Romeo of the piece and a member of the Jets, Larry Kert gives an equally excellent performance, and their scenes together are as tender as the rest of the play is violent.

The casting could hardly have been better. Mickey Calin, Tommy Abbott, Frank Green and Lowell Harris, as the leading gang members, excel both as actors and as dancers. They stage a harrowing gang fight (the rumble), and one encounter with switchblade knives, simulating the duel between Tybalt and Mercutio, is more realistically staged than any theatrical duel within recent memory.

Among the feminine contingent, Chita Rivera provides a fiery substitute for Juliet's nurse and confidante. Art Smith is on hand as the kindly keeper of the store where the gangs assemble, and Arch Johnson and William Bramley play the part of the Law, which is as bewildered as the youngsters over how to handle the passions of the seething city jungle.

There is little preaching in *West Side Story*. There are no social workers to remark on the pity of it all, no lengthy explanations of the young semihoodlums or of how they got that way, although there is one comic scene (about the only light one of the evening) where some of the Jets jeeringly express their reactions to reform. But they are not articulate enough to go beyond the jeer and to examine the furious drives which force the strutting and the fighting.

Instead, Mr. Robbins has translated into physical movement of the most vigorous sort the energies which underlie gang behavior. The Jets and the Sharks not only dance; they leap, they vault high fences, they fight with enthusiasm. Mr. Robbins' choreography is so skillful that one hardly knows where it stops and sheer undisciplined action begins. And there is a single lyric scene where Maria and her lover dream of a different life which is by contrast all the more arresting.

West Side Story, like *Romeo and Juliet,* is a tragedy, and it is tragedy which seems, at least for a time, to settle the boiling spirits of Jet and Shark and move them toward some sort of understanding. Mr. Bernstein can on these solemn occasions relax his strident musical excitements into the calm of a chorale, and I doubt there will be anyone in *West Side Story*'s audiences who will leave the theater without that sense of subdued wonder for which many plays strive but which few achieve.

RICHARD P. COOKE

September 30, 1957

His Town

Under Milk Wood, a play by Dylan Thomas presented at Henry Miller's Theatre by Gilbert Miller, Henry Sherek and Roger L. Stevens. Donald Houston, Diana Maddox, Francis Compton and Powys Thomas head a large cast. Douglas Cleverdon directed and Raymond Sovey did the settings.

The late Welsh poet Dylan Thomas, launched upon the Broadway scene recently by Emlyn Williams in a first-rate "reading" from his works, is back again at Henry Miller's Theatre in a production called *Under Milk Wood.*

Again a theater audience must be impressed with the poet's gift of earthy and lyric language, his interest and delight in people. But as a play, which describes to us one spring day in the life of a small Welsh fishing village, *Under Milk Wood* does not attain the simple poignancy of an American drama which it must inevitably call to mind, namely Thornton Wilder's *Our Town.*

For it is Dylan Thomas' way to touch many characters briefly instead of a few deeply. We are interested, but not strongly, and the poetic rhythms and salty observations alone are not enough to transfer fully to the audience that intimate sense of life which the poet evidently experienced when he was writing *Under Milk Wood.*

A layman, reading *Under Milk Wood* in book form, would have found it very hard to imagine how an episodic play with more than 60 characters and almost as many changes of local site could be made to come alive at all on the stage. It is to the great credit of Douglas Cleverdon that he has accomplished outstandingly this formidable task. With the assistance of designer Raymond Sovey, he has contrived a complex of little rooms (unveiled periodically by curtains), exits, stairs, a local pub, a waterfront, and the trees of Milk Wood itself.

Here in the sleepy early-morning hours the inhabitants of the town of Llareggub dream their dreams, then come awake and go about their tasks, recall their pasts, wrestle with their presents, make love or yearn about it, and so pass through time to the evening, when all is dark again under Milk Wood.

The hodgepodge of incidents is strung together by a character merely called the Onlooker, who is evidently Dylan Thomas himself. A very long part, and one calling for the nicest timing and inflection, it is played very well by Donald Houston, who has to provide more cues in this one play than most actors do in a dozen. Mr. Houston has a firm command of the poet's antic side as well as his lyric feeling, and without a competent actor in this part *Under Milk Wood* could have been almost unintelligible.

The characters are too numerous to list, but it may be said that Diana Maddox, an actress with a lovely voice, made one of the really memorable parts out of Polly Garter, one of those women who seems overgenerous with her loving, but whose heart belongs but to one lover, now dead. This mild touch of sentimentality is also part of the reminiscence of blind Captain Cat (Francis Compton) an old sea rover who communes with his drowned comrades and evokes the shade of his one true love, also now long departed.

The author's most effective male character is the Reverend Eli Jenkins, a gentle old clergyman who, I think, best expresses Dylan Thomas' basically affirmative (although mainly clear-sighted) poetic philosophy. Says the Reverend Jenkins (played by Powys Thomas) in his sunset poem:

> We are not wholly bad or good
> Who live our lives under Milk Wood
> And Thou, I know, wilt be the first
> To see our best side, not the worst.

It's a different note from that sounded by the newly angry young men of the British Isles, and despite its diffuseness as a play, *Under Milk Wood* has a lot of wit and charm to beguile the evening of those partial to Dylan Thomas, or even for those who want to learn about him.

RICHARD P. COOKE

October 17, 1957

Decadent, Beautiful, Obscure

The world of Tennessee Williams, as presented through his plays and stories, can sometimes seem dreadfully strange to those with whom he is trying to communicate. But it is Mr. Williams' great gift that no matter how far from ordinary experience he may stray in his private reaction to life, what he has to say about it is not only beautifully but compellingly said. So it is with *Suddenly Last Summer,* the principal one of the two plays at the nicely refurbished, small York Playhouse on First Avenue at 64th Street.

The scene is a room and conservatory in the Garden District of New Orleans, where a certain Mrs. Venable is consulting a youngish, sympathetic doctor about the possibility of subjecting a deranged niece to a frontal lobotomy which might set at rest the strange delusions which the niece will not abjure and which are poisoning Mrs. Venable's soul. For the delusions, as Mrs. Venable calls them, concern her only son, who had been her constant, carefree companion for twenty adult years and had died under evidently very strange circumstances.

Mrs. Venable is very ably played by Hortense Alden as an ailing, proud woman who will not open her mind to the possibility of truth but is determined to create her own truth by force, if necessary. She sketches out her own portrait of her son Sebastian, who had been content to promenade through the garden spots of Europe with her, leading a singularly celibate, poetic life in search of God. But very soon we are shown the niece, Catherine Holly, who had been selected by Sebastian as a traveling companion for his final summer in preference to his now fading mother, thereby calling down the implacable hatred of that parent upon Catherine.

Catherine's long, difficult part is inspired both in the writing and in the acting. Anne Meacham, as the girl in a mental institution, does much with Mr. Williams' beautifully expounded, deranged notions. She must combat not only the hatred of her aunt, but the greed of her mother and brother, who would benefit if she would recant on the "delusions" concerning Sebastian's real character and his violent, untidy and mystical demise. Finally Catherine, under the influence of a truth drug, drags out painfully a tale of Sebastian's moral degradation and his death at the hands of some infuriated children on a white-hot Mediterranean afternoon. Here is the truth, which sometimes even seems obscure to the playwright himself, which Mrs. Venable will not let enter her mind.

Where *Suddenly Last Summer* and other plays like it fail is in the very privateness of the author's vision. The allusions and motivations are often cloudy, and one never feels sure of just what Sebastian was, how he got that way or just what it was which destroyed him. Such insight as we do get from Miss Meacham's harrowing recital comes as much from the pitch and timbre of the words as from assignable meaning.

The other item on Mr. Williams' bill is a short conversation piece between two aging New Orleans ladies. Some nice touches, but obviously a curtain raiser for Mr. Williams' main event of beautiful, malign obscurity.

RICHARD P. COOKE

January 9, 1958

Character Determined

Sunrise at Campobello, a play by Dore Schary presented at the Cort Theatre by the Theatre Guild and Mr. Schary. Ralph Bellamy, Mary Fickett, Henry Jones and Anne Seymour have leading roles. Vincent J. Donehue directed and Ralph Alswang did the settings.

The new play which opened at the Cort is the dramatic tale of how Franklin Delano Roosevelt was stricken with polio and how in conquering it he further strengthened an already strong character. It is unfolded in a series of family vignettes, beginning with the unhappy August 10, 1921, when the future President felt the first pang of his approaching physical catastrophe following a swim in the cold waters off Campobello Island, New Brunswick. It ends with his triumphant re-entry into political life when, as if sustained almost entirely by his will, he drags himself to the podium to nominate the "happy warrior" Alfred E. Smith for the Presidency in 1924.

Mr. Schary's documentary play is warm and affectionate. He leans much more heavily upon the Roosevelt family relationships, the devotion of his wife Eleanor, the tyrannical solicitude of his mother Sarah, and her frequent brushes with his firm friend and adviser Louis McHenry Howe, than he does upon politics. Politics, to be sure, cannot be banished from the scene, for it is F.D.R.'s determination, reinforced by Howe's solicitude and hardheaded counsel, to get back into national life which is the mainspring of his will to recover. But the best parts of Mr. Schary's play have to do with the more intimate moments of F.D.R.'s life, when he is playing with his children, being consoled by his wife or doggedly fighting the paralysis which threatens to keep him forever from what he loves so much.

With allowances for the aura of future greatness with which the author slightly dusts almost every utterance of Roosevelt, the play admirably succeeds in telling the story of a man's great personal fight. A great measure of credit for this success must be given to Ralph Bellamy in the leading role. He has caught the tilt of the chin with its projecting cigarette holder to perfection. The voice, which swayed so many voters for so many years, comes back almost from the grave, with its characteristic inflections and its laughter. It is a performance restrained to meet the author's concept of F.D.R.'s quieter moments, and yet vital and moving in the moments when the fight against the dread malady is at its height. This is a play which would have made very good campaign material in the thirties, except that F.D.R. hardly needed it then.

Henry Jones makes an excellent Howe, with his asthma, his cigarettes and his unblushing practicality. He helps keep things from getting sticky, something which could easily have happened. Mary Fickett seems to have got hold of Eleanor Roosevelt's character of the day, with her preoccupation with wifely and motherly cares gradually being shifted toward a public life of her own as Louis Howe instructs her in the arts of public appearance. And Anne Seymour is stately and determined enough as the mother Sarah, who wants her son to come back to Hyde Park where he may "rest" and recover his strength. Had he listened to her, the history of the thirties might have been quite different.

Alan Bunce is on hand as Al Smith, but while his characterization makes a few good points, it isn't in the same league with the Bellamy portrait of Roosevelt.

Mr. Bellamy has set a standard in the impersonation of a public figure which it will be difficult to match. For it goes beyond mannerism and into the underlying stuff of personality. As presented by Mr. Bellamy, this portrait could hardly be improved upon for the purposes of Mr. Schary's play.

To be sure, the author gives us F.D.R. in his most favorable light. But I doubt that even strongly Republican members of future audiences will find their sympathy with Mr. Schary's central character much diluted by their politics.

RICHARD P. COOKE

February 3, 1958

Not So "Beat"

It is easy to pan the French and it is easy to pan one of their best-known young authors, François Sagan. Everyone in the United States of course knows that French morals are lax and that Miss Sagan has proved it with her books which sold so well here—*Bonjour Tristesse, A Certain Smile* and *Those Without Shadows*.

This, or perhaps an efficient press agent, may explain all the hullabaloo about *The Broken Date,* Miss Sagan's drama ballet which opened at the off-Broadway Adelphi Theatre with the Ballet-Théâtre Français. The advance publicity included such supposedly devastating reports as one that Prince Rainier of Monaco would not let his wife, the former Grace Kelly, go to see it.

Well, maybe. *The Broken Date* has a couple of scenes that are risqué at the least. But there have been ones as risqué in Broadway reviews and night clubs. And what this ballet had to offer in sex didn't come up, at all, to what has topped the U.S. best-seller book lists in the past year—*Peyton Place* and *By Love Possessed,* for example.

It is entertaining enough ballet but suffers a certain thinness. Leave out the seduction scenes, and this supposed revelation of the "beatest" of the "beat" generation—the French young folks— could just as well have been called Saturday Night on Main Street —and in 1928, '38 and '48, as well as in 1958. Certainly drinking, dancing and love-making, the ballet's main activities, are not monopolies of the "beat."

As a matter of fact, Miss Sagan in her ballet story has eschewed the amorality of her novels. In them, a main quality is the lack of impact on the people involved of their transgressions. But in *The Broken Date,* while we have as the hero a Young Man "consumed with desire for an elegant beauty who is about to return to her husband," we have a Young Man who is also suffering hallucinations, be they from love or guilt. And when his inamorata fails to keep their last date, he is seduced and suffers violent remorse. Finally he commits suicide.

The destruction of personality, and violent death, is a classic way of winding up the story of illicit love. Rooted in Judaeo-Christian morality, it thrives in the tragedies of Shakespeare and other Elizabethans; it is the story line of many a grand opera. It is interesting that—for whatever reason—Miss Sagan's ballet even uses that most classic means of suicide, the poison vial.

Graced with lively choreography by John Taras and Don Lurio, and music by Michel Magne which runs from classic ballet to Dixieland jazz to the dissonant serious modern music, the cast of *The Broken Date* has a good background to cavort against. Adolfo Andrade as the Young Man is a fiery enough dancer for his part. Toni Lander as the elegant young adulteress is quite elegant a dancer and quite a beauty in a cool Scandinavian way. Somehow her motives did not quite come through, though those of the Young Man's seductress were quite clear. Ash-blond Noelle Adam has been

widely publicized as out-Bardoting Brigitte in this role, and yes,
she does.

Edith Allard and Skip Martinsen manage a striking duet in acting out the Young Man's hallucinations in "The Dance of the Hands
of the Clock." And a cast of unusually comely ballerinas, who do
much of their evening's work in leotards, adds attractiveness, as
does Bernard Buffet's décor.

But by and large, a feeling remains of the production's thinness
as a piece of art. As for the meaning of Miss Sagan's drama ballet,
it is as routine as can be, and while there is plenty of entertainment
the dancing does not get much beyond that.

May 22, 1958

JOHN F. BRIDGE

Provocative Première

Since the Metropolitan produced Charles Converse's *The Pipe of
Desire* in 1909 it has had several moderate successes with new American operas—*Peter Ibbetson* and *Amelia Goes to the Ball* are two that
come to mind—but it has found none with the staying power to win
a permanent place in the repertoire.

That record is not likely to be altered by Samuel Barber's *Vanessa,*
which this week had its world première in a sumptuous production
with sets and costumes by Cecil Beaton, music under the direction
of Dimitri Mitropoulos and a fine cast headed by Eleanor Steber
and Rosalind Elias. The work is always intellectually interesting but
only on occasion emotionally compelling.

Its first disappointment is a dull libretto by Gian-Carlo Menotti
with a soap opera plot that would have been tired in the nineteenth
century. The story begins as Vanessa, a lady of middle age, is waiting
for Anatol, the lover she has neither seen nor heard from for 20 years
(why, is never explained). The Anatol who arrives turns out to be the
son, not the old lover. By the beginning of the second act young
Anatol has seduced Vanessa's niece, Erika, and made a bid for
Vanessa's own hand in marriage. By the end of the story the shallow
youth and the shallower Vanessa have married, and poor Erika has
withdrawn from the world to face her own old age alone.

In the writing this plot is not embellished with perceptive characterization, reasonable motivation or poetic expression. And more

importantly, for this listener, Barber's music fails to lift it to any heights.

The music's impression is difficult to convey in words. It is not atonal but in many places it gives the effect of atonality and the ear misses the sense of being anchored to a key or to traditional harmonies. In other places it sounds perfectly conventional in harmonic structure. But the chief impression is one of noise, with the orchestra leaping wildly from instrument to instrument. The decibel level was noticeably—and annoyingly—high during the singing.

In the purely orchestral passages this music can be interesting and provocative. At several of the climaxes it delivers an emotional wallop. By far the most effective scenes are the endings of Acts III and IV when the stage action is largely pantomime and the dramatic movement depends on the pit. An old symphonic hand, Mr. Barber knows how to use the orchestra alone to achieve striking and powerful effects.

But in the vocal passages this kind of music is disconcerting, at least to the unaccustomed ear. Miss Steber, who sang Vanessa, was called upon to make radical jumps of pitch at breakneck speed; this gave an effect of screeching that is not natural to her. In a last-act quintet, obviously intended as a high point in the opera, this departure from normal voice movements plainly gave the singers trouble. Nicolai Gedda, who sang the lover and who has a strong and pleasant voice, got lost, and the others did not seem too sure of themselves.

Lest this sound too discouraging, a real tribute is in order for Rosalind Elias, who sang Erika. Hers is by far the best part and she is the chief beneficiary of the melodic passages. To this she brought a fine voice and the best characterization of any of the principals. As musician and actress, she endowed the role of the unwed mother and abandoned mistress with moving passion.

The principals also get fine support from Regina Resnik, who gave the role of Erika's grandmother a kind of crusty dignity, and from Giorgio Tozzi, as kindly physician and friend of the family. Mr. Tozzi, who possesses a good baritone, injected some light relief into an otherwise somber story.

Fairness also requires mention that this is something of a minority report. Others find Mr. Barber's operatic music impressive in its experimentation with musical forms; some see him as "freeing the voice" from the older rules of progression.

It is true that these things can be appreciated on a cerebral level; there is nothing boring about *Vanessa* as a musical experience. It is also true that composers should be encouraged in experimentation and the Met encouraged in giving them hearings; 11 years is much too long a time between new operas.

Still, when all is done the finished work must be judged against its peers. To this reviewer, *Vanessa* is a work to which all opera lovers should repair at once for the experience of hearing a composer search his way into what for him is a new medium. But the question remains whether the public will find Mr. Barber's first effort a work to which they will return again and again.

VERMONT ROYSTER

January 17, 1958

Aiding the Arts

NEW YORK—Around the green-baize-covered board room table in General Foods Corp.'s Park Avenue headquarters, 15 men and women sat down recently for an unusual conference.

Its subject: "How to ask for a million dollars."

Around the table were the heads of some of the nation's biggest banks, brokerage houses and industrial concerns. The lesson in fund solicitation, conducted by Clarence Francis, retired chairman of General Foods, was part of a meticulously plotted campaign to coax from corporate treasuries contributions to a relatively new venture in business philanthropy: culture.

The executives at this meeting and other volunteer solicitors are seeking $75 million for Lincoln Center, an 11-acre cluster of halls to be built near Manhattan's Columbus Circle. The center eventually may house opera, symphony, dance, drama and other performing troupes. Construction is scheduled to start later this year, with completion of the entire center due by 1964.

It will be the largest privately financed cultural project ever built in the U.S. Some $7.5 million is expected to come from corporations, the rest will be solicited from private, noncorporate sources.

"It bothers some people to ask their friends or associates for a million dollars, especially when they know they are asking for more than their company or they themselves can give," comments John W. McNulty, a fund-raising counselor to the group. "We've tried to show them how."

The culture crusaders' embarrassment, however, isn't the only problem. "Lincoln Center is selling a new idea," says Edgar Young,

*"You know, Gauguin was just my age when he abandoned
the stock market for a career in art."*

associate of John D. Rockefeller III, active head and a promoter of the project. "Business support for the arts now is at the stage where corporate aid to education was 10 years ago and aid to medical and welfare work was 30 years ago. We want to set a spectacular example to establish support for the products of man's leisure and spirit as well as his health and vocational training."

Other cities are watching Lincoln Center's development with keen interest. The decay of downtown areas has long been a major problem for most metropolises. Many experts in urban affairs believe that if downtown areas in cities around the country can re-emerge as places where the best in entertainment and cultural activities is available, it may trigger an over-all revival in commerce, housing and other fields. Thus cities as diverse as Seattle, Pittsburgh and Winston-Salem are planning construction of new civic auditoriums for performing arts companies. Birmingham, Louisville, Boston, St. Paul, Cincinnati and Fort Wayne, among others, are stepping up promotion of arts "festivals" using existing facilities.

In addition, a Fort Wayne group is trying to raise $3 million for a permanent music, drama and dance center.

Behind the increasing zeal of the culture campaigners, too, is a growing respect for other "practical" benefits of ballet, opera and theater.

"We want to attract topnotch technical people here," says a General Electric Co. official in Louisville, "but their wives badger them to settle in New York or some other city where the kids can enjoy the cultural advantages they think we don't have here. What has Louisville got other than horses and whisky, they ask?"

Adds Dr. John E. Bryan, director of Birmingham's "Committee of 100," composed of leading local businessmen: "We want to continue our industrial growth and we have to attract the people to do it. The men our firms want always ask what the community has to offer. And they mean cultural activities as well as good schools and such."

Dr. Bryan, for 11 years superintendent of schools in Birmingham, says over 100,000 persons attended the 75 theater, ballet, opera, orchestral and art programs during the just-completed "Festival of the Arts" in Birmingham.

The Lincoln Center idea already has won widespread praise from New York businessmen. The reason is simple: Planners of the project figure it will attract some 2,500,000 additional persons annually to cultural events—an influx which naturally would be a boon to merchants.

Recently, New York City condemned the land on which Lincoln Center will stand and sold it for $4 million to the nonprofit corporation that will build and operate the enterprise. That was far less than the land cost to the city; the Federal Government makes up two thirds of the city's loss under the slum clearance program.

Lincoln Center's costs so far have been paid from some $15.5 million contributed by three philanthropic foundations. The first unit to be built is a 2,800-seat concert hall, to be ready late in 1960.

According to David Church, director of the American Association of Fund-Raising Counsel, the $7.5 million being sought from business for Lincoln Center probably is more than all U.S. corporations have given directly to the performing arts in any one year. A survey made two years ago of contributions by 138 corporations showed only 2.5 cents of each gift dollar went for "civic and cultural" activities, "and probably only half that went to the arts," Mr. Church notes. American companies gave away some $520 million last year in all forms of philanthropy, the association figures.

There have been some notable cases of corporate financial aid to the arts, to be sure. One came a few years ago when the Detroit Symphony was resuscitated by a $260,000 grant from 26 corporations. The companies pledged to continue the aid for two years.

But many fund managers say business aid has been sporadic and unplanned, at best. Direct grants generally have come only after desperate, "emergency" appeals.

Many communities recently have unified their cultural fund-raising on the lines of local community chest campaigns.

"It is now much easier to solicit gifts from company leaders who formerly were reluctant to give to one organization such as the Louisville Symphony only to be deluged with dozens of requests from other groups," asserts Richard H. Wagerin, director of the Louisville Fund, now busily collecting $131,000 in its annual appeal. The money will help rub out deficits of the Kentucky Opera Association, the symphony, a "junior art gallery" and several other organizations.

Notes Leslie C. White, manager of Cincinnati's Institute of Fine Arts, another united fund: "We collected $250,000 in 1948, our first united drive, about $50,000 more than the total collected by all the individual cultural groups in town the year before." Now the drive garners $325,000 a year and has between 13,000 and 14,000 contributors. About $160,000 was donated last year by corporations and business firms.

Most united fund drives are handled by community "arts councils," which also administer certain office chores and business details of the cultural organizations that are to share in the collected funds. There are some 50 councils now, compared with five or six a few years ago, says Mrs. Helen Thompson, president of the American Symphony Orchestra League, which co-ordinates their activities.

The councils range from new and struggling groups, such as Fort Wayne's Fine Arts Foundation, which has not yet launched a united fund drive and whose director recently painted his own office, to well-oiled organizations such as Winston-Salem's Arts Council. A proud North Carolinian boasts the Winston-Salem group has a volunteer battery of three lawyers to iron out tax tangles and a punched-card machine that will, for example, come up with the names of likely contributors.

Unified funds may help spur culture contributions, but they don't solve all the problems facing the money raisers. Some company executives, for example, fret over possible stockholder opposition to corporate philanthropy. Lincoln Center's directors went so far as to have the New York law firm of Milbank, Tweed, Hope & Hadley draw up a lengthy brief asserting the legality of such grants.

Many business and cultural leaders hope that through centralized private administration of such funds this country can avoid direct government intervention in the arts. Great Britain, France, Italy, Germany and Russia, among others, funnel government funds to "state" opera houses, ballet and theater companies and orchestras and send them abroad as national troupes.

"We hope our groups will fulfill similar functions—and it's fitting they will be privately financed," says Lincoln Center's Mr. Young. Planners hope the Center will serve as a "home base" for touring troupes.

The center also will have an educational role. Some $20 million of the $75 million to be raised will be used for scholarships and subsidies for untried productions. The Juilliard School of Music will cut its enrollment from about 1,400 now in its present quarters near Columbia University to about 400 when it moves into its new plant at Lincoln Center. The change will enable it to concentrate on only the most talented students and to advance instruction to the postgraduate level.

The remainder of the funds raised will be spent to build a new house for the Metropolitan Opera, a replacement for Carnegie Hall for the New York Philharmonic Orchestra, buildings for Juilliard, the first new dramatic theater in New York in two decades, a dance theater, a library, a museum, a band shell and a landscaped plaza. Under the plaza will be an 800-car parking garage owned by the city.

The Metropolitan Opera, the Juilliard School and the other organizations will lease space from Lincoln Center. But rents are likely to be lower than the organizations might pay if they were to rent comparable facilities from a landlord intent on piling up profits. The nonprofit Center is chiefly interested only in collecting enough in rents to cover maintenance of its properties. Also helping to hold down rents will be the fact that all capital costs will have been covered by contributions.

Lincoln Center, like similar but smaller projects in Seattle and Pittsburgh, is part of a broader "urban renewal" project. The New York venture consists of a 45-acre site being rebuilt under Title I of the National Housing Act. Besides the arts facilities, there will be a midtown campus of Fordham University and several housing developments. All of the new buildings will replace tenements and run-down commercial buildings. Estimated cost: $200 million, of which $42 million consists of Federal and city grants for land acquisition.

JEROME J. ZUKOSKY

March 13, 1958

TIME OUT FOR REFLECTION

Eggheads in Action

When Charles André Joseph Marie de Gaulle began to crop up in the news again recently, the background articles made much of the fact that he had written a book. He was described variously as poet, mystic, philosopher, historian, political theorist and visionary.

So no wonder we were startled when De Gaulle went into action. Here, surely, was an intellectual, an egghead. How could he so skillfully outmaneuver the practical politicians in the Assembly and outflank the dashing generals in Algeria?

For it's deeply imbedded in our culture that when it comes to practical affairs eggheads aren't very smart. We are proud of our poets, painters, scholars, writers. They are useful, even necessary; a poet makes people happier and a scientist sometimes invents things. But it took "practical men" to clear the prairies and build the factories out of the wilderness while historians wrote about it and philosophers thought about it. And after Adlai Stevenson it will be a long time before an American political leader lets on he's literate.

Even the eggheads think of themselves as a group apart. The avant-garde in Greenwich Village were as puzzled by the phenomenon of a poet in the insurance business as Wallace Stevens' fellow executives were to find he thought of something besides actuarial statistics. Americans think it an exception to the rule if ever the twain shall meet.

This is certainly one aspect of our culture that is strictly modern and largely indigenous to America. It's an idea that hardly occurred to the ancients, or even to our own forefathers.

To the Greeks, of course, a man wasn't a man unless he was a whole man, both doer and egghead. Nobody thought it strange that Alexander was a star pupil of Aristotle or that Archimedes should be invited into a council of war. It was a journalist, Xenophon, who was called on to save ten thousand Greeks from the Persian army and a dictator, Pericles, who made Athens the city beautiful. Caesar wrote history while he made it and Marcus Aurelius wrote philosophy while, as Emperor, he applied it.

Nor was this just ancient history. Frederick the Great debated philosophy with Voltaire. Napoleon was a man who saw visions and argued the philosophy of the law. The British Empire was built and preserved by men who were novelists, essayists, poets, artists, scholars or philosophers—men of action like Bacon, Disraeli, Gladstone, Balfour and Churchill.

So was America. It would be hard to gather in one place more eggheads than in a reunion of our founding revolutionists: Franklin, Jefferson, Hamilton, Madison and Adams.

This dichotomy between eggheads and "practical men" is partly a result of our history and, one suspects, partly due to a confusion of intellectualism with education.

Pushing westward and building factories left little time for the kind of education we call cultural; a covered wagon has room for few books. The prideful builders in time acquired a scorn for the scholar who couldn't plow a furrow, and the few with leisure for education came to look down their noses at the builders ignorant of Homer and Beethoven.

This separation by cultural exposure, a wider gulf than in the Old World, obscured the fact that "intellectual" describes not education but a quality of mind. The man who thinks from particular problems to general ideas and back again, who has curiosity for all within his purview, who has sensibility for beauty in music or in mountains—such a man is an intellectual whether he digs in ditches or in libraries.

Thus Andy Jackson, roughhewn soldier, was a first-class egghead; we are still influenced by his political theories. So, unquestionably, was Lincoln. So too were the plainsmen who saw more in the West than adventure or the tycoons who saw visions as well as money in the railroads. America would never be if its men of action hadn't included a high percentage of men of speculative mind.

Yet the dichotomy persists. Scholars disdain "practical affairs" and executives hope nobody will notice if they read philosophy at home.

Casey Stengel, the Yankee philosopher, is barred from the fraternity of eggheads just because he garbles his grammar. And radio-and-record crooner Pat Boone dumfounds teen-agers when he graduates from Columbia University magna cum laude.

We don't know whether De Gaulle can do for France what Churchill did for England. But maybe both of them can do something for America. They can remind us that action doesn't require a silencing of the mind. Perhaps they can even lift the impression left by all the many drudges educated beyond their capacity—that all eggheads are incompetent to do anything.

June 24, 1958   VERMONT ROYSTER

Humpty Dumpties

Under the title "Confessions of an Egghead" Malcolm Muggeridge, in the British weekly *New Statesman,* makes an ingenuous confession of personal fallibility that might apply to eggheads, or intellectuals, as a group. And Mr. Muggeridge has every right to be included in this category.

At various times he has been correspondent and editorial writer for such leading newspapers as the *Manchester Guardian* and the *Daily Telegraph;* for several years he was editor of *Punch.*

Mr. Muggeridge recalls how, immediately after World War I, he argued with great passion that the virtuous Germans were being maltreated by the malignant French. Then, a few years later, the virtuous Germans were voting in large numbers for Hitler, while the malignant French were the champions of justice and freedom.

Turning to another part of the world, he recalls how in the days of British rule, he was sure that communal and other troubles in India would vanish with independence. But actually the British Raj ended in a bloody and impracticable partition, with communal massacres on a vast scale.

As for Russia: "I first thought that the Soviet regime had fulfilled all the promises of human felicity ever made, and then, having spent a year in the U.S.S.R., that it must collapse under the weight of its cruelty and oppression."

Muggeridge finally reaches the pessimistic conclusion that eggheads (meaning by this term those who approach life in terms of ideas, rather than of immediate realities) are nearly always wrong. And he finds confirmation for this pessimism in history.

> Past eggheads seem to have been as unfortunate in their prognostications and misguided in their enthusiasms as contemporary ones. They had as foolish expectations and said as foolish things about the French Revolution as we did about the Russian. An egghead like Hazlitt went on regarding Napoleon as the poor man's friend with the same idiot persistence as his like a century later persisted in seeing in Stalin the practical implementer of the Sermon on the Mount.

In this penitential self-flagellation there is a considerable element of truth. For the egghead, the intellectual, the idea man, does have

"Calm! How can I be calm? I send him off to college so he can be useful in the business, and he comes back a Zen Buddhist!"

a tendency to see and judge life, politics, economics in terms of some favored abstract formula which is often tripped up by hard realities which are more easily accepted by simpler, less sophisticated minds. But, while recognizing that the egghead is fallible, it should not be forgotten that he is also indispensable. Without pioneers of new ideas we might still be living in trees or, at best, in the caves of Neanderthal Man.

It is not necessarily a matter for reproach to change an opinion or a judgment in the light of altered circumstances. Opposition to the Treaty of Versailles, for instance, need not involve approval of Hitler. By the same token opposition to Hitler need not imply retrospective endorsement of the Treaty of Versailles, which was not the least of the factors in the emergence of Hitler.

The fact that eggheads have often been demonstrably fallible in their ideas and enthusiasms is no reason to adopt an attitude of hostility to new ideas. The sensible attitude toward the egghead brimming over with original judgments and projects is not to dismiss him and his theories automatically and summarily. It is to examine and test his idea on the basis of inherent soundness and practicality, in the light of what historical experience teaches.

Conservatism, as well as radicalism, needs its thinkers and theorists if it is to remain a living faith for reasonable men, not a mere collection of dogmas and prejudices. As Burke, who would certainly have qualified as an egghead if the term had been known in his age, pointed out so forcibly in his remonstrance with his fellow egg-heads in France who were trying to build a complete new political and social order from scratch, the besetting sin of the intellectual is to assume that society can be shaped by pure reason alone. The inherited experience of the race, emotion, custom, tradition are all necessary ingredients in a workable constitutional society, along with pure reason.

What is most necessary, if the egghead is to fulfill his necessary and valuable function, is to purge the ore from the dross in his theories and, sometimes, to cut these theories down to size. For the type of egghead who has done most harm to his fellow men, and, ironically, often with the best of intentions, is the one obsessed with a single idea which he is determined to impose on others at any cost. At the best this one-idea man is a bore; at the worst and under favoring circumstances he may become a revolutionary dictator.

WILLIAM HENRY CHAMBERLIN

February 5, 1959

Roman Brain Trusters

Theodore Mommsen's *History of Rome,* which was written a cen-tury ago, runs to more than two thousand pages and is probably unknown to ninety-nine out of a hundred present-day college grad-uates. To rescue a great work from the shades, a journalist, Dero A. Saunders, and a professor of classical history, John H. Collins, have teamed up to present Mommsen in a form that is particularly rele-vant to A.D. 1958. They have done this by the simple expedient of shearing away all of Mommsen that has to do with the birth, rise and consolidation of the Republic.

What is left is that part of Mommsen which tells how the nation succumbed to its own dazzling successes, its aristocrats corrupted by easy living and its poor encouraged in chronic mendicancy by free distributions of grain which brought beggars from all over Italy to a capital whose only industry, besides government, was the construction of public works.

Though Mommsen wrote long before there was a New Deal in America or cradle-to-grave security in England, and even before there was a Bismarckian welfare state in his native Germany, his work was as grimly prophetic of the twentieth century as it was evocative of 125 B.C. The Messrs. Saunders and Collins point in their introduction to some of the deadly parallels, notably the "unnerving similarities between the political strategy and tactics of Gaius Gracchus and those of Franklin Roosevelt."

They do not push the parallels as hard as H. J. Haskell pushes them in his delightful *The New Deal in Old Rome,* which presents Gaius Gracchus as the first Henry Wallace (Gracchus instituted an Ever Normal Granary and a Rural Resettlement Administration in his efforts to solve the Roman "farm problem"). But it is obvious that Saunders and Collins are sounding a warning that history will repeat itself if people don't take the precautions to digest its many lessons.

Extending the game of parallels, one can draw all sorts of relevant conclusions from Mommsen. The first lesson is that it is always dangerous to seek the total annihilation of one's enemy. As long as Rome was faced with the competition of Carthage, there was a certain salutary tension in the Republic. A balance of power outside the nation compelled a balance of power within, for rich and poor did not dare turn and rend each other as long as there was a possibility that a Hannibal might descend, elephants and all, on the Italian peninsula.

After Carthage had been obliterated, the members of the Roman aristocracy (who were represented by what H. J. Haskell has called the Roman "Senatorial machine") forgot what it meant to provide disinterested leadership. The poor, meanwhile, succumbed to demagogues and lost all interest in striving for self-respect and independence. It took a dictator, Julius Caesar, to restore the salutary balances to Roman life. Caesar, a man of common sense, refused to push his wars to "total victory"; he had the intelligence to leave the Germans alone as long as they stayed behind the Rhine and the Danube. And he had the audacity to purge the Roman relief rolls of moochers by instituting a means test and by settling the able-bodied poor on overseas farms of their own.

A second lesson to be derived from Mommsen is that it is dangerous for the people of a nation to get rich by political means. Utilizing wealth that poured into Rome from the defeated and despoiled provinces, a new class of capitalists with no traditions of *noblesse oblige* proceeded to buy up the Italian land. They worked this land not by employing free yeomen but by importing vast hordes of slaves—Phoenicians from the east, Numidians from Africa, Celts from Gaul. The free farmers of Italy couldn't stand the competition of the slave-worked latifundia, where men could be used up like oxen.

A third lesson from Mommsen is that reforms, when they are instituted by the methods of the "robber chieftain" (Mommsen's words for a class war politician), end by tearing society apart. The Gracchi brothers, Tiberius and Gaius, tried to solve the land question by extralegal methods, taking land from its owners and giving it away to the poor. The result was a permanent revolution within Roman society that was not brought to a close until Caesar killed the Republic.

It is fascinating to pursue the parallels beyond the scope of Mommsen's own work, into the period of the Empire. Nero tried inflation, and Diocletian tried price fixing. Naturally, neither expedient did a thing to solve the "social question."

The danger of working the parallels between Rome's decline and our own signs of decay is that the ancient world differed from the modern in one important respect. With its slave-worked economy, Rome had no incentive to employ its capital in putting people to work. The booty which the Roman legions brought home was used primarily to buy more slaves, not to create new productive industries. To put it simply, Rome had capital but lacked a capitalistic system of production. It declined and fell because it had no real opportunities for advance. In the last analysis it failed because it couldn't create a real middle class.

JOHN CHAMBERLAIN

December 12, 1958

No Profit in War

There are still some people about who believe the fable that America grows fat on warfare. This notion persists especially in regard to the great industries which must provide the tools for war. Such as U.S. Steel, for instance.

For that reason the remarks by Mr. Fairless, chairman of U.S. Steel, at the stockholders' meeting the other day in Hoboken deserve some comment. He said that U.S. Steel "has never prospered from America's participation in war."

Three times during the company's 53-year history U.S. Steel has been forced to switch over from a peacetime production to a warmaking production. And each time, Mr. Fairless said, the firm "has taken a financial beating from the moment our country entered the conflict."

The reasons are clear. During wartime, production increases enormously, but so do payrolls, taxes and government controls. The company, along with all the others which can produce war goods, is expected to expand and to meet the nation's needs. Though it does so, it is not a normal expansion with all the economic factors that should govern a company's safe growth taken into account. It is rather a "shoot the works" expansion, dictated by the needs of that particular moment of history, and guided by the threat to the country's survival. All of this brings the wartime profit rate of the company to below the peacetime levels.

For example, U.S. Steel's profits in 1941 were $116 millions. But after Pearl Harbor, they began dropping—to $71 millions in 1942 and to a low of $58 millions in 1945.

When peace returned, profits began to rise and in 1950—the year of Korea's beginning—they had reached $215 millions. But in 1951 they dropped to $184 millions and in 1952 to $143 millions. Returns per share of common stock were $6.10 in 1951 and $4.54 in 1952.

Thus the war years prove the case for Mr. Fairless. The Korean conflict also greatly increased capital expenditures while reducing profits. Of it he said:

"It has left no flesh on our financial bones to sustain our health in lean years when it may be difficult to recover our investment in the costly new plants we have built with our own resources."

The figures Mr. Fairless gave in support of his statement make plain what the matter is. Since 1940, the company's employment costs have risen 155 per cent and its payments for goods and services have increased 138 per cent, while the price of steel has risen only 87 per cent. U.S. Steel's tax bill for the first quarter of 1953 is still twice as much as the owners received in net earnings.

Meantime the steelworkers are preparing to demand another advance in wage rates. There will be a lot said on both sides about the financial position of the company and the charges and counters will ring like steel on anvil.

But in the cut and thrust of labor turmoil we hope that the old fable about war profits will have no place at the conference table. For it is a fable that dies hard, and its repetition, like Hitler's lies, gives it a color of truth though it is fable still. Mr. Fairless spoke for more than his company when he said that there is no profit in war.

EDITORIAl

May 6, 1953

Keats and the Beats

Jack Kerouac is a young writer who has been labeled with such extremes as "America's most talented" and "a salesman of smut." He is perhaps best known as being a prophet and defender of something called "the beat generation." And that, in turn, is widely considered to encompass all that anyone happens to consider antisocial in any young adults, from carrying switchblade knives to liking cool jazz.

All of these allegations—lurid magazine articles on "the beats" notwithstanding—contain a high percentage of nonsense. If there is any exception, it is in the fact that Kerouac is indeed a talented writer by such yardsticks as ability to create images, stimulate emotion and intellect, produce believable characters and write to some point; we doubt that he is "the most" talented.

In Kerouac's new book, *The Dharma Bums*, he writes again of that something called "the beat generation." It is not an easy book to read, for it assumes more knowledge of Buddhism than most of us have. But it has about it the same gripping quality as *On the Road*, his best seller of a year or two ago. The subject matter is a little more palatable. One must wonder whether Kerouac isn't mellowing a little, as he reaches the advanced age of 36.

In *On the Road*, Kerouac wrote in the tradition of the great naturalists from Zola to Steinbeck. His central character, Dean Moriarty, had lost his mother in infancy, and his father was a drunken hobo. Barely 20 years old, he has been in prison four times for car stealing, is addicted to dope and alcohol and has been a mental patient. But through Kerouac's careful writing he emerges as a gentle and even likable personality who attracts people to him. As the book progresses, he gradually goes insane. In the process he accumulates several wives and girl friends, dashes frenziedly back and forth across the United States (he drives from Denver to Chicago at an average speed of 70 miles an hour), gabbles profusely if shallowly on many subjects, and avidly pursues a something he knows not what.

Not an admirable character. Yet he is neither mean nor typical of a generation, or even of his group of friends. He is the very wildest, the offbeat product of a sordid heredity and environment, things that Kerouac pointed out. The odd thing is that somehow in the mind of many Moriarty came to stand for a generation, and Kerouac has come to be considered its evil priest.

In *The Dharma Bums* we see further evidence that not all "beats" are Moriartys. True, Moriarty and his friends might have rubbed elbows with the Dharma bums in some San Francisco jazz joint. But they probably would not have known them very well. The "beats" in *The Dharma Bums* are "intellectuals." No, they are not interested in Karl Marx. They are mainly interested in literature, poetry and "essential meanings" of things on the grand scale of man's place in the universe.

Kerouac's main two intellectual "beats" are Japhy Ryder and Ray Smith, university students in the winter and hobos in the summer. The while, they are wrapped in side studies of Buddhism and attempts, sometimes comical, to practice it. They seek "Dharma," or truth. They hate television sets and commuters and are given to mountain climbing and long hikes to seek the lessons of solitude and oneness with nature—which don't make them sound any more sinister than Thoreau or Wordsworth or the late George Apley, birdwatcher. But Kerouac no more makes fun of them than did he rail at Dean Moriarty for being off the deep end into insanity. He writes with sympathy; it's their story, and he tells it as they would.

What all of Kerouac's characters have in common is tremendous youthful enthusiasm, curiosity, energy and, of course, a questioning of things as they are. They are rebels, in short, sharing many of the age-old characteristics of "Bohemians," or the wild groups around Byron and Keats, or of the crowd around Socrates.

In whatever era, most get over their extremism. As *The Dharma Bums* nears its close, Japhy Ryder shaves off his goatee. And though he is going off to Japan on a fellowship for a year as a Buddhist monk, he thinks he will come back and get married and try to make a pile in business.

It is not hard to picture Japhy in a few years. He'll live in Palo Alto or Winnetka or Westport. He'll be an account executive or a book editor with a too-expensive family, a white Jaguar, a collection of Maxwell Bodenheim poems, a Hammond organ, a hi-fi set and a mild delusion he is somehow shaping the future of the world. Then, and only then, will he be really beat.

JOHN F. BRIDGE

October 2, 1958

Of Mice and Women

In England, under certain circumstances, it is perfectly legal for a lady to appear on the stage in her birthday suit, which is a right ladies do not enjoy in this land of the free, even in New Jersey.

The reason it is allowed in England is that the tired businessmen who write the rules have decided that undressed ladies are really a form of art. But they insist that it remain classified as still life, for while the rules say the ladies can appear in just their shoes if they care to, the rules also say the ladies can't move a muscle.

Just the other day a lady was standing right still in keeping with the rules when a mouse, as mice have a habit of doing, changed her plans. The mouse ran across her feet and the lady ganged aft to the wings shaking with fright. This caused quite an uproar in the theater; the customers cheered the mouse and the manager bawled out the lady.

In fact, he ended up firing her for breaking her contract about standing still. Some of the customers demanded in loud voices to know whether the manager himself was man or mouse, but this manager was quite adamant about it. She wasn't supposed to move and she did and the law could take away his license and that, as far as he was concerned, put an end to the matter.

Well, circumstances alter cases and in our view the manager moved too hastily. We doubt if any English court would hold that the lady violated the law; English jurisprudence is built not only on legalisms and justice, but also on habits and mores of the English. And certainly it would recognize that all ladies, no matter how accoutered, are sisters under the skin when it comes to mice. And when mice come around, the ladies can be expected to move mighty fast.

EDITORIAL

January 24, 1956

Senior Delinquents

It will surprise no reader of these essays to know that many of them are based on information gleaned in reading or talking to other people. This one is based on personal experience.

More and more people about this office address us as "Mister." Some of the older hands are on a first-name basis but to the growing young-blood contingent we are "Mister"; at any rate that is what they call us when we are within earshot.

On the eighteenth green the other day we sank a most prodigious putt and someone on the clubhouse porch cried, "Hooray for Uncle Bill."

Then there was the occasion when a nice young man stepped up to help us get a heavy trunk out of the luggage compartment of our automobile. He took one handle and we took another. Then he got a closer look at us. He said, "I'll go get my brother," which he did.

When creaks and aches assailed us our doctor used to go into long explanations of how the body changed as time went on. Now he knows us much better and he merely says, "It's your age."

In short, then, we are, as Mr. Adlai Stevenson puts it, in the "evening of life" or in the "autumn of life." Obviously this is something about which we can do nothing and we would not be inclined to do anything if we could. There are compensations. No one complains if we appear late for work or if we take frequent vacations. We no longer feel extravagant or wasteful when we hire someone to cut the lawn.

Now it is intimated that the "senior citizens" have become a social problem and on that score we wish to register a protest. For that matter Mr. Stevenson is not so junior himself.

On the whole it seems better to have been born around the turn of the century than later. People grew up without knowing that they were problems.

When we were at the age of four or five and did not want to eat very much, no one bothered. They said, "The child has no appetite." When we were half a dozen years older and tried to eat everything in sight, no one thought we were a psychopathic or a glandular case.

If we raided an apple orchard, the man who owned the orchard caught us and applied a corrective to a handy part of our anatomy. No one made us a juvenile delinquent.

Nor were we a "teen-age problem" between the ages of twelve and twenty. At that period we must have done various things which were inexplicable and vexatious to our elders. Certainly our elders did things which were inexplicable and vexatious to us. However, we discovered that if we humored these people we got along fairly well, and perhaps they had the same attitude. We kept our opinions of our elders to ourselves and did not put them in print or air them on radio programs.

Many things have happened to us but we have never been a "social problem." Now comes Mr. Stevenson and says that we are. The Government has to do something about "senior citizens." That is bad enough. But among the other things that Mr. Stevenson wants to do is to increase the capacity of lunatic asylums to take care of the senior citizens. That has ominous implications.

If Mr. Stevenson could fix matters so that we would take a full pivot on the tee, that would be something. If he could arrange so that when we climb the hill to the fourth tee, we wouldn't puff so hard, that too would be something. If we sit up all night at election time to hear the returns, we can't work the next day, as we once could. However, not even Mr. Stevenson who has promised many things can promise everything.

There are some things Mr. Stevenson could do that would be very helpful. They may not be very spectacular things but they lie within the realm of accomplishment.

If Mr. Stevenson would talk about reducing the expenditures of the Government, he could help us seniors by cutting our taxes and if Mr. Stevenson will look at the tax rates he will see that such action would help others than coupon clippers. By the same sort of policy he could avoid the dangers of inflation so that the pension which the seniors now get would not be in danger of buying less and less; he could help to guarantee that the money which the old-age pensioner receives had a value equal to that which the pensioner paid to the Treasury.

A good many of us seniors have sent sons away to far lands and some did not return. Those who did return now have sons of their own. It should be one of Mr. Stevenson's foremost thoughts that those little boys will not be sent to fight. It would add considerably to the peace of mind which Mr. Stevenson wants the seniors to enjoy.

Even in the "autumn of life," many of us worry about what America will be like with the coming of a new spring. Will it be a country cracking up on the rocks of inflation? Will it be one where a government official is always at hand telling the citizen what he shall do and what he shall not? Will it be one where high political office goes to the man who can most successfully set group against group?

We say to Mr. Stevenson that assurance on such points would be more comforting to a great many people than the nebulous promises that the Government is about to do something to see that one is always well fed and well housed.

After all these years we are a "social problem." Congress must pass some laws to do something about us. It will assemble a lot of people in Washington and they will consider our plight.

Among other things Mr. Stevenson says this of the program he proposes: "It will stimulate the training of research workers and social-service personnel."

Most likely we are just an unregenerate old Tory but we warn Mr. Stevenson of this. If he is elected and sends to our house a social-service worker who wants to teach us to weave baskets or engage in the handicraft arts, let that worker be a male.

We request that because it is our firm intention to hit the worker with our crutch.

WILLIAM H. GRIMES

September 27, 1956

A Letter to Our Readers

Yesterday morning just before the Series opener we were chatting with a Dodger fan. We expressed some sympathy with his cause, noting among other things that the Yankees had been too long in power, but observed that there was room for improvement in the Brooklyn pitching.

We probably should have known better. With ire in his eye he attacked us for treason, with a mild suggestion that we were a blithering idiot to boot. This illustrates a political doctrine which Mr. Red Smith, a pundit of the sports pages, reports as "them as ain't for us all the way is against us."

Readers of our Letters to the Editor column will have noted of late that we are simultaneously accused of being blind and stupid to the merits of the Democratic candidate and of trying to undermine the campaign of the Republican candidate.

One of our newsmen reports that one of the candidates is drawing big crowds but reports also there is no clear indication how the

"I guess that was quite a thought-provoking editorial."

crowds will vote; so because the report fails to suggest that all the spectators fell over in a swoon the report is "unfair." Another report says that a candidate's high-sounding phrases didn't get much applause; so the report is "biased" against the candidate.

There will surely be more such letters, and they deserve a sincere and candid reply.

When we send a reporter to a candidate's camp we want him to report back what is happening; what the candidate is doing and saying; what those around him are saying; whom he is talking to and what their ideas are; how big and what kind of audiences he is getting—in short, everything the reporter can find out.

If he finds out something that makes some reader unhappy we may join that reader in his unhappiness, but we think the readers as well as ourselves deserve to know about it. To get information, we think, is why the readers buy the paper and that is why we hire reporters. We very much suspect that if our reporters stop getting information, and if we stop printing it, even if it's about bad weather, we might not be long for the newspaper world.

Our own opinions on this information we express on this page. We have, as we hope our readers have noted, some decided opinions. But they are much more opinions as to principles than they are as to men. When the candidate of either party does, or says, something that accords with the principles we believe in, we remark upon it gratefully. When either candidate espouses ideas we disagree with, we state that disagreement sharply.

Frankly, we have no use for most of what has been done in and to our country by the present Administration and the party presently in power. Much of it has seemed to us foolish economics and immoral politics. But we do not criticize what the Administration does simply because it happens to be a Democratic Administration; we criticize the Democratic Administration because of what it does.

As to the candidates, we do not think it would be honest to withhold a candid opinion, critical or praising, because of the man's party. Neither men nor parties endure unchanging.

Above all, we do not think a newspaper has any business withholding information about the political pitching, be it strong or weak.

But of course, as our Dodger friend reminded us, even that can get you in trouble.

EDITORIAL

October 2, 1952

The Midnight Knock

When there's a law on the statute books it is the obligation and duty of the government to police the people and see that it is obeyed. And with due regard for the constitutional checks, the government's policemen ought to do their duty with diligence.

So purely on the grounds of duty and diligence the policemen of the O.P.S. who swept down at dawn in slaughterhouses in more than a hundred cities are to be commended. If we are going to have federal laws to fix the price of hamburger in Hohokus, N.J., by all means let them be enforced.

But for all this, we find the whole episode very disturbing, not so much for what is but for what it foretells of what may be. Our uneasiness comes from the nature of this law and what will be required to police the people under it.

One of the first things to be noted is that these 500 slaughterhouses which were so dramatically raided were not chosen on the basis of any prior evidence of malefaction on which a warrant could be issued. Some of them, indeed, were not particularly suspected of any specific violations of the law. They were swept down upon merely because there was a possibility that at least some among them were violating the law and on the theory that if enough of them were gathered in the net violations would be found.

This is not unreasonable thinking, as is shown by the fact that quite a few violations were found. It is, indeed, such a reasonable way to catch offenders that many policemen past—and, in some countries, many policemen present—have advocated it with good logic as the most efficient way of nabbing culprits. If the police of any town were to sweep down some dawn upon all the householders, we dare say they could find quite a few chargeable with offenses ranging from building violations to possessing illegal liquor.

We do not believe that in America even policemen would advocate this. Nor is it necessary to resort to the dragnet to enforce most of our laws.

Most of the laws governing the relationships between citizens are to protect one citizen from being set upon by another. If a thief robs you, the police can depend upon you to complain unless they happen to witness the robbery. They do not have to go about pulling in masses of citizens on the general theory that some of them might be thieves, although that would be a reasonable assumption. By failing to do so, of course, the police miss many thieves, but experience has taught men that this is a more happy circumstance than to have the police free to knock at a midnight door.

But price control is a different kind of law. With this particular law, this particular method is almost the only one that will permit the police to apprehend any considerable number of violators. The nature of the law impels the policers to dragnet methods.

This law says it is illegal for two citizens to exchange goods and money except in a ratio fixed by law. To violate this law requires, in most cases, the joint action of two people; the law, incidentally, holds both buyer and seller of the goods jointly responsible. But practically all such transactions are completed on mutually satisfactory basis, or at least an acceptable basis.

So the enforcement problem is much like that of prohibition. If the policers wait for direct complaints, the law will be honored more in the breach. To enforce it, they must use dragnet methods—swooping surprise visits, spot checks, and all the other paraphernalia of what might be called wholesale policing. It is either that or, again as in the case of prohibition, to have a mockery of enforcement.

Now, of course, the spot-checking (to use the milder term) of a few hundred slaughterhouses may not be a matter of great moment, and in a way it is not without precedent. But in its small way, it foreshadows the problems of enforcing this kind of law, affecting as it does not just meat sales but the buying and selling of many millions of items in every village and hamlet.

The policers have already found that routine inspections will not do. They must come by surprise at sunrise. And they will soon find that there must be other surprises. If the offense is an actual sale, must they not surprise buyer as well as seller to capture witnesses and joint culprits?

This is a formidable kind of law we have put upon the books—to regulate each minute mutual agreement between citizens and the kind of enforcement it will take is a forbidding prospect. We do not like to think that after a visit by sunrise loses its surprise we may have to wonder about a knock on our midnight door.

EDITORIAL

September 27, 1951

The Insignificant Few

A basic tenet of the English common law on which part of our own heritage of liberty rests is found in the words: An Englishman's house is his castle.

What this means is that the poorest individual in the meanest kind of home is as secure, under the majesty of the law, as any baron lodged behind a medieval moat and drawbridge. The highest officer

of the law could not enter either place unbidden unless he carried
with him a warrant.

This concept of individual freedom from the harassments of
powerful government is written into our Bill of Rights this way:
"The right of the people to be secure in their persons, houses, papers,
and effects against unreasonable searches and seizures, shall not be
violated, and no warrants shall issue but upon probable cause, supported by oath or affirmation, and particularly describing the place
to be searched, and the persons or things to be seized."

These words, it seems to us, ought to be read only one way. They
mean that where there is no pressing reason, such as a shooting or
other disturbance to the public peace, any man has a right to refuse
entry to his home to a policeman—or any other government official
or employee—who does not bring with him a search warrant. It also
means that the policeman, if he has reasonable cause, can request
and get such a warrant and he can return and search the house.

But the United States Supreme Court has now read the words
another way. It is not always necessary, Justice Frankfurter held in
a 5-4 majority decision, for government to obtain a search warrant
in order to gain entry to a man's house.

The decision came about because a man living in Baltimore
named Aaron Frank refused to permit a City Health Department
inspector to enter his home and search for rats. A Baltimore city
ordinance authorizes inspectors to enter any home during the daytime and makes it an offense to deny an inspector admission.

Justice Frankfurter's majority opinion upheld the Baltimore ordinance, saying that the power to inspect dwelling places is of indispensable importance to the maintenance of community health, and
that this power would "be greatly hobbled by the blanket requirement of the safeguards necessary for a search of evidence of criminal
acts."

Now if we read Justice Frankfurter's words correctly, there seem to
be two errors here. One is that the right of the people to be secure
in their houses really applies only to people suspected of having
committed a criminal act, and that those suspected of a lesser act,
like not catching rats, do not have the same protections. But this
argument must logically conclude, then, that those innocent of any
suspicion of wrongdoing have no protection at all against unin-
vited entry. Can the inspector in the prowl car stop any place he
pleases and demand to see what is being cooked for dinner on the
ground that what is left over may be attractive to mice?

The other error, it seems to us, occurs in the argument that the
"power to inspect dwelling places" might be "greatly hobbled" by

the safeguards of the Bill of Rights. But the intention was to prevent harassment of the people by hordes of government agents—whether they were sheriffs, policemen, tax collectors, or health, truant or welfare inspectors—without due cause.

We do not know why the defendant, Mr. Frank, refused to allow the Baltimore health inspector to enter his house. But he may have had any of half a hundred reasons; he may have been composing poetry or planning to take a shower or talking on the telephone or he may just not have wished a visitor. He may not like government inspectors or he may just have thought the man, in spite of identification, was not an inspector.

Whatever the reason, it is plain that the inspector could have gone away and got his warrant and come back that or another day and the few hours' delay would have endangered neither the public peace nor health. It is also plain that this procedure would have satisfied the "power of inspection" Justice Frankfurter said is "apparently welcomed by all but an insignificant few."

The Bill of Rights, though, was written to protect the insignificant few as well as the many. Its purpose was not to make matters easier for governors to govern or inspectors to inspect. And decisions that grant greater power to government while eroding the rights of individuals do not do injury only to the insignificant few. They breach the threshold of the majority's liberties as well.

EDITORIAL

May 6, 1959

Semantics of Capitalism

The past six years are studded with evidence of how the deterioration of American-Soviet relations has been spurred by snarled semantics. The same word—like "democracy"—often means totally different things to the Russians and to ourselves. What is less generally recognized is that dual definitions of other words—like "capitalism"—similarly breed mutual misunderstanding and distrust between Americans and their friends in Western Europe.

To the average American, capitalism is the system we have here under which many private companies compete in the production and distribution of everything from vacuum cleaners to canned peaches. The firms that turn out the best-quality products at the lowest prices are the ones that get the consumer's dollar. The others usually fall by the wayside sooner or later.

The competition among manufacturers to be most efficient has bred mass-production methods, resulting in comparatively low costs and low prices. It has also bred acceptance of the doctrine that good wages expand both production and sales to the benefit of workers and factory owners alike.

Consequently, the capitalist system has come to be identified here with the streams of shiny new autos that pour from factory gates across the land at the end of every shift, and with the jungle of television antennae on the roofs of workers' homes. It means mechanical refrigerators, telephones and good food inside the homes, too.

The advantages of a system that bears such fruits for the average man seem self-evident to most Americans. They cannot understand why the advantages are not equally apparent to the rest of the world. Yet everywhere we see evidence of capitalism being sneered at or held suspect—and America by association is the butt of much bitterness and suspicion, too.

Why this widespread hostility to capitalism?

Much of the answer lies in the conflict here and abroad between the definitions and connotations attached to the word itself. To the European, no matter in which country he lives, his experience under capitalism is associated with hordes of poorly clad workers bicycling to their jobs in the early morning; cars are only for the rich. Instead of telephones and TV sets, the European worker often can think only of a drab, overcrowded home and how nice it would be to have more fuel for the stove.

To the European, capitalism has become synonymous with cartels—and with the disregard cartels foster for the consumer, the worker and the over-all well-being of a nation's economy.

Competition is something of an ugly word in Britain, France, Germany and, indeed, in most other nations of the world. Trade associations fix prices, impose quotas on output, set quality standards and split up the market by agreement. There are no antitrust laws. The emphasis is on protecting the high-cost, inefficient producer and insuring "stability" for all members of an industry rather than on the improvement of products, plants and prices.

With the spurs to increase efficiency absent, machinery and

methods are allowed to become antiquated and the entire nation's economy suffers in lost production. Industry-wide collusion brings the consumer up against a "take-it-or-leave-it" stone wall when he goes shopping. And as for the worker, there is little recognition by industry of the interrelation between consumers' buying power and wages.

In Britain, for example, each tire distributor is required to buy $560 worth of tires yearly from each of the 14 members of the Tire Manufacturers' Conference. The conference won't let him buy the tires he may prefer from one supplier; he must buy from all.

Before shortages made production quotas temporarily academic, British cement and steel producers were fined if they sold more goods than their quotas called for, and they received bonuses for selling less. Lamp manufacturers are fined for making electric-light bulbs that last more than a specified number of hours.

Qualified authorities agree that such restrictive practices are "practically universal" in most of Europe. The inefficient are sustained, new entrants are kept out of many industries, and the efficient are kept from expanding, lowering prices or improving a product's quality.

The importance of these practices to the U.S. is tremendous.

Europe's production—and hence its dependence on American economic aid—would present a far different picture if the introduction of modern machinery and methods had been encouraged rather than discouraged for so many years. And production could still boom higher today, at much less cost in raw materials and manpower, if competition were allowed to put a premium on efficiency and provide an incentive for improvement.

Socially and politically, the appeal of communism and socialism to Europe's peoples would shrivel up if European capitalism had more in common with American capitalism than the same name. The standards of living there would be closer to what they are here if there were the same incentives there as here to lower prices, improve quality, expand production and pay good wages.

A further contrast must be clearly made if the misunderstanding and distrust through which America is seen by many European eyes is to be dispelled. That is the contrast between the competitive capitalism of the U.S. and the cartel capitalism of Europe. It is as important to mutual understanding among our peoples as a contrast between West and East.

The differences between American and European capitalism are pointed up frequently, of course, to politicians and industrialists. But it has not been grasped by the factory workers, store clerks,

stevedores and coal miners. Perhaps the contrast would put too
much of a strain on the political ties between the U.S. Government
and the governments of our allies, if too clearly drawn as part of a
calculated information drive. The U.S. may as well recognize, however, that so long as the differences in meaning attached to the same
word, "capitalism," are not generally understood, there will be a
wall blocking understanding and trust between our people and the
peoples of Western Europe.

WARREN H. PHILLIPS

December 24, 1951

Morality and the Law

That the ethical standards, and hence the morality, of many of our
public servants have been disgraceful cannot be denied and ought
not to require further proof. Recent court cases and the numerous
congressional investigations offer too many specific examples.

It is natural therefore that many men like Senator Ferguson
should, out of their deep concern, feel that something must be done
about it if democracy is to survive, for a democracy of all forms of
government is most dependent for its very survival upon high standards of public morality. And it is understandable that many should
seek new laws to safeguard those standards.

Something indeed must be done about it. But we believe that
what must be done does not lie in the field of statute-making. We do
not believe that this country can get public morality by law.

In the first place it would take a myriad of laws to define every
act by which a public official might transgress the public interest.
Senator Ferguson, for example, has proposed one law which would
prevent a government official for a period of two years from working
for a company with which his department dealt during the period
of his government service. This law is directed at what appears to
have been an abuse of official influence in several recent instances;
but at best such a law attacks only one possible abuse. This abuse
is, at worst, but one out of many.

In the second place, laws against personal conduct guarantee nothing, safeguard nothing, unless they are as binding in men's minds as they are on the statute books. We have already laws against espionage, against kickbacks on government payments, against tie-ins between government officials and contractors. Yet we have all those things, both at the local level and in high places. And for every case we know, there are doubtless others that we know not of.

In the third place, there is much that cannot be put in any law. The Kefauver investigation sent several men to jail, but what it showed of deeper moment was the nebulous relationship between government officials and men of ill-repute. This no law can touch. You can jail a man for bribery; you cannot pass a law that will abolish all nods, handshakes, and understandings.

Finally, there is a graver matter. Once our lawmakers try to circumscribe every act of personal conduct with a law, we will move ourselves even further to the point where everything is law and where what is not precisely unlawful will not be considered immoral. Then public morality will be truly lost.

Well, if there is no relief in lawmaking, what hope is there?

There is, we believe, a better hope, even though it lies along a harder way. To reach it the people themselves must give a hard answer to a hard question. Why do we have so much of this conduct which so shocks?

The hard answer is that the people asked for it. It is quite true that the people of New York City, let us say, do not choose their Water Commissioner, and they are not responsible for an occasional dubious one. Yet they cannot escape responsibility for a local government which condones and even at times encourages dubious conduct.

It is true also that the electorate did not choose the little men who may barter Federal favors for home freezers or luxury hotel suites. But they—which is to say all of us—cannot escape our responsibility nonetheless. The mental attitudes, the standards and the conduct of those who serve in a democracy are not likely to be higher than those of the people they serve and that is demanded of them by those people.

This is a hard answer, but it points the way to a better one. The way to root out public immorality is to condemn those public servants who condone it, to be intolerant of those who tolerate it. It is not a question of the letter of the law, no matter how many laws we have upon the statute books, but rather of a sense of honor which can be put in no statute.

That may seem a hard way to return to public dignity, but we do not see any other way. If all of us do not demand better when it comes our time to choose again, then afterward we can all expect much worse. Public virtue, like private chastity, will be observed only where it is honored.

EDITORIAL

May 16, 1951

Law and Men

A nation may be governed in two ways.

It may be governed by laws which are adopted in some fashion agreed upon by free men and which are then binding upon the governing officials as well as the citizens until they are changed in the same fashion.

Or a nation may be governed by men having the power, given or seized, to do what they will and as seems best to them at the moment.

The methods by which nations of law make and administer their laws vary. The British and American systems are greatly different in form. So, too, where men govern nations do the methods of governing vary. But the systems of government by law and of government by men are each like unto their own species in substance. They cannot be mixed.

There have been nations governed badly by law. There have been nations governed wisely and justly by men. That over the centuries free men have come to demand government by law is not because government by men cannot be wise nor because government by law cannot be foolish or unjust.

Yet, over the centuries, free men have fought for government by law. The reason is that under government by law bad laws can exist only so long as free men permit them; they can be changed peaceably when the free men choose. While the laws exist, even the bad ones, men know how to order their lives and within the framework of the law can make themselves secure in their possessions and in their lives; the laws protect them not only from injury by their fellow citizens but also from the power of the state. Even the state cannot take their liberty by prison nor their possessions by decree except for a cause and by a method which the free men have themselves agreed upon in advance and made the law.

Under a government by men there may be justice, if the men are just; there may be wise governing, if the men are wise. But what is just and what is wise is a decision alone of the men who have the power to govern. So long as men are governed by men the governing depends upon the nature of the men who govern.

Free men have fought for government by law for the ultimate reason that under government by men the men outside the government cease to be free. And ceasing to be free, they are no longer safe.

For a century and a half this country has fought to be a country governed by law. Its founders fought a bloody war to make it so; since then millions of the old world have fled here from the governments of men in the belief that it is so.

The other day the President of the United States acted without law. He acted, he says, in what he believed to be the best interests of the country. He took the plants that make steel away from the citizens to whom they belong because he felt that the strike which threatened to stop them from making steel would be bad for the country.

He is preparing to take away from the people who own these plants some of the money they receive for selling the steel and give it to the people who work in the plants. He is telling the people who work in these plants that they cannot quit working in an effort to obtain more for their labor.

Both the men whose savings finance the plants and the men whose labor runs the plants are being deprived by order of the President of some of their possessions. Each is to have what the President decrees—no more. And all the state's powers of coercion are to be used to see that the order is carried out.

All this the President does without law. Indeed, he asked for such a law and it was denied him.

Having no law the President rests his authority upon what he says is the inherent power of his office to do whatever he thinks is necessary for the welfare of the country. He claims the power to seize this newspaper, for instance, if he thinks it to the country's welfare—and he may well think that the things we say here are not in the country's welfare.

Having no law, he relies upon precedent to support his claim of unlimited inherent power. He reminds us that other Presidents

have assumed powers they did not have and the precedents are supposed to sanction the present power.

The immediate reply to this is simply that a precedent of an illegal action does not make law.

To say that even a great President, like Lincoln, usurped power
does not prove its rightfulness; it would prove nothing more than
that desperation and great provocation can drive even great men to
overstep the law. To be reminded that Presidents have acted ille-
gally is merely to remind ourselves that to gain truly a government
by law is no easy matter and that we gain it slowly and keep it only
with vigilance.

Beyond this, the precedents cited are a warning of how easy it
may be to have all law usurped by illegal precedent.

If one President's commandeering of the services of a telegraph
line (the owners were not dispossessed) on the eve of battle, is a
precedent for another President's seizure of property when there is
plenty of time for legal process—for a whole new law, if the country
would give it to him—if this is so, then what can follow from this
President's precedent left unchallenged?

Cannot some other President use this President's precedent to
seize a newspaper—one, say, that is disrupting the country by criticizing that President? And if one President can seize a steel mill
and another a newspaper, what can a President not seize from the
citizens when he chooses?

What he seizes today is an entire industry. The enormousness of
the industry and of the act has made it a national issue. Now if so
enormous a deed is justified by precedent and, being unchallenged,
becomes itself a precedent, who can raise a cry afterward if some
President seizes powers of a lesser size against some citizens of smaller
strength?

The enormity of the President's deed is that he has asserted the
superiority of the power of office over law. The particular deed is
a relief to many people; many agree that no steel strike is better
for the immediate welfare of the people involved, and even of the
country, than a steel strike. But the deed is that the President has
asserted that what he thinks should be done for the welfare of the
country can be done by the office, law or no law, and no matter
whether people agree or not.

This act of seizure is not going to wreck the steel industry. It is
not even going to incommode very many people. It is certainly not
going to topple the Republic.

But if this doctrine which the President asserts and gives substance by his deed is true, this doctrine that the powers of the Presidency are limited only by what the holder thinks is the country's welfare, then we cannot long keep government by law. The provocations for power will grow as fast as the precedents.

We may continue to have good and just government. But make no mistake about it—it will be a government by men.

EDITORIAL

April 21, 1952

"By Osiris, I've done it! Full employment!"

THE FRUITS OF FREEDOM

❊

THE FACE OF THE PAST

The Epermanis Story

Early the other morning a Navy transport slipped past the Ambrose Channel lightship, past the Narrows and Bedloe's Island, past the Battery and the towers on the tip of Manhattan. As it nudged its way into a slip, a corps of waiting dignitaries stood bareheaded at attention while a brass band struck up "The Star-Spangled Banner."

The dignitaries and the band were there to meet a twelve-year-old girl from Latvia, Dace Epermanis by name, whom fortune picked as the 150,000th of the new refugees and the uncounted millionth of the exiles that have fled from the ancient lands in the hope of haven.

The little girl in pigtails seemed bewildered by the pomp of the official welcome, which was to include a trip to Washington to meet the President of the United States. But there had been an earlier welcome that was simpler and less bewildering. And one that meant more than pomp to the twelve hundred other homeless who rode with her on the long sea voyage.

The earlier welcome was a glimpse of the Mother of Exiles, the tall, bronzed lady who keeps vigil on an island home, the lady whose towering torch of imprisoned lightning was the harbor beacon for most of those hopes.

Her greeting to the passing ship was little more than an upraised gesture and a few words on a graven tablet. Yet the compassionate lady who lifts her lamp by the doorway knows better than the dignitaries how to welcome the dispossessed. For she too was an immigrant. And she remembers what it is they flee from—and what it is they come here seeking.

417

Dace Epermanis, who by happenstance became a symbol, was born in Jalgava, Latvia, the second child and only daughter of Bernhards and Walda Epermanis, a middle-class farming family who tilled their own land. She was born in the last year of peace for Europe.

Dace—she calls it "dah-chee"—does not remember the family farm as it used to be because when she was two years old the Russians destroyed the Republic and overran the country. Their farm was confiscated by the state and father Bernhards fled with his family to Riga.

A year later it was the Nazis' turn to invade the country. For a brief time the Epermanises went back to the farm, but it was very brief indeed because Bernhards quickly clashed with the new masters and was again driven out of his fields.

Then the war tide turned and the Russians came a second time. This time the retreating Germans seized the whole family for forced labor, and for the next several years Dace wandered in an Odyssey of Europe as her parents were dragged from one labor battalion to another.

Yet perhaps all this was a blessing in disguise. When the liberation came in 1945 it found them not in Latvia with the Russians but in Bavaria, where they were able to get into a refugee resettlement camp. There was suffering behind, but there was hope ahead.

Soon there was an opening for father Bernhards on new fields in New York. They patiently sat out the long waiting period and so arrived on a Sunday morning in the new land.

Twelve years had brought wisdom to Dace. With simplicity she told the dignitaries her desire: "May God help me to find my place among other children."

The Epermanis story is personal and unique. Yet the Epermanis story is also the story of all the homeless and the tempest-tossed.

They all come seeking a place for themselves among men. They are fleeing wars and man-made devastations; they come for peace. They have heard that the Mother of the Exiles does not stand like the ancient colossus with conquering limbs astride, and they are grateful. They have had enough of conquerors and conquering.

They are fleeing oppression and the man-made burdens that crush even hope in a poverty that knows no ending. They come risking new and unknown hardships in an alien land because they have heard that on the shores beyond the statue there is hope for a man and a future in the world for children.

They do not flee because in their native lands they suffer from too little government. They do not come seeking a more attentive state to make them its wards and nurse them till the grave. If they were lured by the vision of the Great Provider they know many other nations where they might journey.

Dace Epermanis and the millions have come trusting in a chance to build destiny with their own hands and the help of God. There is no promise of security written on the pedestal of the Statue of Liberty. Her lamp lights only one hope, but it alone is bright enough to glow world-wide. It is only those too close to it who are blinded and go groping backward in the dark and wasteland.

The Mother of Exiles has watched ships pass with legions of the nameless and she knows what words to speak with her silent lips to bid them welcome. "Give me your tired, your poor," she whispers, "your huddled masses yearning to breathe free." This, and this alone, is the yearning and the promise.

VERMONT ROYSTER

May 18, 1950

A Definition of Democracy

Democracy is that form of social organization in which the laws that provide for the maintenance of the social order and the administration of justice are laid down by consent of the common will of the people itself, and are executed by representatives chosen freely by that will for that purpose.

Man is by his nature social, because only in society with his fellows can he completely fulfill his earthly destiny. His distinguishing characteristic is his personality; the human individual, unlike the rest of the animal kingdom, does not exist for the sake of the *species,* but is himself a *unit* with tremendous unitary value and importance, and society is the natural means for preservation of that value and for providing the means for its full expression in the field of human activities.

The direct purpose of government is to preserve order; the purpose of justice is to secure the necessary liberty for the human person to pursue his destiny in that *freedom* which is due to the dignity and the worth of human personality.

Personal liberty is, therefore, the final objective of democracy as a form of government. The *common good* of the community is neither *distinct* from nor *superior* to individual liberty but is that condition of individual relations which best promotes the maximum of personal liberty for all the people.

Democracy, therefore, connotes a *limitation* upon the *just powers* of government over the actions of the citizen, whose liberty of action may not justly be constrained or restricted except where necessary to prevent similar liberties of others from being violated. Personal rights are not *absolute;* they may, however, be lawfully abridged by the civil authority only where necessary to *protect* other people's personal rights of similar rank. Under certain circumstances the civil authorities may justly take from a citizen both his life and his liberty.

Democracy and *totalitarianism* are, therefore, incompatible: they are mutually exclusive terms. But a totalitarian state is possible under a democratic *form.*

In general, the common *will* of the people, as the source of law, expresses itself by the voice of the *majority* in free and orderly balloting. A simple definition of democracy would be *"Minority rights under majority rule."* For the formation of the *common will* freedom of discussion is indispensable in every form. Men's opinions vary upon everything, and party or group opinions are a normal and indeed inevitable part of democratic government. But underneath these differences, which are mainly as to ways and means, there must be a common faith in the essential—namely in the inviolability of personal liberties.

There must be, therefore, a limitation upon the power of the majority. This limitation may be explicitly contained in a written instrument expressing a general *organic law* or *constitution,* or it may rest upon a solid tradition of the people itself. This law limits the power of the legislature in making new laws, which new laws must not infringe the principles laid down in the organic law.

The organic law does not *grant* the personal rights which it protects; it *recognizes* them as inherent in the natural dignity of the person. While the people, as the immediate *source* of the organic law, has the power to make what law it pleases and change it at will, if it departs from the principle just mentioned it violates the fundamental of democracy itself.

Democracy to be effective must work by a principle of *representation;* the people itself cannot directly legislate; a majority party representing a certain *policy* will elect men to legislative or administrative office who, it believes, will best carry that party policy into effect. The best results are obtained when the representatives are freest to exercise their own judgment as to ways and means for effectuating the party policy and are not subject to the direct dictation of party organizations.

An effective check upon majority action by a vigorous *minority opposition* party is an important, indeed a necessary, factor in healthy democratic government, which works best under a two-party system with more or less frequent alternations in office.

Public opinion, under a system of free discussion, is at all times a mixture of emotion and reason. In all important matters it is vital that common action be taken only in accord with the *considered* will of a *clear majority* of the people, and that hasty action be avoided. Hence, the desirability of bicameral legislatures differently elected and the requirement, in certain cases, of more than a bare majority vote to effect important changes in law—e.g., as in amendment to the Constitution, the overriding of an executive veto or the ratification of a treaty. Under modern conditions of intercommunication the effectiveness of the demagogue has been greatly increased, and demagoguery is one of the greatest dangers to democracy. There has never been a time when it was more necessary than now for the real common will to be distilled from the passing waves of popular emotion.

Mob rule is the result always of mass emotion and is a degeneration of democracy—one, moreover, to which democracy is peculiarly exposed. The reason is that it usually implies a class conflict involving fundamentals and invariably results in one-man rule and a totalitarian state—either of them being necessarily destructive of democracy.

Democracy, as a "way of life" for human society, by its nature is best conducive to the preservation of men's personal liberty and is therefore the most desirable form of government. For its success, however, it demands a high state of civic morality in the people, who must be educated to a relatively high standard of intelligence. In the absence of either it is almost certain to degenerate, and in that process liberty tends to disappear. Forms alone are not sufficient for its preservation; they must be animated by a deep popular faith in principles of liberty itself. These principles, arising as they do from the fact of man's *personality,* are ultimately religious, for man's personality necessarily implies God, the soul and the moral law.

THOMAS F. WOODLOCK

February 14, 1938

The Battles and the Men

"There were these things that happened in one week in the month of May, 1856. The wind was being sown, and the hurricane would come later; . . . ."

There was Kansas, Bruce Catton tells us in *This Hallowed Ground,* and the debate whether it would be slave or free when it became a state. There was the sack of Lawrence, when two men died in the attack on the stronghold of the abolitionists in the disputed territory. There was the caning of Senator Sumner in the Senate for a speech that Representative Preston Brooks of South Carolina said did violence to his kinsman and his state. And there was Pottawotamie Creek, where John Brown led a raid of vengeance that left five bodies to molder in their graves, unmarked by song.

A doom was taking shape, and it seemed to be coming on relentlessly, as if there was nothing anyone could do to prevent it. The Republic that had been born in an air so full of promise that it might have been the morning of the seventh day was getting ready to tear itself apart.

That the Republic could not tear itself apart, though it took four years and five hundred thousand lives before the fact was proved, is something Mr. Catton sincerely believes. Americans had already entered upon a continental destiny; the fears and emotions aroused by the twin questions of slavery and secession could never stop it. For those questions, however morally terrible was one or however philosophically supportable the other, were "sublimely irrelevant" when balanced against other things Americans were doing "that would bind them together forever whether they liked it or not."

The thesis may very well be correct. It is difficult to believe that slavery could have existed very much longer than it did in the South, opposed as many there were even before the war began to the idea that one man ought to own another. And, surely, without that question, the common interests of the sections would have disposed men to join again in one Government.

Though Mr. Catton seems to say that the war was unnecessary, such philosophical points are but the accompanying shadow of his history. It is the history of what happened to those five hundred thousand men from First Bull Run—Manassas—to Appomattox. And if one can take a little of the poet's imagery, the mathematician's preciseness, the historian's dedication to objectivity, add a gift of stage direction and put all these talents into the successful creation of a book, what might result, if one is lucky, would be something like *This Hallowed Ground.*

Mr. Catton's is, of course, no undiscovered talent. Those familiar with his *Mr. Lincoln's Army, Glory Road,* and his Pulitzer Prize-winning *A Stillness at Appomattox,* in which he followed the rise and ebb of fortune's way with the Army of the Potomac, will not have been unprepared for his success in this infinitely more diffi-

cult task. It is one thing to follow one army on the march or in
bivouac; it is far more difficult to place in marching order the whole
vast and violent panorama of the war.

Yet there were light and also gentle touches that broke through the
brooding violence as though human beings were bound now and
then to rid themselves of their own inhumanity. Pickets were
friendly; when there were no battles on there was really no sense
in individual killing.

Mr. Catton's talent for vignettes—for the few deft words that can
bring a historic figure or a situation to life—is what makes his works
more than ordinary history and scholarship. MacKinlay Kantor's
Andersonville and Clifford Dowdey's *The Land They Fought For*
have something like it, too; and it is no reflection on those works to
say that they show it in lesser degree. Dr. Freeman's *Lee's Lieuten-
ants,* that monumental—if granitic—work which all histories of the
time must take into the fullest account, had now and then flashes of
it. But none, to this reviewer's mind, has made the battles and the
men come so clearly through as Catton.

The author says that *This Hallowed Ground* is "the story of the
Union side of the Civil War." This is true only if he means to say
that he views the whole struggle from the seat he took long ago behind Union lines to view the Army of the Potomac from its formation to its last review. It is written the way the Kentucky Senator,
who tried for compromise with reason and understanding and who
at last found his two sons on different sides, would like.

If Mr. Catton has an opinion to offer or a moral to draw, it is that
the war was brought on by the pride and violence of the age, as
Sumner and Brooks and old John Brown inflamed the hatreds of
1856.

And just as men today still sow a century later the winds of un-
reasoning self-righteousness and hot-eyed pride that in the hurricane
of long ago claimed five hundred thousand lives.

WILLIAM H. FITZPATRICK

November 2, 1956

Rugged Constitution

Just 170 years ago, on March 4, 1789, the Constitution of the United
States formally went into effect, ratified by the requisite two thirds
of the colonies after long and sometimes bitter debate.

Two months later, on April 30, George Washington was inaugurated as the first President of the new Republic. The ensuing 17 decades have seen the three million Americans of colonial days, inhabiting the eastern Atlantic fringe of the country, swell to 175 million, filling up a land that stretches from the Atlantic to the Pacific.

This period has also witnessed a tremendous revolution in the daily lives and working habits of the American people. Agriculture has given way to industry as the main source of livelihood. Transportation has advanced from the stagecoach to the jet plane, with a new speed record set almost every year and travel into outer space now regarded seriously. The shrinking in time required for communication makes immediate headlines for events in foreign capitals which would have required weeks or months for transmission.

But the Constitution has stood the test of time and sweeping economic and social change. It has remained the anchor of American political institutions and the shield of American liberties.

And it has measured up to the high test set by John Adams, one of its architects and one of its most learned and eloquent expounders: "The institutions now made in America will not wholly wear out for thousands of years. It is of the last importance, then, that they should begin right. If they set out wrong, they will never be able to return, unless it be by accident, to the right path."

The American Republic, in the inspired phrase of Abraham Lincoln, was conceived in liberty. This was the watchword of the patriot insurgents, sometimes ragged and hungry and ill-paid, often defeated but never crushed, who finally wore down the British determination to put down what was regarded as a colonial rebellion. The men who framed the Constitution knew that liberty is a tender plant which requires careful nurture and ample safeguards.

As Alexander Hamilton made clear in the first of the famous Federalist Papers, which set forth the political philosophy of the Constitution: "Of those men who have overturned the liberties of republics, the greatest number have begun their career by paying obsequious court to the people, commencing demagogues and ending tyrants."

And James Madison, another influential shaper of the Constitution, made a similar point in Number 47 of the Federalist Papers: "The accumulation of all powers, legislative, executive and judiciary, in the same hands, whether of one, a few or many, and whether hereditary, self-appointed or elective, may justly be pronounced the very definition of tyranny."

This definition of tyranny would admirably fit any contemporary dictatorship. The catch phrase "people's democracy" was not unknown in 1789; but the Founding Fathers, one may be sure, would have had none of it. For they were deeply convinced, both as scholars and as men of action, that even the best of men cannot safely be trusted with too much power over their fellows. John Adams summed up this conviction in an admirable epigram: "Power is always abused when unlimited and unbalanced."

Hence the delicate balance in the political provisions of the Constitution. So far as human wisdom could foresee dangers and provide safeguards, the individual was assured against oppression by the central government; the states were left in possession of all the functions which are not clearly the proper concern of the central government. And the powers and limitations of the three co-equal branches of the government are so defined and delimited as to preclude the possibility that one of the three can become all-powerful and reduce the others to nullity.

The ultimate test of a written constitution is workability and the U.S. Constitution has worked so effectively that it stands extremely high in the esteem of the American people. Of course the framers of the Constitution could not foresee all contingencies. The Constitution is silent on slavery, an accepted institution in the Southern colonies. And it neither affirms nor denies the right of one or more states to secede. These two intertwined issues came to a divisive head a century ago and rent the country in what was fortunately its only great fratricidal schism.

There have been times when one or the other of the co-equal branches tended to exceed its powers. Executive acts, especially in time of war or threatened war, have stretched the unspecified powers of the President, as Commander-in-Chief, to the limit. In the period after Lincoln's death it was Congress that threatened to substitute a party oligarchy for proper constitutional government. It is the judicial branch which has incurred most criticism in recent years. The American Bar Association has recently pronounced severe condemnation of Supreme Court rulings regarding Communists in this country. And predominant feeling in the South is certainly that the Court overstepped its proper bounds in denying the right of Southern state legislatures to maintain the previous system of separate schools.

However, public opinion usually rights an unbalance in the distribution of powers. And there is one good reason why the Constitution has stood up well under the test of time and changing folkways.

This is that the Founding Fathers were too wise to go in for promises to make everyone healthy, wealthy and wise. The Constitution assures the citizen against state interference with his natural rights to worship as he sees fit, to express his ideas in print and by word of mouth, and to a fair, independent system of justice. Beyond these assurances, the individual is left pretty much to his own exertions, even though the "general welfare" clause in the Preamble to the Constitution has been stretched to extreme length in modern times. This may seem a negative conception of government to some who like to think of themselves as advanced liberals. But it has served Americans well and has helped to make the United States a magnet for immigrants from many parts of the world.

The nation's second 170 years can be as happy as the first 170 if it continues to be guided by the principles of the Constitution.

WILLIAM HENRY CHAMBERLIN

March 4, 1959

THE FACE OF THE LAND

"Prosperity" Paradox Along Route 40

ODESSA, Mo.—U.S. Highway 40 roams through the mid-continent from Atlantic City to San Francisco, and on its way it cuts through the middle of Missouri in the middle of the Middle West. This is a report on what war and rumors of more wars have done to that small strip in the middle of U.S. 40.

This strip is not a cross section of America. For as the highway crosses the Missouri River at St. Charles, it leaves behind the mills and factories and the dense masses of St. Louis and her kindred big cities. Until it hits Kansas City 264 miles away it runs through a countryside of farms, villages and small towns where 20,000 population is a lot of people, and where just one "town factory" is a thing to talk about.

So the little strip of road can't speak for all of an industrial nation. It can only whisper for itself. But many whispers can speak loudly, and it may be that what is whispered here is whispered elsewhere also.

The new war has brought many changes along and nearby U.S. 40. Yet while they are many in numbers they are all of the same kind, whether seen at a lonc farmhouse beside the road, in Jonesburg village with its 422 citizens, or in Booneville with its 7,000.

U.S. 40 is no longer—if it ever was—aloof from the debates on foreign policy, no longer disinterested in what the captains say on Wake Island or what happens in Indochina. Far Eastern politics is not so far from Centralia since young Arthur Roddy died in Korea, or from Audrain County since Company D, 1st Battalion, 7th Cavalry, lost Bill Cook, just out of high school.

And there is more than a few dead to remind the living that each end of U.S. 40 stretches a long way. No one can have any illusions that settling Korea settles anything when the Headquarters Battery, 128th Field Artillery, Mexico, Missouri, is standing by to shove off, not to fight in Korea but to stand a long guard. Or when in Warrenton the 300 metal fabricators at the Binkley Manufacturing Co. have their take-home pay cut to pay more taxes to prepare for bigger wars.

427

But if middle Missouri no longer hopes to go its own way unmolested, it is puzzled why this is so and uncertain what to do about it.

Indeed, if a stranger gets one dominant impression it is of bewilderment and uncertainty. People are bewildered as to why they have to be fighting in Korea and confused as to what they should do about their personal living and their working.

Ed Robinson, who farms hard by the highway, puts the bewilderment about as well as anyone. "We've got in it and we've got to finish it," he says. "We can't take no licking. But what I don't see is how come we got where we got to do the licking. Somebody was a damned fool and fools is always expensive." Opinions vary along the road as to who's the fool, but nobody seems to see the reasons any better than farmer Robinson.

There is in this little vocal criticism of the actual decision to fight in Korea. If anything, middle Missouri is more virulently anti-Russian than is Washington; as Ervin Hammerer of Columbia states, "We ought to have stood up to them long ago." The resentment, where it shows, is over the earlier placating policy, the decisions that made Korea possible, the military unpreparedness, and above all over what the earlier failures may cost.

Intimations of the cost have hit the people along Highway 40 with a shock. As in the rest of the country, the war's outbreak touched off a buying spree in the roadside towns. From Neal Schowengerdt's old-fashioned general store in little Warrenton to the shiny J. C. Penney chain store in bustling Mexico there was felt that first panicky rush to buy, especially "hard" goods. That tapered off after a while. But now as the radio and the city newspapers make it daily more apparent that the country is going on a "war footing," there has come a new reaction.

The best name for it, perhaps, is "apprehension buying"—different from panic buying in that it is selective, sometimes paradoxical, and oftentimes reluctant. It is significant not only for what it portends for the economy but also for what it reflects of people's minds.

The story is best told by Pete Todsen, a past president of Mexico's Chamber of Commerce and long-time merchant to town and county. "Right now there seems to be more of a shortage of money among the townfolk. September sales just held their own after the boom, and people aren't buying like they were. But they are buying. A woman comes in here to buy three pairs of school dungarees for her boy and when she finds out the price has gone up twice she only buys two pairs, maybe one. But you can tell she wants to buy more because she doesn't know what will happen next, and she'll buy every dollar's worth she can."

At Mexico's Montgomery Ward, sales of durable goods are going up again, but the "soft" goods are off 15 per cent. Many wage and salaried people seem to have loaded up with time payments to beat the restrictions and so are squeezed for the money to buy other things. This is borne out by the fact that a recent wage boost at the A. P. Green Firebrick Co. was followed almost immediately by an increase in installment commitments. Glenn Torreyson, Ford salesman, can just sit and wait for his customers while the department and clothing stores have increased advertising linage in the newspaper.

The apprehension buying is marked in farm real estate. The little Warren County Trust Co. has had a sharp boost in its loans since June, practically all in real estate. "We've noticed a decidedly new interest in farms," says president Otto Eisenstein. "Folks here think we are going to have a lot more inflation."

Yet there are bits and pieces that don't fit the pattern. For instance, Claude Schroff, who sells tractors throughout Montgomery County, averaged eight sales a month this year until August. For September he had exactly one sale, "and I had to push that." In Booneville the Kemper State Bank had a 50 per cent decline in its installment loans even before the second government restrictions were clamped on. The Slumbertown Motel east of here has been doing a pretty brisk business—with salesmen hitting the road.

Without question this bit of Highway 40 has all the earmarks of prosperity. Farm crops are good and prices high; it looks like a rich autumn. Wages in the factories are up or going up. Retail sales, despite rising prices and some odd inconsistencies, are high. These speak of prosperity. But every storekeeper notices that his customers clutch the dollar while spending it. Some fixed-salary workers are actually hard up. Three banks on the wayside report a heavy cash-in of savings bonds. None of this speaks true prosperity.

What all these things together say is that here is something that looks like prosperity but here is no peace of mind. Pattern and paradox are both explained by inflation present and inflation feared. The people along the highway are confused and apprehensive about the future, for once fearful of "prosperity."

And what is true in this is true in other things. The new war has not left many dead along the wayside here, but it has brought the fear of more dying in more wars. It has not brought hardship, except to a few, but it has left with many an apprehension as to how they will fare tomorrow. It has done little to upset the actual living plans of most of the people, but it has thrown all planning into confusion. And unlike World War II, this new kind of warring has brought both apprehension and confusion as to how and when it will ever end.

Apprehension and confusion. These things strike the stranger as the two big gifts that war and rumors of war have brought to U.S. 40.

VERMONT ROYSTER

October 20, 1950

Revolution on Route 40

SWEET SPRINGS, Mo.—U.S. Route 40, for a little less than 260 miles of its cross-country length, catches much of America in microcosm. Old St. Louis on the Mississippi is "East," a place of factories, sophisticates and slums. Newer, perhaps sharper, Kansas City with its great livestock yards is "West." And in between are "North" and "South" and people who partake of some of those sectionalisms and yet share something that defies them.

The thing shared by the people in the scores of towns along this highway is all but a revolution. As recently as World War II, many of them were fairly isolated, physically and intellectually, from the world around them. They had a point of view all their own. But today the visitor to these towns, chatting casually with the citizens, finds that any especially "rural" viewpoint has largely disappeared.

The views of the white-haired dentist's wife, rocking on her porch on a Sunday afternoon in Warrenton, a town of some 1,600 population, are much the same as those of a housewife met over cocktails in a middle-class suburb of a big Northern city.

True, this small-town Missourian has much less of a shared viewpoint with a fellow townsman, once a farmer, who now commutes 100 miles daily in his auto to an industrial plant. But the ex-farmer, in what he says and thinks, could fit quite nicely in a neighborhood of industrial workers in the East.

What are some of these views? The middle-class people, in whatever location, generally have a fairly keen interest in American involvements around the globe. High taxes, high government spending, growing "socialism" often are anathema. Among the industrial workers and many of the small merchants, on the other hand, there is less concern with these things. The big worry is "inflation" and how to cope with it.

*"Emily, I don't know whether I shoulda let you talk me into
getting a convertible instead of a pickup."*

Naturally there are very considerable individual exceptions to
such general impressions. In fact, a frequently heard comment among
citizens along U.S. 40 is "Well, things around here sure must be a
lot different than in the East."

One certainly can agree that the small town appears much as it
did a decade ago, and thus on the surface has little in common with
the East. Yet there are many—and growing—surface things the "ruralist" holds in common with the city dweller. In his Fords, Cadillacs
and occasional Volkswagen, or in his prepackaged ranch house or
chocolate cake, he is one with Chicago and Pittsburgh as well as
Seattle and Dallas.

In the field of foreign affairs the disappearance of the rural view
—so long equated with "isolationism"—is perhaps most dramatic.
For one sample, come along to Sweet Springs, a pleasant place of
1,300 population. At the white frame Methodist Church it is lay-

man's Sunday and four leading citizens each deliver a short sermon on the text, "Seek ye first the Kingdom."

By and large the speakers' comments are concerned with things that seem closer to the peaceful daily life of the congregation than world turmoil. But the next morning the visitor finds the remarks of Dr. R. L. Yoder have stuck most firmly in the minds of the listeners. He has talked about the global crisis and the threat posed by missiles and atomic weapons—that "mankind could be wiped out in thirty minutes" by atomic war.

And the visitor must wonder if the fear of personal destruction, so long foreign to this town, is not one reason why foreign affairs are as close to many citizens of Sweet Springs as to the citizens of bigger coastal cities.

A conversation with a young woman working behind the soda fountain at the Bumgarner Pharmacy in Odessa (pop. 2,000) gives another reason for the interest in world affairs. She is worried about the renewed Red Chinese shelling of Quemoy. "People my age are all worried; my husband just got out of service, but he might have to go back if there's a war." But she shows no sign of wishing a U.S. withdrawal from such places around the globe as Quemoy. "We can't let them run over us," she says. And when she adds that "we've got to stop Communism somewhere or we'll be the only ones left," one must recall how a series of arguments for "stopping" this aggressor or that, "or we'll be the only ones left," has since 1917 become firmly embedded in the American mind.

This is not to say that "interest" in world affairs is synonymous with firm endorsement of "interventionism." There are plenty of people hereabouts, though perhaps a minority, who believe the U.S. is too much involved.

A young college student at the University of Missouri, at Columbia, is one; he faces military service on foreign shores and would rather marry his girl and stay in Missouri. There are others who think the basic philosophy of the current interventionism somehow is impractical. "You just can't police the world the way we are trying to," states a hardware store operator. Too, there are encountered some few who want no part of intervention or any talk of it. "I don't want to think about it, and I don't," says a woman clerk in a variety store.

The moral aspects of U.S. intervention bother Frank Farmer, editor and publisher of the Sweet Springs *Herald*. "Americans don't behave abroad; they go abroad and run over the people. Our people don't set a proper Christian example," he declares.

This theme is rather common hereabouts; some speakers of it have read the current novel *The Ugly American,* or its serialization in a national magazine. One gets the feeling that morality and honesty, abroad or among officials in Government and in labor unions, is an issue of more weight among these Missourians than in bigger cities. It's the country's "biggest issue," for example, to Marvin Unnerstall, a Washington (Missouri) service station operator. Another thing that has him riled: too many foreign imports, especially cars, which "caused the business recession."

A businessman in another small town assigns another cause for the recent recession. He says it's taxation, which bears too heavily on the average small-town dweller whose income is often less than the big city dwellers'.

"Despite the renewed farm prosperity many businessmen here have stopped looking at new cars and are searching around for good used ones," he says as a case in point. He explains that the farmer's prosperity is partly absorbed in taxes. He adds that the small-town dweller's taxes stay high though his cost of living rises while his wages lag, cutting the amount he can spend for things other than necessities. "That continues to hurt many small-town businessmen," he states.

The squeeze on the small-town dwellers is frequently mentioned in talks with them. As they see it, costs of the things they buy are hiked by wage increases to labor unions in big cities, plus costlier distribution. But the small-town dweller does not participate in the rise in wages.

Still and all, the general impression along U.S. 40 is one of prosperity, particularly among the farmers. One must doubt, however, that this abundance is enough to turn this generally Democratic state into a Republican one. "God made the farmer prosperous, not Benson or Eisenhower," says banker Richard Wall of Sweet Springs, in a rather typical comment.

And one must wonder whether, barring a deep farm depression, such a typically "rural" issue as the farmer's economic health can again have the impact it used to have in the small towns.

For their inflation-changed economy is more a reflection of the whole national economic health than ever before. And beyond that, there is the indisputable fact that rural horizons have been widened vastly in many other ways.

The sons of the small towns have covered the globe in uniform. The TV aerials atop the houses and the abundant national magazines and newspapers bring to the small town the same encapsuled news and views of the wide, wide world that they do to the big cities. And in many of the towns, at both the St. Louis and Kansas City ends of U.S. 40, there are the commuters. For more than two thirds of the length of Missouri along U.S. 40, one encounters these daily travelers, barreling up to 100 miles each day to work in one of the cities, and 100 miles home again at night.

These are all things that have made in America, for better or worse, a "ruralist" who is vanishing—in his views he is becoming almost indistinguishable from the rest of the country.

JOHN F. BRIDGE

October 24, 1958

Frontier Revisited

Six years ago Lucius Beebe, confidant and chronicler of New York's *haut monde,* threw in his cocktail napkin, packed up his beluga, Mumm's Extra and other necessities, and headed West. Mr. Beebe's destination was Virginia City, Nevada, where he was to be the publisher of that state's oldest newspaper, the *Territorial Enterprise.*

The transition from his white tie at "21" and the Colony to the five-gallon hat he now sports in the wide-open spaces doubtless confounded many of Beebe's Smart Set friends. The siren's call to the West would soon die down, they thought, and he would return to his leading role among the first-nighters.

It is safe to say now that Lucius Beebe's change of venue has been a success. In *The American West,* Mr. Beebe offers an exciting pictorial view of the glory of America's adventurous expansion era which so enticed him. The affectionate and often salty copy which accompanies the abundant drawings and photographs makes the Far West so inviting it might well inaugurate another mass movement in that direction. (In which case Mr. Beebe will certainly pack up once more and head north, probably toward the old diggings of the Hudson's Bay company.)

Assisted by Charles Clegg, the editor of the *Territorial Enterprise,* Beebe has accomplished a magnificent job of ferreting out old prints, paintings and photographs from their own collections, museums, private sources, newspapers and other archives. The publisher has fulfilled his end of the bargain by providing a handsome example of book production.

The book begins with a chapter on the Long Hunters, of whom Kit Carson was the most famous. In the 1830s this restless crew of nomads on the search for hunting grounds "made the West their back yard." The West was truly wild and wooly then. "The gateway to the land" for nearly a century was the Mississippi and Ohio rivers, and in a wonderful chapter we are shown the turmoil and turbulence around these rivers during the fifties and sixties. The magnificence and luxury of some of the river queens was amazing, but the treacherous Mississippi eventually claimed them all. Over 600 vessels have been counted lost through collisions, snaggings and fire.

During this era the "West" continued to recede. But it took the discovery of gold at Sutter's Mill in California to shrink our borders overnight. And when, in 1869, the rails of the Union and Central Pacific railroads converged at Promontory Point in northern Utah, "the American Frontier was a thing of the past."

But the West remained "wild" for many years to come. Eventually, it became possible to predict the pattern of events: first, discovery of gold or silver, then a tide of miners, merchants and madames. If the lode was plentiful, permanent buildings would arise and almost overnight another city was born. It required men of tough spirits and adventurous souls to make up such a city—and contribute so much to the development of the West.

Beebe's adopted Virginia City—the archetype of the Western mining town—is treated with warmth and a tender air of nostalgia in the chapter on "The Comstock." It was in 1859 that the heavy blue ore in the Washoe Diggings, as the future Comstock was first known, was assayed as silver of "almost unbelievable richness." In the space of a few weeks the camp site in the foothills of Mt. David-son, now known as Virginia City, grew to 5,000 people; it hit its zenith in 1875 with 25,000 residents.

At its peak of prosperity, Virginia City was a bustling community with permanent homes, stores, hotels; indeed at one time six Shake-spearean companies were playing the Comstock at the same time and the number of minstrel shows and tent shows were past counting. Its International Hotel boasted the first elevator west of Chicago's Palmer House. The second telephone exchange west of the Missis-sippi (the first was in San Francisco) served its growing businesses and residences. Wine and champagne flowed and the wives of speculators and mine superintendents wore gowns which came from Worth's in Paris.

Unlike the fate of most mining towns which become ghosts im-mediately on the exhaustion of their lodes, death came slowly to the Comstock. Though the resources were still there, the recovery of silver became too costly. The Comstock lode did not "give out." It simply became unworkable.

In his subtitle introducing the Comstock chapter, Beebe describes the old Virginia City as the "Cosmopolis of the Western World." At the close of the day as he sips his champagne in the office of the

Enterprise, Lucius Beebe can probably still hear the miners' wagons rolling down C Street against the background of raucous applause echoing through from Maguire's Opera House.

CHARLES PRESTON

March 30, 1956

Taos Mixes Art and Credit

TAOS, N. M.—The president of a large Eastern corporation strolled with his wife across the plaza of this bustling little town and stopped a tall, sun-tanned stranger to ask some advice.

"I've just arrived in town and want to buy a water color," said the corporation president. "Where can I find some good paintings for about $35?"

"Follow me," said the stranger. Fifteen minutes later the corporation president emerged from the stranger's art studio richer by one water color—but poorer by $600.

The stranger was Emil Bisttram, one of the best-known artists in Taos, a town which is almost completely dependent on perhaps the most unpredictable of all industries—art. Like many of the other 200 or so artists in this town of 3,500, Mr. Bisttram is more than art-conscious. He is also extremely sales-conscious. Thanks to this factor and to a great upsurge of interest in painting around the U.S., Taos artists are selling more of their work today than they ever dreamed possible.

Taos artists miss few sales opportunities. The town's 60-odd studios and 18 galleries are selling more than half their paintings on time with no interest charged and only a small down payment required. Customers can take paintings home to "try them out," with no deposit demanded. Several artists tour the U.S. during the winter months, displaying and selling their paintings. At least one artist has retained a public-relations agency to publicize his work.

"Some people call this an art colony, but I describe it as an art mart," remarks Arthur J. Merrill, who, like several of his Taos colleagues, paints during the winter and presides over his art gallery during the summer season.

There are no national figures available on total sales of paintings. But many galleries report sharp sales increases. "Our dollar sales have doubled since 1950," says Miss Edith Halpert, manager of

New York City's Downtown Galleries. "Dollar sales are up fifty per cent since 1950," reports W. R. Fine of Fine Galleries in Dallas.

Sales of art materials are rising, too. Permanent Pigments, Inc., of Cincinnati reports 1955 sales of paints, brushes, easels and canvas reached a new high, 15 per cent ahead of 1954. New York City's M. Grumbacher, Inc., a major producer of artists' supplies, says its volume has "at least tripled" in the past 10 years.

Lee Gross, Grumbacher's advertising manager, attributes much of his firm's sales gain to a rise in the numbers of amateur artists. Among these weekend painters are such well-known individuals as President Eisenhower, Sir Winston Churchill and movie stars Jane Russell and Gary Cooper.

Taos sales, according to authoritative guesses, are also on the upbeat. Town officials say about 300,000 people visited Taos during the 1955 summer season alone and purchased at least $150,000 worth of paintings plus almost that much in Indian arts and crafts.

"In the art field Taos' sales rival any other community except New York," says Leone Kahl, director of the Stables Gallery. "Art is both our livelihood and our way of life," she adds.

Booming art sales in Taos have been the biggest news for the town since Coronado's men came tramping up the Rio Grande Valley four centuries ago. The visitors were disappointed with what they found, however, and Taos soon slipped back into obscurity.

In 1898 two gifted young artists, Ernest L. Blumenschein and Bert Phillips, who were journeying across New Mexico in search of new subjects to paint, broke a wagon wheel and found themselves stranded near the dusty village. Their dismay gave way to delight, however, when they examined their surroundings: the timeless Indian pueblos, the dark mountains of the Sangre de Cristo range, sagebrush-lined plains, majestic aspens and cottonwoods, and a general variety of landscape capable of inspiring any artist's paintbrush.

Messrs. Blumenschein and Phillips decided to remain in Taos, and they were soon joined by other artists. Their numbers have been swelling ever since. Townspeople guess there are now about 60 painters of national or international reputation settled in and around Taos, plus at least 150 more "unknowns" who are striving to gain recognition. Smaller but still notable colonies of artists have taken up residence in Santa Fe and Albuquerque.

"When I see that a customer is interested in a painting, I tell him, 'Don't look at the price; if you want the painting we'll make it possible through our payment plan,'" says Leone Kahl. Mrs. Kahl, former author of an advice column in the Houston *Post*, can be seen presiding over the Stables Gallery attired in a flowing white gown, a brown Navaho fiesta robe and giant silver-and-turquoise earrings and bracelets.

Mrs. Kahl estimates that 75 per cent of the Stables' dollar volume is on time. The gallery charges no interest and is "flexible" about the amount of down payment demanded. "Instead of sending bills to remind a customer of a payment, I mail little personal notes saying 'Hope you come back soon,' or something like that," she explains. "I've never had a check bounce and rarely had any difficulty with a customer."

Under Mrs. Kahl's direction, the Stables grossed $25,000 on 482 paintings sold in 1955, including $9,000 grossed on a tour of the Southwest. This compared with $18,500 on 305 paintings sold in 1954, including $3,200 grossed on tour.

The Stables' "easy-terms" policy is followed by nearly all other galleries and studios in Taos. "I let the customer name his own terms, but I like to get twenty-five per cent down on a painting," remarks Charles H. Reynolds, who owns the Reynolds Gallery.

"You can sell for cash to collectors, but with the tourists you must resort to credit and other incentives," says Alfred Rogoway, a modernist painter who until recently managed the Ruins Gallery.

Besides offering helpful credit terms, gallery managers also make every effort to bring customer and artist together—something that is rarely done in big-city galleries. If a prospective buyer inquires about a painting and indicates any interest in purchasing it, gallery managers hasten to the phone. Either the artist will come down to the gallery or the customer will go out to the artist's studio. "Meeting an artist teases the vanity of a customer," says Eulalia Emetaz, the pale, petite manager of La Galería Escondida.

"The tourists shake a few artists' hands and that gives them a veneer of culture—something to tell their friends," observes Howard Cook, one of Taos' outstanding painters. "When they stare at a painting you've worked on for weeks and ask, 'Is that hand-painted?' you just learn to shrug it off," he adds with a suppressed wince.

Painters who maintain their own studios recruit their customers from among old admirers, persons directed to the studio by friendly galleries or art enthusiasts who saw their work at museums or special shows.

Most Taos artists can relate tales of quick sales similar to the experience of Emil Bisttram. As a rule, however, the dollars don't flow so freely. The majority of Taos' artists must settle for incomes that range from $1,500 to $6,000 a year. Nearly all complain that their incomes fluctuate wildly from year to year.

"The other day a geologist bought one of my abstracts for $500;

I figure that will be twenty-five per cent of my 1956 earnings," observes Mr. Rogoway, staring glumly across the sparsely furnished living room of his adobe home which has no running water.

Says the pioneering Mr. Blumenschein, still spry and alert at 82: "I've earned a total of $10 in the last twelve months. But some really good years I've sold as much as $12,000 worth of paintings. Whenever I have a good year I return to Europe to study."

To supplement their incomes most Taos artists assume teaching positions. Some take on odd jobs around town, bartending or sign painting. Others do professional illustrating for publications.

"The nicest thing about New Mexico is that you can be poor without standing out like a sore thumb. You can live like an artist without everyone saying you're trying to be Bohemian," says Howard Schleeter, an abstract painter, as he pushes one of his seven cats off the only chair in his living room.

PETER B. BART

July 27, 1956

Life on the Farm

PEORIA, Ill.—The strike here at Caterpillar Tractor Co. couldn't have come at a more convenient moment for employee Norman Jepson. The walkout of his fellow United Auto Workers is giving arc welder Jepson time to finish harvesting corn and soybeans on his 80-acre farm just southwest of town.

Mr. Jepson, who had long hankered after rural life, became a parttime farmer five years ago, moving from a Peoria suburb to a ramshackle farmhouse at the end of a muddy country lane. "There was no plumbing and all we had for heat was a potbellied stove," recalls Mrs. Jepson. "It was so cold we had to wear almost all our clothes to bed."

Today, the old farmhouse is gone. The Jepsons live in a snug new ranch-type home, complete with two-car garage, picture window and flamboyant lampshade. Except for the cows grazing out back and a cornfield on one side, the place has the appearance of a subdivision residence anywhere.

The Jepsons' desire for a suburban standard of living amid the rustic setting of an honest-to-goodness working farm points up a significant change sweeping America's hinterland: the breakdown of the dividing line between farm and city styles of living.

"Farm life is gradually assuming a character that's typical of many suburban areas," says Dr. Clinton L. Folse, a University of Illinois associate professor of rural sociology.

Adds M. S. Hadley, an agricultural economist at Purdue University: "Farmers are losing their identity as a class. In the past, they kept pretty much to themselves. Now they're beginning to live like other people."

This disappearance of such urban-rural boundaries is working profound changes in the way farmers accumulate household gadgets, buy cars, shop for groceries, educate their children and spend their increasing hours of leisure time. To see where these changes are leading, consider three Midwestern farm families. One family, Mr. Jepson's, lives on a part-time farm; a second family operates a corn-hog farm in central Illinois; the third, a Wisconsin dairy farm.

Part-time farmers such as Mr. Jepson are perhaps the most direct embodiment of the intertwining of rural and urban life. Born in England 48 years ago, Mr. Jepson has been a Caterpillar employee for 17 years and has never been laid off. "We've always wanted to live on a farm," he explains. "When we came here, there was nothing. We started from scratch."

The place now is equipped with a 10-year-old used tractor, a combine and two-row tillage implements. A hay baler probably will be purchased next. The soil has been limed and fertilized to the point where the Jepsons get around 75 bushels of corn an acre—pretty respectable for that rough, wooded area.

Mr. Jepson, his wife and their 20-year-old son Norman all hold down outside daytime jobs. Mrs. Jepson works at the Agriculture Department's big research laboratory in Peoria; Norman recently has gone to work for a road contractor. Mr. Jepson works the 7:30-to-3:30 daylight shift at Cat; his farm chores are squeezed into about three hours each night and on weekends.

An estimated 30 per cent of the nation's farm operators now spend 100 days or more each year at off-the-farm pursuits, compared with only 16 per cent in 1939. Farmers collected a total of $6.7 billion in income from nonagricultural sources in 1956, up from $2.5 billion in 1939. Last year, however, the recession helped knock the non-agricultural income harvest to an estimated $6.3 billion.

This extra income reaped by farmers who double as factory workers, of course, helps fatten the bankroll available for cars, washing machines, vacations, schooling and other trappings of an urbanized, middle-class society.

But the mixing of traditional patterns of rural and urban life is by no means confined to areas close to industrial centers. Meet Russell Perkinson, a 38-year-old hog raiser with a round, bespectacled face who farms 240 acres near Buckley, Illinois. Mr. Perkinson got a master's degree in agricultural economics at the University of Illinois in 1941, then went to Washington for a stint in the Agriculture Department's Bureau of Economics. He returned to Buckley to take over the family farm when his father retired. Mr. Perkinson now calculates he puts in a 10-hour day, much of it in active labor. "But I think I got just as tired working eight hours a day in that office in Washington," he says with a grin.

Mr. Perkinson, his wife Arvella and their three sons moved into a new $25,000 magazine-cover home last March. It's specially designed for farm living, but the trilevel, three-bedroom dwelling would blend nicely into 'most any commuter neighborhood in the land.

Inside, the living room is paneled with mahogany; in a corner near the front entry is that horticultural symbol of suburbia, a brick planter sprouting with wax-leaved philodendra. Mrs. Perkinson's modern kitchen is outfitted with a pastel-green refrigerator, a dishwasher, a clothes washer and drier and an electric range, all bought from a nearby John Deere farm equipment dealer. The back door leads to a concrete-floored patio.

While few farmers are as elegantly housed as the Perkinsons, their array of creature comforts illustrates the improvements in rural living standards elsewhere. The Agriculture Department has a statistical yardstick to measure this; called the "farm operator family level of living index," it includes the percentage of farms with telephones, electricity and automobiles, plus a measurement of gross farm income.

With 1945 as the base year (100), this index for all U.S. farmers had climbed to 122 by 1950, to 140 by 1954, and to 145 by 1956, the last year computed. It almost surely stands higher now. In 1956, for example, an estimated 52 per cent of all farms had telephones. Bell System officials now believe this has climbed to 56 per cent.

In items outside the formal index, the Agriculture Department estimates 90 per cent of all farm homes had mechanical refrigerators in 1956, compared with 32 per cent in 1945; 53 per cent had TV sets (the Census Bureau figures this now is about two thirds), compared with 3 per cent in 1950; 39 per cent had home freezers, up from 12 per cent in 1950; 64 per cent had running water, compared with 29 per cent in 1945; 74 per cent had passenger cars, up from 63 per cent in 1950.

There are striking regional variations within the nation-wide figures, with the South still showing the closest resemblance to what sociologists call "peasant" agriculture. Only 39 per cent of the farm homes in Kentucky, Tennessee, Mississippi and Alabama had running water in 1956, compared with 98 per cent in the Pacific Coast states. Only 27 per cent in that central Dixie area had telephones, compared with 73 per cent in the eastern Corn Belt.

Agricultural economists note that the image of Old MacDonald's farm, with its wide variety of livestock and field crops, is fading, as farmers become more specialized in the production of foodstuffs. The usual example cited is "integrated" broiler farming, where the grower spends his time on chickens and little else. But specialization also is narrowing the array of livestock on the independent so-called "family farm."

Mr. Perkinson's specialty is hogs. "I used to have a lot of other things besides," he recalls. "I had chickens, beef cattle, and a good many sheep. Then I decided I could make more money on hogs year in and year out. We cut out all the hens, and that gave us time to take care of two extra litters of pigs. We don't have any more cattle, and we only keep a few sheep to eat up the weeds around the yard. They're a lot better than a mowing machine."

This has cut down the variety of food the Perkinsons produce for their own table. "We generally buy our beef from a neighbor, and we get our eggs from Arvella's folks, who raise a lot of chickens. We very seldom butcher our own hogs. I usually take them to town to the locker plant. Butchering takes time, and it's more economical to let somebody else do it."

The Perkinsons' garden supplies them with such summer staples as tomatoes, sweet corn, broccoli, radishes and onions, but the family doesn't look upon this as a money saver. "It probably costs us just as much as if we'd buy vegetables at the store, but we do get a better-quality product," Mr. Perkinson says. The family keeps no dairy cows, but milk is produced on the place—goat's milk. "That keeps us supplied for most of the year, but we do occasionally buy milk in town," he says. "And I suppose it's heresy to say this, but we use oleo instead of butter. It's just as good, and besides, this is soybean country here anyway."

The Agriculture Department says about 60 per cent of the food consumed by farm families in 1941 was produced at home. By 1955, the year of the latest survey, the balance had been precisely reversed: 60 per cent of all food on the farm family's table was bought from outside sources, while only 40 per cent was produced at home.

In the 1955 survey year, the average farm family spent $223 per person on food from outside sources. That's still below the estimated per capita food expenditure of $415 in the average city family. But in 1941, farm families were spending only $62 per person for food bought in town or from neighbors.

"Farmers are living just as well as city people, and they're certainly eating just as well. The biggest difference is that farmers don't have as much ready cash jingling in their pocket," says George Merwin, a towering 41-year-old dairyman who lives near Lake Geneva, Wisconsin.

The Merwins get clear television reception from Chicago, Milwaukee, Madison and Rockford, Illinois. They bought their first set seven years ago ("It sure spoiled book reading around here," Mr. Merwin notes) and are now on their second. The family owns two radios; one is kept in the barn, where Mr. Merwin picks up the early-morning market reports.

Next month, Mr. Merwin plans to join a band of neighborhood cronies for a week of deer hunting in northern Wisconsin. "I go up every year, and that's about all the vacation I take," he says.

Part-time farmer Jepson's family also is partial to northern Wisconsin vacations, but they go fishing. The Jepsons didn't make it this summer, though. Rain delayed the harvest schedule, and Mr. Jepson spent most of his three-week leave from the factory combining wheat.

"I really don't think I need a vacation," protests hog farmer Perkinson. "When our corn is in, I plan to start building a new barn for fattening hogs. I enjoy that kind of work, and that's all the change I need." But Mr. Perkinson isn't loath to take off for a day to a machinery exhibit in Indiana, or to slip up to Chicago occasionally to watch the White Sox play.

ARLEN L. LARGE

October 21, 1958

Television Sets Outnumber Phones
Down on the Farm

As the American farmer rushes to add city comforts, the television set is becoming a good deal more prevalent than the more routine telephone.

Census Bureau officials estimate that about two thirds of all farm families now own TV sets. That compares with a Bell System estimate of 56 per cent for telephones. As recently as 1950, only 3 per cent of all farm homes had television sets, according to the Agriculture Department.

One reason for TV's greater percentage, according to a spokesman for Illinois Bell Telephone Co., is purely technical: Some farmers live in areas which are reached by TV but have no telephone lines. "Then, too," he says, "there are farmers who simply don't want a telephone. They've never had them before, and they see no reason to get one now."

THE FACE OF POLITICS

The New Deal: Did Roosevelt or
Popular Demand Create It?

WASHINGTON—Like every President of the United States since the Government became too big and complicated for any one man to understand all its manifold activities, the Franklin D. Roosevelt that the general public knows is a composite personality. He is the product of what he sees, what he reads and what he is told by those who have his confidence. As what he sees, what he reads and what he is told by those he trusts changes the composite changes.

This is not a new phenomenon.

Mr. Roosevelt personifies, to most of his enemies and many of his friends, a great many economic- and social-reform experiments that he did not originate. For this reason, he probably has been the recipient of both praise and blame far beyond his just deserts.

Some of Mr. Roosevelt's more outspoken opponents in business and financial circles frequently have become almost hysterical in their more or less personal attacks upon him. This is sheer nonsense, but it has contributed to one of the greatest political build-ups this country has ever seen and it is partly responsible for the myth of "one-man government."

Fundamentally, this thing called the New Deal seems to have grown out of deep-seated popular dissatisfaction with affairs as they were and were becoming between the peak of the boom in 1929 and the bottom of the business depression in 1932. There is evidence to show that this dissatisfaction outran Mr. Roosevelt on more than one occasion.

His campaign for the Presidency in 1932 did not indicate that he fully sensed it.

If the origins of the New Deal lay in what the politicians are wont to describe as the grass roots, its formulation into a series of none too harmonious reform programs to deal with specific economic difficulties was more the result of pressure-group activities than it was the work of any single individual.

These facts are important, because they help explain the deadlocks of 1937 and 1938 and they point to the factors that will determine the final outcome—namely, a shift in public opinion, the realignment of pressure groups and the emergence of more effective leadership.

It seems somewhat improbable that such a shift and realignment would push a second-term President—any second-term President—to the front as the leader of one of the two alternative movements which we have described as Reconstruction and Revolution.

Leaving definitive analysis to that shadowy figment of almost any distracted commentator's imagination, the Historian of the Future, it would appear that Mr. Roosevelt's strength, during his first term, largely was the result of his ability to grasp and express in effective language the hopes and aspirations of a whole people. His weakness, as his second term got under way, would appear to have been the result of an unwillingness or inability to resolve the inevitable conflicts among those hopes and aspirations and to carry forward the enormous task of administering economic- and social-reform projects.

It has been asserted frequently that Mr. Roosevelt has been more popular than his program. If that program be stated only in terms of its broad objectives, this is probably untrue.

Even the Republican National Convention of 1936 found it difficult to pick suitable quarrels with those objectives. But growing differences of opinion as to methods have disrupted the President's own party since the 1936 elections.

And the most serious criticism that can be chalked up against Mr. Roosevelt arises out of his failure, on several critical occasions, to exert the strong guiding influence which his high office and the devotion of his followers would have enabled him to exert.

Where was the "leader" of the New Deal when popular dissatisfaction with the scheme of things needed to be directed into more practicable channels (demands for social-security legislation, for example)?

Or when public interest in basic economic problems lagged (as was the case with respect to the railroad situation in 1936)?

Or when conflicting views within his circle of administrative officials and advisers tended to produce stalemates leading to uncertainty and delay (such as was inevitable in the absence of any decision on national power policy in 1937)?

The answer is that there was no leadership in the New Deal when a real directly exerted influence was most needed.

BERNARD KILGORE

April 14, 1938

Third-Term President

WASHINGTON—The first man ever to be elected President of the United States for the third time held his first regular press conference as third-term President-elect yesterday in the circular executive office of the White House.

Sensing the importance of the occasion and the particular significance of anything Mr. Roosevelt might say, as well as the meaning of the manner in which he might say it, newspaper correspondents crowded into the room. Close to 200 men and women were present, half again as many as usually attend and twice as many as have shown up on dull days. Despite the chilly November weather outside, the French doors on one side of the office overlooking the gardens behind the White House were thrown open to provide extra needed ventilation.

So far as news was concerned, the conference could be described as only mildly interesting. There were a few matters of considerable importance discussed but nothing world-shaking. On the general question of how does a third-term President-elect act just after the election, the press conference atmosphere could probably be best described as pretty businesslike. It was not as boisterous as some and not as serious as others.

The President was calmly smoking a cigarette when the reporters trooped in. An attendant, as usual, called "All in" and a period of anticipatory quiet ensued.

The President broke it by remarking, as he has remarked dozens of times, that he didn't think there was any particular news. Ofttimes when he has said this, there wasn't any news. Other times there has turned out to be some. The correspondents never turn around and prepare to leave the room empty-handed just because Mr. Roosevelt doesn't begin the conference with an announcement of some sort.

In line, too, with custom, were the President's next comments. He told about his plans for the immediate future—Press Club party Saturday night, speech on Armistice Day, cornerstone to lay, and next week three or four days of rest and sleep on the *U.S.S. Potomac,* cruising river and bay. There are also, he said, a lot of documents that haven't been read.

There followed a brief discussion of new War and Navy department buildings of interest only to local newspapers.

Raymond P. Brandt brought up the first question of wider news value. He asked whether the President had done better than Dr. Gallup in forecasting the election.

Calling the correspondent by his nickname, which is Pete, Mr. Roosevelt admitted that he was 'way off. He had guessed last August that he would get 340 electoral votes and had seen no reason to change the estimate. He lost out also, he admitted, in the Hyde Park election "pools" made up by newspapermen assigned to cover the windup there.

"What states surprised you?" somebody asked.

The President declined to comment, cheerfully stating that he had been surprised by about 110 electoral votes' worth.

Mr. Roosevelt thought it was awfully nice that a Pan-American group had gone on record as congratulating him. No, he hadn't heard from Herr Hitler and Mussolini.

BERNARD KILGORE

November 9, 1940

In Behalf of Politicians

In his cabinet appointments to date Mr. Truman has selected politicians. Each appointee has at some time been elected to office or has had experience equivalent to that gained in running for office. It seems unlikely that the President will make any radical departure from that practice and we think he acts wisely in that respect.

In this country the word "politicians" has grown to be a term of opprobrium often preceded by indelicate adjectives. A few people may really be convinced that politicians are an unworthy lot, but most of the condemnation probably is only parrotlike repetition. Whatever the cause, the practice ought to be stopped. It can be and very probably has been destructive because it builds a distrust for those who are the most capable of conducting governmental processes in an orderly manner.

The politician is a man who is a specialist in public affairs. He has in the first place some traits which incline him in that direction. In due time he runs for office or he becomes a leader in the deliberations of some group or party. If he does neither of those things, he is not successful and is soon forgotten. If he does them, he accumulates experience. If he takes the next step and is elected to office,

"See what it was I promised the voters last election."

he gains more experience and this he may quite legitimately employ to gain still higher office.

By some curious, illogical process of reasoning there has grown up in this country the theory that the men who have gone through this experience are the least fitted to conduct government. There was a time when it was fashionable to advocate that businessmen should be elected to high public office. The modern idea is that government is a job for the "expert" or the "technician," although it has never been very clearly specified just how one manages to get into either category.

In this country the job of a government official is:

1. To carry out an action which the people want taken;

2. To restrain the people from hurried, unwise action, or,

3. To persuade them into a course of action which the sponsor believes will be constructive.

Observe that nothing can be done unless the people by expression of the majority want it done. The wisest and most noble program is valueless unless it can be carried out and it cannot be carried out unless the people approve. There have been attempts to cram things down the people's throats and for a little bit those attempts seemed successful, but in the end the people will wreck them.

Obviously the person best able to sense and thus to guide public sentiment is the politician. He must have and he must have developed the traits that enable him to do that. Unless he had, he would not have been elected to office, certainly he would not stay in office for any length of time. The fact that he has succeeded in remaining in office is proof of his capabilities in this respect.

Mrs. Perkins was a labor expert. She had spent her life in studying labor statistics and the details of labor relations. In a discussion of those things her successor, Mr. Schwellenbach, probably would be outshone by her. But Mr. Schwellenbach has another kind of training which should lead him to know what can and what cannot be done in dealing with the people with whom he has to deal. He understands them and so is in a position to administer where their interests are involved, and this understanding came through seeking their support.

Mr. Wickard was a trained farmer and a student of agricultural conditions. Mr. Anderson, his successor, is not wholly ignorant on the subject, of course, but he has not devoted his time to agricultural theory as Mr. Wickard had. But Mr. Anderson has something that was lacking, and that is a sense of what the people will allow to be done. Again he got that through contact with people by running for office.

Mr. Hull as Secretary of State had no detailed knowledge of diplomacy when he took office. He was a master politician. Mr. Hull knew how to win the support of all factions and to bring them into agreement so that American adhesion to the United Nations Charter was assured. At the beginning, the job he undertook looked vastly more formidable than that assigned to either the Department of Labor or the Department of Agriculture.

There is a know-how to government just as there is in building a house or playing a violin, and, generally speaking, the performance will succeed in proportion to the experience of the performer.

For ten years we have had government by the experts and technicians, and, whatever may be history's verdict on the period, no one living through it will deny that it has been marked by disruption and animosities which hindered progress toward economic recovery before the war and which have interfered with the full prosecution of the war.

Your successful politician possesses something that the expert lacks—many other people lack it too. It may be described as tolerance or restraint. If he is a reform politician, and is wise, he does not push his reforms too fast. Restraint is to him a matter of self-preservation. He knows that as far as the people swing in one direction, they are likely to swing back in another. He knows that the law of averages someday will put him out of office. He does not want to stay out and he does not want to see the pendulum swing so far that it will not swing back within the time that he may seek office again.

Even the venal politician—there are many of him just as there are shyster lawyers and quack doctors—has this quality of restraint. If he grafts, he does not steal too much or too brazenly.

It was once assumed in this country that if a man made a great deal of money, he must know the answers to everything. Lately it seems to be assumed that if a man or woman is a movie star, they must know a good deal; that they are wise in international affairs as well as having the solutions to domestic problems. And there never has been a time when it has not been assumed that all classes could run the Government better than the politicians who had made a study of the matter. None of these things are so.

Like the rest of us, the politician needs criticism and he needs prodding and there is little danger that he will escape either. But in our opinion President Truman is right when he turns to him for assistance.

July 9, 1945

EDITORIAL

Self-Portrait of a Man
Who Happened to Be President

Poets and psychiatrists have long known that if you set a man to talking about himself he will in time tell you more about himself than he intended. That is part of the interest in Shakespeare's soliloquies, Browning's poetic monologues and the revelations of the analyst's couch.

It is also the major attraction in the first volume of the memoirs of Harry Truman. No future biographer is likely to do half so well as he has done himself in revealing what sort of man it was that became 33rd President of the United States. And none will make half so interesting a tale of it. The reader who turns to the Truman memoirs for startling new information on the facts of history or new insights into the meaning of history, as to the memoirs of Churchill or Eisenhower, will be disappointed. There are, it is true, some new bits and pieces to the puzzle of Yalta in the recorded conversations of what was said afterward by the surviving principals. Also, historians interested in the minutiae of the Presidency can make use of the carefully detailed reports on what happened day by day, and on who said what to whom, in the White House.

But the substance of that story is already known. The Truman memoirs will not alter the picture in any major way nor likely change anyone's previous judgments. The insights in this book are not so much into history as into Harry Truman. The portrait may not be exactly the one Mr. Truman intended. He is obviously writing a defense of his Administration, and he seems to look upon himself as the forceful Captain who stepped into the breach and vanquished all; there is no instance in which he entertains the suggestions he might have been wrong in any major action.

Yet for all that, another and warmer portrait shows through. Mr. Truman was honest enough, or ingenuous enough, to try to tell his story exactly as he saw it, including many of the things he wrote at the time not for history but for his family. It makes a story that cannot be read without understanding and even admiration for the man.

For here is the story of a man pushed by destiny into a role he never made. Harry Truman never aspired to be President; indeed, he never really expected to be Vice-President. Yet one day the sun and the moon and the stars fell down on him and there he was, President of the United States. He was, plainly, overwhelmed by the magnitude of the job, overcome by the astounding fact that he, Harry Truman, was "Mr. President." Again and again he refers plaintively to the "constant pressure and necessity of making decisions" and marvels that he could make them. "Six days President of the United States!" he wrote home. "It is unbelievable."

It is always an interesting study in human nature to watch a man who does not feel quite up to a job face up to its burdens. Mr. Truman knew little of our military position, less of the problems of foreign policy, nothing of the atom bomb. In his first uncertainty he relied almost entirely on Roosevelt's old advisers and policies. Yet he did not duck the hard decisions when they had to be made, even though he relied more on intuition than knowledge.

He did cast the atom bomb. He greatly influenced the disposition of troops when the war ended in Europe. He changed the policy on the surrender of Japan. He stood up to Churchill over Germany and to Stalin over Poland. He dismantled the armies and he completed the United Nations.

Quite often, truth to tell, his instinct was better than the involved logic of others. An early memo to the State Department, after Potsdam, shows he quickly got "tired of babying the Soviets." In this case it may be a pity that he did not gain confidence quicker in his instincts.

He did gradually gain confidence, and the change can be easily followed in his letters home and in the changing character of his instructions to his subordinates. This volume ends after the first year, but already you can see the uncertain Mr. Truman emerging as the cocky Mr. Truman. It looks as though having painfully acquired the confidence to make decisions he could not have that confidence threatened by any suggestion that a decision might be wrong.

While these self-revealed attributes are not good qualities for a President, they will nevertheless strike many readers as very human. Many a citizen would be just as startled as Harry Truman to find himself suddenly President—and just as overwhelmed, too. A reader may not excuse the blunders but he can understand them. "There but for the Grace of God go I."

That President Truman was not always adequate to the tasks at hand will affect his place in history. But that final verdict does not affect the drama of his story.

Reading Harry Truman's memoirs in the tranquillity of different times you cannot help but feel a sympathy for this man who did as well as he was able.

VERMONT ROYSTER

November 7, 1955

Politician Ike

DENVER—How is General Ike making out as a politician?

It's been only two weeks since Ike shucked his Army uniform—with all of the protections it offered—and plunged so abruptly into politics. It's too early to tell how he'll fare in the fight for the Republican nomination next month. It's not even clear whether Ike has won more than a handful of delegates since his return.

But this much is certain: As a politician, Ike is making out fine—under circumstances so difficult that Ike himself has been sorely tempted to give up the idea altogether.

Since his return, Ike—for forty-one years a somewhat insulated military man—has been badgered by newsmen and photographers, besieged by politicians. He has answered, sometimes two or three times a day, the same questions on a raft of subjects unfamiliar to him. He's been bombarded with conflicting and often bad advice from the mixed assortment of supporters and advisers who make up the campaign organization he inherited lock, stock and barrel.

His press relations have been handled in such a fashion that newsmen assigned to his headquarters here found themselves running around in circles a few days back, interviewing each other because some had been granted a hush-hush interview and others had been excluded.

Ike has been advised to speak out more bluntly, to say almost nothing about the issues, to embark on a "whistle-stop" campaign, to settle down and talk only to delegates. On just about all the hot issues, he's gotten conflicting counsel. He's been urged to take varying points of view on farm price supports, labor legislation, so-called tidelands oil and a host of other knotty problems.

Yet Politician Ike has committed almost no real blunders—at least none that are generally recognized as such at this point.

How has Ike managed to handle his sudden transition from soldier to politician with such apparent success? The answer is simple: To Ike, being a politician comes naturally.

The explanation for the answer is less easy, but if you put the question to anybody who has seen the General in action the past two weeks, you'll probably get much the same response: "Ike does by instinct what professional politicians take a lifetime to cultivate. This is so because he is a passionately honest man."

This is the view of political observers who have seen a lot of politicians come and go, and developed a healthy cynicism in the process. Most are convinced that Candidate Ike is the rarity on the American political scene who means it when he says, "If speaking from my heart is a gamble then I'm that sort of a bettor."

Ike's determination to "gamble" in this fashion gives his advisers anxious moments. Some would rather have the General read carefully prepared political speeches than shoot from the hip as he did in Detroit a week ago. But others recognize a natural hitter when they see one, and, like a smart baseball manager, they aren't inclined to tamper with his swing.

The same qualities that seem to be making Ike's new job come easily to him are the ones that got him into the race for the Republican nomination, and almost got him out, in the view of many around him. It was more a sense of obligation to his backers than a real desire to be President that led him step by step into an active political role. When each successive step created new conflicts with his official job at SHAPE headquarters, he admitted he had made a "bad mistake" by giving the Ike bandwagon a push while proclaiming he wasn't in politics.

Those who were with Ike in Paris and have seen him recently will tell you his last six months in SHAPE were "terrible" and Ike would not deny it. The first two weeks in the U. S. have not been much easier for Ike, his close advisers admit.

There was a brief time when the General was on the verge of abandoning his new profession before he got in any deeper. The low point came shortly before the Detroit speech. Confronted suddenly with over a half-dozen drafts, he decided he couldn't deliver any of them—"They don't sound like me." For a time his aides weren't absolutely sure he'd go through with the speech after all.

Ike has chafed under the omnipresent eyes of newsmen and the ever popping flash bulbs. The General's hot temper, something that apparently more than one junior Army officer can testify to, might have wrecked his campaign on two occasions, once at his Morningside Heights home at Columbia University, and once at his Gettysburg farm, when he came close to "blowing up" at photographers.

Yet you have to conclude that career soldier Ike has turned politician with astonishing ease, despite these crises. And whether you're convinced of his sincerity, there's no denying the celebrated Eisenhower charm, the forthright manner, the willingness to plead ignorance on such crucial topics as farm price supports, all stamp him as somewhat of a "hot article" in the political trade.

You have only to watch Ike standing easily before a group of visiting delegates, some friendly, some not so. The General never ducks a question in the usual sense—never refuses to comment. He sometimes gives a reply so well hedged that it is almost meaningless, but somehow he leaves the questioner with a satisfied look.

A delegate inquiring about the General's views on statehood for Alaska and Hawaii, to take one example, is satisfied to learn "you bring up that question for the first time." Then the General discusses the pros and cons and winds up: "I would say, as a matter of sentiment, I would be instinctively in favor of it, but I would want to verify it with real study on the situation." No commitment there, but supporters of statehood for Alaska and Hawaii are comforted that, at least, the General's instincts are right.

Or consider how the General opens a meeting with a delegate group: "The meetings are the height of informality," he tells the Oregon delegation. "Their purpose is an exchange of views, and out of them I have certainly derived a lot more information than I have ever been able to give."

A final case in point: the General's reiterated insistence that he will ask the support of no delegate, and wants the support of none that aren't chosen by the "will of the people." Certainly this is good politics for Ike; his strategists are out to discredit Taft forces on the grounds that rival Candidate Taft has "stolen" delegations in Texas and other states.

But when Ike says it, it sounds convincing, and more than one delegate has come away thoroughly convinced by such disarming declarations as this: "I will say this, I have said it from the beginning, I believe it and I mean it, and I can't help whether it is a thing that a politician is not supposed to say or not. I want no delegate who is unduly influenced toward the Eisenhower camp. . . ."

Is Ike sincere about that?

This being a political campaign, and Ike being a candidate, there's bound to be more than a little disagreement on that point.

But those who've seen Candidate Ike in action at close range are pretty generally convinced that they're looking at a completely honest politician.

PHILIP GEYELIN

June 25, 1952

Nixon: A Man in Motion

WASHINGTON—The nation's capital these days is witnessing a subtle but nonetheless real shift in the center of political gravity—from President Eisenhower to Vice-President Nixon.

The Republicans have for a long time looked to Mr. Nixon, not to the President, as their party leader. Now they're beginning to think of Mr. Nixon as the leader of Government as well as the G.O.P. The Vice-President, let it be said, did not usurp this power; it has, instead, been thrust upon him by force of events and circumstance.

What is Mr. Nixon's role and how did he acquire it?

The explanation of how the Vice-President arrived at his present status is not a simple one. Mr. Eisenhower's age and health supply only part of the answer. As some observers see it, what is even more basic is that the people think times have changed, and the President has not been fully aware of the change in the public mood. Or if he has, that he has not kept pace with it.

What this means is that Mr. Eisenhower was the political product of years in which the voters wanted to take a recess from depression, war and then inflation of the 1930s and 1940s. In the 1952 campaign, one did not have to talk with many voters or be very discerning to sense that what they wanted was not more crisis but a holiday from two decades of crises. Candidate Ike's conservative campaign six years ago did not create that mood; he sensed it and reflected it.

The first Eisenhower years, which were not too eventful, no doubt reflected this state of national contentment. He steered clear of dazzling new Federal programs. The Korean War ended. The fear of future wars subsided. The country prospered—and Mr. Eisenhower's popularity rating curved ever upward.

Aside from his illnesses, the President's political troubles didn't really begin until, first, Russia signaled what's now known as "the space age," and, second, the present recession became evident. As best one can judge from Washington, including the reaction of Congress, the mood of the country suddenly changed. The lawmakers may not always accurately mirror their constituents, but usually they try to. And suddenly they demanded action, first on defense, then on recession.

In both instances, Mr. Eisenhower held back. Even after he shifted ground on the defense issue, he still, relatively speaking, was disinclined to hit any panic buttons. Now, the President is holding back on drastic antirecession measures, including tax relief. The result is that, for the first time, lawmakers feel free to attack the President on his military judgment, which was supposed to be his forte. And once again the G.O.P. is threatened with the "Depression Party" label which it took them 20 years to shake off.

Moreover, Mr. Eisenhower's advancing years and declining health have forced him to reduce his activity, leaving increased responsibility to his subordinates. He never did, of course, relish his role of party leader. The bulk of that responsibility fell to Mr. Nixon right from the beginning. Furthermore, the Constitution bars the President from running for a third term. The question of whether he will be able to serve out his present term is openly discussed in Washington.

The Vice-President is a study in contrasts. He is young and vigorous. He is ambitious for himself and his party. He has been and is impatient to build up the nation's defenses and fight the recession. His tax policy statement was just the latest example of his effort to seize the initiative for himself and his party on the recession issue.

The Vice-President cannot, to be sure, make the big policy decisions. What he is doing, though, is making decisions inevitable by supplying the drive Mr. Eisenhower has lost through advancing years and failing health. As one White House intimate put it, "Nixon is the activist of this Administration."

Mr. Nixon's role can best be described, perhaps, in terms of the events of the past six months. Last fall, after Russia launched the first sputnik, White House aide Clarence Randall referred to it as "a silly bauble." Sherman Adams spoke derisively of the "space basketball game." The President declared the Soviet achievement made "not one iota" of difference so far as national defense was concerned. Whether such remarks were right or wrong, manifestly they were out of tune with the times.

And sensing this, Mr. Nixon spoke what pretty soon became Administration policy—that the U.S. could make no greater blunder than to laugh off Russia's venture into outer space. It no doubt would be an exaggeration to assign to Mr. Nixon all the credit for this major policy shift; but it would be equally erroneous to underestimate his influence in bringing it about.

The same sort of thing is happening right now on the recession issue. More than any other Administration official, Mr. Nixon is furnishing the push for government action to deal with the business slump. The result is that G.O.P. lawmakers, state party leaders and in some instances even members of the Eisenhower cabinet—seeing the G.O.P. again threatened with the "Depression Party" label—are gravitating toward the Vice-President as the one to guide them out of the depression danger zone.

This was dramatized just the other day with Mr. Nixon's statement supporting tax relief as the next big antirecession move. His pronouncement was clearly in line with Administration thinking; the difference was that no one else had bothered to state it with such clarity and force.

In taking these forward positions, the Vice-President studiously tries not to further his own political interests alone, even though Mr. Eisenhower has explicitly given him a free hand to develop his own positions. But in doing so, Mr. Nixon is always careful to promote the interests of the Administration and the G.O.P. as well as his own.

The fact nonetheless remains that Mr. Nixon is a man in motion. So politicians who think in terms of the future, as most of them do, perforce must look not to the White House; they must look elsewhere. And right now, there is no other place to turn but to Richard Nixon.

ALBERT CLARK

March 17, 1958

Sherman Adams: The Sad Part of the Story

We are sure it's true that the departure of Mr. Sherman Adams is going to be a loss to President Eisenhower. Mr. Adams, whatever his faults of judgment in his personal affairs, impresses us as an extremely capable administrator, and his years of service with the President have given him a familiarity with the job which another cannot quickly acquire.

Yet we find it strange, and even a little sad, that the departure of any one man from the White House staff should be a loss of such proportions as it is said to be by the President's associates.

And if this is the case, then it seems to us that it raises some important questions about the whole concept of a White House staff and its role in the executive branch.

Presidents have long had some personal assistants—a press secretary, an appointments secretary and a few general administrative helpers to shoulder some of the drabber chores around the office. All this is understandable and its desirability is unquestioned.

But this is not what is meant in the present talk about organizing a White House staff. More recently Presidents have taken to appointing people whose jobs are commonly labeled "assistant Presidents" and whose function is to serve in the manner of staff officers in an army, each with his own particular field of policy. The practice began with President Roosevelt, was continued by President Truman and has been enlarged by President Eisenhower.

Besides "the" assistant to the President, there is presently a deputy assistant and nearly a score of special assistants. There is, for example, a special assistant for national security, a special assistant for economic affairs, for science, for certain aspects of foreign policy, and so on.

Now, whatever may be intended in theory, in practice all these people have great influence in determining what matters relating to a particular field are brought to the President's attention, whom he sees about what, and the manner in which ideas are presented to him. And it is bound to happen—again whatever the intent—that these people, this inner staff, will come to have great influence upon what is decided. In extreme cases, they could even make such and such a decision inevitable.

This tendency, to be sure, exists even without a staff. The Secretary of the Treasury, for instance, influences economic decisions;

so does the Secretary of Commerce. But at least these are public officers, confirmed in their appointments by the Senate, and they operate in the public limelight. They are also, and this is an important difference, operating heads responsible for carrying out the decisions that are made.

The growth of the staff system inserts a sort of personal bureaucracy between the cabinet officers, or other department heads, and the Chief Executive. The inevitable effect will be to downgrade the cabinet. This effect, already noticeable, will be intensified by any of the various suggestions for creating formal administrative "Vice-Presidents" and giving them specific legal authority.

We are aware of all the arguments for doing this, and some of them sound plausible. The Presidency can be a man-killing job and it does require its holder to make many decisions on matters about which he is not deeply informed. So he must rely on others for information and, to some extent, for advice.

But the President of the United States is not a constitutional monarch whose role is only to be kept informed and to give authority to staff decisions. His main duty, and almost his only governing function, is to make decisions. And the country ought to think a long time before it adopts the practice of having a Secretary of Defense, let us say, with responsibility for military operations and then removing him by one functionary a farther distance away from the President.

We sympathize with Mr. Eisenhower over the circumstances that cost him the services of an able assistant. But we sincerely hope it is not true that this resignation is going to cause all the dislocation in the White House that some suggest. At least it should not be true, because the people of the United States did not elect Mr. Sherman Adams to do anything.

EDITORIAL

September 24, 1958

Rockefeller's Ambition

NEW YORK—Nelson Aldrich Rockefeller, a man who will never know what it's like to make his first million, has spent a lifetime looking for success in other quarters. He has been a business executive, a philanthropist, a civic leader, and an appointed functionary in local, state, and Federal government.

Now he is trying politics. As Republican candidate for governor of New York, Mr. Rockefeller is attempting not only to win an important office for his party but apparently also to prove himself in a dramatic and very personal way. And in the process he hopes to give new meaning to the Rockefeller name.

The race for governor provides him with a rare opportunity. It pits him against Averell Harriman, a fellow millionaire and social equal, a foe who cannot easily put Mr. Rockefeller in a position where his wealth might be politically embarrassing.

Who is this newcomer, why is he there, and what does he really want?

Mr. Rockefeller, at a youthful 50, is the second eldest of five grandsons of the late John D. Rockefeller, the billionaire oil tycoon who at one time in his life was described as the richest man in the world. The Rockefeller legend has hung—sometimes heavily—over the movements of this family since the late nineteenth century. The family has for decades concentrated on wide humanitarian activities designed, at least in part, to remove whatever public impression of ruthlessness remains from the elder Rockefeller's business maneuvers.

To this end the current Republican candidate has worked diligently for most of his adult life. The minimum estimate of his personal wealth places it at $150 million, but some put the figure at two or three times that amount. He has given away many millions himself to continue the family's philanthropic tradition, and he has supplemented his charitable activities with service to both community and nation.

But his philanthropy and even his public-service record were made possible largely because he was a Rockefeller—not necessarily because he was Nelson A. Rockefeller. Although his proven executive ability led to his high advisory posts in the Roosevelt, Truman and Eisenhower administrations, these posts did little to improve the public image of him as the conscientious, rich man's son who could have just about anything that money and influence could buy. Mr. Rockefeller, in the judgment of men who have known him over the years, is not satisfied with that appraisal.

In running for governor Mr. Rockefeller would seem to risk nothing. At best, he could upset Governor Harriman and become an important political force in the nation. At worst, it might be thought, he would lose only a difficult race in which he was the underdog, and he could always salve his pride with a new estate, a trip around the world, or some other material delight. But Nelson Rockefeller does not look at things that way. Victory for him would have a special personal importance over and above what it would have for many other men.

Mr. Rockefeller, personally, comes to politics with several built-in assets. He has an easy manner in public and handles people with the polite dispatch of a man accustomed to receiving attention. He is solidly built and walks as though he were already a little late for something, and his energy has a contagious quality about it. There is an on-the-level air about him that is difficult to define but none-theless a characteristic which, according to several leading Republicans, is likely to enhance his political salability. On the debit side (maybe) he is only mediocre as a public speaker.

Philosophically, Mr. Rockefeller has strong humanitarian feelings and he is regarded as a liberal "modern Republican," a definition that to some G.O.P. conservatives makes him dangerously close to being a Democrat. Mr. Rockefeller, for instance, predicts he will have to raise taxes somewhat if he's elected, and he has come out against a measure which would require people to be state residents for a year before becoming eligible for welfare assistance. On other occasions he speaks at length about the "dignity of the individual" and of the need for economy in government. Thus, it is difficult to pinpoint Mr. Rockefeller's attitudes—possibly because he has yet to decide himself exactly what these attitudes are.

Friends say he is a dynamic executive and note his experience as chairman of Rockefeller Center and his overseeing part of the family empire. His foes see him as a personable man who has always had his own way, a man untested in any situation where his name and money couldn't have come to the rescue.

Mr. Rockefeller himself has compared being a Rockefeller to living in a goldfish bowl. But, he adds, like the fish "you get used to it." And people are easily moved to prejudge a man who must ascribe his position in life so much to the chance of birth. But in Washington, where prejudging comes especially easy, most of Mr. Rockefeller's associates in Government regarded him with friendliness and respect.

As a family man the candidate provides a good picture. He is married to the former Mary Todhunter Clark of Philadelphia, and the couple now has five grown children, two of them married. Friends say they are a closely knit family, a fact stemming not only from domestic rapport but from the somewhat isolating factor of all being named Rockefeller.

Aside from wealth and family, what were the other influences that helped mold the man?

Mr. Rockefeller, like a child of royalty, was conditioned early to the meaning and responsibilities of his birthright. His father is John D. Rockefeller, Jr., who was far more interested in giving away his fortune than in increasing it, who instituted the restoration of Colonial Williamsburg and contributed millions to medical, cultural, and social charities. His mother was the late Abby Greene Aldrich Rockefeller, a woman of strong character who brought up her children close to the Bible and the Baptist Church. Both parents feared what enormous wealth might do to the characters of their sons, and they instilled in them an appreciation for financial prudence and a desire to serve the community. And the children were carefully kept away from the public spotlight until they were grown.

As boys, the Rockefeller brothers are said to have received allowances of 25 cents a week, out of which a portion was set aside for church and for savings. So with at least a few coins to jingle, young Nelson grew up at the family's sumptuous, rolling estate at Pocantico Hills in New York's Westchester County.

Friends who knew him as a boy say he was good-humored and bright, with an interest in boating and athletics. He attended the Lincoln School in New York and Dartmouth College, where he earned a degree in economics and was a better-than-average soccer player.

The family tells the story of how Mr. Rockefeller coasted through his first three college years without distinguishing himself academically. Then, in his senior year, with his roommate heading for Phi Beta Kappa, young Nelson turned on the steam and won the coveted key himself. In competition, Mr. Rockefeller seems to find a fourth gear.

Six days after he was graduated he married and with his bride took a trip around the world, meeting along the way leading personages such as Mahatma Gandhi. The tour was a wedding present from his father. When he returned home he went to work as a clerk in the old Chase National Bank and was given a minor executive role at Rockefeller Center. During the thirties, also, he spent several years in South America watching over oil wells and other family interests.

Those who knew him during the late thirties say that it was his experiences in Latin America that spurred his interest in the economic development of backward countries. With his own money and later as a State Department aide he was instrumental in building low-price housing developments and industrializing underdeveloped areas in South America and Puerto Rico.

When World War II broke out, President Roosevelt named him Assistant Secretary of State for Latin American Affairs. He served in other advisory posts under Mr. Roosevelt and President Truman, and in 1953 President Eisenhower made him Under Secretary of Health, Education and Welfare. Later the same year he was appointed special assistant to the President. But even this wide service failed to provide the kind of intense personal satisfaction that Mr. Rockefeller seems to need.

It was not enough for him to be wealthy or famous or merely to do a job well. Something was still missing and that something is the sense of achievement that could only come by stepping off the Rockefeller pedestal and slugging it out in an arena where his name might even be a liability.

Mr. Rockefeller says he is running for governor because he is dissatisfied with Governor Harriman. And as far as it goes this is undoubtedly true. But perhaps behind this conscious reason for entering the political wars lies a deeper, more impelling reason— that even after a diverse and demanding career, Nelson Rockefeller is not yet satisfied with himself.

EDWIN A. ROBERTS, JR.

September 2, 1958

Mr. Wallace Is Dismissed

The criticism offered here of Henry Agard Wallace, Vice-President of the United States, is aimed at Mr. Wallace not as an individual but as the representative of a type of thought.

This type of thought has a desire—in the case of Mr. Wallace at least a purely unselfish desire—to do good. That is all very well. But the adherents of the school are prone to believe that they know, and know surely, what is good. From this it is a short step to reason that any who differ with them must be against good and in favor of evil. It matters not that their proposals are vague. It matters not that when they become specific they also envisage a degree of paternalism which will go to the extent of proposing the harshest punishment for those who may reject their good offices.

This type of thought has never been absent from American public life, but it is only in recent years that men holding such beliefs have found their way into high administrative posts of the Government. In those posts they have contributed just two things: futility and disruption.

For two terms Mr. Wallace—and again we speak of him as a representative of a type—was Secretary of Agriculture. Under his regime the farms of this nation were brought under a degree of control and regimentation that was hardly rivaled in some of the totalitarian countries. We are now seeing the results of that in a demoralized agriculture and a shortage of food in a nation where potential production of food is almost limitless.

During the course of war preparations Mr. Wallace was given other administrative posts from which he was unostentatiously shifted. He finally wound up as the head of the Board of Economic Warfare. There he became embroiled in a controversy with Secretary of Commerce Jesse Jones, and the President has now withdrawn the functions of B.E.W. from both Mr. Wallace and Mr. Jones, an action which is highly encouraging if it means that the bickerings and the rivalry among Washington personages are at last to be ended.

It was not some "economic royalist" or some "reactionary" that found Mr. Wallace an unstable administrator. It was the man who has a deep personal affection for him and who forced an unwilling convention to eliminate him for the office he now holds.

This newspaper hopes that Mr. Wallace and those like him will continue to voice the idealism that is a credit to them. As idealists they have their place and function in American life. But what has happened to Mr. Wallace is a lesson that that place and function is not responsible administrative office.

EDITORIAL

July 17, 1943

Taft Phenomenon

A pre-election wanderer along the diagonal of Ohio, from Cincinnati to Cleveland, could find no one who would not take violent issue on some particular with that state's singular statesman, Robert A. Taft.

Yet there was no difficulty at all in finding violently pro-Taft partisans who with eagerness and enthusiasm were out working for the re-election of this same Robert Taft. Curiously, many of these apostles were not merely advancing Taft to avoid some other evil. By some political alchemy they had been made "for" the man whose opinions they were oftentimes against.

And when the roll was called more than a million and a half Ohioans cast their lot with this strange politician, giving him an amazing plurality of 430,000 votes over his opponent.

So the man without glamour, the man without political sex appeal, the man without tact, indeed the man without anything supposedly needful for political success, had once more baffled all the rule makers.

Now everyone is trying to explain it. Possibly there is no explanation in familiar terms; Taft may be a phenomenon, to be perceived and perhaps catalogued but never quite comprehended. Nevertheless, an autumnal visitor in Ohio could catch glimpses that might be clues for some more astute philosopher.

The first glimpse came at the Cincinnati station. Earlier, some 1,500 miles of Midwest touring had uncovered much concern over the makings of politics—war and inflation—but very little over the personalities of the politicians. The Cincinnati taxi driver, abruptly and without prodding, launched into a tirade against Mr. Taft. Now, the driver, it is true, was against and not for, but the significant thing was that he was aroused.

Cab driver, foundryman, farmer, housewife, bank clerk, lawyer, doctor and merchant—all were aroused, for or against. To a weary wanderer it was like stepping from a room of stale and lethargic air into a refreshing breeze. So, to begin with, Mr. Taft is no man to leave apathy in his wake.

In the general rousing, Mr. Taft had aroused the very people hardest to stir, the vast majority of the citizens who belong to no pressure group, who do not look for preferential treatment from political action. These are the people too often complacent.

"That's a letter from a constituent who doesn't ask for anything."

Also in this general rousing—and here Mr. Taft was helped by his enemies—it was proved that pressure groups are only people. Within these groups, too, there are the quiescent who let the few speak and act for them. But once pushed to the poll gate they showed much aroused admiration for Mr. Taft's independence, or at least aroused anger at their labor bosses who would deprive them of voting independence.

That Mr. Taft can arouse the countryside can be understood. Since he rarely ducks any controversy, what he says always arouses somebody. Yet that leaves the phenomenon still unexplained. Whom Mr. Taft pleases today he angers tomorrow, and soon he has said something to anger everybody. The mystery is why so many of those angered end up, in violation of all the rules, voting for him.

There are clues to that, too. Mr. Taft can, as he did, tactlessly tell farmers they ought to have fewer government benefits or union members that their union ought to have more regulation and yet still walk away with the votes of both. The answer may be that deep in his heart the farmer is uneasy at big government handouts and the union member uneasy at the actions of his own union. Each is shocked by the tactlessness, but each admires the integrity and decides finally that here is a man to be trusted.

It is this sense of trust that most impressed the pre-election visitor. After awhile it was no longer surprising to find a man damning Taft's views on this or that and yet saying: We need Taft.

If Senator Taft were a mere officeholder, if he valued political success for its own sake, he would not do and say what he does, unnecessarily charge into controversy. Politicians say this is just because he lacks political sense. But there is something deeper and the people feel it: Here is a man who when he speaks does not weigh his words for votes.

This makes him, oddly enough, both glamorous and appealing. There are many people who oppose all the things summed up in the phrase "welfare state" but who for years have felt lost and leaderless. Here comes the knight in shining armor valiantly slugging at the seemingly unconquerable hosts; the very nature of the fight makes the plodding warrior glamorous. These people rallied to Taft as they have been able to do to no man in a generation.

Nor were these all. There are many more in the ranks of labor and other pressure groups who have grown vaguely distrustful of politicians who promise everything and brook no questioning. There was great appeal in a man who promised nothing except to be honest and as wise as he knew how. And there was even more appeal in a man who would do this in defiance of enemies who would have him recant or be politically executed. Courage is an old ingredient in sex appeal.

Perhaps these people might not vote for another man expressing these same opinions. At least the impression on one visitor was that many people were voting for the man, not necessarily for all his opinions. It seemed to echo the days before the demagogues when men cussed their way to the polls to vote for Webster or Clay or Calhoun because they trusted them while they cussed them.

Indeed, in retrospect the real mystery of Taft may not be so much in his winning as in the fact that he ever appeared in the lists at all. The true phenomenon to be explored is not the victory but how Mr. Taft got loose from the nineteenth century and into the twentieth.

VERMONT ROYSTER

November 16, 1950

Adlai E. Stevenson

History is rich with men of stature whose own hour and that of destiny did not run together; their lives and the times were out of joint.

One such man was a Democrat from the state of Illinois who ran for President of the United States. Stephen A. Douglas was a man of good character, of great ability and one with as deep a belief in the nation and the need to preserve her as had his Republican opponent.

But across the land there was a great ferment, and the people chose a man who advocated little that was different in specific programs but who knew that differences in attitude can be fundamental. Earlier or later the people might have chosen differently.

Adlai E. Stevenson did not, we think, lose this election for himself; he did not lose, as some may say, because he did not fight hard enough or because he fought with the wrong weapons. He did not talk over the people; the people understood what he was saying. But the people were no longer attuned to what he was saying.

Adlai Stevenson was defeated because he was forced to go the wrong way on the tide. He was defeated by his own party, which though it once spoke for the people, and will do so again some day, no longer does now. Mr. Stevenson's attitude and the attitude of his party was perforce one of approval of all that is and has been in the Democratic Administration, and in this attitude there was a fundamental difference with Mr. Eisenhower and, as it turned out, with the people.

The supporters of Mr. Stevenson have nothing to be ashamed of in him and much, we think, to be proud of. No man could have better stated the cause of his party; no man could have so well demonstrated that his is a party that can claim allegiance from men of stature.

And not the least of the things Mr. Stevenson's supporters have to be proud of was what he said in his dark hour of yesterday morning. His words, of course, were molded to a long tradition which accepts political defeat graciously, but those words also told of him that he understood the wisdom of that tradition. That which unites us is greater than that which divides us.

With no sense of disparagement but with a deep pride in the

quality of men that this country can uncover in its crucial days, we think that nothing better revealed in Mr. Stevenson a quality for leadership than the manner of his yielding it.

VERMONT ROYSTER

November 6, 1952

Knowland: A Political Figure Reflects

OAKLAND, Calif.—The political tom-toms were still, the bitterness of the campaign long past.

He had come home as assistant publisher of the family-owned newspaper. In this industrial city, his name was admired and respected despite the final defeat.

As on those broiling autumn days of electioneering, he was shirt-sleeved and smiling. The cast of his bearlike shoulders, the deliberate power of his handclasp were unchanged. And yet there was a perceptible difference about the man.

Somewhere along the corridors of defeat Bill Knowland had shed his Senatorial robes. His simple and unpretentious desk was bare save for an open appointment book. There were no autographed portraits of famous figures along the walls. Only a wood plaque embossed with a few lines of poetry.

The office was an oasis. No phones rang, no eager secretaries bustled in with messages. Four flights down the presses roared, but in the room there was only the gentle hum of conversation.

Tanned and relaxed, he rocked back in his swivel chair, hands clasped behind his head. The stern belligerence of his features had mellowed. He no longer delivered speeches, but spoke as one newspaperman to another.

The causes of his defeat for the California governorship, and for the defeat of many other Republican candidates last fall, still perplexed him. "Some of the early columnists tried to oversimplify it," he said, "as a problem in one area or branch of the party. But in reflection that is not the case."

Pro-Benson and anti-Benson Congressmen were beaten. Republicans with "good" labor records and Republicans who were bitterly opposed by the A.F.L.-C.I.O. lost. "There was no fixed pattern or reason for it," he insisted.

As for his own campaign, one that probably cost him his political career, he had no misgivings. He spoke with the resignation of a man who had played for high stakes and lost. "I frankly have no regrets whatsoever in raising the issues I did and making the fight I did. I think that is what campaigns are for."

Then he added, with a touch of the crusader still, "I think it will help alert the people of California to some of the dangers ahead. History shows that the issue of slavery wasn't solved the first time Lincoln and Douglas debated it. Douglas won and Lincoln lost." He referred to the proposed right-to-work law which he vigorously supported as a union reform measure, but which was defeated along with him.

He had gained, however, a grudging respect for the political effectiveness of the unions. "Organized labor," he conceded, "certainly did give the Democrats a highly efficient, well-organized in most cases, intelligently led and well-financed group able to do much more than the party could."

As a politician, the Senator rarely talked about himself in his speeches. As a private citizen he is much less reticent.

The single greatest change in leaving public life, he said, was that time was suddenly his own. At the Capitol his workday usually started with a 7:30 A.M. breakfast with perhaps members of the White House staff, or cabinet officers, or other Congressmen. It rarely ended in less than 12 hours. In election years he campaigned through 12 to 14 meetings a day.

He plans to take a personal interest in the editorial department of his newspaper. "I've been associated with the paper for thirty years. I'll do some editorial writing from time to time as I feel the situation warrants it. I'll keep in constant touch with the editorial department, go over editorials, make suggestions," he said.

Democrats and Republicans would fare alike. "There will be no carping criticism," he insisted. "I don't believe in it and never have." He said the *Tribune* will continue to do two things: first, cover the news, and second, comment on it constructively. "We'll be free to praise any Democratic official regardless of who he is. And if he happens to be a Republican who merits condemnation, we'll be critical," he declared.

The toughest question was saved for the last. What of his future—did he plan to seek public office again? "I have no present intentions," he replied firmly. "Right now I expect to be deeply involved in the newspaper business and my family. There is no appointment that I seek or would accept."

Then for a fleeting moment he gazed contemplatively out over the Oakland horizon. He mused. "Having been an active participant in history in the making for thirteen crucial years, it will be very interesting to watch these events from three thousand miles across the country."

And perhaps it will.

JONATHAN SPIVAK

January 20, 1959

THE FACE OF THE FUTURE

The World of Buck Rogers

NEW YORK—In laboratories across the nation, scientists are painstakingly fitting together bits and pieces of knowledge to create in the world of tomorrow science fiction of today.

"If you look at the Buck Rogers comic books you'll get a pretty good idea of what's coming," explains a top industrial research director. "These comic characters usually are doing the things that represent the desires of people." And today's industrial research is aimed mainly at learning how to make things folks want, no matter how fanciful.

Many of the desires seem fanciful indeed, but they are matched by expectations of some top-ranking researchers. Here are some of the things these men of science and industry expect around 1960–65 and later:

Individual flying machines to help conquer problems of traveling in congested areas.

Chemicals that can radically influence the growth of plants and animals, even perhaps remove some of the physical dangers of infancy and old age.

Plastics to replace many of today's nonferrous metals, plus new rubberlike materials to fill a host of yet undefined needs.

Chemical means of producing electricity, and vastly improved methods of storing and transmitting energy.

New metal alloys for high-temperature, high-pressure applications in jet aircraft, guided missiles and industrial processes.

These peeks at the future were made at a round-table meeting of some of the nation's top industrial research directors and editors of *The Wall Street Journal*. The directors included Dr. Edgar Bain, vice-president of U. S. Steel; Dr. William Baker, vice-president of Bell Telephone Laboratories; Dr. Samuel Lenher, vice-president of Du Pont; Dr. E. D. Reeves, executive vice-president of Esso Research, and Dr. C. Guy Suits, vice-president of General Electric.

Future products require ideas and manpower even more than materials. But somewhat surprisingly, the research chiefs agreed getting scientific manpower is not one of their major problems.

472

"Study of the Cepheid variables in the system indicates its distance from us to be twenty million light-years, give or take a million light-years."

"Keeping your creative people happy, productive—and creative—is the toughest job," commented one researcher. (It was agreed the members of the round table would not be quoted directly.)

Ironically, it is the scientist himself that science knows the least about. "We're trying to use scientific techniques in analyzing what makes men creative," commented a research boss. "One man stops creating when you move him and another starts. My trouble is I can't tell in advance who will start and who will stop when they're moved around." Each spring rank after rank of university graduates are handed scientific and technical degrees but, another research director noted, probably less than one in ten is a creative person. "The creative people were in short supply ten years ago," he continued, "they're short now and they'll be short ten years from now. Since that's the kind of man it takes for industrial research, we've got to learn to make full use of the ones we've got."

Most of today's laboratory work, by creative people as well as the scientific plodders, is evolutionary, not revolutionary. It is keyed to improving existing products and processes. Success of these experiments won't give consumers radically new products, but it will mean better, cheaper goods. It was evolutionary progress, for example, that perfected a polyethylene "squeeze" bottle that can be boiled, thus vastly increasing the uses of the container.

But in many areas of research, such as direct conversion of atomic radiation into electricity, the most creative men in research are looking for a "breakthrough" idea that will open up a new field to commercial exploitation. A recent breakthrough was the discovery of a way to make synthetic diamonds. Scientists are not yet sure how these heretofore impossible pressures will be utilized, but they are certain the techniques will have applications.

Development of safe, lightweight, high-energy fuels is one of the keys to individual flying machines—the flying platforms of the comic books—one research scientist noted. Such fuels now are being studied intensively by workers in missile and rocket fields; it is possible that a flying platform might utilize tiny rocket motors.

"I'd be surprised if there are not flying platforms by 1965," observed a researcher. Experimental models of flying platforms, or one-man flying machines, already have been tested under government research contracts.

Chemical control of plant life is another rapidly growing area of research. Weed killers used by professional and amateur gardeners are only the beginning, researchers predicted.

"Startling effects on plant growth are being obtained," commented one scientist. Compounds are being investigated that make plants grow slower or faster, taller or shorter, increase flowering, grow more beans or fewer beans.

The most exciting basic research, however, is centered on the amino acids, 20-odd complex molecules that are the essential building blocks of the proteins found in every living cell. Eight of these acids are essential to human nutrition. Absence or presence of certain amino acids in diets affects animals' growth. But much more important is the possibility that a few of these acids may exert profound influence over the body.

Some scientists, for example, believe amino acids may help solve some problems of senility and make possible a reasonably fruitful life at advanced ages. Chemicals to alter or change animal behavior, including the possibility of curing mental disorders in human beings, now are in the discussion stage.

The industrial researchers noted that development is under way of plastics and elastomers (rubberlike synthetic materials) that can withstand temperatures and working conditions that now require metals. Plastics that can hold up under temperatures of several hundred degrees seem quite likely in the near future.

Plastics research is being pushed hard along lines that might lead to replacements for scarce, strategic nonferrous metals. "People are trying to conquer their environment," explained one scientist, "and one way is to make themselves independent of natural resources as much as possible. A lot of work is being done to make us independent of nonferrous metals to a large extent." The United States has only limited supplies of such key nonferrous metals as nickel and tin.

Development of rubbery synthetics for special applications is progressing—and in one facet introducing another kind of "people" problem. There have long been suggestions, for example, that auto bumpers should be made of natural rubber. This is perfectly possible and undoubtedly would reduce contact damage of even head-on collisions. But if the car hit a tree or another auto, the impact might bounce it across the street. Some of the new elastomers have such a high "energy-absorbing" capacity that they would simply halt the car if it hit a tree. But there's another problem: The people inside might bounce around like ping-pong balls unless they wore seat belts.

Various means of producing electricity that would not require huge installations of steam power plants and their dependence on fuel supplies are under serious study. Of particular interest in this field is the fuel cell. In such a cell, different chemicals or gases are combined to produce free electrons, which can be channeled to produce an electric current. The idea of a fuel cell is by no means new; the first one was made in 1839. The problems are the long-familiar ones of combining high efficiency with low cost. (A fuel cell is not a storage battery; it actually produces energy instead of holding it in chemical form.)

Industrial researchers, however, are equally interested in the battery and possibilities of coming up with a greatly improved means of storing energy. If it were of sufficient size and high efficiency, some type of storage battery could be charged by off-peak electrical power, as in the early-morning hours in a city, and used during periods of peak demand. But for either an efficient fuel cell or a much improved storage battery, basic new discoveries will be required, the industrial scientists agreed.

A much better means of transmitting electrical energy from areas of cheap power generation to areas of demand may be much closer. Refrigerated transmission lines may solve this problem.

Fundamental studies in the structures of solid materials, particularly crystals, have in the past few years led to discoveries that may make it possible to prevent the type of metal fatigue that caused the crashes of the British Comet jetliners.

For many years metallurgists were concerned only with the "atoms that are there," a scientist explained. "Now it turns out you also have to worry about the atoms that aren't there."

The "atoms that aren't there" actually are vacancies in the atomic structure of metal. Under constant vibration, these vacancies can move toward the surface of the metal while the atoms remain fixed. This movement can lead to cracking and eventual failure of the metal. Scientists now are beginning to learn how to lock "atoms that aren't there" in place as well as the atoms that are there.

Several research directors were optimistic that the high-temperature metal alloy problems of turbines and jets will be solved in the near future. Part of this problem is to find alloys that will maintain their strength as the metal approaches its melting point.

In addition to better turbines, such metal development would lead to significant improvements in many industrial processes. Development of chemical and metal processes calling for superpressure and extra-high temperatures depend on new metals. Such processes would yield better plastics, for instance, and superpressure already has been used to produce diamonds.

October 5, 1956

A Bald-Headed Bird

NEW YORK—The Yul Brynner of the bird world, a gregarious little guy known as the wattled starling, may hold some fresh clues to the age-old mystery of the vanishing male hairline.

The wattled starling, it's just been learned, goes bald in much the same manner as humans. Only the bird, of course, sheds feathers.

Dedicated doctors and scientists who specialize in baldness problems claim the wattled starling is the first creature they've found that might be used in controlled laboratory studies of natural baldness. Such studies, they cautiously predict, might eventually lead to a method for arresting disappearing hair.

News of the wattled starling's potential service to the world's bald-headed men was but one morsel of heartening intelligence to come out of a weekend conclave of university and industrial hair experts at the New York Academy of Sciences.

These experts confirmed again that there is no known "cure" for most cases of baldness, and many pointed to their own heads as proof. But some progress is being made.

Dr. Richard A. Ellis of Brown University, for example, has been making microscopic studies of bald pates. He told the meeting that even in the most extreme case of baldness, he has found some hair follicles—the small cavities out of which hair grows—that are still connected to a nourishing blood supply. "This keeps alive the hope," says another scientist, "that even in cases of complete baldness, there may be something left that might grow hair."

Just what could induce this hair to sprout is unknown, but researchers are investigating the problem. Hair specialists have discovered, however, that a crop of new hair can be raised in certain special types of baldness.

Dr. Irvin I. Lubowe, a New York dermatologist who was conference chairman, told the meeting he had watched new heads of hair grow on 68 patients afflicted with "spotty" baldness—where handfuls of hair begin falling out overnight—after they had been treated with synthetic hormones.

"Hormonal changes, heredity and neurogenic changes resulting from nervous tension seem to be related to baldness," says Dr. Lubowe. Hormonal changes are suspect because many times more males than females suffer from baldness, which suggests male sex hormones may play a part. Tension, he notes, apparently causes constriction of the blood vessels in the scalp, which cuts down on the flow of blood that can reach the hair. "Heredity, of course," he adds, "is something we can do nothing about.

"Studies are now under way to determine which of these factors are basic," Dr. Lubowe says, "and whether there is any possibility of offsetting or delaying their effects." Stopping the loss of hair when it first begins to disappear, rather than struggling to regrow hair on a dome that's already bald, is the first aim of the research, according to Dr. Lubowe.

Scientists hope the wattled starling will prove helpful in furthering this aim. Dr. James B. Hamilton, chairman of the State University of New York's anatomy department in Brooklyn, has been experimenting with these gray-and-black birds and is presently awaiting another shipment of them from Africa.

In his paper entitled "General Aspects of the Problem of Baldness," Dr. Hamilton told the meeting the common baldness pattern in male wattled starlings is "symmetrical and progressive," as in men. He also noted that although "baldness occurs normally in many adult male" birds, it does not take place in immature males, female birds, or wattled starlings that have been turned into eunuchs. "We hope we might find methods that would interfere with the baldness in this bird," Dr. Hamilton said.

While doctors and scientists are battling to solve the baldness problem that plagues in varying degrees an estimated eight out of every 10 American men over age 25, their efforts are being matched by researchers employed by firms producing hair preparations. Americans' outlays on such preparations run at the rate of nearly $390 million a year, according to *Drug Trade News*.

Colgate-Palmolive Co., which produces Halo Shampoo and is in the process of acquiring Wildroot Co., Inc., which makes Wildroot Cream Oil Hair Tonic, has several researchers at work, as does the Warner-Lambert Pharmaceutical Co. and Gillette Co.'s Toni division.

In the background of the growing search for a baldness cure is a subtle shift in the American male's attitude toward baldness that may help him endure his infliction until the researchers find a cure. "Baldness is no longer as embarrassing as it once was," says one scientist attending the conference. "A bald man today can look at such famous men as Eisenhower, Sam Rayburn and Yul Brynner and say to himself, 'If these baldies can make good, so can I.'"

JERRY E. BISHOP

February 2, 1959

Skimpy Astronomer Supply

LOS ANGELES—Professor Samuel Herrick, a red-haired specialist in the motions of astronomical bodies, is a busy man these days. He's consulting with six space-age companies, teaching courses in astrodynamics and rocket navigation at the Los Angeles campus of the University of California and, on top of all this, is putting the final touches to a new text on celestial mechanics.

Things were not always so hurried for astronomer Herrick.

His scientific schedule once provided room for such matters as studying the orbits of three minor planets (one of them named for his wife, Betulia) which are whirling around the sun between Mars and Jupiter.

The exploration of space has boosted industry's demand for astronomers—and increased their pay. U.C.L.A.'s Dr. Herrick, for example, a few years back received $50 to $80 a day for consulting with North American Aviation, Inc. Now Aeronutronic Systems, Inc.,

Ford Motor Co.'s space-age subsidiary in nearby Glendale, pays him $200 a day.

One of the reasons for this pay boost is the scarcity of professional stargazers. There are only about 800 astronomers in the United States, according to the American Astronomical Society. Of this number a mere handful are trained in the currently timely field of celestial mechanics, which deals with the orbits of planets and provides, among other things, the information needed to chart a rocket course to the moon, Mars and Venus.

"Few astronomers have gone into this field, because it has been considered somewhat of a substandard occupation. The attitude has been that it has nothing new to offer," explains Dr. Leland Cunningham, a University of California astronomer. He estimates there are only a half-dozen specialists in the country and less than 50 astronomers with any training in the field at all.

As a result, in the Los Angeles area, where much space research is concentrated, such outfits as Aeronutronic, Northrop Aircraft, Inc.'s Nortronics division, and Space Technology Laboratories, Inc., have found few astronomers trained or willing to work for them. "I could use right now about ten celestial mechanicians if I could find them. People who can do precise orbit studies are very scarce," comments Dr. Louis Walters, head of Aeronutronic's astrodynamics department.

Space Technology Laboratories' guidance and navigation department recently hired its first astronomer, a woman. "We welcome people of this sort," says Dr. Arnold Rosenblum, the department's assistant manager. "A lot of their training is applicable to our work. And the kind of things we are doing are so new it's hard to find people with the proper training."

Northrop even set up its own observatory equipped with a 12-inch telescope in Flagstaff, Arizona, to develop a guidance system for the Snark intercontinental missile.

Industry wants astronomers most urgently now for the calculation of trajectories of space vehicles. The first rockets to the moon and planets, once boosted above the earth's atmosphere, will depend upon gravitational attraction to hit their target. For more than 200 years since Newton outlined his gravitational theory, astronomers have been working out just such orbit problems with planets and asteroids and with comets that wander into the solar system. In addition, astronomers are sought for the light they can shed on conditions on the planets and for advice on the type of instruments to send up into space.

This movement of astronomers from science to full-time jobs in industry is a recent development and still is only a trickle. "I would guess there are probably only a dozen astronomers working full-time for industry in this country," says Dr. A. G. Wilson, an astronomer who is employed by Rand Corp., a scientific research company in Santa Monica, California. Until 18 months ago, he was director of the Lowell Observatory in Flagstaff, a center of solar system research. Why did he make the switch? "There is a sizable difference in industry offers, salarywise, and salaries you can make with the observatories and universities. Most astronomers, if the jobs are available, can raise their salaries fifty per cent or more," he says.

Despite such inducements, many are reluctant to give up the freedom to do unrestricted research at an observatory. Often, however, they're eager for part-time consulting work.

This can be fairly lucrative ($100 to $200 a day), but it has not developed without some criticism from the universities. For example, six months ago, the University of Colorado's High Altitude Observatory at Boulder adopted a stern policy requiring that all consulting fees be paid to the observatory and not the staff members who do the work. The purpose, explains Dr. Walter Orr Roberts, observatory director, is to discourage astronomers from taking on consulting jobs that divide their efforts, just for the extra money.

The observatory's executive officer, Robert Low, adds, "You find if one person consults, the others see it and say to themselves, 'I'd better get some of that gravy.' When there's a new course to be taught, they'll say, 'I can't do it, I've got too much consulting.' "

Growing interest in space, not surprisingly, is boosting high-school and college attendance at astronomy classes.

Enrollment in the University of California's Astronomy Department has increased sharply. "At the present time some students who might have gone into geology and physics are now going into astronomy. In a few years, this will be reflected in an increase in the number of graduate students," comments Dr. Otto Struve, chairman of the department.

Even some high schools are offering full-fledged courses in astronomy. The Los Altos (California) High School last fall added a college-freshman-level course in astronomy to its curriculum. It attracted no less than 27 students. And, in addition, the high school purchased a $500, six-inch reflector telescope for its sky-minded students. "If you had tried to do this a few years ago in most schools, someone would have thought you had a hole in your head," comments a pleased science teacher.

JONATHAN M. SPIVAK

January 15, 1959

The Function of a Newspaper

For some elections past the majority of the newspapers have in their editorial pages supported the Republican candidate. In these same elections the majority of the people have voted for the Democratic candidate.

Wherever editors gather, these incontrovertible statistics—which might be verified again this year—are repeatedly brought forth and used as a springboard to some remarkable conclusions.

Frequently our own colleagues use them for self-flagellation; should they not do so, some outside critic is sure to seize upon them as a whiplash for shortcomings. The latest to fret over the sad estate of the fourth estate is Governor Stevenson.

The newness of what Mr. Stevenson says lies only in the urbanity of his wit. For the burden of it is again that newspapers have a duty to influence as well as to enlighten the people and that since the statistics show a failure to influence there is demonstrated thereby a failure to perform their duty. In Mr. Stevenson's bright phrase, we have not lived up to our invitation to greatness.

Of course one might comment that what Mr. Stevenson complains of is good fortune for Mr. Stevenson. If the statistical majority of newspapers were able to influence public opinion, which he says is their proper function, then his party would not now be in power and Mr. Stevenson's own political chances would be poor instead of good.

Or if one assumes—as Mr. Stevenson possibly does—that the majority of the people in this case are wise and the statistical majority of newspapers are foolish, then his argument really is that the newspapers should be influenced by the people, that they should endorse ideas because of their popularity. Yet this is the reverse of the argument that Mr. Stevenson pretends to make.

But we are not concerned so much with the inconsistencies that glitter through Mr. Stevenson's shining phrases. What interests us is the underlying assumptions in all this talk about the duty of a newspaper and the "public responsibility" of an editor commenting upon the passing scene.

The primary function of a newspaper is to tell people what is happening in the world be it good, bad or neither. In our own field we report bankruptcies as well as successes, "bad government actions" as well as "good government actions." We do it not to perform a duty but to fulfill a function. We have no duty to print a

"I wonder how long it will take us to invent an H-bomb again?"

newspaper at all, but if we do and fail to carry out the function of one we would quickly find the readers going elsewhere.

A newspaper editor who becomes overwhelmed with his sense of duty and decides that some news ought not to be printed because it would be bad for the public to know about it will quite likely find that he has no newspaper to be an editor of. The graveyards are littered with the wreckage of newspapers that tried to censor news instead of printing it.

A secondary function of a newspaper is to offer judgments and opinions on the passing events. And it is here that the critics of newspapers most often bring up such phrases as "duty" and "public responsibility."

The thought seems to be that an editor has a responsibility for what his readers think, that he has a duty to mold public opinion, and that if the editor and his readers get out of step, then the newspaper has failed in its duty. As a corollary it is said too that the editor has a duty only to utter "responsible" thoughts—an irresponsible thought being generally one that runs counter to the great public policies of the day.

We do not think that an editor has any duty to mold public opinion. Indeed, when he conceives this to be his duty and to think that he can do it, he is in the greatest danger of ceasing to perform his editorial function. It is only in totalitarian countries, in the realms where there is dogma, that such a "duty" is accepted and attempted.

The function of an editor is to express an opinion which the reader can judge. And that function is properly performed only if the opinion is an honest one. The minute an editor withholds an opinion for fear that someone may think it "irresponsible" or that he may be "out of step with the times," he ceases to perform his function.

If an editor believes, say, that a policy of government deficits is bad, he should say so, and continue to say so, though for twenty years the government with the acquiescence of the people continues to depreciate the money with government deficits.

A newspaper editor who becomes overwhelmed with his sense of duty to uphold, say, the foreign policy of his government and suppresses his thought that it is bad out of fear of "irresponsibility," that editor has ceased to perform his function. So has he too if he yields up his opinion because somebody tells him editors are getting too "one-sided" and he thinks it his duty to redress the balance.

The reason he has ceased to perform his function is that he has ceased to give an honest opinion. And in due time his readers will find him out, and his editorial page, for all his sense of duty, will join the graveyard of the discredited.

EDITORIAL

September 10, 1952

In Hoc Anno Domini

When Saul of Tarsus set out on his journey to Damascus the whole of the known world lay in bondage. There was one state, and it was Rome. There was one master for it all, and he was Tiberius Caesar.

Everywhere there was civil order, for the arm of the Roman law was long. Everywhere there was stability, in government and in society, for the centurions saw that it was so.

But everywhere there was something else, too. There was oppression—for those who were not the friends of Tiberius Caesar. There was the tax gatherer to take the grain from the fields and the flax from the spindle to feed the legions or to fill the hungry treasury from which divine Caesar gave largess to the people. There was the impresser to find recruits for the circuses. There were the executioners to quiet those whom the Emperor proscribed. What was a man for but to serve Caesar?

There was the persecution of men who dared think differently, who heard strange voices or read strange manuscripts. There was enslavement of men whose tribes came not from Rome, disdain for those who did not have the familiar visage. And most of all, there was everywhere a contempt for human life. What, to the strong, was one man more or less in a crowded world?

Then, of a sudden, there was a light in the world, and a man from Galilee saying, *Render unto Caesar the things which are Caesar's and unto God the things that are God's.*

And the voice from Galilee, which would defy Caesar, offered a new Kingdom in which each man could walk upright and bow to none but his God. *Inasmuch as ye have done it unto one of the least of these my brethren, ye have done it unto me.* And he sent this gospel of the Kingdom of Man into the uttermost ends of the earth.

So the light came into the world and the men who loved darkness were afraid, and they tried to lower a curtain so that man would still believe salvation lay with the leaders.

But it came to pass for a while in divers places that the truth did set man free, although the men of darkness were offended and they tried to put out the light. The voice said, *Haste ye. Walk while you have the light, lest darkness come upon you, for he that walketh in darkness knoweth not whither he goeth.*

Along the road to Damascus the light shone brightly. But afterward Paul of Tarsus, too, was sore afraid. He feared that other Caesars, other prophets, might one day persuade men that man was nothing save a servant unto them, that men might yield up their birthright from God for pottage and walk no more in freedom.

Then might it come to pass that darkness would settle again over the lands, and there would be a burning of books, and men would think only of what they should eat and what they should wear, and would give heed only to new Caesars and to false prophets. Then might it come to pass that men would not look upward to see even a winter's star in the east, and, once more, there would be no light at all in the darkness.

And so Paul, the apostle of the Son of Man, spoke to his brethren, the Galatians, the words he would have us remember afterward in each of the years of his Lord:

Stand fast therefore in the liberty wherewith Christ hath made us free and be not entangled again with the yoke of bondage.

EDITORIAL

December 24, 1951